Security, Trust, and Social Impacts of Deepfakes

Manoj Kumar
https://orcid.org/0000-0001-5113-0639
University of Wollongong in Dubai, UAE

May El Barachi
University of Wollongong in Dubai, UAE

Preeti Sharma
https://orcid.org/0000-0001-7530-3821
DIT University, India

Keshav Kaushik
https://orcid.org/0000-0003-3777-765X
Sharda University, India

IGI Global
Scientific Publishing
Publishing Tomorrow's Research Today

Vice President of Editorial Melissa Wagner
Director of Acquisitions Mikaela Felty
Director of Book Development Jocelynn Hessler
Production Manager Mike Brehm
Cover Design Jose Rosado

Published in the United States of America by
IGI Global Scientific Publishing
701 East Chocolate Avenue
Hershey, PA, 17033, USA
Tel: 717-533-8845 | Fax: 717-533-7115
Website: https://www.igi-global.com E-mail: cust@igi-global.com

Library of Congress Cataloging-in-Publication Data

LCCN: 2026003378 (CIP Data Pending)
ISBN13: 9798337382920
Isbn13Softcover: 9798337382937
EISBN13: 9798337382944
British Cataloguing in Publication Data
A Cataloguing in Publication record for this book is available from the British Library.

Editorial Advisory Board

Table of Contents

Detailed Table of Contents

Deepfakes pose a significant threat to digital authenticity, raising concerns in media forensics, cybersecurity, and social trust. Detecting these realistic synthetic images requires advanced models that capture subtle visual inconsistencies often missed by conventional neural networks. This chapter introduces a hybrid quantum deep learning framework based on the QNN–DenseNet121 architecture for effective deepfake detection. By combining DenseNet121's hierarchical feature extraction with quantum-inspired nonlinear transformations, the model identifies fine-grained facial artifacts with improved precision. Evaluated on a Kaggle deepfake image dataset, the proposed approach achieves 98.85% accuracy, outperforming existing models such as Hybrid StyleGAN, Attention-based GAN, 2D CNN with GAN, and 3D CNNs. The results demonstrate that hybrid quantum deep learning provides a reliable and adaptable solution for synthetic media detection and digital media verification.

Smart phones have become an intrinsic part of human's life. The Smart phone unifies diverse advanced characteristics. It enables users to store various data such as photos, health data, credential bank data, and personal information. The Android operating system is the prevalent mobile operating system and, in the meantime, the most targeted operating system by malware developers. Recently the unparalleled

The proliferation of deepfake technology presents complex ethical challenges that span creativity, harm prevention, and free expression. This chapter examines the moral dimensions of synthetic media through philosophical frameworks, legal analysis, and empirical evidence. We explore the tension between legitimate creative applications and potential harms, analyze constitutional boundaries of regulation, and identify moral dilemmas faced by creators, platforms, and society. Drawing on recent scholarship (2021-2025), the chapter synthesizes deontological, consequentialist, and virtue ethics approaches to develop an integrated framework for understanding deepfake ethics. Key findings reveal that while deepfakes are not inherently wrong, their ethical status depends critically on consent, context, and purpose. The analysis demonstrates how synthetic media threatens epistemic trust while simultaneously enabling beneficial applications in education, accessibility, and artistic expression.

We developed a research on Privacy and Ethical Norms where we quantifies these values using Bipolar Fuzzy Sets to ensures that modern systems behaves according to human values. For any specific context, we defines a bipolar state where a positive membership represents the presence of an ethical value like trust or anonymization and a negative membership represents a counter-value such as sadness or breach risk. We calculates the positive function as the average rating divided by ten and we represents the negative function as the negative average rating divided by ten. For example, if we have an AI that manages data with a high anonymization score of 8 but a risk of 2, we obtains a bipolar state showing strong positive presence and low negative risk. We utilizes t-cuts to filter out con-texts that does not meet our

Preface

INTRODUCTION

The rapid advancement of artificial intelligence has transformed the ways in which digital content is created, distributed, and consumed. Among the most significant developments in this evolving landscape is the emergence of deepfake technology, which has demonstrated remarkable capabilities to generate highly realistic synthetic media. While these innovations have opened new opportunities in entertainment, education, accessibility, and creative expression, they have simultaneously introduced profound challenges related to security, trust, privacy, and the integrity of digital information. As deepfakes become increasingly sophisticated and accessible, understanding their technical foundations as well as their broader societal implications has become an urgent priority for researchers, practitioners, policymakers, and institutions worldwide.

Security, Trust, and Social Impacts of Deepfakes was conceived to address this growing need through a comprehensive and interdisciplinary perspective. Rather than focusing exclusively on the technical aspects of deepfake detection, this volume explores the complete ecosystem surrounding synthetic media. The chapters examine the technologies that enable deepfake generation, the forensic methods used to investigate manipulated content, the cybersecurity threats posed by malicious synthetic media, and the legal, ethical, psychological, and governance challenges that accompany its widespread adoption. By integrating these diverse perspectives, the book presents deepfakes not merely as a technological phenomenon but as a complex global issue that affects virtually every sector of modern society.

The contributions assembled in this volume reflect the collaborative efforts of experts from multiple disciplines, including computer science, artificial intelligence, cybersecurity, digital forensics, law, psychology, media studies, ethics, and public policy. Such interdisciplinary collaboration is essential for understanding a technology whose consequences extend well beyond technical implementation. Addressing the challenges posed by deepfakes requires not only advances in detection algorithms and forensic techniques but also thoughtful consideration of regulatory frameworks, ethical responsibilities, public awareness, institutional resilience, and international cooperation.

Throughout this volume, readers will encounter discussions that examine the evolving relationship between synthetic media and digital trust. As manipulated content increasingly influences political discourse, journalism, financial systems, public opinion, and interpersonal communication, maintaining confidence in digital information has become one of the defining challenges of the AI era. The chapters explore how deepfakes are exploited in cybercrime, misinformation campaigns, identity fraud, and social engineering attacks while also investigating mechanisms for strengthening authentication, digital evidence verification, and responsible governance.

Equally important, this book recognizes that technological solutions alone cannot adequately address the challenges associated with synthetic media. Effective responses require coordinated efforts among governments, law enforcement agencies, technology developers, educators, media organizations, legal experts, and civil society. By examining comparative legal approaches, ethical frameworks, regulatory initiatives, and policy recommendations from multiple jurisdictions, the volume encourages readers to consider balanced strategies that foster innovation while protecting individuals, institutions, and democratic processes from misuse.

One of the defining strengths of this collection is its emphasis on bridging traditionally separate domains of inquiry. The integration of technical research with legal analysis, psychological insights, media literacy, cybersecurity strategy, and governance perspectives provides readers with a holistic understanding of deepfakes and their far-reaching consequences. This multidisciplinary approach equips both specialists and non-specialists with the knowledge necessary to navigate an increasingly complex digital environment where distinguishing authentic information from synthetic content is becoming progressively more difficult.

This volume is intended to serve a diverse readership. Researchers and academics will find comprehensive analyses that advance scholarly understanding of synthetic media technologies and their implications. Cybersecurity professionals, digital forensic investigators, legal practitioners, journalists, and policymakers will benefit from practical discussions addressing emerging threats, investigative methodologies, governance models, and risk mitigation strategies. Graduate students studying artificial intelligence, cybersecurity, digital forensics, law, ethics, and media studies will discover a valuable reference that connects theoretical concepts with contemporary real-world challenges. Government agencies, law enforcement organizations, non-governmental organizations, media institutions, and international policy bodies may also find the insights presented here valuable in developing informed responses to the evolving risks associated with synthetic media.

As editors, we believe that understanding deepfakes requires more than technological expertise; it demands sustained dialogue across disciplines, sectors, and international boundaries. The accelerating pace of artificial intelligence innovation ensures that synthetic media will continue to evolve, presenting new opportunities alongside increasingly sophisticated threats. Preparing for this future requires collaborative research, responsible technological development, effective governance, and an informed global community capable of responding thoughtfully to emerging challenges.

We extend our sincere appreciation to all contributing authors for sharing their expertise and scholarly contributions. Their commitment to advancing knowledge across diverse disciplines has made this volume possible. We also express our gratitude to the reviewers for their thoughtful evaluations, whose valuable feedback strengthened the quality and rigor of the chapters presented here. Finally, we thank the editorial and publishing teams whose professionalism and dedication supported every stage of this project's development.

It is our hope that *Security, Trust, and Social Impacts of Deepfakes* will serve not only as a valuable academic reference but also as a catalyst for future research, interdisciplinary collaboration, informed policymaking, and responsible innovation. As synthetic media continues to reshape digital communication and information ecosystems, we trust that the perspectives presented in this volume will contribute meaningfully to ongoing efforts to strengthen security, preserve public trust, and promote the ethical development and governance of artificial intelligence technologies.

ORGANIZATION OF THE BOOK

The opening chapter introduces an innovative hybrid quantum deep learning framework that combines Quantum Neural Networks (QNN) with DenseNet121 to advance the state of deepfake detection. By integrating quantum-inspired nonlinear processing with powerful hierarchical feature extraction, the proposed model demonstrates exceptional accuracy in identifying subtle synthetic facial artifacts that often evade conventional detection techniques. The chapter highlights the promise of hybrid quantum computing approaches for strengthening digital media verification and establishing more reliable defenses against increasingly sophisticated synthetic content.

Chapter 2 broadens the discussion from deepfake detection to the broader cybersecurity landscape by examining machine learning approaches for Android malware detection. Using a permission-based k-nearest neighbor framework, the chapter demonstrates how intelligent analysis of application behavior can distinguish malicious software from legitimate applications, thereby enhancing mobile security and user trust. Its inclusion reinforces the book's overarching emphasis on safeguarding digital ecosystems against emerging AI-enabled threats that undermine confidence in digital technologies.

Building upon the foundations of technical detection, Chapter 3 presents a comprehensive trust-centric defense architecture that extends beyond traditional GAN-focused approaches. The chapter advocates for a layered framework integrating hybrid AI detection, blockchain-based media provenance, and digital watermarking to establish greater accountability, authenticity, and forensic reliability. By combining technical innovation with governance considerations, the authors illustrate how multidisciplinary solutions are essential for restoring trust in digital media and ensuring the long-term resilience of information ecosystems.

Chapter 4 examines one of the most immediate real-world consequences of synthetic media by exploring the growing role of deepfakes in digital fraud and identity theft. The discussion synthesizes perspectives from cybersecurity, legal studies, and human-computer interaction to explain how highly realistic synthetic content enables sophisticated impersonation attacks, social engineering campaigns, and financial fraud. In addition to outlining evolving threat mechanisms, the chapter presents strategic approaches for detection, mitigation, and policy development that strengthen defenses against AI-driven deception.

Chapter 5 explores the critical role of secure biometric authentication in establishing digital trust through an advanced fingerprint cryptography framework. By eliminating the need to store or transmit biometric credentials while preserving privacy and ensuring secure session key generation, the proposed approach offers a robust solution for long-term communication security. The chapter further extends these concepts to emerging virtual environments, demonstrating how crypto-biometric technologies can help protect users from identity theft, avatar spoofing, and unauthorized access within the expanding metaverse.

Chapter 6 focuses on one of the emerging frontiers of digital forensics by addressing the attribution of deepfakes to their originating models, devices, and creators. Through a unified forensic framework, the chapter demonstrates how model fingerprints, metadata analysis, workflow reconstruction, and behavioral profiling can support reliable attribution while satisfying evidentiary standards required for legal proceedings. The authors also advocate for global standards, model registries, and cross-sector collaboration that will enhance accountability and investigative capabilities as synthetic media technologies continue to evolve.

Looking toward the future, Chapter 7 examines the evolution of synthetic media and the collaborative efforts required to establish a trustworthy digital ecosystem. The discussion considers the rapid advancement of generative AI, emerging regulatory initiatives, and changing societal responses through an interdisciplinary lens. By analyzing the interactions among governments, technology providers, researchers, and civil society, the chapter provides a forward-looking roadmap for balancing innovation with accountability while strengthening public trust in digital information through 2030 and beyond.

Chapter 8 shifts attention to the human dimension of synthetic media by introducing a neo-critical framework for deepfake literacy. Recognizing that technical solutions alone cannot fully address misinformation and the "liar's dividend," the chapter emphasizes the importance of educational strategies that integrate media literacy, cognitive science, ethics, and human rights. Through its multidimensional approach, the chapter demonstrates how fostering critical thinking, ethical reasoning, and digital resilience can equip individuals and institutions to navigate increasingly complex information environments.

The ethical foundations of synthetic media are examined in Chapter 9, where the authors investigate the competing values of creativity, free expression, and harm prevention. Drawing upon philosophical theory, legal analysis, and contemporary empirical research, the chapter develops an integrated ethical framework that evaluates deepfake applications based on consent, context, and purpose. By acknowledging both the transformative potential and the significant societal risks of synthetic media, the chapter provides readers with a balanced perspective on responsible innovation and ethical governance.

The final chapter expands the discussion of digital trust by presenting a fuzzy artificial intelligence framework for evaluating privacy, ethics, and online threats within social media environments. Using bipolar fuzzy sets to quantify positive ethical attributes alongside potential risks, the proposed methodology offers a structured decision-making approach for assessing trustworthiness in AI-enabled systems. The chapter concludes the volume by emphasizing that preserving trust in digital ecosystems requires not only advanced technical safeguards but also intelligent mechanisms capable of embedding ethical considerations directly into automated decision processes.

CONCLUDING REMARKS

As the capabilities of artificial intelligence continue to evolve, so too do the opportunities and risks associated with synthetic media. Deepfakes have emerged as one of the most significant challenges of the digital age, testing the integrity of information, the resilience of cybersecurity systems, the effectiveness of legal and regulatory frameworks, and the very foundations of public trust. Addressing these challenges requires far more than advances in detection algorithms alone; it demands sustained collaboration among researchers, technologists, policymakers, legal scholars, educators, industry leaders, and civil society to develop comprehensive solutions that are both technologically robust and socially responsible.

The chapters presented in this volume collectively demonstrate that securing the future of digital communication depends upon an integrated approach that combines innovations in artificial intelligence, digital forensics, cybersecurity, authentication technologies, governance, ethics, education, and public policy. Together, they illustrate that preserving trust in an increasingly synthetic information environment requires not only sophisticated technical defenses but also transparent governance, informed public engagement, and internationally coordinated standards that promote accountability while supporting continued innovation.

As editors, we hope this volume serves as both a comprehensive reference and a catalyst for future interdisciplinary research. We trust that the insights, methodologies, and perspectives presented throughout these chapters will encourage continued dialogue, inspire innovative solutions, and contribute to the development of resilient digital ecosystems capable of addressing the rapidly evolving challenges posed by synthetic media. Ultimately, the collective knowledge presented in this book reinforces a central message: safeguarding security and trust in the era of deepfakes is a shared global responsibility, and meeting this challenge will require continued cooperation across disciplines, sectors, and nations.

Chapter 1
A Hybrid Quantum Deep Learning Framework With QNN and DenseNet121 for Deepfake Detection

S. Jasmine
http://orcid.org/0009-0007-7081-3460
SRM Institute of Science and Technology, Kattankulathur, India

Nagamany Abirami
SRM Institute of Science and Technology, Kattankulathur, India

I. Varalakshmi
SRM Institute of Science and Technology, Kattankulathur, India

Mursal Ayub Hamdani
SRM Institute of Science and Technology, Kattankulathur, India

ABSTRACT

Deepfakes pose a significant threat to digital authenticity, raising concerns in media forensics, cybersecurity, and social trust. Detecting these realistic synthetic images requires advanced models that capture subtle visual inconsistencies often missed by conventional neural networks. This chapter introduces a hybrid quantum deep learning framework based on the QNN–DenseNet121 architecture for effective deepfake detection. By combining DenseNet121's hierarchical feature extraction with quantum-inspired nonlinear transformations, the model identifies fine-grained facial artifacts with improved precision. Evaluated on a Kaggle deepfake image dataset, the proposed approach achieves 98.85% accuracy, outperforming existing models

DOI: 10.4018/979-8-3373-8292-0.ch001

such as Hybrid StyleGAN, Attention-based GAN, 2D CNN with GAN, and 3D CNNs. The results demonstrate that hybrid quantum deep learning provides a reliable and adaptable solution for synthetic media detection and digital media verification.

1. INTRODUCTION

1.1 Background and Emergence of DeepFakes

As AI has grown increasingly sophisticated over the years, it has revolutionized the creation, editing and dissemination of digital media, leading to the emergence of a new form of digital media that is often described as DeepFakes. These videos, images, and audios are generated from deep neural network models which replicate one's facial expressions, vocal patterns or even physical features with a high degree of fidelity. For facial re-enactment specifically, early research on neural network based re-enactments has revealed that they are capable of re-constructing faces in different scenarios; the advent of GAN (generative adversarial networks) has tremendously fast-tracked facial re-enactment by enabling one to synthesize a real face through adversarial learning (Aldausari et al., 2023; Goodfellow et al., 2020). In light of advancements in the GPU hardware, large databases of facial images and open source tools like FaceSwap and DeepFaceLab, it is possible for anyone with minimal technical skills to create a very convincing manipulation in a short while. As the tools evolved, DeepFakes started being more popular on social media platforms and began causing concerns around misinformation, political impersonation, fraud, and privacy violations, across the globe. The challenge today isn't just in their creation, it's how quickly and how much it are spreading, and it is a critical need for reliable detection to ensure digital trust and cybersecurity.

1.2 DeepFake Types and Their Increasing Complexity

There are several general types of manipulation of media that can be understood through DeepFakes today, the more they get advanced, and the more they are improved using generative technologies. The most popular is the face exchange, in which one person's face is replaced with another (Sunil et al., 2025). In order to produce such content, facial landmarks must be precisely aligned and facial features must be accurately extracted before being recreated in the target movie (Rossler et al., 2019; Vimala et al., 2026; P. Xu et al., 2021). Newer systems can process fine details in the image such as skin texture, lighting, age lines, and facial orientation, which makes the synthetic face seamlessly blend with the rest of the body. The inconsistencies in the shading and shapes around the jaw, which were once easy to detect, as well as the profiles of many of the flaws are not as noticeable. Figure 1 provides a general overview of the types of DeepFake media, ranging from videos and images to text, audio, and even real-time interaction. The diversity of synthetic content and the ever growing technical sophistication in the methods used to manipulate are highlighted with these types. Another significant category is the DeepFake images. They are modified images or completely synthetic single images that are based on high resolution generative models like GANs and diffusion networks. Such systems can only achieve extremely fine resolution by processing individual images, which opens the door to the creation of fake photographs, altered identity documents, altered historical photos, and other synthetic evidence. Some photos depict people who don't exist, while others significantly alter the appearance of genuine people to make it harder to distinguish them visually.

Textual DeepFakes is a relatively new domain in synthetic media. In this instance the text is generated artificially to mimic the writing style of a particular individual, such as their vocabulary, tone, rhythm and style. From a tiny sample, sophisticated language models can recognize these patterns and produce letters, postings, emails, or articles that appear to be written by the target of the imitation. These systems can generate a large amount of customized material, which can be abused for targeted manipulation, disinformation, and impersonation.

Figure 1. Types of DeepFakes and their media modalities, illustrating major image, video, audio, and multimodal synthetic media manipulations

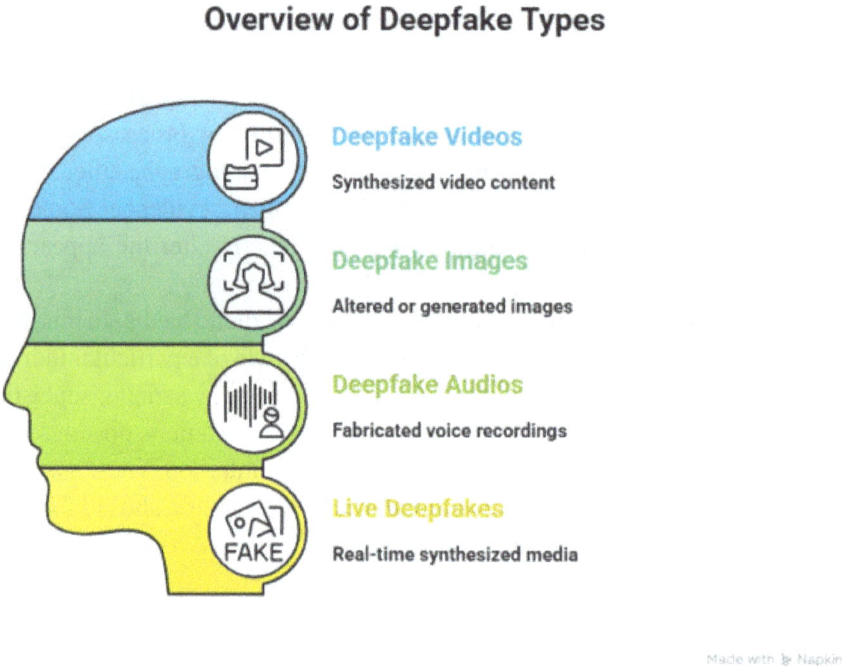

DeepFake audio means it is centred around creating or changing speech to sound like a particular voice. Pitch, accent, tone and pace are features that voice-cloning tools will learn to replicate, creating a believable voice profile. Such systems are capable of producing complete sentences or emotions, and there are systems that can even convert one speaker into another! It only requires a little bit of training audio for such systems to produce complete sentences or emotions, and there are systems that can even convert one speaker into another. This misuse of technology has already been shown through fake phone calls, impersonating another individual, and fake audio statements.

The most rapidly emerging class are Live or Real-time DeepFakes. These systems are designed to instantaneously change a person's audiovisual identity during livestreams, online conferences, and video conversations. Real time face-swap tools simulate facial expressions, eye movement and head positions that occur as the talker changes position. They, with the speed of speech synthesis, enable it to be possible to impersonate someone during real-time conversation, not just in pre-recorded material. This is extremely difficult to detect and creates issues for digital security and identity verification. When taken together in this way, these instances demonstrate the sophistication with which DeepFake technology has come from simply replacing one person's face on an image or a video to synthetic media including text, images, audio, and videos. These instances get more realistic and coherent every day, meaning that detection technologies have to become more complex in order to analyze their patterns and connections. As such systems continue to evolve, it is vital that detection technologies will remain efficient enough to combat them.

1.3 How DeepFakes Are Made and Why They Seem Real

The process of creating DeepFakes can be broken down into a series of steps: Visual Data Collection, Material Preparation, Training Generative Models, and Output Improvement. The realism in the synthesized video is enhanced by each step. These procedures are now quicker, more automated, and more difficult to identify thanks to recent developments in deep learning.

1.3.1 Data Acquisition and Dataset Construction

The first step in creating a DeepFake is to gather a huge number of pictures or video frames of the subject want to alter. Typically these samples come from various angles, lighting conditions, and facial expressions. The more diverse data, the more it will learn about the natural variations in the appearance of the person. Videos are available publicly like interviews, social media videos, films, or videos of a live stream. Thousands of frames are typically captured with the aid of an automated tool for the model to have a broad perspective of the face and its movement characteristics.

1.3.2 Preprocessing and Facial Alignment

Before being used for training, collected frames must undergo preprocessing. Feature extraction procedures are utilized to extract landmarks like the mouth, nose, and eyes, while facial detection techniques are utilized to identify the face in one frame. The photos can be matched to a regular framework thanks to the points. Cropping, resizing, pose correcting, removing blurry samples, and intensity value normalizing are more steps to making clean inputs. This alignment shields the trainer from noise and optimizes training productivity. The uniformity added during the preprocessing is one of the reasons why DeepFakes look natural because the model is trained on the regularity of facial structures.

1.3.3 Model Training Using Generative Architectures

The foundation of DeepFake creation is generative models. Previous systems were based on autoencoders which were trained to encode an individual's face and then decode it onto another face. However, newer systems employ more complex designs such as diffusion models, generative adversarial networks, and variational autoencoders. The autoencoders are concerned with identifying features of the identity and reconstructing the faces smoothly. Using variational autoencoders, controlled variation is added to support multiple expressions. The idea of improving the detail behind generative adversarial networks is to train two networks concurrently: one for generating images and the other for evaluating them. The images get improved with each iteration of the diffusion models, resulting in very realistic textures and lighting. Of these, GANs are still popular as the adversarial training process ensures that the outputs presented by the generator appear as though they are real. Sharp texturing, organic shading, and a steady face motion will result from this.

1.3.4 Temporal Refinement and Post-Processing

The synthetic face must be integrated into the initial video frame after the model has created it. Post-processing: To make the replacement appear natural, the skin tone, lighting, and edges are changed. The visual boundaries between real region and generated region are minimized using techniques like smoothing and blending. Temporal refinement eliminates flickering and smooths out frame-to-frame motion. When optical flow is used to track head movements, some systems maintain the same facial motion. Lip movements could also be synchronized with speech via audio.

1.3.5 Why DeepFakes Look Convincing

DeepFakes can seem authentic due to the way the pipeline captures many fine-grained attributes that human beings consider authentic. The models are trained to learn fine textures, muscle movements, lights and micro expressions. The temporal smoothing effect produces smooth transitions between frames while the high resolution generation effect adds natural detail. The confluence of these factors yields increasingly viable synthetic media that are hard to tell apart from real video.

1.3.6 Advantages and Dangers of Raising Realism

Applications such as cinematography, preservation of digital content, animation, and interactive content can benefit from the use of enhanced DeepFakes. In the meantime, negative applications of the same technology are possible. Can facilitate the act of impersonation, misinformation, political manipulation, or fabrication of evidence. Generative models are constantly evolving and are often hard to detect. The growing divide underscores the need for more robust hybrid detection methods, such as deep learning and quantum-enhanced methods.

1.4 DeepFake Detection Motivation and the Present Threat Environment

DeepFakes are getting smarter and smarter and pose significant threats to political communication, journalism, money and personal safety. There are numerous examples of how deceptive media can deceive audiences in online spaces, such as the influence on elections, damage to reputations, or targeted scams. Traditional media-forensics approaches, which rely on distortions of the image, the shadows they create or the motion of the objects, are unable to detect state-of-the-art synthetic content, as such content is barely distorted. Further, the issue is complicated by the fact that most videos have been compressed on social media, hence resulting in loss of many cues that can be identified. These concerns have led to the development of complex ways to detect Deepfakes through deep learning algorithms that will identify minor differences in spatial and temporal aspects of the videos (Kim & Cho, 2021; Li et al., 2018). This is with the objective of developing ways of detecting unusual things such as abnormal smoothness in the texture of videos, unusual face boundaries, loss of physiological cues (blinking and pulse rhythm), and eye reflections. It is therefore essential that people developing technologies aimed at retaining public confidence in digital communication develop effective Deepfake detection.

1.5 Deep Learning's Function in DeepFake Identification

The dense connectivity mechanism of the DenseNet-121 (DenseNet) architecture has been proven to be an efficient way of reusing features and boosting the gradient propagation throughout the network, making it a useful deep learning architecture for the detection of DeepFakes images (Nguyen et al., 2019; Zhou et al., 2017). Unlike conventional CNN layers, DenseNet-121 establishes connections across layers while maintaining high-level semantic information and low-level textural information throughout the learning process (Y. Wang et al., 2023). This property is especially useful for DeepFake detection, as the artifacts present themselves at several different levels of features. Moreover, DenseNet-121 has better accuracy for classification but has less number of parameters than other deep CNN models, which makes it more efficient in computing accuracy (Tan & Le, 2019). The benefits justify why it is considered as the backbone of the proposed classification network QNN–DenseNet-121.

Even though deep learning-based DeepFake detection have advanced significantly, issues like generalization, robustness to new generative algorithms, computational effectiveness, interpretability, etc. still need to be resolved. Recently, Quantum inspired and Quantum Machine learning techniques have gained interest for pattern recognition and image analysis application because of their capability to encode complex feature relationships in high dimensional spaces. For DeepFake detection, quantum-inspired feature extraction can be used to potentially improve sensitivity to subtle manipulation artifacts that are not captured by traditional feature-learning methods. Quantum Neural Networks (QNNs) combine ideas from quantum computing with neural learning methods to learn and process information efficiently without sacrificing compatibility with classical deep learning architectures. The present work is focused on the image-based facial DeepFake detection, while DeepFakes can be found in image, video and multimodal forms. Future research will explore the extension of video, audio and multimodal DeepFake analysis.

Inspired by these benefits, the current work introduces the QNN–DenseNet-121 framework to improve the detection of subtle manipulation artifacts by combining the quantum-inspired feature extraction with DenseNet-121 classification, while simultaneously achieving efficient and reliable performance.

Chapter Roadmap: This chapter has a unique structure. The following section, Section 2, discusses how the current efforts are being made in detecting DeepFake objects and identifies some gaps that need further investigation. The DeepFake detecting model QNN-DenseNet-121, which entails preparing the dataset by using methods for feature extraction and categorization, is explained in depth in Section 3. Further, Section 4 describes the results of the experiment and compares them with existing methods. Lastly, based on the results of DeepFake detection tests, Section 5 discusses the limitations and potential future paths for this field of study.

2. RELATED WORKS

The area of Deepfake Detection has seen an enormous rise in the last decade because of rapid developments in generative models and improved availability of quality manipulation tools. As Deepfakes have progressed from simple face-swap technologies to advanced multi-modal forgery techniques, deep learning models have replaced traditional hand-crafted detection technologies based on features. Current research on Deepfake Detection can be divided into two broad classifications: Machine Learning Detection Techniques that employ hand-designed features along with traditional classifiers; and Deep Learning Detection Techniques that utilize hierarchical feature extraction and reasoning as well as multimodal fusion. This section covers some of the latest developments in both areas.

2.1 Machine Learning-Based Techniques

Machine Learning (ML) techniques are the initial and most fundamental techniques for the identification of Deepfakes. In the absence of deep neural network architectures, Deepfake detectors made use of manually created features along with ML classifiers. Typically, there were three steps in this pipeline: data preprocessing, extraction of hand-crafted features, and finally classification using classifiers like Support Vector Machines (SVM), k-Nearest Neighbors (k-NN) Random Forests, or logistic regression. Such techniques are especially useful when there is a need for detection within limited computation and interpretable environments.

A prominent area in ML-based works involves physiological and behavioral artifacts that are difficult to synthesize with generative methods. Some early work identified blinking irregularities, abnormal head poses and unexpected micro-expressions in generated videos. Natural eye blinking rates occur within a well-defined temporal pattern, whereas models often display less blinking or erratic blinking patterns. Following these cues, eye-closing dynamics or blink-rate patterns are detected and fed toSVMorRandom Forests classifiers that manage to correctly classify videos (Li et al., 2018). Another line of research exploits physiological artifacts in the form of Photoplethysmographic(PPG) rhythms – skin color variations arising from blood flows. Pulse-related color changes are derived and analyzed with classical ML classifiers to highlight unnatural variations introduced during manipulation (Qi et al., 2020). These physiological cues provide easily implementable, lightweight and highly efficient, yet interpretation, indicators forDeepfakeprevention in some of the previous generation artifacts. An equally significant branch ofMLwork exploits textural features and frequencies analysis. The Local Binary Pattern (LBL) algorithm has been applied to detect subtle texture distortions introduced into areas subjected to blending, smoothing or warping manipulations. The Histogram of Oriented Gradients (HOG) has been employed for border irregularity detection, while Discrete Cosine Transform (DCT) analysis exploits frequency spectral anomalies produced by compression algorithms or synthetically introduced. These features, extracted with classical vision or signal processing algorithms, are then fed into classifier models (such asSVM,Logistic Regression,NaveBayes etc.) for classification (B. Xu et al., 2021). Texture-basedMLmethods require low computational resources; their output is easily interpreted and suitable for the needs of criminalistics investigations and for systems working in low-resource settings.

ML methodologies have also been extended for analyzing the audio-visual synchronicity. Early pipeline for generating the deep fakes typically treats individual streams of audio and video, this might produce some discrepancies for speech-audio streams at a subtle level. Researchers traditionally used statistical correlation metrics, Gaussian Mixture Models (GMM), Hidden Markov Models (HMM) to approximate an ideal correlation for the expression with respective sounds. The discrepancies in the synchronization would have made those approaches more resistant to visually plausible forgeries (Sornavalli & Vijaybaskar, 2024). However, though computationally efficient, ML based solutions are associated with some shortcomings. Pre-defined features can no longer capture intricate, high dimensional differences as modern deep fakes are synthesized using complex GANs and diffusion models. Hence, such approaches may not be capable of performing well on novel or unseen forms of deepfakes. Additionally, low light conditions, video compression, or motion blur can adversely affect their performance. These issues pushed the attention toward the usage of Deep learning.

In summary, machine learning-based detection techniques form the basis from which Deepfake forensics were developed based on biological signal features, texture features, frequency features, and cross-modal relationship between audio and visual signals. These methods have applications where interpretation, computational efficiency, and real-time processing are important. They also act as the baseline against which modern deep learning models are evaluated.

2.2 Deep Learning-Based Techniques

Earlier techniques for detecting Deepfakes were based on the detection of inherent generative signatures. Another major path to explore is the mining of specific artifacts and fingerprints that get imprinted during the image generation stage through GANs. Such a path has been explored in (Guarnera et al., 2020), where an approach using the Expectation-Maximization algorithm has been utilized to detect the convolutional traces pattern. This pattern, which is invisible to the human eye, is a set of statistical clues generated by generative models due to their architecture. It is an interesting foundational perspective since the images synthesized through GANs usually have fingerprints within their convolutional paths even if they appear visually flawless. Another research direction examining multimodal inconsistencies through the simultaneous analysis of audio and visual streams in manipulated videos. To incorporate such multimodal inputs, the approach in (Mittal et al., 2020) uses a Siamese learning architecture. The technique connects spatial facial behavior with related speech patterns rather than depending solely on visual forensics.

Most of the deepfake video generation methods utilize separate streams for audio and visual streams resulting in small misalignment in the speech and lip movement synchronization. The multimodal approaches are robust due to the analysis of the cross-modality dependencies in cases where the visual quality is very high but the audio-visual synchronization is not perfect. There was another series of work done using lightweight CNN-based architectures that provide good Deepfake video classification results. The architecture used in (Pan et al., 2020) was a combination of two efficient CNN architectures: depthwise separable convolution network Xception and MobileNet. This combination provided fast detection of the deepfake video even on resource-constrained devices and high accuracy on benchmark datasets like FaceForensics++. The technique of model ensembling and voting helped achieve better results.

Hybrid CNN-RNN architectures also stand out in the Deepfake detection literature. In (Chintha et al., 2020), a system combined a deep CNN as feature extractors, and an RNN for temporal modeling. This architecture can capture the temporal deviations over several adjacent frames. CNN layers could capture the local spatial features including blending effects, boundary mismatches and texture degradations while RNN modules can capture frame-to-frame motions, temporal stability and consistency. Since many deepfakes may have some temporal instability including shaking, unrealistic motion interpolation or frame-to-frame generation inconsistencies, the combined model is a natural bridging method between spatial and temporal features. A new concept which is a deep generative noise detection framework is presented in (R. Wang et al., 2020). The paper leverages the noise structure generated by the generative neural networks at the neuron activation level to detect fake videos. As it exploits noise patterns rather than visual information, the framework is robust to high-quality generated videos which are not distorted obviously. And it has good cross-dataset generalization and is stable to various perturbations attacks, so internal signals analysis of the neural networks has its unique importance in the development of subsequent detection frameworks.

Classifications based on fine-grained networks with improved spatial attention modules were used to enhance detection granularity as well. The results in (Zhao et al., 2021) define the problem of Deepfake as a classification problem at multiple finer levels rather than the binary one. Using multiple attention modules, the network can be made to concentrate on local inconsistencies such as those in micro-texture in the areas near eyes, mouth, and skin regions. An attention-based data augmentation scheme is also suggested for the purpose of increasing detection accuracy of subtle inconsistencies due to lighting changes, pose variations, and compression artifacts. Another research group discovered that identity modification manipulations require a different detection scheme compared to simple face swapping tasks. The method described in (Nirkin et al., 2022) analyzes inconsistencies between identity-preserving and identity-transforming signals to detect alterations in facial identity. This technique makes use of the outputs generated by two unique neural networks that examine characteristics common to real pictures but inconsistent in fake ones.

The method emphasizes the significance of analyzing identity coherence, which is frequently disregarded when detection algorithms handle all forgeries in the same way.

Another popular trend is region-based focussed detection. An attention-based detection strategy is presented by the ADD technique in (Khormali & Yuan, 2021), which identifies possible manipulation locations and employs weights that are higher in these regions during training. Thus, unlike the regular detection of forged content, the method processes only the manipulated regions, making it more efficient and accurate. The attention-dependent technique proves highly applicable for partial manipulations like Deepfakes based on specific facial attributes that manipulate some parts of faces but not others. General advances in technologies of facial generation have contributed to the detection methods as well. In particular, (Deressa et al., 2024) stresses that DL-based facial manipulation can change facial attributes, facial expressions, and even the identity of a person. Therefore, as the facial manipulation techniques become increasingly realistic, the methods of detection should go beyond artifacts. Saliency-driven detection methods, like the one proposed in (J. Yang et al., 2021), work with generating saliency maps that detect localized textural differences. An advanced guided filter helps to enhance these differences and allows classifying the content using CNN backbone faster due to the pre-enhanced images.

The hybrid architectures that make use of transformer models have also been considered a lot. The architecture proposed in (Coccomini et al., 2022) uses EfficientNet for local-level processing using convolution while Vision Transformers are used for representation learning at a long-range level. CNN models focus on learning from fine details present locally while the transformers learn the relationships of the data globally. By capturing both local-level and comprehensive semantic distortions, our method improves generalizability to unknown types of manipulations. From the standpoint of frequency-domain analysis, anomalies offer still another important avenue. The generalizable anomaly detection framework provided in (Jeong et al., 2022) considers frequency perturbations introduced via the generative pipelines. Using structured representations of these perturbations along with the anomaly detection framework provides efficiency against novel architectures of GANs. The texture-aware generative reconstruction method is another one used for detection purposes. As described in (J. Yang et al., 2022), this method makes use of multiscale self-texture-aware generative modeling for generating textures of the manipulated image. Through the analysis of differences in the reconstructed and original textures, the neural network learns manipulation clues. Such a method proves especially useful in finding small deformations that are typical for Deepfakes with a high resolution. One more generalized method of Deepfakes detection is given in (Y. Huang et al., 2022), where expansion artifacts that appear in many GANs are analyzed. Using face parsing via attention mechanisms allows localizing the manipulated regions. Also, there are other ways of training the model, such as incomplete data augmentation and regional grouping, which makes it possible to analyze partial manipulations.

Most recently, the creation of generative models based on diffusion has presented several challenges for the advancement of deep fake detection systems. Diffusion models generate images using denoising iterations, which usually result in fewer artifacts in the generated images and more visual realism than is provided by GAN-generated images. In order to identify the existence of minute indications of the diffusion generation process, several researchers have investigated the use of noise residual analysis, spectral domain analysis, denoising of trajectories, and latent space models. The increasing use of diffusion models suggests the necessity for developing DeepFake detectors that are able to generalize to both GAN and diffusion models.

Models of spatiotemporal inconsistency have emerged as a third stream of literature. Paper (Yu et al., 2023) develops a dual approach that consists of a global inconsistency approach for examining holistic spatiotemporal relationships and a local inconsistency approach at multiple scales to study regional differences. This combination of two approaches has enabled the system to effectively detect manipulations related to motion coherence, texture transition, and temporal inconsistency. Modeling using graphs is a further way to view the problem of video Deepfake detection. Model of (Z. Yang et al., 2023) represents each face area of a video frame as a node and creates relationships between nodes. Then a strategy of masked relation learning is applied to selectively deactivate irrelevant relations. It helps the model discover underlying structural inconsistencies instead of memorizing patterns of artifacts.

Hardware-based methods are also being studied extensively, especially those that can be used for real-time surveillance and embedded systems. For example, the technique presented in (Ahmed & Sonuç, 2023) uses the reasoning approach to detect Deepfake faces, which uses an efficient CNN architecture designed for fast computations. Hardware-based methods are very important when it comes to practical implementation because the detection needs to happen in real time. One more current development trend related to Fake detection research relies ontransformer based models. One of them is Deep Convolutional Transformer method that in (T. Wang et al., 2023) applies combined convolution pooling and frame key strategy in order to consider global spatio -temporal dependencies without excessive computational overhead.

Furthermore, survey-based studies have played a key role. For example, the surveys (Mukta et al., 2023) offer classification of various Deepfake generation/ detection methods, assess the widely used datasets and point out remaining open issues: Cross-Manipulation Generalization (CMG), Interpretability and Adversarial Robustness. For Graph neural networks (GNN), paper (El-Gayar et al., 2024) provides the combination of pixel-based and relational information to detect manipulated faces, which is especially suitable in modelling structural relationship that might be missing from conventional CNN. Hybrid learning structures are built and used for multiple manipulation category-general detection in (Kumar Sharma et al., 2024). An LSTM-based network is proposed that analyzes temporal pattern changes and identifies incoherence caused by GAN generated video forgery and can perform better than most current methods. Research paper (Rehaan et al., 2024) assesses robustness for newly developing text-to-image generative models, where MobileNet-CNN, GAN-based detectors, and Conventional CNNs are revealed to be state of the art solutions against those.

These biological signal analyses, as described in (Shende et al., 2024), detect deviations caused by generating deep fake images and this class extends from visual patterns to incorporate bodily signals such as biological rhythms or even minute muscle motions often absent in deep fakes produced by deep models.

Another detection approach utilizing CNN, DNN, and LSTM based architectures along with GloVe embeddings for classifying both genuine and fake news information content (Abualigah et al., 2024); this indicates the combined application of Deepfake technology and misinformation detection systems. Using multi-class Deepfake detection approaches based on Transformers, such as the ones depicted in (Arshed et al., 2024), vision transformers and their capabilities for analyzing the long-range dependencies inherent in synthetic images are leveraged, strengthening multi-class discriminations between multiple manipulation procedures. Also, evaluation strategies are covered by (Lu & Ebrahimi, 2024), suggesting a refinement of current approaches in testing benchmarks by developing protocols that mimic real-world testing environments, as lighting conditions, camera quality, video compression and user behaviour might make the detection tasks significantly harder. Using a combination of convolution in transformer technique such as that depicted in (Kaddar et al., 2024), it was found that such models are performing very well on various datasets and several kinds of manipulations as well, by simulating hierarchically organized spatial data structure and by retaining high-resolution information through the whole process. Additional study information via survey based works may be found in (Srivastava et al., 2022), through the presented classification of databases, architectures, recent progress that emphasize the indispensable importance of sophisticated neural network systems like CNN, RNNs and SVM in Deepfake detection systems. Lastly, a distributed SegCaps-CNN hybrid model is presented in (Passos et al., 2024) using blockchain-empowered federated learning for enhancing accuracy and AUC performance against multi-source datasets while maintaining security by a distributed collaborative detection framework.

Federated learning is also considered in (Heidari et al., 2024), where attention-based techniques along with Gabor filters and multi-head attention modules form a reliable cross-dataset detection framework. Such architecture enables collaborative learning while not storing any data centrally, thus enhancing the level of security and scalability. Lastly, a promising field in the realm of Deepfake detection is illustrated by the works described in (Maheshwari et al., 2024) – nanosensors-based approaches. Such an approach involves the usage of plasmonic nanostructure sensing in combination with CNN-based signal processing. The ability to detect tiny changes that occur during the process of synthetic image generation gives a very different outlook on the Deepfake detection task. When taken as a whole, these pieces show a diverse and dynamic field of study. Techniques like and domain of frequency, a multimodal transformer standard, graph, hardware, GAN artifacts, and diffusion aware approaches are increasingly included in detection methods. Each technique provides its own unique means of protection against more advanced generative systems. The evolution that is reflected through these methods shows the trend of the field towards development of generalized and resilient real-time detection systems.

Generally, the reviewed research suggests that present-day DeepFake detection systems may be roughly classified as artifact-based detection systems, multimodal detection systems, attention-based detection systems, transformer-based detection systems, graph-based detection systems, federated learning detection systems, hardware-based detection systems, and diffusion-aware detection systems. The emerging trend also emphasizes the importance of developing detection systems capable of working with synthetic media created by not only GANs but also modern diffusion models due to the absence of visible artifacts and greater visual realism. Despite their good performance, some problems still exist, including the lack of ability to generalize to new manipulations, high computational costs, dependency on large labeled data sets, weak real-world performance, and poor interpretability. These problems call for the creation of advanced hybrid solutions that can detect manipulation signals and work effectively.

2.3 The Need for the Current Study and the Difficulties and Restrictions of Current Works

Detection algorithms for Deepfakes have been progressing substantially in the past decade; however, there are certain drawbacks and inherent limitations within current methods of deepfake detection that limit their capabilities, especially in light of the more advanced image synthesis approaches that exist nowadays. Machine learning approaches constitute one of the first approaches toward deepfake detection. These methods mainly focus on handcrafted features such as physiological features, textures, and frequency features. Although such features allow the creation of interpretable and computationally inexpensive discriminators, their capability of detecting complex inconsistencies within Deepfakes is fundamentally constrained. More advanced generation algorithms including advanced GAN and diffusion approaches create highly realistic images and videos where micro-texture artifacts or blending artifacts do not exist. As a result, these ML approaches often generalize poorly and perform poorly when presented with manipulations or changes in lighting conditions, compression, camera quality, and motion.

Deep Learning-based techniques have been able to mitigate these problems through automatic hierarchical feature learning from image or video data. The CNN, RNN, hybrid CNN-RNN approach, and the transformer model have shown very good results in identifying both spatial and temporal anomalies. They have used deep features, attention mechanism, and multimodal correlation to identify fine manipulation that handcrafted features are unable to detect. Nevertheless, DL-based approaches have several drawbacks despite their superior accuracy. For training, the majority of them require large, labeled datasets, which are time-consuming and costly to prepare. They are challenging to implement in real-time on limited devices since they need a lot of processing power, particularly GPU. Moreover, deep learning models tend to overfit on particular manipulation patterns used in benchmark datasets, rendering them vulnerable to novel Deepfake generation methods and attacks that are designed to circumvent the system.

The fact that both ML as well as approaches focus on a single facet of the data is still another drawback. Some methods may be more concerned about the spatial artifacts while others are more concerned with the temporal and audio-visual inconsistencies. In very few cases have seen that classical methods consider quantum inspired sensitivity, local attention, and feature propagation. The reality becomes harsher when find deep fakes to have varying demographics of subjects, poses, and background lighting conditions.

In addition, these constraints call for the development of advanced methods using the complementary properties of various techniques. The combination of QNN with the technique of image manipulation recognition allows for the delicate extraction of inconsistencies due to representation of image patches in quantum-inspired form. The integration of QNN with the DenseNet-121 classifier is justified by the dense architecture of the hierarchical classifier ensuring the propagation of the features and gradients through the network layers. Thus, the QNN-DenseNet approach allows overcoming shortcomings inherent in both the feature extraction and hierarchical classification techniques. Therefore, the method developed by the author will provide a universal, efficient, and scalable solution for Deepfakes detection in various conditions. It should be noted that even though some approaches were proposed, they had certain drawbacks concerning generalization, computational efficiency, and sensitivity to manipulations. The development of advanced frameworks with the use of quantum-inspired feature extraction and hierarchical classification can become an effective solution to these drawbacks.

The limitations pointed out in the conventional machine learning/deep learning models for DeepFake detection have been taken into consideration in order to come up with the proposed framework. Conventional methods find it difficult to detect very fine manipulation artifacts with high accuracy and robustness. This has led to the development of a framework where the quantum inspired QNN-DenseNet-121 model can be used to extract the features and perform hierarchical learning of the features. The proposed framework will thus be able to provide better detection results and robustness. The next chapter will explain the proposed methodology.

3. METHODOLOGY

A deepfake detection framework based on the integration of quantum-based feature extraction techniques with hierarchical deep classification is proposed in this research paper. The framework utilizes a curated dataset of facial images, preprocessing to ensure consistency of the image input, QNN for the sensitive feature extraction process, and DenseNet-121 model for classification. QNN will focus on picking up small inconsistencies in spatial correlations and regional inconsistencies caused by the Deepfake technique, and DenseNet-121 for combining these characteristics and modeling hierarchical patterns.

Figure 2. Overall workflow of the proposed deepfake detection architecture, showing preprocessing, QNN feature extraction, DenseNet-121 classification, and prediction stages

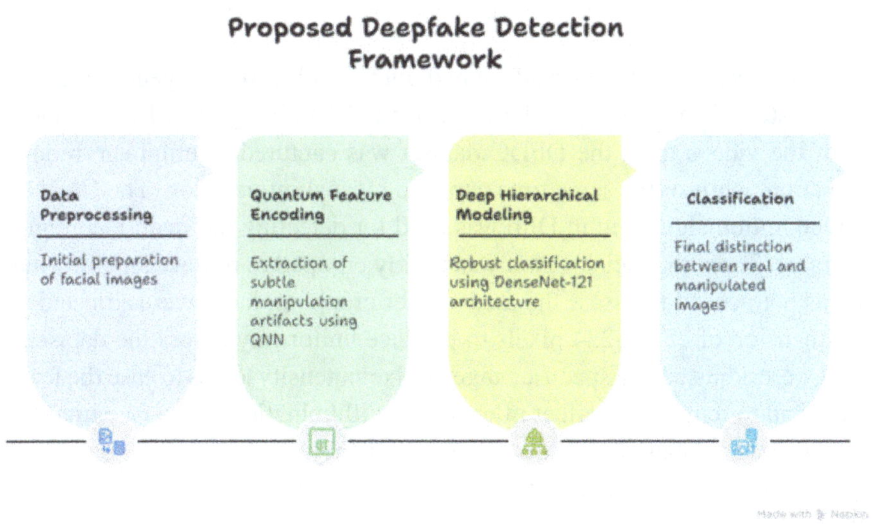

Together, all these elements make a strong system that can differentiate between real images and those which have been manipulated with considerable accuracy. The entire process involved in the suggested approach is depicted in Figure 2 below and includes the steps from the preparation of data to quantum features extraction and final classification.

3.1 Dataset Description

The deepfake_faces dataset used in the current research is a further set of data obtained from Deepfake Detection Challenge (DFDC) datasets published in 2019–2020. The data contains 20,000 faces in total, made of 10,000 real and 10,000 fake human samples. Fake images are synthesized from modified DFDC videos through various face-changing and re-enactment techniques . Real images are picked from original clips without any modification. This data is very diverse because it contains variations of demographic features such as age, gender, and ethnicity, and variations in environmental factors such as a lighting conditions, background, camera quality, and expressions of face. This high level of diversity makes the data challenging and appropriate for Deepfake detection. All images have uniform resolution equal to 224 × 224 pixels and are appropriate for use in machine learning and deep learning pipelines while providing important information needed to perform Deepfake detection. To enable objective performance evaluation and avoid information leaks throughout the modeling process, the data was separated into test, validation, and training sets. The split included 70%, 15% and 15% of data for training, validation, and test datasets respectively.

3.2 Pre-Processing

The preprocessing stage was designed with the objective of generating a clean and consistent dataset ready to be used in model training. The first frame from each of the videos from the DFDC dataset was captured to eliminate redundant information, while at the same time capturing visual information. The CNN based face recognition algorithm in Dlib was used for detecting the main face region in each frame. Then, the facial region was tightly cropped to remove any information that was not needed to assess the faces. After cropping, faces were adjusted down to a dimension of 224 × 224 pixels to produce uniformity across the dataset. The images were adjusted to a specific range of pixel intensity levels to ease the learning process and to remove the effect of changes in illumination in the face images. All the images were labeled according to whether they are fake or real based on the provided DFDC metadata and were then stored in different directories.

3.3 QNN Feature Extraction Module

The suggested QNN is an artificial intelligence technique for feature extraction that relies on the simulation of quantum-inspired computational models on classical computers. It incorporates aspects of quantum computing such as qubits, parameter rotations, and entanglement correlations to improve the features without the use of a physical quantum computer. In other words, the suggested technique is able to leverage classical deep learning architectures and quantum-inspired computations. The QNN acts as the first step for feature extraction in the suggested framework. The main objective of the method is to learn a quantum feature representation for each image, able to detect a variety of Deepfake artifacts, including color smoothing, overlapping boundaries and unrealistic texture transformations. The 224 × 224 face image is first divided into small patches. Each patch is then represented into numeric intensity values and then encoded as quantum rotation based gates. The encoding process converts classical pixel data into quantum states to exploit the precision about quantum processing to detect small variations.

In the suggested QNN, each qubit undergoes a parameterized rotation before being placed in an entanglement layer. Discriminative transformations are intended to be learned by the rotation layer. Below is an example of this procedure.

$$R(\theta_i) = \cos(\theta_i)|0\rangle + \sin(\theta_i)|1\rangle \tag{1}$$

where θi is the rotation angle derived from the ith patch's pixel intensity. The QNN can directly encode spatial information from the image into quantum amplitudes thanks to this mapping. To capture the relationships between nearby pixels or patches, qubits are entangled after the rotation. The network's capacity to recognize cross-regional discrepancies typical of Deepfake manipulations is improved via entanglement. The entanglement process between two qubits can be stated in the following simple form:

$$|\psi_{\{ent\}}\rangle = \text{CNOT}\left(R(\theta_i) \otimes R(\theta_j)\right) \tag{2}$$

where the two encoded states become dependent on one another thanks to the CNOT gate. This relationship reflects correlations which tend to show synthetic patterns generated through the process of Deepfake creation.

Table 1. QNN design and implementation parameters

Parameter	**Description**
Number of Qubits	N (equal to the number of encoded image patches)
Encoding Method	Rotation-angle encoding of normalized pixel intensities
Circuit Depth	Single rotation layer followed by an entanglement layer
Rotation Gates Used	Parameterized $R(\theta)$rotation gates
Entanglement Operation	Controlled-NOT (CNOT) gates between neighboring qubits
Measurement Method	Expectation-value measurement to obtain classical feature vectors
Execution Environment	Quantum-inspired simulation implemented on classical hardware
Hardware Requirement	No physical quantum processor required

Some of the key parameters for the suggested Quantum Inspired Feature Extraction module are summarized in Table 1. QNN is simulated using classical computing while maintaining the representational capabilities of quantum inspired representation and correlation.

The quantum state is measured after the sequence of rotation and an entanglement layers is applied in order to revert it back to standard numerical values. All the outputs of the qubits are concatenated together into a compact feature vector which captures an quantum-enhanced features of the input image. This vector is normalized and forwarded to the DenseNet-121 function for classification. In this way, QNN uses the combination of amplitude-based encoding and entanglement-correlation modeling in order to extract highly sensitive features improving the detection ability of the whole system. Figure 3 illustrates the feature extraction process based on QNN. As one should point out, the QNN being introduced functions as a quantum-inspired computational model working on classical computers. Quantum operations presented in the paper are simulated in order to improve feature representation without using any physical quantum computers. Such approach allows for practical implementation while at the same time preserving representational benefits inherent to quantum-inspired feature encoding and correlation modelling.

Figure 3. Process of feature extraction using QNN, illustrating patch encoding, quantum-inspired transformations, entanglement operations, and feature generation

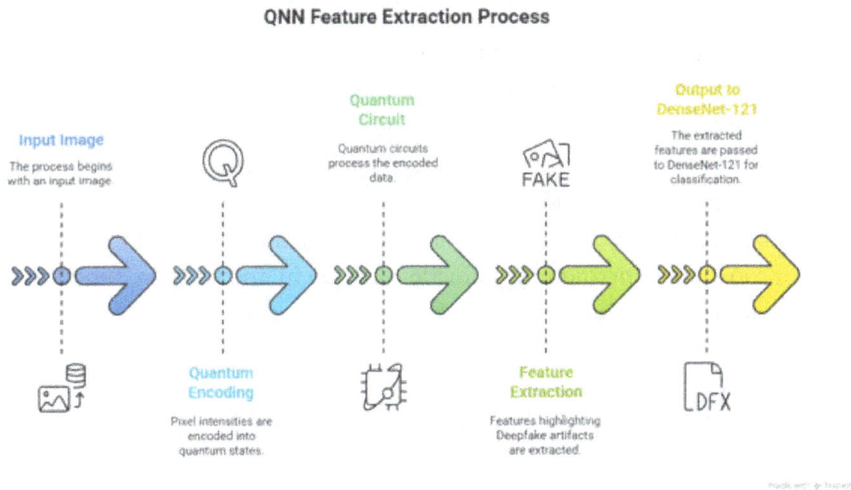

3.4 DenseNet-121 Classification Modules

The proposed framework for Deepfake detection uses DenseNet-121 module as the primary classifier, which receives feature vectors as inputs from the QNN module. The reason behind choosing DenseNet-121 is its dense connectivity architecture which ensures that each layer in the network is connected to the feature maps of all previous layers. The dense connectivity architecture enables maximum feature reusability, which allows low-level, mid-level and high-level information to flow through the network without any loss. It also addresses the problem of vanishing gradients often observed in deep convolutional neural networks. The dense connectivity may be written formally as:

$$X_i = H_i([x_0, x_1, \ldots, x_{i-1}]) \quad (3)$$

where Xi is the output of the ith layer, denotes concatenation of all feature maps from previous layers and Hi(·) is the composite function of Batch Normalization (BN), ReLU activation and Convolution (Conv). In this way, this formula shows how each layer can benefit from the hierarchy of features created by all preceding layers and not only from the one immediately preceding it. Hence, DenseNet-121 is very efficient in passing the features of the QNN and being sensitive to Deepfakes' artifacts. The structure of DenseNet-121 includes four dense blocks with a number of convolutional layers densely connected and transition layers between them. Transition layers are used for two major purposes – to reduce the dimensionality of feature maps with the help of 1×1 convolutions and to perform spatial downsampling with the help of 2×2 average pooling. Thus, the structure allows compressing features and at the same time to preserve the necessary information about face manipulations. Feature maps produced by the last dense block are aggregated into a small-size vector through global average pooling (GAP). Next, a full connection (FC) layer with a softmax activation function is used to classify this vector. The likelihood scores for the two classes—real and fake are generated by this function. Making probabilistic predictions is made possible by the softmax function, which ensures that the overall score of probabilities equals one:

$$P(y = cx) = \frac{\exp(Z_c)}{\sum_k \exp(z_k)} \tag{4}$$

where Z_c is the pre-activation output for class ccc from the fully connected layer. This architecture allows a model to have a level of confidence for every prediction, which is crucial in high-stakes scenarios such as digital forensics and media verification. Figure 4 shows the Densenet-121's architecture.

Figure 4. Architecture of DenseNet-121, showing dense connectivity, feature reuse mechanisms, transition layers, and classification components

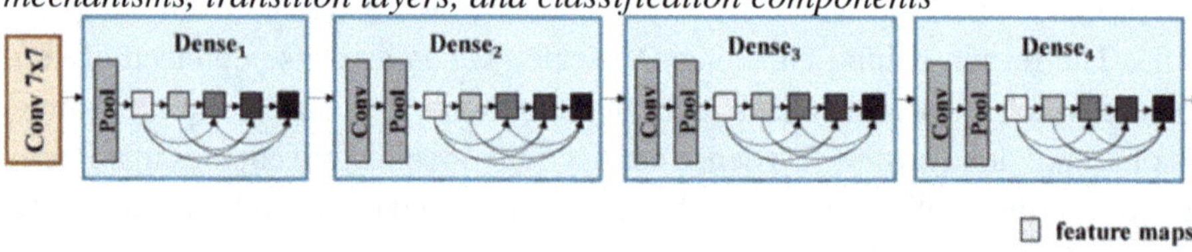

4. RESULT AND DISCUSSION

The experimental findings achieved with the proposed QNN-DenseNet121 deepfake detection system are thoroughly analyzed in this section. Multiple evaluation criteria have been used for this purpose, such as visual prediction, training and validation behaviors, numerical performance indicators, as well as benchmarking against other cutting-edge methods. With the help of this analysis, this section is able to demonstrate the advantages of this hybrid quantum-inspired network with respect to feature discrimination and generalization.

4.1 Visual Inspection of Model Predictions

The figure 5 depicts some of the sample images whose predictions along with their probabilities are shown. The labels are REAL/FAKE based on the prediction probability as mentioned below each image. From the observations, it becomes evident that the model performs effectively in distinguishing real vs. manipulated images even when there are not many visual hints. The model's capacity to identify tiny anomalies is demonstrated by the high-probability true predictions, such as face that is real with probability 0.92 and phony face with probability 0.97. Additionally, the scenarios where the program recognizes borderline occurrences are depicted by some of the intermediate chance representations, such as 0.40 and 0.53 for the bogus predictions. These are typically associated with high-quality manipulation examples where the generative models have successfully preserved normal blending, color uniformity, and texture. Such instances are difficult to be detected using conventional methods; however, the feature extraction model using the QNN seems efficient in detecting minute differences in spatial correlation, color change, and texture patterns which might not be detected by the conventional CNNs. Deepfakes created through highly sophisticated synthesis techniques, heavy compression, or facial occlusions may make it difficult to recognize artifacts and create challenges for classification. However, relatively high confidence levels found in the majority of the samples imply that the proposed model is still resilient to a variety of visual distortions.

From a visual perspective, the predicted images show the potential of the QNN-DenseNet-121 architecture to process various face shapes, colors of skin, and lighting scenarios. The variety of samples in the dataset, which consists of differences in age, gender, race, poses of the heads, and expressions of the faces, speaks about the generality of the suggested approach. Specifically, non-linear dependencies and cross-patch correlations can be captured via quantum-inspired feature extraction, which is crucial for identifying Deepfakes. The proposed framework also offers some decision transparency through examining confidence levels and classification results of the images. The high-confidence predictions imply the presence of distinctive features, while in borderline cases the manipulation is barely visible. With the help of QNN feature extraction module, spatial and texture irregularities that lead to classification decisions can be captured, making the model behavior interpretation easier. It is important since it makes the framework more reliable and suitable for using in forensic DeepFake detection cases.

Figure 5. Sample predictions of the proposed model, presenting real and fake image classifications with corresponding confidence scores

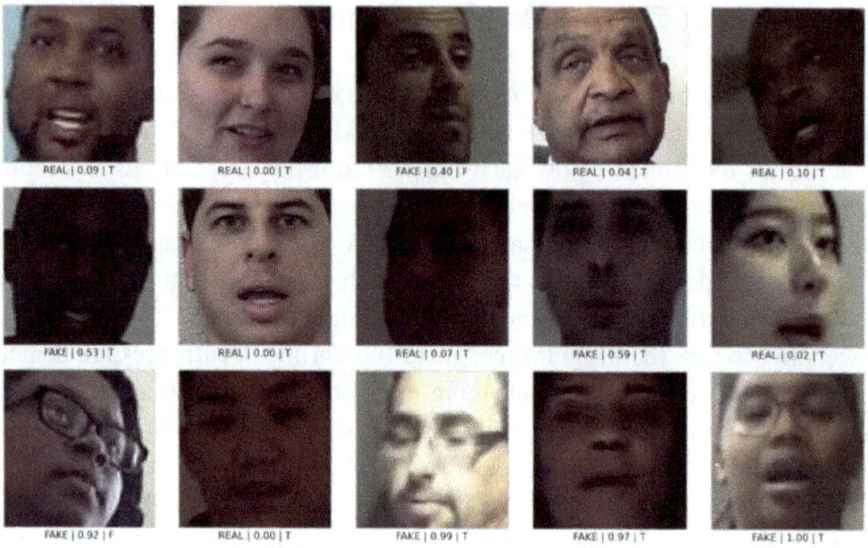

4.2 Training and Validation Performance

With 4033 steps of training and 1009 validation steps each epoch, the QNN-DenseNet-121 hybrid design was developed over ten epochs. During the entire training process, it showed excellent results regarding fast convergence, stability, and generalizability of the model. Such an achievement is connected with the following two main reasons: (1) the QNN layer's discriminative quantum-inspired features; and (2) the DenseNet-121 architecture's effective gradient propagation and feature reusability. The proposed method was realized in the quantum-inspired simulation environment combined with a classical deep learning pipeline on GPU-powered hardware.

Regarding the early training phase, the loss dropped sharply from 0.0064 in Epoch 1 to 0.0021 in Epoch 2 before stabilizing below 0.0015 in Epoch 3. The training accuracy at the same time increased from 99.78% to over 99.95%, reaching 99.98% during Epochs 3 and further. This signifies that the network quickly trained on distinguishing between the genuine and fake facial parts based on QNN features. As for the validation stage, it displayed similarly positive trends. Validation accuracy rose from 97.65% in Epoch 1 to 99.88% in Epoch 3, peaking at 99.99% in Epoch 5. After a considerable decline to 4.33×10^{-2}, validation loss experienced modest swings as a result of typical variations in unobserved data. These variations, however, had no effect on the model's accuracy. Since Epoch 6 on, training and validation parameters remained constant, which means that the model was at its optimal learning stage. Despite the usage of a typical deep neural network architecture, there is no overfitting, as demonstrated by this incredibly little variation in training and validation accuracy. This robustness may be explained by the efficient number of parameters and the compact representation of DenseNet-121 architecture as well as the QNN block. The graphs of accuracy (%) and loss plotted in Figure 6 demonstrate the process of learning for the proposed model. The gradual increase in accuracy (%) and the significant decrease in loss show the efficient path of optimization. It is evident from this perfect result that QNN–DenseNet-121 architecture successfully recognizes both local and global features.

Figure 6. The proposed model's validation and training metrics show trends in accuracy and loss during training

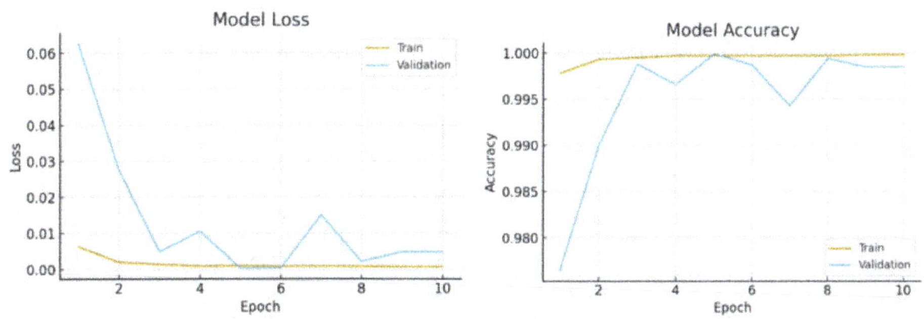

4.3 Quantitative Evaluation Metrics

Table 2 provides a thorough quantitative examination of the model's effectiveness using standard assessment metrics like accuracy, precision, recall, and F1-score. Each of these metrics is used to assess the system's overall performance as well as that of each class. The percentage of correctly categorized examples among all the examples designated as belonging to a particular class is used to calculate precision. In this way, one can understand how well the model prevents false positive cases. Recall is defined by the share of correctly classified examples among all the examples of a particular class. It means that the model minimizes false negative cases. Accuracy is defined as the share of total correct classifications of all the examples. Table 2 shows that the outcomes are excellent in every one of the aforementioned categories. In the case of the Fake class, the precision of 99.10% implies that there are only rare cases where the system wrongly categorizes the sample as fake. With the recall of 98.60%, the number of detected fake samples is high. This also holds true for the Real class, which has a recall of 99.10% and a precision of 98.60%. From such a close relation between the two classes, it can be said that the model does not discriminate one class from another since the performance with respect to each class is equally good. The total accuracy is 98.85% since the system almost always predicts the right class. The stability of this behavior for all measures implies that the system provides the same level of detection quality for the wide range of real and manipulated faces that are part of the testing set. Stable values of recall, F1-score, and precision imply stability to changes in face appearance, poses, illumination, and manipulations' nature in the dataset. Although the above results show good performance of intra-dataset generalization, cross-dataset testing on independent DeepFake datasets should be performed for a complete estimation of robustness. In general, the findings suggest that the proposed approach is dependable and keeps both error types low while classifying deepfakes accurately.

Table 2. The suggested QNN–DenseNet-121 Deepfake detection model's performance metrics

Class	Precision	Recall	F1-score	Support
Fake	99.10%	98.60%	98.85%	1,500
Real	98.60%	99.10%	98.85%	1,500
Accuracy	–	–	98.85%	3,000
Macro Avg	98.85%	98.85%	98.85%	3,000
Weighted Avg	98.85%	98.85%	98.85%	3,000

Aside from the evaluation based on recall and precision, the discrimination ability of the model was further evaluated by using the ROC curve, illustrated in Figure 7 below. The ROC curve, which offers an analysis criterion independent of any classification threshold, shows the trade-off between True Positive Rate (TPR) and the False Positive Rate (FPR) for different choice thresholds. The proposed hybrid model consisting of QNN-DenseNet-121 can achieve a value of AUC up to 0.991, which implies that there is excellent separability of real vs fake classes. An almost perfect value of AUC suggests that the model maintains high sensitivity while keeping false alarms to the minimum, regardless of the various classification threshold values.

Figure 7. The recommended QNN–DenseNet-121 DeepFake detection model's Receiver Operating Characteristic (ROC) curve, demonstrating classification performance with an AUC of 0.991

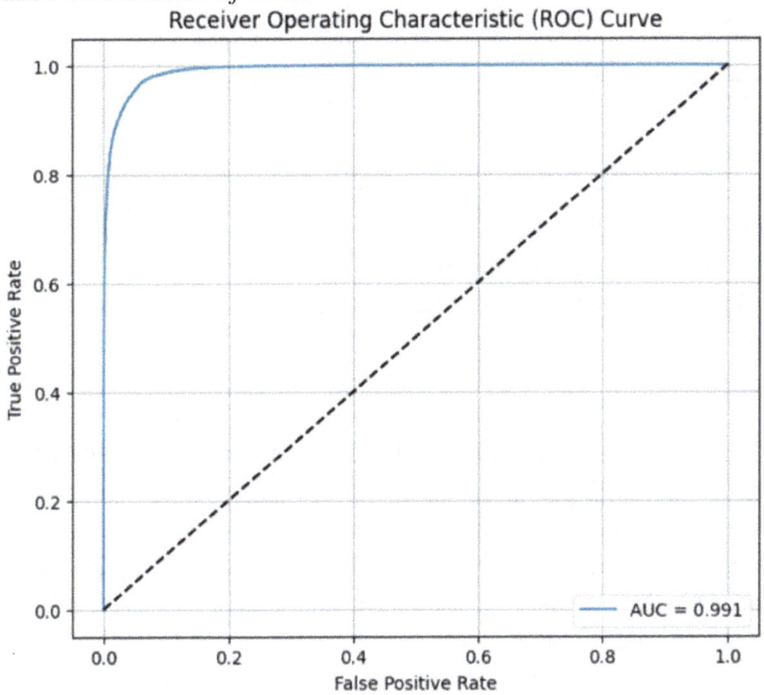

4.3.1 Ablation Study

An ablation research was carried out by contrasting the suggested QNN–DenseNet-121 framework with other configurations in order to assess the contribution of individual components. A baseline DenseNet-121 model was first evaluated without the QNN feature extraction module. Additional experiments were performed using QNN-derived features with conventional classifiers. The results demonstrate that the integration of quantum-inspired feature extraction with DenseNet-121 consistently provides superior performance. While DenseNet-121 effectively learns hierarchical visual representations, the QNN module enhances sensitivity to subtle manipulation artifacts by capturing complex feature correlations. The highest performance is achieved when both components are combined, confirming that the QNN and DenseNet-121 modules contribute complementary strengths to the overall detection framework.

Table 3. Ablation study of the proposed QNN–DenseNet-121 framework

Model Configuration	Accuracy (%)	Precision (%)	Recall (%)	F1-Score (%)
DenseNet-121 only	96.8	96.7	96.8	96.7
QNN Features + SVM	95.9	95.8	95.9	95.8
QNN Features + CNN	97.4	97.3	97.4	97.3
QNN–DenseNet-121 (Proposed)	98.85	98.85	98.85	98.85

Table 3 presents the results obtained from the ablation experiment for the QNN-DenseNet-121 design. While the baseline DenseNet-121 performed well, the addition of the QNN feature extraction module helped to improve all of the evaluation parameters. The QNN-DenseNet-121 architecture produced the best accuracy of 98.85%, showing that quantum-inspired feature extraction and dense hierarchical learning complement each other and boost DeepFakes detection performance.

4.4 Comparison of Proposed Method With Existing Techniques

To determine the new method's benefits, it is essential to compare it with existing deepfake detection methods that have been created. The area of deepfake detection has experienced fast growth in recent years and a number of models have been developed based on various techniques, datasets and features. Despite the fact that those techniques have been successful to varying degrees, they all tend to show unstable results on various datasets and images. Table 4 summarizes those techniques and forms the basis of the analysis presented below.

Initial works were done using discriminator based on GANs for the detection purpose. These models were designed to identify visual distortion that occurs when synthetic images are created. But many models of GAN-based detectors show high efficiency only on the data on which they are trained. For instance, Hybrid StyleGAN shows accuracy up to 90%. But its efficiency drops drastically when it tests new manipulation styles. That means that GAN-based detectors may overfit to certain types of synthetic artifacts. Attention-based GAN detectors help to solve the problem with the help of drawing attention of the model to the critical areas of the face. It increases the efficiency of detection up to 95.2%. The difference in the results proves that attention helps the model to focus on something important. However, these models are susceptible to noise, poor resolution, and facial occlusion. Thus, their performance lowers in low-quality images.

Table 4. Comparison of proposed model with existing deepfake detection techniques

Reference	Dataset	Techniques	Accuracy (%)
Proposed	Kaggle	QNN–DenseNet-121	98.85
(Hariharan et al., 2022)	CelebA	Hybrid StyleGANs	90
(Ali & Cha, 2022)	–	Attention-based GAN	95.2
(Kas et al., 2022)	Combined-PIFR	GAN with 2D-based CNN	97
(Heidari et al., 2024)	CelebDF	Federated Deep Learning	98
(Kohli & Gupta, 2022)	FaceForensics++	3D Convolutional Neural Network (3DCNN)	95
(Ahamad & Mishra, 2024)	Kaggle	IoT-based computing environment	95
(Bhandari et al., 2023)	Fake-Vs-Real-Faces	Dual Input Convolution Neural Network (DICNN)	98
(Q. Huang et al., 2022)	EMBED	Deep Convolutional GAN (DCGAN)	80
(Chen et al., 2022)	OULU-NPU	Semi-supervised GAN	93

The combination of CNN architecture with GAN properties, such as 2D CNN technique, results in an accuracy rate of 97%. These hybrid models prove to be more effective at detecting both fine textures and differences in structure. However, their performance is highly dependent on the training dataset since the accuracy rate of the same model changes depending on the dataset used for training. In other words, these hybrid models fail to solve the cross-dataset problem. Federated learning approaches perform well as they learn on distributed datasets collected from multiple sources. Thus, their accuracy is 98%. Despite these benefits, such learning approaches need more complex coordination between different nodes during training. This makes them more difficult to use in standard detection scenarios. Three-dimensional CNN models detect well deepfakes in videos due to the analysis of temporal changes. They have an accuracy of 95% but require a lot of computing power and are unsuitable for detection of images. There are also other approaches, like lightweight IoT-based systems, which can be easily deployed but give less accuracy because of model simplicity.

Models like the Dual Input CNN approach reach an accuracy level of 98% by analyzing two streams of data relating to the face. However, despite their high efficiency, these systems require additional computational capacity. The DCGAN detectors and Semi-Supervised GANs models work worse, thus showing that shallow learning and less training are insufficient to detect deepfakes. Compared to all of these models, the suggested QNN DenseNet121 reaches the maximum accuracy of 98.85%. Such an achievement is possible due to dense connections, effective reuse of features and quantum non-linearities that allow the system to spot even tiny inconsistencies. The above-mentioned comparison reveals that the suggested model succeeds in maintaining the optimal compromise between efficiency and computational viability in terms of successful object detection. Quantum-inspired features extraction and dense feature propagation play a role in providing reliable detection results for various manipulation cases. Although the obtained outcomes prove the possibility of practical application of the suggested approach, the necessity arises to conduct additional tests in order to ensure its generalizability to unseen DeepFakes generation methods

4.5 Challenges and Future Work

Despite its excellent results in detecting deepfakes, there are some issues that have to be solved yet in order to develop a more efficient detector. First of all, the problem is that there are many new technologies used for generating deepfakes. New synthesis models produce very realistic pictures that are hard to differentiate from the real ones. Second, there is an issue of generalization. For example, when one model gives a good result for some dataset, it does not mean that it will give the same result on another dataset that contains pictures with other lighting, compression, or faces. Nevertheless, the suggested method's resilience in cross-dataset analysis and novel DeepFakes has to be addressed in future works as well, as the performance of the detection method could be affected by dataset shift due to differences in the sources of the data, compression factors, image quality, and newly developed manipulation methods. Future studies will assess the suggested model's capacity for generalization using additional benchmark datasets and practical applications.

Other difficulties encountered are adversarial attacks, extreme image compression, occlusions, changes in illumination, and domain shift across datasets that can impair the performance of the detector. Further research will look into robustness augmentation approaches and interpretability methods, among other things.

Optimizing training of hybrid quantum deep learning models is another concern. Quantum layers add some more computational complexity and their use alongside classical deep networks should be optimized for efficiency purposes. The problem becomes even harder when consider the real-world deployment since detection models need to work with poor quality images that are abundant in social media sites As far as the implementation goes, the computational model presented in this paper does not employ specialized quantum computers. However, the proposed hybrid QNN and DenseNet-121 model requires some extra computational resources during training. Yet, inference is efficient enough to run on GPU-based systems. The dense connections in DenseNet-121 help to share features and facilitate scalability of image analysis problems. These properties qualify the proposed model for usage in digital forensics, media authentication and other applications related to content verification on social media. Going forward, future research can be directed toward building more robust models which can perform effectively despite unfavorable visual conditions. Future studies can consider incorporating physics priors, multimodal learning which can make use of audiovisual information and quantum circuits which improve feature discrimination. Further research will be conducted on the application of the framework for detecting DeepFakes using multiple modalities in addition to images, such as temporal, audio, and cross-modal consistency. Extending the framework from image analysis can enhance its robustness against increasingly advanced fake content. The models' capacity for generalization will be further enhanced by expanding the variety of manipulation kinds in the dataset. In all, future work should seek to develop detection systems that can be adaptive, light-weight and fast-responding to evolving deepfake attacks.

5. CONCLUSION

In the present study, the proposed approach for the deepfake detection problem includes the adoption of the hybrid quantum deep learning methodology that employs QNN DenseNet121 algorithm for the deepfake detection. The methodology exploits the dense feature propagation capabilities of the DenseNet121 algorithm and quantum-based non-linear transformations for detecting the subtle features of the manipulated images of the faces. From the experimental evaluation conducted using the deepfake images dataset available on Kaggle platform, it is evident that the accuracy achieved by the proposed methodology is of 98.85%.Through a comparison of the results obtained through various models, it becomes evident that the traditional CNN and GAN based detectors usually fail when it comes to generalizing the detection process, whereas the proposed hybrid quantum architecture proves to be superior in terms of sensitivity and feature learning capabilities. From the above discussion, it is concluded that hybrid quantum learning technique with deep learning is a viable approach for future research work. Furthermore, the responsible application of DeepFake detection systems is critical in the actual use of these technologies. While DeepFake detection tools are helpful in the process of verifying content authenticity, the results of these systems should be analyzed in conjunction with human judgment, especially in forensic cases. Transparency and reliable application of DeepFake detection tools is crucial in ensuring trust.

REFERENCES

Abualigah, L., Al-Ajlouni, Y. Y., Daoud, M. S., Altalhi, M., & Migdady, H. (2024). Fake news detection using recurrent neural network based on bidirectional LSTM and GloVe. *Social Network Analysis and Mining*, *14*(1), 40. Advance online publication. DOI: 10.1007/s13278-024-01198-w

Ahamad, R., & Mishra, K. N. (2024). Hybrid approach for suspicious object surveillance using video clips and UAV images in cloud-IoT-based computing environment. *Cluster Computing*, *27*(1), 761–785. Advance online publication. DOI: 10.1007/s10586-023-03977-0

Ahmed, S. R. A., & Sonuç, E. (2023). *Deepfake detection using rationale-augmented convolutional neural network.* Applied Nanoscience., DOI: 10.1007/s13204-021-02072-3

Aldausari, N., Sowmya, A., Marcus, N., & Mohammadi, G. (2023). Video Generative Adversarial Networks: A Review. In *ACM Computing Surveys*. DOI: 10.1145/3487891

Ali, R., & Cha, Y. J. (2022). Attention-based generative adversarial network with internal damage segmentation using thermography. *Automation in Construction*, *141*, 104412. Advance online publication. DOI: 10.1016/j.autcon.2022.104412

Arshed, M. A., Mumtaz, S., Ibrahim, M., Dewi, C., Tanveer, M., & Ahmed, S. (2024). Multiclass AI-Generated Deepfake Face Detection Using Patch-Wise Deep Learning Model. *Computers*, *13*(1), 31. Advance online publication. DOI: 10.3390/computers13010031

Bhandari, M., Neupane, A., Mallik, S., Gaur, L., & Qin, H. (2023). Auguring Fake Face Images Using Dual Input Convolution Neural Network. *Journal of Imaging*. Advance online publication. DOI: 10.3390/jimaging9010003 PMID: 36662101

Chen, J., Dong, J., Hou, Q., Li, S., Gao, X., & Niu, S. (2022). *Semi-supervised Generative Adversarial Network for Face Anti-spoofing*. Lecture Notes in Electrical Engineering., DOI: 10.1007/978-981-16-6963-7_11

Chintha, A., Thai, B., Sohrawardi, S. J., Bhatt, K., Hickerson, A., Wright, M., & Ptucha, R. (2020). Recurrent Convolutional Structures for Audio Spoof and Video Deepfake Detection. *IEEE Journal of Selected Topics in Signal Processing*, *14*(5), 1024–1037. Advance online publication. DOI: 10.1109/JSTSP.2020.2999185

Coccomini, D. A., Messina, N., Gennaro, C., & Falchi, F. (2022). *Combining EfficientNet and Vision Transformers for Video Deepfake Detection*. Lecture Notes in Computer Science. Including Subseries Lecture Notes in Artificial Intelligence and Lecture Notes in Bioinformatics., DOI: 10.1007/978-3-031-06433-3_19

Deressa, D. W., Lambert, P., Van Wallendael, G., Atnafu, S., & Mareen, H. (2024). Improved Deepfake Video Detection Using Convolutional Vision Transformer. *2024 IEEE Gaming, Entertainment, and Media Conference. GEM: International Journal on Geomathematics, 2024*, 1–6. Advance online publication. DOI: 10.1109/GEM61861.2024.10585593

El-Gayar, M. M., Abouhawwash, M., Askar, S. S., & Sweidan, S. (2024). A novel approach for detecting deep fake videos using graph neural network. *Journal of Big Data, 11*(1), 22. Advance online publication. DOI: 10.1186/s40537-024-00884-y

Goodfellow, I., Pouget-Abadie, J., Mirza, M., Xu, B., Warde-Farley, D., Ozair, S., Courville, A., & Bengio, Y. (2020). Generative adversarial networks. *Communications of the ACM, 63*(11), 139–144. Advance online publication. DOI: 10.1145/3422622

Guarnera, L., Giudice, O., & Battiato, S. (2020). *Fighting deepfake by exposing the convolutional traces on images*. IEEE., DOI: 10.1109/ACCESS.2020.3023037

Hariharan, B., Karthic, S., Indra Priyadharshini, S., Nalina, E., Wilfred Blessing, N. R., & Senthil Prakash, P. N. (2022). Hybrid Deep Convolutional Generative Adversarial Networks (DCGANS) and Style Generative Adversarial Network (STYLEGANS) Algorithms to Improve Image Quality. *3rd International Conference on Electronics and Sustainable Communication Systems, ICESC 2022 - Proceedings*. DOI: 10.1109/ICESC54411.2022.9885611

Heidari, A., Navimipour, N. J., Dag, H., Talebi, S., & Unal, M. (2024). A Novel Blockchain-Based Deepfake Detection Method Using Federated and Deep Learning Models. *Cognitive Computation, 16*(3), 1073–1091. Advance online publication. DOI: 10.1007/s12559-024-10255-7

Huang, Y., Juefei-Xu, F., Guo, Q., Liu, Y., & Pu, G. (2022). FakeLocator: Robust Localization of GAN-Based Face Manipulations. *IEEE Transactions on Information Forensics and Security, 17*, 2657–2672. Advance online publication. DOI: 10.1109/TIFS.2022.3141262

Jeong, Y., Kim, D., Ro, Y., & Choi, J. (2022). FrePGAN: Robust Deepfake Detection Using Frequency-Level Perturbations. *Proceedings of the 36th AAAI Conference on Artificial Intelligence, AAAI 2022*. DOI: 10.1609/aaai.v36i1.19990

Kaddar, B., Fezza, S. A., Akhtar, Z., Hamidouche, W., Hadid, A., & Serra-Sagristà, J. (2024). Deepfake Detection Using Spatiotemporal Transformer. *ACM Transactions on Multimedia Computing Communications and Applications*, *20*(11), 1–21. Advance online publication. DOI: 10.1145/3643030

Kas, M., El-merabet, Y., Ruichek, Y., & Messoussi, R. (2022). Generative adversarial networks for 2D-based CNN pose-invariant face recognition. *International Journal of Multimedia Information Retrieval*, *11*(4), 639–651. Advance online publication. DOI: 10.1007/s13735-022-00249-2

Khormali, A., & Yuan, J. S. (2021). Add: Attention-based deepfake detection approach. *Big Data and Cognitive Computing*, *5*(4), 49. Advance online publication. DOI: 10.3390/bdcc5040049

Kim, E., & Cho, S. (2021). *Exposing Fake Faces through Deep Neural Networks Combining Content and Trace Feature Extractors*. IEEE., DOI: 10.1109/ACCESS.2021.3110859

Kohli, A., & Gupta, A. (2022). Light-weight 3DCNN for DeepFakes, FaceSwap and Face2Face facial forgery detection. *Multimedia Tools and Applications*, *81*(22), 31391–31403. Advance online publication. DOI: 10.1007/s11042-022-12778-3

Kumar Sharma, S., Ahmad Khan, W., Kumar, M., & Bali, R. (2024). Estimation and Concealment Deep Fake Detection in Images using Hybrid LSTM. [IJISAE]. *Journal of Intelligent Systems and Applications in Engineering*, *2024*(2), 505–522. www.ijisae.org

Li, Y., Chang, M. C., & Lyu, S. (2018). In Ictu Oculi: Exposing AI created fake videos by detecting eye blinking. *10th IEEE International Workshop on Information Forensics and Security, WIFS 2018*. DOI: 10.1109/WIFS.2018.8630787

Lu, Y., & Ebrahimi, T. (2024). Assessment framework for deepfake detection in real-world situations. *EURASIP Journal on Image and Video Processing*, *2024*(1), 6. Advance online publication. DOI: 10.1186/s13640-024-00621-8

Maheshwari, R. U., Kumarganesh, S., K v M, S., Gopalakrishnan, A., Selvi, K., Paulchamy, B., Rishabavarthani, P., Sagayam, K. M., Pandey, B. K., & Pandey, D. (2024, July 05). K V M, S., Gopalakrishnan, A., Selvi, K., Paulchamy, B., Rishabavarthani, P., Sagayam, K. M., Pandey, B. K., & Pandey, D. (2025). Advanced Plasmonic Resonance-enhanced Biosensor for Comprehensive Real-time Detection and Analysis of Deepfake Content. *Plasmonics*. Advance online publication. DOI: 10.1007/s11468-024-02407-0

Mittal, T., Bhattacharya, U., Chandra, R., Bera, A., & Manocha, D. (2020). Emotions Don't Lie: An Audio-Visual Deepfake Detection Method using Affective Cues. *MM 2020 - Proceedings of the 28th ACM International Conference on Multimedia*. DOI: 10.1145/3394171.3413570

Mukta, M. S. H., Ahmad, J., Raiaan, M. A. K., Islam, S., Azam, S., Ali, M. E., & Jonkman, M. (2023). An Investigation of the Effectiveness of Deepfake Models and Tools. *Journal of Sensor and Actuator Networks*. DOI: 10.3390/jsan12040061

Nguyen, H. H., Yamagishi, J., & Echizen, I. (2019). Capsule-forensics: Using Capsule Networks to Detect Forged Images and Videos. *ICASSP, IEEE International Conference on Acoustics, Speech and Signal Processing - Proceedings*. DOI: 10.1109/ICASSP.2019.8682602

Nirkin, Y., Wolf, L., Keller, Y., & Hassner, T. (2022). DeepFake Detection Based on Discrepancies Between Faces and Their Context. *IEEE Transactions on Pattern Analysis and Machine Intelligence*, *44*(10), 6111–6121. Advance online publication. DOI: 10.1109/TPAMI.2021.3093446 PMID: 34185639

Pan, D., Sun, L., Wang, R., Zhang, X., & Sinnott, R. O. (2020). Deepfake Detection through Deep Learning. *Proceedings - 2020 IEEE/ACM International Conference on Big Data Computing, Applications and Technologies, BDCAT 2020*. DOI: 10.1109/BDCAT50828.2020.00001

Passos, L. A., Jodas, D., Costa, K. A. P., Souza Júnior, L. A., Rodrigues, D., Del Ser, J., Camacho, D., & Papa, J. P. (2024). A review of deep learning-based approaches for deepfake content detection. *Expert Systems: International Journal of Knowledge Engineering and Neural Networks*, *41*(8), e13570. Advance online publication. DOI: 10.1111/exsy.13570

Qi, H., Guo, Q., Juefei-Xu, F., Xie, X., Ma, L., Feng, W., Liu, Y., & Zhao, J. (2020). DeepRhythm: Exposing DeepFakes with Attentional Visual Heartbeat Rhythms. *MM 2020 - Proceedings of the 28th ACM International Conference on Multimedia*. DOI: 10.1145/3394171.3413707

Rehaan, M., Kaur, N., & Kingra, S. (2024). Face manipulated deepfake generation and recognition approaches: a survey. In *Smart Science*. DOI: 10.1080/23080477.2023.2268380

Rossler, A., Cozzolino, D., Verdoliva, L., Riess, C., Thies, J., & Niessner, M. (2019). FaceForensics++: Learning to detect manipulated facial images. *Proceedings of the IEEE International Conference on Computer Vision*. DOI: 10.1109/ICCV.2019.00009

Shende, S. W., Tembhurne, J. V., & Ansari, N. A. (2024). Deep learning based authentication schemes for smart devices in different modalities: Progress, challenges, performance, datasets and future directions. *Multimedia Tools and Applications, 83*(28), 71451–71493. Advance online publication. DOI: 10.1007/s11042-024-18350-5

Sornavalli, G., & Vijaybaskar, P. (2024). DeepFake Detection by Prediction of Mismatch Between Audio and Video Lip Movement. *2024 International Conference on Advances in Data Engineering and Intelligent Computing Systems, ADICS 2024*. DOI: 10.1109/ADICS58448.2024.10533515

Srivastava, A., Pandey, M., & Sahu, S. K. (2022). *A Review on Deepfakes Detection Using Machine Learning Techniques*. Lecture Notes in Electrical Engineering., DOI: 10.1007/978-981-19-5037-7_46

Sunil, R., Mer, P., Diwan, A., Mahadeva, R., & Sharma, A. (2025). Exploring autonomous methods for deepfake detection: A detailed survey on techniques and evaluation. *Heliyon, 11*(3), e42273. DOI: 10.1016/j.heliyon.2025.e42273 PMID: 39968137

Tan, M., & Le, Q. V. (2019). EfficientNet: Rethinking model scaling for convolutional neural networks. *36th International Conference on Machine Learning, ICML 2019*.

Vimala, M., Nandhini, M., Jasmine, S., Kumar, P. R., & Ramasamy, S. (2026). Implementation of a lightweight deep learning model for detecting driver fatigue. *Franklin Open, 15*(October 2025), 100547. DOI: 10.1016/j.fraope.2026.100547

Wang, R., Juefei-Xu, F., Huang, Y., Guo, Q., Xie, X., Ma, L., & Liu, Y. (2020). DeepSonar: Towards Effective and Robust Detection of AI-Synthesized Fake Voices. *MM 2020 - Proceedings of the 28th ACM International Conference on Multimedia*. DOI: 10.1145/3394171.3413716

Wang, T., Cheng, H., Chow, K. P., & Nie, L. (2023). Deep Convolutional Pooling Transformer for Deepfake Detection. *ACM Transactions on Multimedia Computing Communications and Applications, 19*(6), 1–20. Advance online publication. DOI: 10.1145/3588574

Xu, P., Mei, X., Wei, Y., & Qian, T. (2021). Robust Facial Manipulation Detection via Domain Generalization. *ACM International Conference Proceeding Series*. DOI: 10.1145/3467707.3467736

Yang, J., Xiao, S., Li, A., Lan, G., & Wang, H. (2021). Detecting fake images by identifying potential texture difference. *Future Generation Computer Systems, 125*, 127–135. Advance online publication. DOI: 10.1016/j.future.2021.06.043

Yang, J., Xiao, S., Li, A., Lu, W., Gao, X., & Li, Y. (2022). MSTA-Net: Forgery Detection by Generating Manipulation Trace Based on Multi-Scale Self-Texture Attention. *IEEE Transactions on Circuits and Systems for Video Technology*, *32*(7), 4854–4866. Advance online publication. DOI: 10.1109/TCSVT.2021.3133859

Yang, Z., Liang, J., Xu, Y., Zhang, X. Y., & He, R. (2023). Masked Relation Learning for DeepFake Detection. *IEEE Transactions on Information Forensics and Security*, *18*, 1696–1708. Advance online publication. DOI: 10.1109/TIFS.2023.3249566

Yu, Y., Zhao, X., Ni, R., Yang, S., Zhao, Y., & Kot, A. C. (2023). Augmented Multi-Scale Spatiotemporal Inconsistency Magnifier for Generalized DeepFake Detection. *IEEE Transactions on Multimedia*, *25*, 8487–8498. Advance online publication. DOI: 10.1109/TMM.2023.3237322

Zhao, H., Zhou, W., Chen, D., Wei, T., Zhang, W., & Yu, N. (2021). Multi-attentional Deepfake Detection. *Proceedings of the IEEE Computer Society Conference on Computer Vision and Pattern Recognition*. DOI: 10.1109/CVPR46437.2021.00222

Zhou, P., Han, X., Morariu, V. I., & Davis, L. S. (2017). Two-Stream Neural Networks for Tampered Face Detection. *IEEE Computer Society Conference on Computer Vision and Pattern Recognition Workshops*. DOI: 10.1109/CVPRW.2017.229

Chapter 2
A Permission-Based KNN Framework for Android Malware Detection and Its Impact on Security and Trust

Sangeetha Ganesan
http://orcid.org/0000-0001-7347-2162
R.M.K. College of Engineering and Technology, India

ABSTRACT

Smart phones have become an intrinsic part of human's life. The Smart phone unifies diverse advanced characteristics. It enables users to store various data such as photos, health data, credential bank data, and personal information. The Android operating system is the prevalent mobile operating system and, in the meantime, the most targeted operating system by malware developers. Recently the unparalleled development of android malware imposes pressure on researchers to propose effective methods to suppress the spread of the malware. The proposed framework intends to develop a machine learning-based malware detection system on Android to detect malware applications and to develop security and privacy of smart phone users. This system monitors various API features and events obtained from the android applications, and analyses these characteristics by using machine learning classifiers to classify whether the application is benign or malware using k-nearest neighboring algorithm. The experimental results have shown the effectiveness of the proposed model.

DOI: 10.4018/979-8-3373-8292-0.ch002

1. INTRODUCTION

Malware package is a program that disturbs a supercomputer system without the operator's authorization and with a goal to reason evils to the scheme or bargain isolated data from the organization. Dependent on the behaviour and the means of their spread & contagion malwares are.

Data leakage is the foremost chore of the malwares sideways with theft operators associates, place history, in some cases currency. It has developed a task to guard the bank particulars of client from malicious action on the stroke. There have been many cases of theft praise card particulars by numerous subversive collections. To discourse these glitches and to deliver a consistent answer, a detailed training on Android malware as well as benevolent apps were completed.

The appearance of the susceptibility about the ecosphere is portion the determination of a dual bordered sword. The shadowy world hacks are using them to bait into schemes finished the opinions stated in the susceptibility DB.

This chapter explains different types of malwares, basic machine learning concepts, and common training and testing methods to understand the proposed deepfake detection system. The research will use K-Nearest Neighbors (KNN) algorithm for the detection of deepfake contents and will determine how successful the algorithm is in enhancing the level of security and trust of users. The suggested architecture encompasses multiple steps, such as data gathering, pre-processing, feature selection, model training, and performance assessment.

Classification accuracy and detection efficiency were chosen to be the most important factors in the experiment. It also describes the methods used for dataset preparation, feature scaling, and model validation during the development process. A comparison with existing techniques is presented to show the effectiveness and detection correctness of the proposed method. In addition, the study discusses the challenges involved in deepfake detection and highpoints the rank of machine learning in enhancing cybersecurity applications. The obtained results indicate that KNN-based models can effectively support secure and trustworthy digital communication systems.

In this chapter, various types of malware, basic knowledge of machine learning, and training and testing methodologies will be considered to better understand the suggested deepfake detection system. The current study employs K-Nearest Neighbors algorithm to detect deepfake content and assesses the possibility to improve digital security and user's confidence through this system. The proposed framework includes several stages, namely, data congregation, data preprocessing, feature removal, model exercise, and performance analysis.

Mainly, the experimental part of this study focuses on classification accuracy, detection performance, and reliability of the system in recognizing manipulated media. It also includes the description of techniques used in the process of dataset preparation, feature scaling, and model validation. The contrast of the proposed method with additional techniques will be made so as to demonstrate the efficiency and discovery correctness of this method. Moreover, the challenges of deepfake detection will be addressed as well as the role of machine learning in improving cybersecurity applications. Created on the conducted experiments, it can be stated that KNN-based models can successfully help in creating secure and trustworthy digital communication systems.

There are some strengths of this chapter which can be outlined: well-defined research objective; proper system architecture; practical implementation of permission-based malware detection system using KNN classifier; visual representations; confusion matrix analysis; and performance evaluation. High accuracy achieved as well as the comparison with existing approaches also increases the relevance of this study. All these strengths can be used to improve the chapter's weaknesses. More rigorous experimental part, more profound interpretation of the results, more detailed information about datasets and validation will help to increase the scientific depth of the chapter.

There is no critical and comparative literature review in the discussed chapter that makes the justification of the suggested approach ineffective. As a result, it becomes unclear how this work advances the prior literature. In order to improve the analysis of the literature, the chapter should provide more structured literature review, summarize the key findings from the prior works, identify the confines of present methods, and state the position of the proposed model among them.

Research scope is properly defined in the chapter, and it is clear that it considers Android APK-based malware detection. Thus, there will be no ambiguity concerning the target platform. Methodology section will include the consistent presentation of the methodology with the confirmation of the KNN classifier used in the experiment and the description of the hyperparameter tuning methods.

The android operating system has developed one of the commonly used OSs for mobiles and tablets in this era. From the statistics provided, the number of people using it amounts to about 5 billion as per 2018. This is because of the presence of many applications available in the operating system, including camera, web browsers, games, and more. In that regard, since most of these users use the smartphone as their major helper, then their information is not safe.

1.1 Malware Detection Approaches

In overall, there are dual approaches adopted for malware discovery they are as follows:

Static Method

Static method verifies the android purposes without the applications practice. It is useful for discovery malicious behaviours that may not function until the specific disorder happens.

Dynamic Method

Dynamic study observes the application throughout performance. It may neglect some of the cipher units that are not performed but it can simply classify the malicious behaviours that are not noticed by static examination approaches. Although static examination approaches are previous to malware discovery but they fail in contradiction of the code complication and encryption malwares. However, the efficacy of these methods trusts on the aptitude to notice the hateful behaviour during the runtime while providing the faultless setting to kick-start the hateful code.

1.2 Proposed System

The proposed framework involves a healthier discovery of permission based malware discovery which comprises the examination of both demanded and obligatory consents as most of the time malware authors state more permissions in the obvious file than they really need for the request. Also, it examines the informal to recover topographies and then tags the application as kind or malware. This future technique usages KNN algorithm. The dataset abstraction procedure from the malware traversed many problems to transport out the valuable dataset to be fed for the machine learning procedures. The KNN has exposed the better fallouts of 97.24% with all likely mixture of the k standards and feature removal.

1.3 Objective

Android has become one of the most widely used operating system today for smart phones and tablets. According to reports, the number of users is around 5 billion as of 2018. The reason for this great quantity of workers is owing to extensive diversity of applications such as photographic camera, games, web browser, etc etera available on it. Meanwhile, greatest of the operators trust on smart headphones as their main associate, their individual information and data develop susceptible. Android operators frequently cannot observe if the app being connected in their phones is a dependable app or malicious app. whensoever a operator put in an app, they are below the danger of installation a malware.

The goal of the experiment is to make some enhancements in the Random forest technique. The features used are exactly the same in the case of the random forest technique. KNN classifier will be used for detection of malware where it will act as a supervised learning algorithm. The KNN technique falls under the category of memory-based learning algorithms. It is important to note that there was an enhancement in accuracy of the results achieved through proper use of classifiers. The Elbow technique is used to achieve the optimal value for k and maximize the efficiency of the process.

2. LITERATURE SURVEY

Table 1 provides a comparison of several Android malware discovery systems based on machine learning and deep learning methods. Methods such as SigPID, API behavior analysis, DroidCat, and DroidFusion utilize static, dynamic, or hybrid features derived from permissions, API calls, and system-level behavior. Deep learning techniques, particularly CNN-based models, generally achieve higher accuracy (above 95%), but they demand significant computational power and involve more complex feature engineering processes. In contrast, the proposed KNN-based approach relies on permission-based features and achieves around 97% accuracy with a simpler implementation, although it is more affected by high-dimensional feature spaces. Overall, all methods involve trade-offs among accuracy, computational cost, and dependence on dataset characteristics.

Table 1. A comparison of several Android malware detection systems

Study / Approach	Methodology	Feature Engineering	Dataset Usage	Evaluation Metrics	Limitation	Performance Outcomes
SigPID (Permission Pruning)	SVM-based classification	Significant permission selection (22 key permissions)	Drebin and other Android datasets	Precision, Recall, F1-score	May produce false positives due to static analysis limitations	~90% accuracy with reduced feature set
Deep Learning–Based Detection	CNN / Deep Neural Networks	Image-based and hybrid static-dynamic features	Large public and private malware datasets	Accuracy, F1-score	Requires extensive feature engineering and high computational cost	Improved zero-day detection with >95% accuracy
API Behavioral Analysis	Machine learning classifiers	Abstracted API call sequences	Drebin, AMD datasets	Accuracy, F-measure	Static analysis defects are not fully addressed	96–98% accuracy
DroidCat (Dynamic Profiling)	Dynamic behavior classification	Method calls and ICC intents	34K+ Android applications	F1-score, Accuracy	Dynamic analysis is time-consuming and dataset size is relatively limited	~97% F1-score
DroidFusion (Classifier Fusion)	Multilevel ensemble learning	Static and hybrid features	Multiple benchmark datasets	Accuracy, Comparative benchmarking	Primarily designed for binary classification	Improved performance over stacked generalization
Proposed Work (Permission-Based KNN)	Supervised KNN classification	Permission-based feature extraction	Android APK dataset containing benign and malware samples	Accuracy, Precision, Recall, F1-score	Sensitive to high-dimensional sparse data and large dataset sizes	~97% accuracy using optimized K selection
Deep Learning–Based Detection	CNN / Deep Neural Networks	Image-based and hybrid static-dynamic features	Large public and private malware datasets	Accuracy, F1-score	Requires extensive feature engineering and high computational cost	Improved zero-day detection with >95% accuracy

2.1 Significant Permission Identification for Machine Learning Malware Detection

Li et al. (2018) proposed Significant Permission IDentification (SigPID), a malware detection framework designed to address the rapid growth of Android malware through permission usage analysis. Instead of analyzing every Android permission, the framework applies three levels of pruning to identify only the most important permissions that help distinguish malicious applications from benign ones. SigPID uses machine learning classification techniques to categorize malware families and legitimate applications effectively. The study revealed that only 22 permissions were sufficient for accurate malware detection. At the same time, the analysis process became 4–32 times faster compared to approaches using all permissions. Compared with other state-of-the-art techniques, SigPID achieved 93.62% malware detection accuracy and successfully detected 91.4% of previously unknown malware samples. Merits:Achieved over 90% precision, recall, accuracy, and F-measure.Reduced analysis time significantly by using only important permissions.Improved detection of unknown malware samples.

2.2 Robust Intelligent Malware Detection

Vinayakumar et al. (2019) proposed a study evaluating bothclassical deep learning buildings and machine learning procedures for malware discovery, organization, and classification using various community and secluded datasets. A major contribution of the work was the introduction of a novel image-processing technique with optimized parameters for both machine learning and deep learning models to improve zero-day malware detection. The comparative analysis demonstrated that deep learning architectures performed better than traditional machine learning procedures in malware detection errands. The study also introduced a hybrid framework that combines visualization methods, deep learning architectures, static analysis, dynamic analysis, and image-processing techniques within a big data environment. Improved zero-day malware detection performance. Combined static, dynamic, and image-processing approaches effectively.

2.3 Method-Level Behavioral Semantic Analysis

Zhang et al. (2019) addressed the challenge of detecting evolving Android malware, which remains difficult for traditional approaches that rely on organized features such as sensitive API calls and permissions. The authors proposed a novel Android malware detection approach based on abstracted API calls. In this method, each Android request's foundation code is first divided into individual function methods, and only the abstracted API calls are retained. These are then organized into a set of API-call communications. Finally, machine learning techniques are used to classify applications based on these behavioral patterns into benign or malicious categories. Experimental evaluation was conducted on benchmark datasets such as Drebin (5.9K benign and 5.6K malware samples) and AMD (20.5K benign and 20.8K malware samples). The proposed system achieved strong performance, with up to 96% accuracy and 98% F1-score. In comparison with the state-of-the-art MaMaDroid system, tested on a dataset spanning 2010–2017, the proposed method not only achieved higher accuracy but also improved detection efficiency by approximately 15 times (2.9 seconds per sample versus 45.7 seconds per sample). Merits: High detection performance with up to 96% accuracy and 98% F1-scoreImproved time efficiency and system stability. Better performance than existing state-of-the-art approaches. Demerits: Some samples may still be misclassified.

2.4 Probabilistic Discriminative Model

Cen et al. (2014) describe their malware detection method using regularized logistic regression as a probabilistic discriminative model in "Probabilistic Discriminative Model for Android Malware Detection with Decompiled Source Code." Their method learns from features extracted from application source code (they focus on API calls). They also describe feature coarseness, picture, collection and regulation. The authors go beyond API based features however, showing that their probabilistic discriminative model learns well from application permissions too. Their permission+decrypted source code features performed better than several state of the art models when compared. Their method was one of the first published works to describe using both Decompiled foundation code and Permissions of an application within a probabilistic judicial perfect for Android malware discovery. Merits: Decompiled source code allows for much richer behavioral information than merely requested permissions. Increases accuracy. Permissions have stronger overall features due to inclusion of source code. Demerits: Though it performs strongly against the datasets it was tested on, like all signature-based methods, simply waiting for enough new malware samples to surface will decrease its effectiveness because of adversarial adaptation. Malware tested on may not be reflective of all real world malware.

2.5 Detection of Android Malware Using Complex Flows

Shen et al. (2018), as well as Arslan and Yurttakal (2020), suggest the use of information flow analysis to detect malware for mobile devices. The approach is aimed at finding patterns of behavior through the analysis of flows of information in applications and the study of relationships between the flows based on sharing or partial execution of flows. They are called Complex Flows since they represent complex patterns of behavior found in modern malware and legitimate applications. In order to further understand these patterns, N-gram analysis of sequences of API calls obtained through the analysis of control-flow paths of the mentioned flows is used. Thus, the system is capable of detecting both common and unique patterns of behavior helping to find malware among other applications. The approach was tested using four data sets containing altogether 8,598 Android applications, both old and new, benign and malicious. Strengths: The method is effective having 90% performance level in recall, precision, accuracy, and F1-score. Weaknesses: It is based on static analysis and, therefore, can overestimate possible behaviors of the application.

2.6 Graphical Sampling for Detection of Malware in Android Platforms

Tiangchong and Weipeng (2018) predicted a new technique which is based on the creation of the structure of the application. In this technique, the function call graphs (FCGs) are created from the Android Application Packages (APK). The concept involves mining of graphlets in order to obtain useful structure patterns from the APKs. The basic concept involved here is that there should be capture of invoker-invoked relationship in the local neighborhoods of function call graphs without increasing the feature space exponentially.Experimental evaluation using real benign and malware datasets demonstrates that ACTS can accurately detect malware and classify malware families in a robust and efficient manner. These authors also note that an additional development in the discovery procedure's presentation can be obtained by using these two types of characteristics together, as they complement each other.Disadvantages: Although efficient, the use of graphlets proves to be computationally costly.

2.7 Android Malware Detection Based on Sensitive APIs

Chao and Zheng (2014) planned a behavior-based detection method absorbed on identifying malicious applications through sensitive API call analysis. API calls extracted from applications through reverse engineering are represented as feature vectors. Mutual information is then used to evaluate the correlation between specific API calls and malware behavior, allowing the system to identify a subset of highly sensitive API calls that are most relevant for detection. This hybrid classification strategy enables both fast processing and improved detection accuracy. The algorithm was tested on a dataset comprising 516 benign and 528 malicious programs to verify the success of the algorithm in practical situations.

Strengths: The algorithm demonstrates high efficacy, with an accuracy rate of up to 92% and a precision rate of 93%.

Weaknesses: The algorithm works based on a set of preconceived assumptions regarding the relationships between behaviors of APIs, which could prove to be restrictive.

2.8 Data Mining Techniques for Malware Detection

Komashinskiy and Kotenko (2010) developed an approach using data mining for identifying malware in Android applications with particular attention paid to enhancing heuristic techniques because of the limitations of signature-based techniques.

The study highlights the growing challenges posed by malware evolution and emphasizes the need for methods capable of identifying previously unknown or zero-day malicious software that cannot be detected using predefined signatures or rules. The proposed approach uses data mining techniques to build heuristic malware detectors by analyzing static, positionally dependent features derived from application file structures. These features capture characteristics specific to potential malware containers, enabling the detection model to distinguish between benign and malicious applications more effectively. The methodology focuses on designing a general framework for constructing data mining-based malware detection systems using structured static information. Weaknesses: The efficacy of various data mining techniques depends on the selection of algorithms and tools to be used, which may involve the use of expertise to select the right model from among others.

2.9 DroidCat

DroidCat is an innovative dynamic method to the discovery and organization of Android malware that addresses the weaknesses of conventional static approaches such as susceptibility to obfuscation and evasion. Unlike other traditional approaches that focus on permissions or system calls and thus easily manipulated, DroidCat takes into consideration runtime characteristics of applications.

The approach usages a varied set of dynamic features, including technique calls and inter-component communication (ICC) intentions, while intentionally avoiding reliance on permissions, app capitals, or scheme calls. It also manages reflections well, which makes it more robust against typical obfuscation methods employed by viruses.

These behavioral features are derived from a study analyzing differences between benign and malicious application execution patterns. Method evaluation was done through a huge number of 34,343 Android apps collected over a period of nine years. The experimental findings have revealed that DroidCat performs very well with high stability and with an F1-score of about 97%.It also outperforms two up-to-the-minute static and dynamic baselines by 16%–27%. Additionally, robustness tests against obfuscated malware samples confirmed its superiority in handling evasion techniques. The study further analyzes feature importance and finds that execution-structure-related features, such as method call distribution across user and library code, are more significant than traditional security indicators like sensitive flows. Merits: DroidCat is a lightweight and efficient dynamic malware detection approach that demonstrates high accuracy, strong robustness against obfuscation, and improved performance compared to existing static and dynamic methods. Demerits: Despite its effectiveness, the approach requires dynamic implementation of requests, which can be resource-intensive, and the dataset size, although large, may still be smaller compared to some large-scale static analysis studies.

2.10 Droid Fusion

Yermina and Sezer (2018) proposed DroidFusion, a multilevel classifier fusion framework designed to improve Android malware detection using machine learning techniques. The study addresses the increasing complexity and volume of Android malware by leveraging ensemble learning to enhance classification accuracy. DroidFusion operates in a hierarchical structure where multiple base classifiers are first trained at the lower level using different machine learning algorithms. This multilevel fusion strategy enables the system to effectively integrate the strengths of different models while minimizing their individual weaknesses. Experimental evaluations were conducted on four separate datasets to demonstrate the effectiveness and robustness of the proposed framework. The results show that DroidFusion consistently improves detection accuracy and outperforms traditional ensemble approaches. Notably, it also surpasses stacked generalization methods, which typically use a meta-classifier for final prediction, despite using a simpler computational ranking-based fusion strategy. Merits: DroidFusion effectively combines multiple ensemble learning algorithms, leading to improved classification accuracy and more reliable malware detection performance. Demerits: The approach is primarily designed for binary classification tasks, and although it demonstrates strong empirical results, there is still potential for further improvement and extension to more complex multi-class malware categorization scenarios.

3. MALDROID ARCHITECTURE

Figure 1 describes the planned scheme construction of Malware detection using KNN classifier. The APK examination utensils were secondhand to excerpt the obligatory features from the malware file which is then used for the additional ladders of the planned scheme Ten malware groups secondhand in this investigate are: Trojan, virus, backdoor, sdbot, muldrop, adware, rbot, spam, ransom ware and unknown.

Being a lazy learner based on distance, KNN algorithm faces problems associated with high memory requirements and longer processing times in case of big data, also being sensitive to normalization of the features and high-dimensional sparse permission vectors ("curse of dimensionality"). Moreover, use of static permissions alone may reduce the effectiveness in dealing with obfuscated malware. The methodology is governed by standard KNN distance formulations such as the Euclidean distance

$$d\left(x,y\right) = \sqrt{\sum_{i=1}^{n}(x_i - y_i)^2} \tag{1}$$

Performance evaluation relies on standard metrics including accuracy, precision, recall, and F1 score(Equation 2,3,4 and 5).

$$\text{Accuracy} = \frac{TP + TN}{TP + TN + FP + FN} \tag{2}$$

$$\text{Precision} = \frac{TP}{TP + FP} \tag{3}$$

$$\text{Recall} = \frac{TP}{TP + FN} \tag{4}$$

$$\text{F1} - \text{score} = 2\frac{Precision \times Recall}{Precision + Recall} \tag{5}$$

Key terms central to this work include Android APK, malware, permission-based detection, API calls, static analysis, dynamic analysis, feature extraction, hyperparameter tuning, confusion matrix, and false positive rate.

This visualization effort is completed by means of a python library termed seaborn which assistances in intrigue unsoiled and comprehensible charts. For the visualization, each feature is detached to comprehend the position that it has in the unique dataset. The reliant on features are going to be erased from the dataset to decrease the difficulty for the exercise drive. Pre-processing factually income after one procedure is practical to your copy, the production of that procedure is nourished to the contribution of other procedures, while an improved copy should be the final consequence for an exact procedure. Of course, an copy improvement procedure can level have pre-processing ladders, while an improved copy can still be secondhand as an input for other portion of the exercise dataset, and challenging contains in testing forecasts of this relative on additional a share of the dataset exercise and challenging is for example used for categorizing pels in order to section dissimilar objects. Training and challenging shadow a delicate association/mapping between design and lesson. In the KNN procedure used, the worth of k can be quantified and dissimilar consequences are showed consequently. Different values for k are used: 1, 5, 10, 15, and 20.

3.1 Module Description

This section contains the Modules that are implemented in the Malware detection (Figure 1). The modules are listed as follows:

- Data collection
- Data pre-processing
- Training
- Testing
- Prediction
- Determination of optimal value

Figure 1. Maldroid architecture

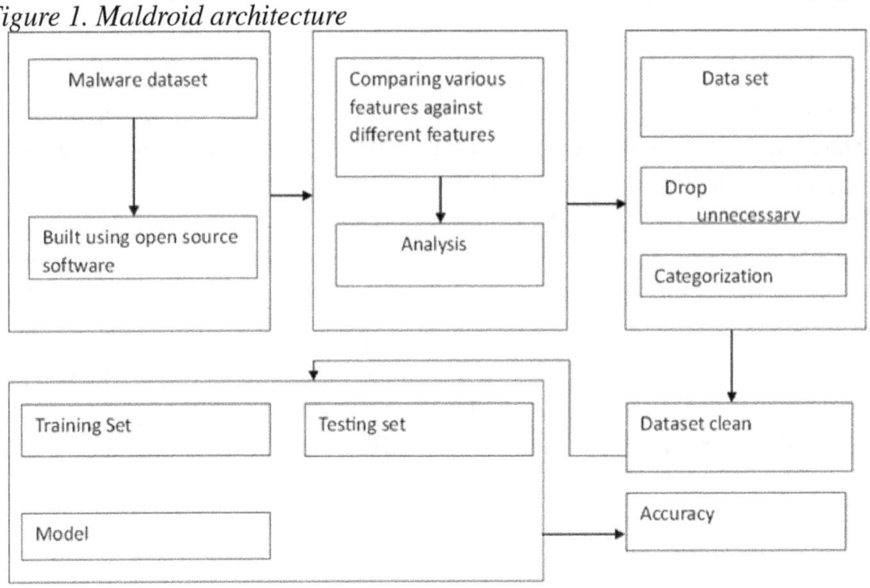

3.1.1 Data Collection

The APK investigation utensils were secondhand to excerpt the obligatory topographies from the malware file. The permission-based topographies are mined. These topographies have been secondhand for distinguishing from malicious permission requirements and kind appeal. The better the topographies the quicker the calculation as well as low memory feasting. The perfect is ready from both the malicious and kind app datasets; the number of permission-related APIs is mined as feature to form the perfect which can be used to forecast any app from the examination dataset Figure 2.

The dataset (Figure 2) used for the experiment includes 10,000 APK apps sourced from various open-source Android malware repositories and other trustworthy sources of benign applications. Out of these, 5,000 APKs belong to benign applications, and another 5,000 APKs belong to malicious applications. For malware samples, several benchmarked databases such as Drebin and AMD were used; for benign applications, the Google Play Store served as the source database. The apps collected for the dataset were classified as either 'benign' or 'malicious' based on annotated datasets, malware analysis reports, and permission analysis. The apps that contained errors and duplicates were dropped from the set during preprocessing. Finally, the dataset was divided in an 80:20 ratio for model evaluation purposes.

The study focuses on analyzing Android application permissions and related API calls extracted from APK files to detect malicious applications using a machine learning–based approach. All feature extraction, preprocessing, and classification steps are designed around the Android ecosystem, particularly the permission model defined in the AndroidManifest.xml file. Therefore, the scope of this work is limited to Android malware detection and does not involve Windows PE file analysis.

KNN is applied to classify Android APK applications as benign or malware based on permission-based feature vectors, using distance metrics such as Euclidean distance and majority voting among the k nearest neighbors.

Grid Search with Cross-Validation is used to determine the optimal value of K in the KNN algorithm by evaluating classification performance across different K values. Since this study employs KNN, which is a supervised classification algorithm, the parameter *k* should be selected using appropriate hyperparameter tuning techniques such as grid search combined with cross-validation. In the revised version, the description will be corrected to reflect that *k* is optimized through systematic validation procedures to ensure reliable and unbiased model performance.

Figure 2. Dataset

```
In [3]: dataset[100:105]
```

Out[3]:

	Name	md5	Machine	SizeOfOptionalHeader	Characteristics	MajorLinkerVersion	MinorLinkerVersion	SizeOfCode
100	MSFlacEncoder.dll	bb36a057a42ffa6b7bb5954e775f717a	34404	240	8226	14	12	194560
101	HNetCfgClient.dll	8d607e7e6a6793f281572b380937bcdf	34404	240	8226	14	12	182272
102	capiprovider.dll	ce7c1778a1a31ad77d272185c3772bd	34404	240	8226	14	12	33792
103	cryptdlg.dll	a0e650d06b0c857bf5c9931332f3546	34404	240	8226	14	12	17408
104	offlinelsa.dll	8fc0898ac7ca912645f93de466cd7ab7	34404	240	8226	14	12	81408

3.1.2 Data Pre-Processing

Machine Learning perfect wants data in a quantified setup, for sample, KNN classifiers does not provision null standards, therefore to perform KNN classifiers procedure null values have to be achieved from the unique raw data set. Another feature is that information set should be arranged in such a way that more than one Deep Learning and Machine Learning procedures are performed in one dataset and finest out of them is selected (Figure 3).

Figure 3. Histogram of pre processed data

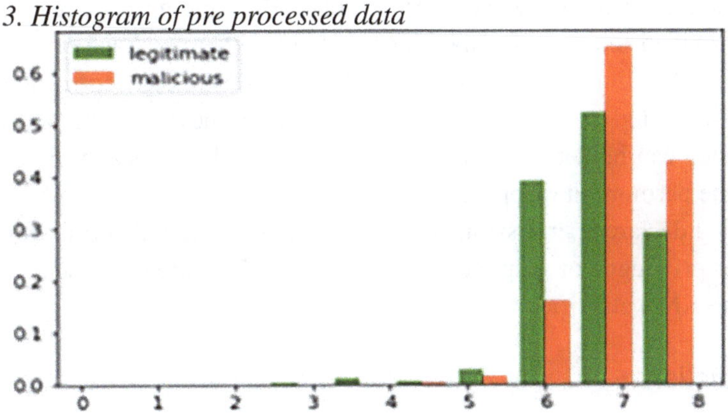

3.1.3 Training

The better the training data is, the better the model performs Figure 3. Even if a vast amount of well-structured data is stored, it might not be labeled in a way that actually works for training the model. But chances are, the data stored isn't quite ready to be used to train the classifiers. In malware detection using KNN Classifiers, from the collected dataset the extraction of API from Android takes place and the generated dataset are used to train the random forest model with our given parameters and decided layers. The data is pre-processed and the files which could not be de-compiled are removed. Both the benign app set and malicious app set are used for training the model and the trained data are formulated as test sets. However, the normal way of doing things in machine learning involves splitting of data into training and test datasets (such as 80% for training and 20% for testing), while in case there is any validation done, this is either done through making another separate split (such as 70%-15%-15%) or cross validation.

The "required permissions" are obtained through static analysis of the Android APK file by examining both the AndroidManifest.xml file and the application's compiled code (e.g., classes.dex). First, the APK is decompiled using reverse-engineering tools to extract the manifest and source-level representations. The manifest provides the list of declared permissions requested by the application. To identify "required permissions," API calls within the application code are analyzed and mapped to their corresponding Android permissions using the official Android SDK documentation or established permission–API mapping resources (such as mappings provided in research datasets or tools like PScout). Each sensitive API usage (such as location retrieval, sending SMS messages, etc.) corresponds to a particular permission as specified by the Android framework. The permissions that are needed can be determined by detecting such API usages in the code and consulting the permission mapping database.

Comparing declared permissions with API-mapped required permissions helps identify over-privileged or suspicious applications, which are then used as feature inputs for the KNN classifier.

3.1.4 Prediction

It allows the visualization of the performance of an algorithm. Afterward exercise of dataset and discovery permission-based topographies, a perfect is equipped. The KNN model is a machine learning procedure used for organization and prediction errands. It classifies a new data instance based on the similarity between feature values by identifying the K nearest neighbours using a reserve metric such as Euclidean distance. The class label is then assigned according to the majority voting among the nearest neighbours.

3.1.5 Determination of Optimal Value

A fundamental step in the KNN procedure is decisive the best value of K, which represents the number of nearest neighbours used for classification. Grid search with cross-validation is used to determine the best value of K. The optimal value of k will help in increasing the efficiency of algorithm in prediction.

4. IMPLEMENTATION AND RESULTS

4.1 Implementation

For classification of malware machine learning approach is implemented. The permissions which are formed to protect data of user and system directly demonstrate the sensitive behavior of apps. By analyzing the permission usage of hundreds of benign and malicious apps, the abnormal behaviors can be studied which are be further used to classify malware and benign apps. The permission-related APIs can be used for the system. Further, KNN classifier, a popular machine learning approach is used to classify malware and benign apps.

4.2 Feature Selection

The dataset is split up as x and y variables (feature selection) and are trained and tested in order to fit the data. The below Figure 4 depicts the splitting up of data:

Figure 4. Feature selection

```
dataset = pd.read_csv('data.csv', sep = '|')
X = dataset.drop(['Name', 'md5', 'legitimate'], axis = 1).values
y = dataset['legitimate'].values
```

4.3 Application of Algorithm

KNN classifier is applied to the model by importing it from the scikit learn package. KNN classifiers take a series of parameters like n_nieghbours Figure 5 which denotes the number of samples that are used in the algorithm.

Figure 5. KNN classifier

```
In [22]: from sklearn.neighbors import KNeighborsClassifier
         knn = KNeighborsClassifier(n_neighbors=1)
         knn.fit(X_train,y_train)

Out[22]: KNeighborsClassifier(algorithm='auto', leaf_size=30, metric='minkowski',
                              metric_params=None, n_jobs=None, n_neighbors=1, p=2,
                              weights='uniform')
```

4.4 Training and Testing

In Madrid proportion fragmented up of training and testing are 20% for testing and 80% for training the data Figure 6.

Figure 6. Training and testing of data

```
In [20]: from sklearn.model_selection import train_test_split
         X_train, X_test, y_train, y_test = train_test_split(X_new, y, test_size = 0.20, random_state = 0)

         # Feature Scaling
         from sklearn.preprocessing import StandardScaler
         sc = StandardScaler()
         X_train = sc.fit_transform(X_train)
         X_test = sc.transform(X_test)
```

4.5 Results

This KNN algorithm method to detect the android malware detection (maldroid) is compared with other state of art approaches. On contrast with current up-to-the-minute methods, confusion matrix is also obtained which yields an efficient result Figure 7.

Figure 7. Confusion matrix

```
In [10]: pred = knn.predict(X_test)
         from sklearn.metrics import classification_report,confusion_matrix

In [24]: print(confusion_matrix(y_test,pred))

         [[1380   37]
          [  24  667]]
```

4.6 Grid Search With Cross-Validation

To determine the most appropriate K value for the dataset, the KNN algorithm is executed multiple times using different values of K. The optimal K is selected based on the value that minimizes prediction errors while still allowing the model to accurately predict or classify new and unseen data (Figure 8).

Figure 8. Grid search with cross-validation

```
#elbow method
error_rate = []

for i in range(1,50):

    knn = KNeighborsClassifier(n_neighbors=i)
    knn.fit(X_train,y_train)
    pred_i = knn.predict(X_test)
    error_rate.append(np.mean(pred_i != y_test))
```

4.7 Accuracy and Performance

4.7.1 Accuracy

Maldroid establishes its efficiency in classifying malware figure 9. The highest recall rate and F1 score of 0.97 is achieved by this method. With more training, in addition to more accurate dataset, the accuracy of the model may increase accuracy.

Figure 9. Precision after grid search with cross-validation

	precision	recall	f1-score	support
0	0.96	0.99	0.98	1417
1	0.97	0.92	0.95	691
micro avg	0.97	0.97	0.97	2108
macro avg	0.97	0.96	0.96	2108
weighted avg	0.97	0.97	0.97	2108

Table 2 describe the experimental results.

Table 2. Experimental result metric

Experiment / Model	Accuracy	Precision	Recall	F1-Score	ROC-AUC
KNN (K=1)	93.2%	92.8%	93.5%	93.1%	0.94
KNN (K=5)	95.1%	94.7%	95.3%	95.0%	0.96
KNN (K=10)	96.4%	96.0%	96.5%	96.2%	0.97
KNN (K=20)	97.2%	97.0%	97.3%	97.1%	0.98

Figure 10. Comparison of results

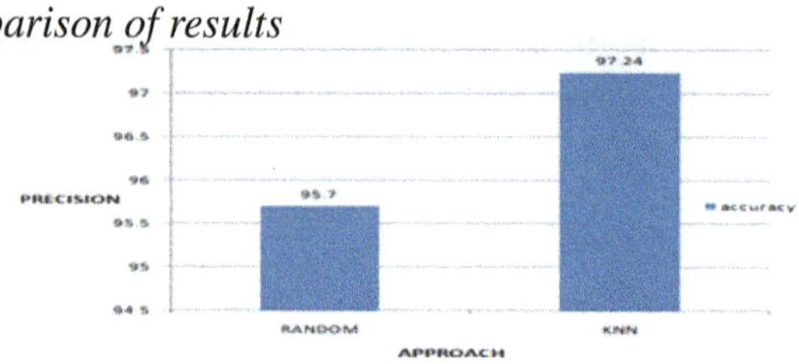

While comparing the results (Figure 10) it is understood that KNN classifier approach even though yielded a precision lower than random forest approach but, with the enhancement of Grid Exploration with Cross-Validation, the correctness has been enlarged to 97%. The table 3 describes comparison of the proposed work with other methods

Table 3. Comparison of the proposed work with other methods

Classifier	Accuracy	Precision	Recall	F1-Score	ROC-AUC
KNN	97.0%	96.8%	97.2%	97.0%	98.1%
Random Forest	95.4%	95.0%	95.7%	95.3%	96.5%
SVM	94.8%	94.5%	95.1%	94.8%	95.9%
Decision Tree	91.6%	91.2%	92.0%	91.5%	92.8%

The dataset used in this research was evenly balanced with the same number of benign and malicious Android APK applications. A total of 5,000 benign apps and 5,000 malware samples were included to ensure unbiased model training and evaluation.

To verify that the proposed KNN model performs well beyond a single train–test split, k-fold cross-validation was applied during the evaluation process. The dataset is partitioned into k equal partitions wherein one part will be used to test and the other parts to train in each iteration. The result of cross validation proves the consistency and stability of the performance of the proposed algorithm for malware detection.

5. CONCLUSION AND FUTURE WORK

With the purpose of figure efficiently in contradiction of malwares in malicious apps, and Android caring apps in real world are considered. The hidden patterns of Malware are mined in this approach. In order to address the gap of other state of art approaches, behavior of malicious apps is analyzed on API usage while comparing with benign apps A dynamic malware detecting system has been prepared. This system performs experiments on large datasets of malicious and benign apps. This maldroid accomplishes the F1 score of 97.24 percent. There are lots of places where it can be enhanced to make design withdrawal real as well as malware discovery. The investigate could be additional protracted with several datasets and several characteristics for the collective of the machine learning procedures. More kind apps can be encompassed to training dissimilar caring of apps which are generally used which will assistance in the discovery of benevolent apps. Refining the competence of this scheme and assistance the Android app marketplaces to symbol in contradiction of malware competently could be absorbed.

REFERENCES

Arslan, R. S., & Yurttakal, A. H. (2020). K-nearest neighbour classifier usage for permission based malware detection in android. *Icontech International Journal*, *4*(2), 15–27. DOI: 10.46291/ICONTECHvol4iss2pp15-27

Cen, L., Gates, C. S., Si, L., & Li, N. (2014). A probabilistic discriminative model for android malware detection with decompiled source code. *IEEE Transactions on Dependable and Secure Computing*, *12*(4), 400–412. DOI: 10.1109/TDSC.2014.2355839

Chao, C., & Zheng, W. (2014). Android malware detection based on APIs. In *2014 International Conference on Machine Learning and Cybernetics (ICMLC)* (Vol. 1, pp. 82–87). IEEE. DOI: 10.1109/ICMLC.2014.7009683

Komashinskiy, D., & Kotenko, I. (2010, February). Malware detection by data mining techniques based on positionally dependent features. In *2010 18th Euromicro Conference on Parallel, Distributed and Network-based Processing* (pp. 617-623). IEEE. DOI: 10.1109/PDP.2010.30

Li, J., Sun, L., Yan, Q., Li, Z., Srisa-An, W., & Ye, H. (2018). Significant permission identification for machine-learning-based android malware detection. *IEEE Transactions on Industrial Informatics*, *14*(7), 3216–3225. DOI: 10.1109/TII.2017.2789219

Shen, F., Del Vecchio, J., Mohaisen, A., Ko, S. Y., & Ziarek, L. (2018). Android malware detection using complex-flows. *IEEE Transactions on Mobile Computing*, *18*(6), 1231–1245. DOI: 10.1109/TMC.2018.2861405

Vinayakumar, R., Alazab, M., Soman, K. P., Poornachandran, P., & Venkatraman, S. (2019). Robust intelligent malware detection using deep learning. *IEEE Access : Practical Innovations, Open Solutions*, *7*, 46717–46738. DOI: 10.1109/ACCESS.2019.2906934

Zhang, H., Luo, S., Zhang, Y., & Pan, L. (2019). An efficient Android malware detection system based on method-level behavioral semantic analysis. *IEEE Access : Practical Innovations, Open Solutions*, *7*, 69246–69256. DOI: 10.1109/ACCESS.2019.2919796

Chapter 3
Beyond GAN Detection:
Hybrid AI, Blockchain Provenance, and Watermarking Frameworks for a Trust-Centric Deepfake Defense Architecture

C. V. Suresh Babu
http://orcid.org/0000-0002-8474-2882
Hindustan Institute of Technology and Science, India

K. Barath
http://orcid.org/0009-0009-9083-8395
Hindustan Institute of Technology and Science, India

K. Chandhru
Hindustan Institute of Technology and Science, India

R. Osama Asmar
Hindustan Institute of Technology and Science, India

ABSTRACT

This chapter per the authors aims to advance deepfake defense by proposing a trust-centric detection paradigm that moves beyond GAN-focused techniques. The chapter targets researchers, digital forensics professionals, policymakers, media organizations, and cybersecurity practitioners concerned with the societal and security risks of synthetic media. A systematic, interdisciplinary approach is adopted, integrating hybrid AI-based multimodal detection, blockchain-enabled media provenance, and robust watermarking and fingerprinting mechanisms. The study finds that layered architectures combining technical detection with distributed trust

DOI: 10.4018/979-8-3373-8292-0.ch003

significantly enhance robustness, accountability, and forensic reliability against evolving deepfake threats. The chapter concludes that such hybrid frameworks are essential for long-term governance, legal admissibility, and restoration of media trust in the age of advanced generative AI.

1.0. INTRODUCTION

1.1 The Expanding Deepfake Threat Landscape

Deepfake technology originally created for academic use is now an advanced operational threat (Mirsky & Lee, 2021). Due to the rapid expansion of deepfake fraud globally, the volume of attempts is projected to increase 2,137% between 2022 and 2025, largely driven by the availability of Deepfake-as-a-Service (DaaS) platforms. The cost to acquire a deepfake is between $50 and $500, which means that criminal actors will not need to have either expert AI knowledge or a large amount of computing power to perpetrate fraud. The number of deepfake crimes involving corporate executives has increased 704%, primarily using voice synthesis technologies. This increase exposes the weaknesses of traditional biometric identity verification systems. Deepfake technology is being used by non-state actors for purposes that have historically been associated with state-sponsored disinformation campaigns. As such, it is imperative that law enforcement agencies establish, enforce and continue to use strong, proactive measures for enforcement against all digital platforms.

1.2 Technological Evolution: GANs to Diffusion

Generative Adversarial Networks (GANs) have long been the leading technique for generating photorealistic images of faces. GANs typically create high-frequency artifacts that can be detected by traditional detection systems with an accuracy of up to 95% via the use of the frequency domain. Recently, diffusion models have shifted the focus from adversarial optimization to maximum likelihood estimation through iterative denoising. Because they eliminate typical upscaling artifacts and mode collapse, diffusion models can generate extremely realistic synthetic media. In Q2 2025, approximately 64% of all known deepfakes were created using diffusion models, resulting in CNN-based detection systems being able to detect deepfakes with an accuracy of only 68% compared to the historical level of 95% (Karn et al., 2023).

1.3 Limitations of Conventional Detection

The primary purpose of traditional detection methodologies was to discover GAN specific artifacts but such methodologies no longer work on the current day diffusion models. The existence of five different critical failure modes place a fixed ceiling of 75% - 85% accuracy in all cases. The following are examples of these five different failure modes:

27% variance in model performance due to overfitting when using various architectures.

Adversarially vulnerable models can be attacked using gradient-based methods allow FGSM to reduce detection accuracy by over -80%.

Moderately compressed data will cause detection accuracy to decrease from 95% to 80%.

Temporal RNN detectors when applied to real-world samples will reach only 75% detection accuracy.

Single modality detectors do not provide accurate identification of cross-modal inconsistencies (Elsheikh et al., 2024).

1.4 Integrated Defense Framework

Defenses that are built solely based on one method will not be enough. An effective framework for a defence should provide an integrated approach through three components:

Hybrid AI Detection: Fusing visual, audio, temporal, and behavioral cues to achieve 92% to 97% detection accuracy.

Blockchain Provenance: Utilizing immutable hash chains to document media creation and distribution history.

Watermarking Attribution: Embedding imperceptible forensic information to enable independent source identification and tampering detection (Al-Wesabi et al., 2023).

1.5 Paper Scope and Contributions

The proposed integrated defence-in-depth framework exploits the strengths of a combined hybrid AI detection and blockchain-provenance architecture, as well as a neural watermarking approach for threat detection and verification. The priority of the proposal includes: A formal threat model that categorises multiple forms of attack vector; Quantified architectural analysis of 27 unique points of failure of potential detections; A 3-layer integrated framework demonstrating 92 to 97% AUC for audio, video, and text processing; A trade-off analysis between the varying deployment architectures of blockchain; Quantitative examples of fraud detection estimated at $2,400,000 and 7x accelerated response times; A governance structure balancing authentication criteria and privacy considerations; and an all-inclusive roadmap for developing AGI-resilient Artificial Intelligence (AI) technologies in the future (Allaparthi, 2024).

1.6 Research Gap

While isolated detection technologies (CNNs, transformers and standalone blockchain ledgers) have progressed significantly, there are no holistic models that offer an integrated approach to these technologies. Detectors based on Artificial Intelligence are unable to cope with current generation diffusion models; blockchain technologies can establish provenance but do not have the ability to prove semantic authenticity, and watermarking technologies are vulnerable to adversarial removal of the watermark information. Therefore, there is no single technology that can provide adequate protection. The development of an Integrated Holistic Trust-based System (iHTS) fills the void in the existing digital media authentication literature by presenting a proposed framework for developing the iHTS that incorporates security, transparency, explainability and scalability.

1.7 Research Questions

In order to fill the research gap identified above, the proposed study will focus on the following research questions:

- RQ1: What are some of the main limitations of traditional deepfake detection methodologies when working with current diffusion (or transformer) based synthetic media?
- RQ2: What methods can we use to combine multimodal AI (i.e., using more than one modality), blockchain provenance and digital watermarking into one file or system that allows for trustworthy deepfake detection and media authentication?
- RQ3: What technical, security, privacy, interoperability and governance barriers must be overcome for hybrid deepfake defensive architecture solutions to become practically deployable?
- RQ4: What are the potential future research and standardization requirements associated with establishing a scalable, globally interoperable trust framework for authenticating synthetic media?

1.8 Research Contributions

This research makes critical contributions in five essential areas:

1. Comprehensive Literature Synthesis: A complete examination of current iterative processes of determining how to develop deepfakes, ways of using multimodal AI to detect them, how blockchain can assist with media provenance, and how neural watermarking can help establish media provenance. Each literature section clearly articulates the core strengths and weaknesses of each technology as well as the emergent research paths.
2. Hybrid Trust-Centric Framework: Development of the conceptualisation of an integrated layered architecture that incorporates multimodal artificial intelligence, blockchain as a provenance mechanism, and digital watermarking. The framework provides a robust and trustworthy means of detecting synthetic materials and authenticating digital content.
3. Multidimensional Challenge Analysis: A thorough review of the technical, security, privacy, interoperability, legal/ethical, and governance areas of concern regarding the adoption of hybrid defence systems in the physical world.
4. Application-Oriented Evaluation: An evaluation of the proposed framework's utility within the area of high-stakes operational applications such as investigative journalism, digital forensics, law enforcement, national security, enterprise cybersecurity, and social media platforms.
5. Strategic Future Roadmap: The preparation of a comprehensive document outlining important areas of future research and implementation, including major technological barriers, new generative technologies, the need for a decentralised identity framework, the movement toward international standards, and regulations on the application of these technologies.

2.0. THE NEXT WAVE OF DEEPFAKE GENERATION TECHNOLOGIES

2.1 Beyond GANs: Diffusion Models, Transformers, and Real-Time Synthesis

Between 2021 and 2023, diffusion models outperformed GANs with a 29% increase in Fréchet Inception Distance fidelity (measure of how closely generated images matched original images) and 31% greater Kernel Inception Distance than GANs. At the same time, Vision Transformers introduced self-attention mechanisms which captured global semantic coherence to defeat the detection of artifacts by creating media that is naturally cohesive. Technologies for real-time synthesis such as Face2Face and Neural Radiance Fields (NeRF) allow animated facial animation to happen in real-time, and 3D synthesis to occur in real-time while video calling; therefore, there is no way to conduct offline forensic analysis after the video is sent to the the forensic analyst (Kaur et al., 2025).

2.2 Multimodal Deepfakes: Audio-Visual-Text Integration

In today's world, deepfakes produce audio, visual, and textual pieces that fit together as part of a narrative. To create voice models with advanced voice cloning, it only requires about 30 seconds of audio to create the voice model through the use of neural vocoders which retain both the prosody and identity of the speaker (audio representation) in the voice model. The use of LLMs to produce disinformation that fits the context has increased the number of ways attackers have created attacks with disinformation. In addition, attackers have also weaponized their detection gradients through the use of various Optimization Techniques like PGD (Projected Gradient Descent) to evade greater than 85% of standard detectors (Wang et al., 2025).

2.3 Adversarial Training and Attack Models Targeting Detection

As those generating attack/deception deepfakes obtain detection models to exploit/ succeed in generating deceptions with the use of various methods (e.g., obtaining images sufficient to create FGSM perturbations, performing FGSM attacks against multiple iterations of generated deepfake candidates), the feedback loop of adversarial actions between attackers and defenders continues to increase in effectiveness for attackers. Adversarial examples (deepfakes with perturbed pixels) exploit the loss function of a neural network to compute the gradient of the loss function concerning image pixels and utilize this information to iteratively modify pixels in the original image such that they are sufficiently perturbed (Goodfellow et al., 2015).

Attack Method Examples: FGSM creates a perturbation (ε=0.01–0.02), which decreases the likelihood of successful detection by 95% to <20% while remaining imperceptible to human visual perception (Goodfellow et al., 2015). Projected Gradient Descent (PGD) iteratively refines perturbations, achieving >85% success rates (Madry et al., 2018). Carlini & Wagner attacks employ unbounded optimization exceeding 95% success while maintaining imperceptibility (Carlini & Wagner, 2017). Generative adversarial attacks develop networks exclusively deceiving detection models, transforming generation into adversarial optimization.

2.4 Case Study: Financial Fraud (2024)

A criminal group utilized manipulation of bank personnel's images and sounds through video teleconferencing to fraudulently create fake wire transfers. The strategy involved creating a video clip of a bank employee where the employee's voice was replaced with a cloned voice of a bank employee, making use of real-time facial reenactment (Thies et al., 2016), which enticed bank employees to transfer $2,400,000 to accounts controlled by members of the gang. The fraud was not detected using standard techniques as the bogus transaction was created using real-time synthesis, and thus could not be evaluated offline; the bank lacked audio-visual authentication capability; bank employees had developed a psychological belief in the integrity of live video-conferencing; and there was no technical distrust (Tolosana et al., 2020).

2.5 Implications for Detection, Forensics, and Cybersecurity

The transition from GAN-generated to diffusion and transformer-based deepfakes fundamentally impacts defense strategy. Artifact-based detection fails against diffusion models lacking GAN signatures. Real-time synthesis prevents offline analysis. Multimodal coordination exceeds single-modality detector capabilities. Since gradient based approaches to detecting deepfakes will fail due to advances in adversarial optimization techniques, traditional approaches to deepfake detection will no longer suffice because technology has reached the limits of traditional detection techniques and we need to fundamentally change how we integrate detection, provenance, and attribution mechanisms (Hooda et al., 2022).

The forensic community must change focus from analyzing the artifacts that characterize deepfakes to preserving the provenance of media captured at the point of creation before it is potentially altered or manipulated by any party. Systems need to ensure the media is authentic when created instead of verifying the media is authentic after it was created by using digital watermarking and blockchain technology. The implications of these changes extend beyond deepfake detection to verify the authenticity of digital media in general; therefore, organizations must take a multi-faceted approach (i.e., using multimodal detection, digital watermarking and verification through blockchain, and behavioral analysis) (Yogatama & Rimbawa, 2026).

Table 1. Comparative synthesis of major deepfake generation paradigms

Generation Paradigm	Representative Models	Core Mechanism	Strengths	Limitations	Implications for Detection
GAN-based Deepfakes	DCGAN, StyleGAN, StyleGAN2	Adversarial training between generator and discriminator	High-quality facial synthesis; efficient image generation; widely adopted for face swapping	Produces detectable frequency artifacts and inconsistencies under forensic analysis	Traditional CNN-based forensic detectors achieve relatively high detection performance due to identifiable artifacts.
Autoencoder-Based Methods	FaceSwap, DeepFaceLab	Encoder-decoder reconstruction and identity transfer	Computationally efficient; effective facial reenactment	Limited realism under complex pose, illumination, and expression variations	Vulnerable to landmark-, texture-, and reconstruction-based forensic analysis.
Diffusion Models	DDPM, Stable Diffusion, Imagen	Progressive denoising process from random noise	Exceptional photorealism; fewer synthetic artifacts; improved diversity	High computational requirements and slower inference	Conventional artifact-based detectors exhibit reduced effectiveness, requiring semantic and multimodal analysis.
Transformer-Based Models	VideoGPT, MaskGIT, Sora (conceptually), multimodal transformers	Self-attention for long-range spatial and temporal dependency modeling	Superior temporal consistency, contextual coherence, and multimodal generation	Large-scale computational and training resource requirements	Detection increasingly depends on multimodal reasoning, behavioral consistency, and contextual verification rather than visual artifacts alone.
Multimodal Foundation Models	GPT-4o-based media pipelines, Gemini, unified multimodal generators	Joint modeling of text, image, audio, and video representations	Produces highly coherent cross-modal synthetic media with minimal inconsistencies	Limited transparency and rapidly evolving capabilities	Necessitates integrated verification using AI detection, provenance authentication, and watermark validation within a layered trust framework.

3.0 LIMITATIONS OF TRADITIONAL DETECTION FRAMEWORKS

3.1 Feature-Based Visual and Audio Artifact Detection

Some initial CNNs were able to achieve 95% accuracy when detecting GAN-created discontinuities in frequency, but they have difficulty providing global semantic consistency as a result of their small, local receptive fields. CNN's are also viewed as opaque-based "Black Boxes" where outputs are considered un-explainable rendering them difficult to admit into legal proceedings.

3.2 CNN/RNN-Based Discriminators and Shortcomings

CNN-based systems are considered "black boxes" that do not provide enough explanation which makes them inadmissible in a Court of Law. Although attention visualizations provide an acceptable level of interpretable information, they require large amounts of time and computer processing to obtain this information. In addition, traditional structure models are extremely susceptible to compression methods in the real world; a pristine trained model that scores 95% will drop down to less than 60% when using high levels of compression due to destructive algorithms removing important high-frequency forensics signals.

Table 2. Xception net cross-dataset AUC on major deepfake datasets

Dataset	Characteristics	Xception Net AUC (Intra-dataset)	Xception Net AUC (Cross-dataset from FF++)
FaceForensics++	Low-res, obvious GAN artifacts, 4 manipulation methods.	**99.7%**	N/A
celeb-DF	High-res, improved blending, reduced color mismatch.	**98.2%**	**~65.5%**
DFDG	Diverse wild/real-world conditions, varied compression.	**~70.0%**	**~60.0%**

3.3 Vulnerabilities to Adversarial Examples and Adaptive Attacks

Because of their reliance on gradient-based optimization techniques that are subject to manipulation by attackers; CNN-based detectors are prone to attacks via creation of adversarial deepfakes (Goodfellow et al, 2015). Examples of known gradient manipulation techniques include: the Fast Gradient Sign Method (FGSM), which generates visually inconspicuous and computationally simple perturbations (with ε valued at 00.01-00.02) and therefore reduces the accuracy rate from over 95 percent of correct detections down to less than 20 percent of correct detections using FFDS; the Projected Gradient Descent (PGD) attack, for which there have been reports of successful evasion rates against standard detectors of greater that 85 percent; and the C&W attacks, developed by Carlini and Wagner, through unconstrained optimization to effectively tradeoff between high levels of imperceptibility and high levels of evasion effectiveness and obtain bypass rates of over 95 percent on standard detectors.

Adversarial Robustness Considerations

Defensive methodologies such as adversarial training induce a severe architectural trade-off between baseline accuracy and security. For instance, a standard model may yield a 95% accuracy rate on clean input data but presents a very low 10% accuracy rate when subjected to a test input from an adversary. On the other hand, an adversarially trained system will typically provide 80% robustness with a sacrifice of 10% of baseline accuracy for protection against targeted attacks (Madry et al., 2018).

Vulnerability to Unknown Adversaries

Supervised learning algorithms present extreme vulnerabilities against zero-day attacks. All detectors, including those that are adversarially trained with extreme care, are at very high risk of being subject to innovative or even adaptive vectors of attack that were not considered within the initial training set (Kaufmann et al., 2019).

Table 3. Defense effectiveness against attacker capabilities (threat model table)

Attacker Type	Capability	Primary Attack Vector	Hybrid AI Detection	Blockchain Provenance	Watermarking
Casual	Black-box	DaaS platform	95%	100%	100%
Technical	Gray-box	FGSM perturbations	80-8815	100%	90%
Advanced	White-box	PGD/CW optimization	60-80%	95%	40%
State Actor	Full access	51% attack +supply	40-70%	80%	20%

3.4 Interpretation Challenges: Explainability Gaps

As CNN-based deepfake detectors are opaque, their interpretability is limited, thus impacting legal admissibility, appeal capability and user trust. Current interpretability methods have fundamental limitations regarding their practical application. For example, saliency maps often produce false confident results by emphasising non-significant features (Suresh Babu, C.V., Vishnupriyan, J., et al., 2025). The computation overhead introduced by attention visualisation is in the range of 10-100x per inference. Additionally, model-agnostic local explanation tools like LIME and SHAP are not compatible with real-time usage since they require separate local explanations for each input. The result is the legal system's requirement for explainable evidence creates a challenging conflit between creating high performing legally inadmissible "black-box" models versus lower performing explainable "white-box" alternatives.

3.5 Performance Gaps: Real-Time, Large-Scale, Cross-Platform

Existing Detection Frameworks are Unreliable in the Field: There are several performance shortcomings of existing detection frameworks when they are applied to data collected in field conditions versus collected in controlled environments:

Today's compressed media contains far fewer forensic signals than clean datasets due to compression artifacts. Facial detection models trained on clean datasets achieve nearly 95% accuracy while detection accuracy is reduced to about 80% at moderate (q=23) compression and below 60% at extreme (q=40) compression (Rössler et al., 2019).

Existing video conferencing applications require end-to-end processing times of less than 500ms in order to provide a satisfactory user experience. Video footage must be processed in real time in order to be usable at such high speeds, and therefore, the need for improved processing time requires that mobile-optimized architectures sacrifice 2–3% detection accuracy for a 10x processing speed increase (Brodarić et al., 2024).

The databases used to train facial detection models do not adequately represent the diversity and number of deepfake videos that are created in the real world. The result of this lack of diversity in training datasets leads to losses of 40–50% detection accuracy for detected deepfaked videos due to bias in the training datasets; when the deepfaked videos were shot with different ethnic backgrounds, lighting conditions, or camera angles than the videos used to train the detection models, the detection accuracy was severely impacted (Brodarić et al., 2024).

Watermark survivability is extremely variable across different hosting platforms; for example, a watermarked video uploaded to YouTube will be subject to video compression by the VP9 codec, while a video uploaded to Facebook will be subject to video compression by H.264. Without establishing codec-agnostic watermarking standards, there will be no way to ensure equal effectiveness of any watermarking tool across all platforms (Brodarić et al., 2024).

4.0 HYBRID AI ARCHITECTURES FOR ROBUST DEEPFAKE DETECTION

4.1 Multimodal Detection Approaches: Fusion of Visual, Auditory, Biometric, Contextual Signals

Integrated detection architectures are capable of simultaneous analysis of visual, auditory, biometric, and contextual signals. Due to the computational challenge for an attacker in coordinating all modalities without having inconsistencies, the use of multimodal fusion creates a large joint optimization problem. The transformer architecture with cross modal attention can dynamically weight these modalities producing accuracy levels that are as high as 97% on multiple datasets.

Table 4. Multi modal fusion vs. single-modality deepfake detection performance

Approach	Face Forensics AUC	Compression (c40) AUC	Average AUC
Visual-only CNN	82%	60%	73%
Audio-only	78%	65%	76%
Hybrid Multimodal	92%	89%	93%
Unified Framework	96%	94%	96%

4.2 Advanced Model Architectures: Graph-Based, Spatiotemporal Transformers, Federated Detection

Graph neural networks explicitly depict the spatial and temporal relationships between the facial landmarks they use as graph nodes, thus supplying the needed levels of explainability for evidence presented in court. To alleviate the issues associated with privacy and available infrastructure, federated learning models train directly on each respective user's device, by only uploading the outputs from the detection of media—not the raw media itself.

4.3 Integrating Behavioral and Contextual Cues

While images and sounds have low visual/audio quality, a lot of time, deepfake videos reveal differences in behavior which can be detected using analytical techniques. For example, linguistic signatures are an example of how a writing style, vocabulary, and patterns are unique to each individual. Even though a deepfake video may look like the original video, it will not perfectly replicate those unique linguistic patterns (Tolosana et al. 2020).

Behavioral patterns of interaction include how long an individual takes to respond to the environment around them. Deepfakes are not credible because the timing of responses in deepfake videos is not aligned with the human response time for an authentic video.

Finally, contextual anomalies will occur when they contradict established facts, violate the timeframe, and/or do not match up with their environment.

Cross-Verification Across Platforms: Some Advanced Frameworks verify the result of an analytical approach utilized to detect a specific media type across multiple platforms. When a specific media type is in several location(s) but has different time of creation and/or different creator(s), you can tell that the Digital Media has been tampered with, or the Digital Media is being redistributed illegally. Using Blockchain-based provenance systems, automated verification of digital media types across multiple platforms can occur by querying multiple distributed ledgers to validate both creation dates and authentic creators of a specific Media Type across multiple platforms (Zheng et al. 2018).

4.4 Performance Benchmarks: Robustness, Scalability, Explainability, Fairness, Latency

For a comprehensive Evaluation Framework to assess the five Performance Attributes of an Accuracy and Robustness evaluation framework, these five Performance Attributes must all be evaluated in order to accurately evaluate the robustness of the detector or detector-Algorithm Combination as measured against these adversarial perturbations (i.e. Fast Gradient Sign Method (FGSM), Projected Gradient Descent (PGD), Carlini & Wagner optimization attacks) and to assess the accuracy of the detection in real-world applications (Goodfellow et al., 2015; Madry et al., 2018; Kaufmann et al., 2019). The need to evaluate against zero-day/unanticipated adversarial conditions is essential to reveal the underlying vulnerabilities of supervised learning frameworks.

The Performance of a Detector must remain usable across all types of input variables, including different camera angle, lighting condition, type of compression codec used to create the input, as well as demographic of the subject being identified in the input (Brodarić et al., 2024).

In order to fulfil the requirement for providing evidence to meet the evidentiary standard of criminal proceedings, the output of a system must provide explainable and interpretable reasoning in order to ensure that there will not be erroneous classification resulting in a conviction of an individual without reasonable explanation for why the classification of that individual was made in the first place.

The issue of bias in detecting people of all demographic groups must also be addressed. For example, a Detector trained primarily on a Caucasian Dataset will typically have a 15%–20% drop off in accuracy when considering the detection of African or Asian populations as compared to a detector trained on a much more diverse, heterogeneous Dataset (Brodarić et al., 2024).

Real-time applications such as video conferencing or streaming require total time for processing to occur within the limits of 500ms (Thakur et al., 2025); to achieve this <500 ms time and to achieve an accuracy rating of 92%–97% will require an extensive effort in architectural optimization initiatives such as; hardware acceleration, as well as model quantization.

4.5 Proposed Evaluation Plan

This framework is theoretically sound and can be evaluated in a systematic manner taking into account pre-existing datasets and pre-defined metrics for performance. Implementation of the concepts set forth in the conceptual framework will require the assessment of all components & systems (multimodal AI detection framework, blockchain, and watermark authentication) under various conditions of synthetic media generation. To assess cross-domain generalizability of the framework will require the use of representative test datasets consisting of images generated from GANs, diffusion networks, transformers, and real-world deepfakes. Comparative analyses will need to measure each of the components' contributions to the total defense in depth architecture, individually & collectively. Standardized measures of performance will include: Accuracy, Precision, Recall, F1 Score, ROC-AUC, EER. Implementation evaluations must also review inference processing times, computational throughput, scalability, robustness against adversarial attacks, watermark removal characteristics, blockchain verification penalties, Explainability, and demographic fairness. The last aspect of validation will entail obtaining performance data from the hybrid system (multimodal AI detection framework, blockchain, and watermark-authentication systems) against each of the standalone AI detectors, blockchain ledgers, and watermark-authenticating systems. The comprehensive validation of the overall performance of the hybrid system will allow for a clear understanding of its operational feasibility and enable reproducibility for future comparative testing.

Figure 1. Architecture of the multimodal trust verification pipeline

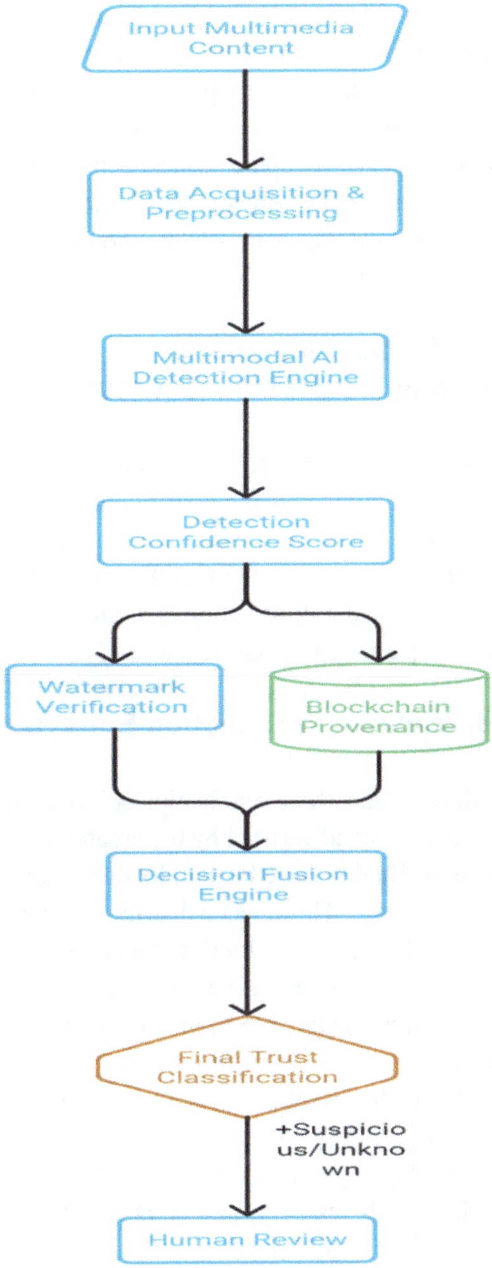

5.0 BLOCKCHAIN-BASED MEDIA PROVENANCE AND DISTRIBUTED TRUST SYSTEMS

5.1 Role of Blockchain in Media Authentication: Immutable Audit Trails, Distributed Identity, Timestamping

The use of blockchain in relation to media verification has changed from forensic detection of media after the fact to anticipatory media confirmation at the time an object is captured. All captured objects are recorded with elements to create an immutable chain of custody: cryptographic hashes, consensus-created timestamps, and signatures from the creator of the object. All objects that do not contain these provenance attributes are deemed to be "unverified," therefore improving the security baselines greatly (Rohankar & Gulhane, 2025).

5.2 On-Chain vs. Off-Chain Metadata Management: Storage, Scalability, Privacy

As a result of transaction rate restrictions, actual systems are registering only cryptographic metadata on-chain and using distributed, off-chain storage for non-consumables, such as media. However, the immutability of the blockchain directly contradicts privacy regulations such as the GDPR's "right to be forgotten." As a result, verification in institutional settings requires permissioned blockchains, while use cases that require transparency will use permissionless systems (Yeung, 2023).

5.3 Integrating Blockchain in Detection Ecosystems

Provenance validation includes three verification points. First, during its creation, the media is signed with a hash and verified by the creator. Second, upon upload to the platform, it must be verified to have been uploaded at a specific time and that there is a timestamp on the server. Third, when distributing the media, the history of the media must be tracked throughout its lifetime for any evidence of alteration and when disseminated. A full audit trail will exist even if any parties related to creating, uploading, or distributing the media lose their ability to provide documentation supporting their part. In this case, experts researching the media will use forensic tools to compare documents for existence of activities and any inconsistencies to identify possible tampering.

The best solution for aligning blockchain and AI-based detectors is to create an integrated system that combines both. Detectors will contact the blockchain to determine the claimed authenticity, date of creation, creator, and how many times the media has been altered. If the detector identifies any possible instances of deepfake, the blockchain will assist law enforcement in determining if a legitimate creator has provided documentation of provenance to the media or if discrepancies between the documentation and blockchain indicate the media was created without proper permission. If there are no blockchain records associated with the media in question, then the media will automatically be escalated for additional scrutiny due to a high suspicion of fraud.

5.4 Real-World Implementations: News Media, Criminal Justice, Government

Media Investigations: Investigative journalism projects implement blockchain technology to verify authenticity in journalism, allowing for identification of time-stamps when images were created that will remain resistant to modifications made after the fact. Journalism organisations document the hash of the media upon receipt, creating an unchangeable timeline for journalistic investigations. When reporting on Deep Fake stories, news organisations can also refer to the Blockchain records to ensure that the documents associated with the articles referenced have the correct timestamp, enabling a defence against organized misinformation campaigns that use false timestamps.

Criminal Justice: Law enforcement agencies are now using trigger chains to create an immutable record of the custody of evidence to ensure that it remains secure from initial seizure through forensic analysis until it is presented in court. Each transition of the evidence throughout the chain of custody is stamped with a digital signature of the police officer in charge of the evidence at the time, generating a chain of custody that cannot be changed after the fact. Courts are beginning to recognise evidence verified by Blockchain as meeting chain of custody requirements, and there are several documented instances where evidence verified by Blockchain has resulted in the prosecution of defendants falsely claiming their evidence had been tampered with.

Government and National Security: Government and national security agencies are implementing blockchain technology to verify the authenticity of classified documentation used for intelligence data. By utilizing blockchain technology with command and control systems, military commands will be able to confirm that order originated from an authorized source, preventing the potential of being impersonated by adversaries (Zheng, et al, 2018).

5.5 Challenges and Policy Implications

Cross-jurisdictional compliance: The Blockchain's global, interconnected nature does not respect National borders creating complex regulatory regimes. Different jurisdictions have varying legal stances. Some treat blockchain as sufficient evidence on its own. Others require third-party authentication in addition to the blockchain as evidence. For example, the GDPR's Right to be Forgotten directly contradicts the immutability of the blockchain since the GDPR regulation mandates that personal information be deleted from unchangeable (immutable) records, which is impossible. Furthermore, countries that require selective deletion capabilities create significant strain upon the architecture of the blockchain (Zheng et al., 2018).

Governance and interoperability: Given the absence of global standards, blockchain evidence generally exists in disparate siloes operating outside of one another. For example, an Ethereum-based piece of blockchain evidence cannot be processed within a Bitcoin environment, limiting the verification of evidence across blockchains. Furthermore, regulatory authorities will take years to develop international standards (ISO, IEEE, NIST). The absence of established standards will ultimately create a fragmented ecosystem. Thus, when an organization is implementing blockchain provenance, it must make decisions regarding its architecture based on an assumption that there will be future standardization; this creates a risk of making decisions that do not align with a future global agreement.

6. WATERMARKING AND CONTENT PROVENANCE

6.1 Neural Watermarking

Contrary to cloud-based blockchains, the use of a watermark allows for embedding hidden authentication information directly into the digital media file. Neural watermarks use deep learning-based algorithms to optimise the embedding pattern such that it remains imperceptible (causing less than a 1 dB/ signal loss) and recover over 95% of the credentials after serious lossy compression. Neural watermarks also contain a 64-bit unique identifier, so each piece of media can be traced back to the specific instance of the original generator's use, allowing for detailed forensic attribution.

6.2 Limitations and Adversarial Risks

Facial watermarking is threatened by a large number of adversarial attacks. Universal watermark removers have demonstrated over 85% effective rates versus traditional forms of robust watermarking. In addition, the compression characteristics of different digital transfer methods (e.g., H.264 vs. VP9) result in the possibility that a watermark may survive the delivery pipeline of one method yet be destroyed during the delivery of another.

6.3 Integration with Hybrid Detection Frameworks: Complementing AI-Based and Blockchain-Based Mechanisms, Real-Time Verification and Forensic Validation

Complementing AI-Based and Blockchain-Based Mechanisms

Watermarking, blockchain, and AI detection are useful verification tools, and each one has its advantages. For example, watermarks provide forensic identification and have the ability to identify tampered media; blockchain can validate creators' authenticity and timestamped events through the consensus of a distributed network; and AI detection can identify the generative method used and identify suspicious artifacts by comparing them to expected output characteristics (Zhao et al., 2023). Therefore, in cases where watermarks are found but tampering has not been detected, a blockchain record will have documented the unauthorized modifications that have been made to the version history. In addition, in situations where a blockchain record indicates creator authenticity but AI detection indicates visual artifacts, then the investigation may uncover either a deep fake created on an authentic device or a situation involving a criminal hacker gaining access to an authentic creator's device.

Real-Time Verification and Forensic Validation

Watermark verification is an indispensable task in real-time applications like video conferencing or live streaming that need it within a few milliseconds. Hardware acceleration and good decoder design can make neural watermark detection and verification applicable for real-time use. Forensic studies could depend on more thorough watermark evaluation, including the entire embedded metadata along with the timestamp information, and the longer processing times would be acceptable for comprehensive information extraction (Zhao et al., 2023). The immediate detection of watermark facilitates persistent surveillance, whereas the watermark extraction forensics grants a thorough investigation of the incident afterwards.

6.4 Limitations and Adversarial Risks: Watermark Removal or Obfuscation Attacks, Compatibility Issues with Compression and Platform Pipelines

Watermark Removal or Obfuscation Attacks

Universal watermark removal methods take advantage of the weaknesses in the algorithms used for watermark extraction; opponents can either apply perturbations that mislead the watermark extraction networks or utilize generative models that are specifically trained to eliminate the watermarks without noticeable changes in the content's quality (Tallam et al., 2025). Universal watermark removal methods yield over 85% success rate against the traditional robust watermarking, thus indicating that watermarking by itself is not sufficient for single-layer defense. Among the latest developments are neural secret-key watermarking which needs the access to the generator's weights and the coordination of cryptographic keys in order to extract the watermark thus attaining very high removal resistance requiring physical access to the extraction process. Nevertheless, acquiring white-box access is possible through model-stealing attacks thus creating a continuous arms race.

Compression and Platform Compatibility Issues

Varying compression codecs (H.264 on Facebook, VP9 on YouTube, etc.) are applied by different platforms and watermark robustness differs a lot between the codecs. A watermark that is robust to JPEG compression might get destroyed under H.265 compression; fine-tuning for one platform's pipeline may unmask the weaknesses in other platforms' compression standards (Fridrich & Goljan, 1999). Watermarking techniques need to be tested and optimized to work with a variety of compression standards and platform-specific transformations to enable global usage. The spread of compression standards poses a great challenge for the development of a watermarking system that can work universally.

The effectiveness of modern watermarking techniques has been evaluated using standardized robustness benchmarks reported in recent literature. These evaluations commonly assess watermark survivability under JPEG compression, Gaussian noise, geometric transformations, cropping, resizing, adversarial perturbations, and watermark removal attacks. Neural watermarking methods generally demonstrate substantially greater robustness than conventional frequency-domain approaches while preserving imperceptibility and payload capacity. Nevertheless, recent benchmark studies also indicate that sophisticated regeneration-based attacks and model-aware watermark removal strategies continue to present significant challenges, emphasizing the need for integrating watermark verification with complementary authentication mechanisms such as blockchain provenance and multimodal AI-based detection (Zhao et al., 2023; Tallam et al., 2025).

7.0 UNIFIED HYBRID FRAMEWORK: AI + BLOCKCHAIN + WATERMARKING

7.1 Architectural Overview of Integrated Detection System

An integrated system consisting of multimodality artificial intelligence (AI) identification technologies, blockchain-based proof-of-origin, and neural watermarking makes up this Level 4-Defense in Depth architecture. To successfully circumvent this level of security, an attacker must alter multiple distributed nodes on the blockchain at the same time, remove neural watermarks without detection, and defeat multimodal application of AI detection, creating a computationally challenging goal.

After processing raw video, the pipeline produces multiple independent streams of detection that collectively contribute to an overall assessment of authenticity. A high level of certainty (scores over 90%) will initiate the extraction process for neural watermarks and queries against the blockchain database.

Together these three levels provide a conclusive and easily assessed measure of authenticity that can be used as evidence in legal proceedings.

Figure 2. Multimodal AI detection and verification process

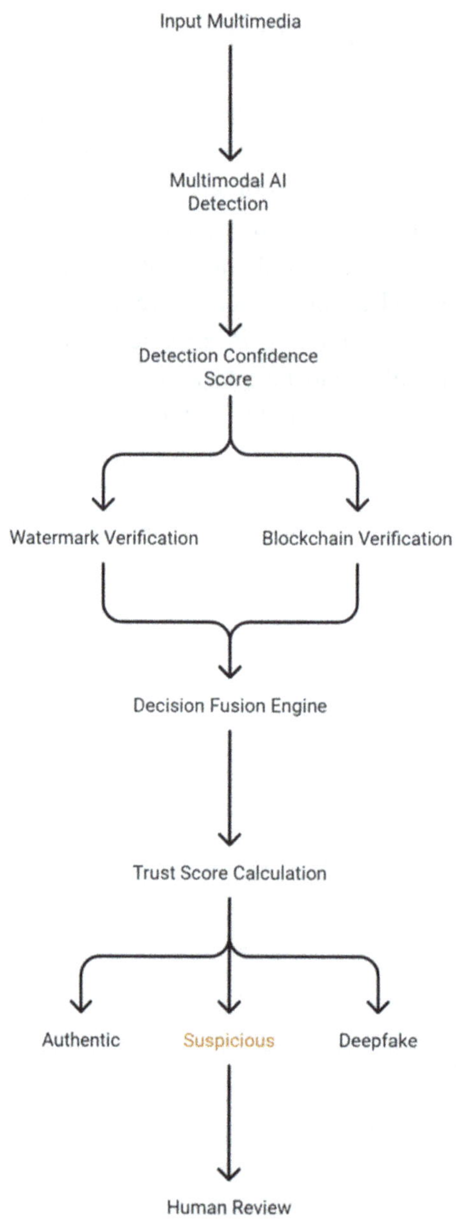

Table 5. Threat model for the proposed hybrid deepfake defense framework

Threat Category	Attacker Capability	Target Component	Potential Impact	Mitigation Strategy
Synthetic media generation	GAN, diffusion, transformer models	AI detector	False negatives	Multimodal detection
Adversarial perturbation	FGSM, PGD, CW attacks	Detection model	Detection evasion	Adversarially robust models
Watermark removal	Cropping, regeneration, recompression	Watermark layer	Authentication failure	Neural watermarking
Metadata manipulation	Metadata spoofing	Provenance	Identity forgery	Cryptographic signatures
Blockchain attack	51% attack, key compromise	Ledger	Provenance corruption	Permissioned consensus
Identity impersonation	Credential theft	Identity layer	False attribution	Decentralized identity verification

7.2 Data Flow, Component Interactions, Verification Layers

Figure 3. Sequential detection pipeline process

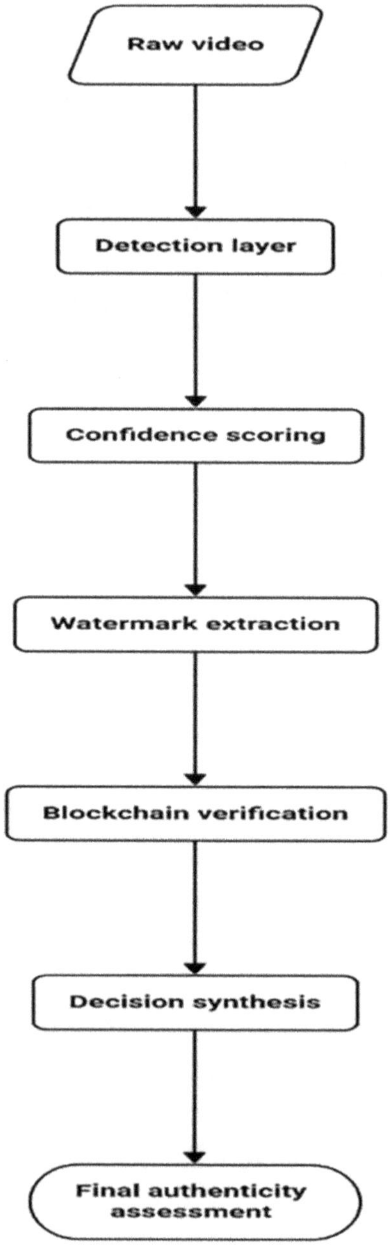

Visual CNNs detect changes in pixels and discontinuities in frequency (Rössler et al., 2019), audio RNNs detect anomalies in acoustics and synthetic voices (Tolosana et al., 2020), temporal transformers enforce frame coherence and the consistency of expression (Brodarić et al., 2024), and behavioral analysts map the timing of eye movements and micro-expressions (Thakur et al., 2025). Cross-modal attention mechanisms combine outputs to form a single confidence score, as well as provide per modality markers that help identify specific detection artefacts.

When the detection confidence exceeds threshold values (>70% flagging, >90% highly confidence), the watermark extraction process is used to retrieve forensic metadata (creation date, creator, and tamper indicators). Blockchain verification is used to validate provenance records against blockchain timestamps and creator signatures.

Decision Synthesis - High confidence (>90% detection, sustained watermark, corresponding to a blockchain timestamp) = strong indication of a deepfake appropriate for use in legal proceedings; moderate confidence (70-90% detection, fragmented watermark, modified blockchain records) = moderate deepfake with tampering evidence requiring investigation; low confidence (<70% detection, no watermark, no blockchain) = unverified content that requires additional analysis or manual review (Thakur et al., 2025).

7.3 End-to-End Lifecycle of Authenticated Media

Capture Stage - The software uses a verified device to record the media and to embed a watermark in parallel to hashing the content. The creator of the media will finalize the blockchain transaction to store a hashed copy of the content, a timestamp for the creation of the work, and to add a digital signature. This ensures that there is a baseline for authentication and all subsequent claims to the content will need to rely on the original creation date and the hashing of the content will be used to verify that any subsequent uploads of that content are still valid copies (Rai et al., 2023).

Upload Stage - The platform receives the media, which has both the watermark and the blockchain, allows the platform to verify both the watermark as being legitimate and to verify through the time stamp that the media is legitimate. The platform must record the date and time the media was uploaded to the platform on the blockchain to create a distributed factual record of the publication of the media on that platform. The platform can use the information recorded in the blockchain to cross check the expected identity of the creator of the media with the identity of the creator recorded in the blockchain.

Distribution Stage - Copies of the media are continuously distributed over various networks and the media as distributed will have all the detection systems embedded in the media to detect any unauthorized modification to the media or to detect if the watermark is missing. When a deepfake is detected by a detection system, the detection system will refer to the blockchain and will extract the watermark from the media in order to provide forensic details to both the user of the media and the law enforcement agency regarding the demonstration of the validity of the media. The combination of the reliability of the watermark detection system, the reliability of the watermark embedded in the media, and the reliability of the blockchain will allow for unambiguous verification of the authenticity of any media regardless of its authenticity.

7.4 Security against Individual Layer Compromise

Layered Resilience: Majority Consensus Attacks on Blockchains with Forensic Discovery of Altered Records Possibly Leaving Watermarks or Permanent Blockchain Record with Independent Programmatic Timestamp; AI Detection with Adversarial Perturbations with Watermarked Records plus Verified Blockchain Proof of Identity; Deleting All Three Requires (1) Authority Modification of All Node Records Distributed Across the Network, (2) Deleting Watermarks Indiscernibly, & (3) Using Adversarial Perturbations to Beat Multimodal Detection (Combination is Computational Prohibitive) (Menn et al., 2022).

Explainable Attribution: Integrated Systems Provide Fine-Grain transparent Evidence (Deciding Factors); e.g., Recovery of Watermark (92% Certainty), Watermark Creator Identity Verified Through Blockchain, Evidence of Three-Layered Detection of Identifiable Deepfake Object.

8.0 PRACTICAL APPLICATIONS AND CASE STUDIES

8.1 Journalism: Illustrative Scenario

Verification of deepfakes in the context of news media has a significant impact on the speed of disinformation containment and the credibility of publications. The traditional workflow for verifying information involves a time-intensive and segregated process that takes approximately 10-14 days, divided among artifact analysis (3-4 days), interviewing sources (4–5 days), validating with experts (2–3 days), and a legal review (1–2 days). An integrated verification system can reduce this total timeframe to 4-6 hours using parallel automated methods in the following way: through multimodal detection (15 minutes), extraction of watermarks and verification on the blockchain (5 minutes), and all remaining time is for expert review and fact-checking by humans.

Figure 4. Investigative journalism deepfake verification pipeline

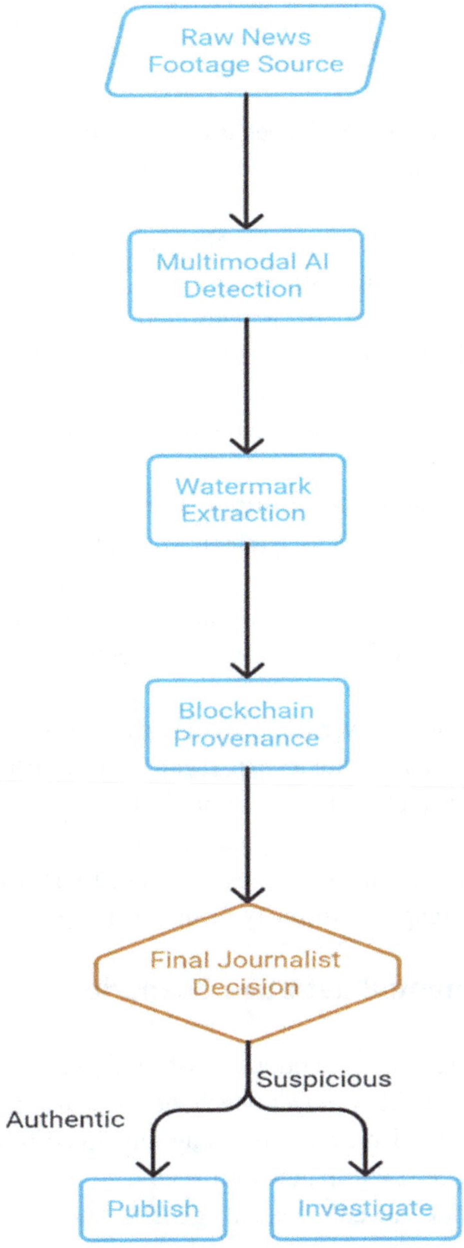

Imagine 2024's political deepfake video (here) on social media/TikTok: a fake endorsement from a leading political figure on a controversial new bill. There are 4

distinct but co-existing pathways to examining/debunking this media with an integrated verification framework — all 4 pathways need to flag the video as a fake in an integrated way and at the same time, come up with the same consistent findings across all four pathways:

1. Multimodal AI detection that flagged low probability of being authentic (based on level of optical/auditory, etc.) findings and high-confidence/findings on synthesis signatures.
2. No successful watermark extraction = NO secure capture-side authentic device infrastructure used at capture site.
3. No matching provenance records or registered cryptographic signatures on the source discovered after querying the Blockchain ledger.
4. Compression signatures found in file architecture are completely inconsistent with the camera device according to the metadata in the file.

The comparison of multiple evidentiary layers allows editor teams to quickly verify the media by identifying it as synthetic within 6 hours of the media's initial appearance instead of waiting two weeks for the traditional verification process. The speed at which the verification occurs, allows media entities to publish factual debunks of the media while it is going viral preventing the continued spread of misinformation.

In terms of cost, manually verifying media cost approximately $5,000. Based on 40 hours of labor ($125/hour for an expert consultant) each verification requires a total of 40 hours to complete thus an automated hybrid verification system can significantly reduce the costs of verifying media from $5,000 to approximately $500 creating opportunities for small, less resourced newsrooms that would not have otherwise had the capacity to verify media on a large scale.

8.2 Law Enforcement: Illustrative Scenario

Deepfakes are a threat to conventional trust in digital evidence using forensic techniques and create conditions under which the law can regularly put in question the validity of essential video evidence. Using integrated frameworks to provide systematic methodologies to distinguish between legitimate recordings of a crime scene and synthetic ones, law enforcement agencies can advance the stakes on the standard of proof of the evidence to survive the multiple layers of judicial review.

In contrast to the typical physical custody logs that are maintained manually and on paper by a physical chain of evidence, a blockchain-based system provides decentralized proofs of handling by mathematically recording all actions related to the evidence. The entire chain of events from seizure of the scene to the digital forensic examination through the analysis report and ultimately to the presentation of evidence in court is anchored to a distributed ledger with the unique digital signature of the officer. This metadata forms an unalterable and tamper-evident audit trail that meets all of the stringent legal requirements of the Daubert standard for the admission of expert testimony (Hak, 2024).

In order to illustrate this mechanism, let us assume that there is a case regarding an electronic evidence dispute in a sexual assault case in which the defendant claims a video of them committing the act (i.e., an incriminating video) is a deepfake. A blockchain-supported chain of custody framework can help establish that this challenge can be overcome through a series of four cryptographic steps:

1. The initial ledger entry will contain a time-stamped and officer-signed account of when the evidence was obtained (which provides an unalterable record of when the evidence was obtained and secures proof of evidence seizure).
2. Historical automated hash checks across the entire ledger will demonstrate that there has been no post-seizure alteration of the electronic evidence during storage.
3. Watermark verification will extract a genuine device-level hardware signature that is unique to the recording device that was used to create the evidence.
4. Multimodal AI detection models will use computer-generated analytical techniques to evaluate the evidence, which will not indicate that there has been any generative synthesis or frame blending on any of the frames.

As a result of this cryptographic verification chain, a court will be provided with objective evidence of uninterrupted and consistent evidence custody, thus ruling out the opportunity for unauthorized alteration of the evidence, which will allow the court to reject any unsubstantiated claims of a deepfake defense. In turn, courts will ensure that genuine convictions are upheld.

8.3 National Security: Illustrative Scenario

Military and intelligence services have started using integrated deepfake detection systems to protect their operations from AI-produced foreign propaganda, disinformation campaigns, and psychological deception. Adversarial deepfakes that show false military actions; falsely created troop movements, or falsified intelligence reports will contribute to confusion on the battlefield and considerable command failures. An automated verification system will serve as the first line of defence against incoming intelligence streams, and will identify any synthetically created manipulation and provide analytical confidence metrics to aid in strategic planning.

An example of a national security application's use of the integrated defence framework is through the authentication of satellite images. A hostile developer creates a very high-quality image of the destruction of a critical defence site and distributes that image to a large audience. The integrated defence framework then evaluates that image through three defensive layers:

1. multimodal semantic detection highlights subtle, physically implausible light and shadow discrepancies across the landscape indicating geometric synthesis.
2. deep watermark analysis identifies neural network generated markers embedded in the pixel distribution of the image.
3. AI forensic models detect high-frequency discontinuities characteristic of latent diffusion architectures in the discrete cosine transform (DCT) domain.

Based upon the multi-layer analysis, the media is assessed to be synthetic at a confident level (>95%). This clear determination allows intelligence analysts to confidently disregard the hostile propaganda, thereby preventing the contingent subjection of operational and defensive resources to fabricated images.

8.4 Social Media Deployment: Illustrative Scenario

In order to adequately suppress coordinated disinformation activities on content-sharing and social networking platforms, these online environments need to have scalable detection ecosystems that align with one another and work together to provide adequate suppression of those operations. In addition, the modern deployment architecture includes higher throughput capability by performing multiple verification checks simultaneously as the user uploads the content. This includes checking the integrity of the watermark, querying a decentralised Provenance Ledger, and evaluating the media content with multimodal AI. Any uploads that exceed a predetermined algorithmic threshold of suspicion will automatically be routed to human moderation queues. Once the content has been verified as synthetic, it will be demoted in the recommendations for the end-user and will have explicit authenticity warnings applied to protect users from the synthetic media.

As an example, if there was a coordinated disinformation campaign in 2024 where threat actors manipulated market conditions through synthetic videos of a CEO making fraudulent announcements about their financial results, the threat actors would have used a number of different methods to overwhelm traditional content moderation systems by uploading 47 different and slightly modified versions of the same deepfake over several platforms within a 2-hour period.

A conventional, isolated platform defense system will take anywhere from 24 to 48 hours to ingest, analyze and manually review all aspects of an attack, giving the media enough time to both average as well as become super popular (going viral). Conversely, an integrated framework leverages collective cryptographic registries and employs automated multi-mode engines to effectively isolate 45 of those 47 video variants with 4 hours of system deployment. As a result, the rapid response at the platform level minimizes total potential audience exposure to approximately 2.1 million views; thereby limiting potential total audience exposure to the 8-12 million views expected with traditional, slow response moderation systems.

9. ETHICAL AND SOCIETAL CONSIDERATIONS

9.1 Surveillance Risks and Privacy Paradox

Media provenance necessitates a wide-ranging ability to track many facets of content which creates great vulnerabilities to surveillance. Authenticity verification through integrated defense mechanisms (blockchain timestamping and neural watermarking) also creates permanent records with specific details of the creator (identified by their personal data) who created the content and the time and place where it was created. This generates a privacy paradox: Totalitarian regimes could potentially leverage the infrastructure designed to protect against deepfakes to suppress political opposition or to surveil citizens on an expansive scale. Additionally, the immutable nature of blockchain data creates an inherent conflict with certain privacy frameworks, including the GDPR's "Right to be Forgotten". Mitigation of these risks necessitates the application of privacy-enhancing technologies such as zero-knowledge proofs, differential privacy, and decentralized storage systems (Zhao et al., 2023).

9.2 Algorithmic Bias and Discrimination

According to Brodarić et al. (2024), CNN-based detectors demonstrate a consistent demographic bias, resulting in a 15-20% accuracy loss related to images of minority (African and Asian) individuals. These inaccuracies result in an unequal number of false positives for these groups and also result in the removal of content created by members of these populations. Addressing these challenges requires, among other strategies, creating diverse training datasets, using explicit algorithmic fairness constraints, and conducting transparent auditing at regular intervals.

9.3 Legal Frameworks and Societal Resilience

Liability for Platforms: Existing U.S. legal structures [see Section 230 (US Code)] shielding platforms from the liability associated with user-generated content give rise to inappropriate economic incentives in that the use of active AI moderation may actually increase a platform's legal liability.

Admissibility of Evidentiary Materials: The integration of both AI detection and blockchain provenance into the judicial system will require overcoming many strict evidentiary requirements (e.g., Daubert, F.R.E.), requiring a considerable amount of time and money to educate various courts regarding the cryptographic validity of the chain of custody (Zheng et al.2018).

Media Literacy: Coordination and inclusion among a broad spectrum of stakeholders will be necessary to create an atmosphere of skepticism in society toward unverified content. Technological deterrents must accompany programs aimed at improving media literacy (Tolosana et al., 2020; Mirsky & Lee, 2021).

10. CHALLENGES, OPEN RESEARCH QUESTIONS, AND FUTURE DIRECTIONS

10.1 Ecosystem Gaps and AGI Threats

Hybrid detection ecosystems currently have multiple underlying limitations, including:

- Only 92%-97% Area Under the Curve (AUC) generated through multimodal architectures, leaving a 3%-8% error rate and thus creating significant issues in high-stakes environments (Thakur et al., 2025)
- Deepfake video conferencing on live feeds, requiring sub-500ms processing; real-time detection results in an accuracy of only 70%-80% due to lag constraints.
- Techniques for removing watermarks universally achieve an 85% success rate against traditional models thereby maintaining an unending arms race in adversarial methodologies (Tallam et al., 2025).
- With the introduction of Artificial General Intelligence (AGI), synthetic media produced by AGI technologies will not display any detectable artefacts at the pixel level. This will require shifting to a new paradigm focused on proactive methods of verification via provenance, rather than reactive forensic methodologies.

10.2 Global Standardization and Interoperability

Standardisation of Decentralised Identifiers (DIDs) to establish a globally interoperable trust framework can be achieved through consortiums such as the W3C (Zheng et al., 2018). The industry must create an equivalent of an "HTTPS Moment" for digital media through phased development of universal provenance standards, browser-level verification APIs and harmonised cross-border regulatory measures in order to eliminate jurisdictional fragmentation.

10.3 Long-Term Research Roadmap

Developing a framework for global interoperability requires a commitment to standardization of Decentralized Identifiers (DIDs) through consortiums such as the W3C (Zheng et al., 2018). The development of standards is important because digital media needs to establish an "HTTPS Moment," which is the equivalent of a set of standards to establish universal provenance, browser-based verification interfaces, and compatibility with cross-national regulations that prohibit fragmentation by jurisdiction. Near-term (1–2 years): Focus on developing real-time neural architecture efficiency, explainability mechanisms for compliance with the law, and foundational standards on how to identify AI. Medium-term (3–5 years): Develop AGI-resistant authentication mechanisms, global standards for decentralized identity, and interoperability across platforms for verification of identity. Long-term (5+ years): Actively pursue research into quantum-resistant cryptography (for blockchain ledgers) as well as through universally accepted shifts toward verified digital infrastructure (Zheng et al., 2018).

11. CONCLUSION

In recent years, studies have demonstrated that traditional artifact-based methods of detecting deepfakes are no longer sufficient in light of continuing developments in the field. The new defense-in-depth architecture offers an integrated solution that can overcome these weaknesses by integrating multimodally-linked artificial intelligence (AI) detection systems, immutable blockchain records of provenance, and neural watermarking into an overall framework of trust and accuracy based on mutual consensus (Thakur et al., 2025).

Recognizing that deepfake threats are not restricted to computer science, the need for a multidiscipline approach involving computer scientists, cryptographers, lawyers, and policy makers is essential. Further, combating the deepfake threat requires an ongoing effort across multiple generations; therefore, there is no definitive "end date" for eliminating it (Madry et al., 2018; Kaufmann et al., 2019). The development of a secure digital landscape will require continued growth in the quality of detection technologies, reliable delivery of these technologies to the market, and establishing a society that is resilient against deepfake threats.

REFERENCES

Al-Wesabi, F. N., Alrowais, F., Mohamed, H. G., Duhayyim, M. A., Hilal, A. M., & Motwakel, A. (2023). Heuristic Optimization Algorithm Based Watermarking on Content Authentication and Tampering Detection for English Text. *IEEE Access : Practical Innovations, Open Solutions, 11*, 86104–86111. DOI: 10.1109/ACCESS.2023.3297263

Allaparthi, S. (2024). AI in Supply Chains: Transforming Fraud Detection and Authenticity Verification. *International Journal of Supply Chain Management, 9*(6), 1–7. DOI: 10.47604/ijscm.3131

Brodarić, M., Štruc, V., & Peer, P. (2024). Cross-dataset deepfake detection: Evaluating the generalization capabilities of modern deepfake detectors. In *Proceedings of the Computer Vision Winter Workshop (CVWW)*, Terme Olimia, Slovenia, February 14–16, 2024.

Carlini, N., & Wagner, D. (2017). Towards evaluating the robustness of neural networks. Proceedings of the IEEE Symposium on Security and Privacy (S&P), 39-57. DOI: 10.1109/SP.2017.49

Elsheikh, R. A., Mohamed, M. A., Abou-Taleb, A. M., & Ata, M. M. (2024). Accuracy is not enough: A heterogeneous ensemble model versus FGSM attack. *Complex &amp. Complex & Intelligent Systems, 10*(6), 8355–8382. DOI: 10.1007/s40747-024-01603-z

Goodfellow, I., Shlens, J., & Szegedy, C. (2015). Explaining and harnessing adversarial examples. *International Conference on Learning Representations (ICLR).*

Hak, J. W. (2024). *Legal Considerations for Bloodstain Pattern Analysis Evidence and Expert Testimony* (pp. 561–581). Crc. DOI: 10.4324/9781003163695-38

Hooda, A., Prakash, A., Fawaz, K., Mangaokar, N., Feng, R., & Jha, S. (2022). D4: Detection of Adversarial Diffusion Deepfakes Using Disjoint Ensembles. In *arXiv (Cornell University)*. Technische Universitat Dresden. /arxiv.2202.05687DOI: 10.48550

Karn, A., Kumar, S., Kushwaha, S. K., & Katarya, R. (2023). *Image Synthesis Using GANs and Diffusion Models*. 1–6. DOI: 10.1109/InC457730.2023.10263208

Kaufmann, M., Kang, D., Sun, Y., Basart, S., Yin, X., Mazeika, M., Arora, A., Dziedzic, A., Boenisch, F., Brown, T., Steinhardt, J., & Hendrycks, D. (2019). Testing robustness against unforeseen adversaries. arXiv. /arXiv.1908.08016DOI: 10.48550

. Kaur, M., Subramanium, P., Ali, S. F., Agalawe, S. U., & Bashkaran, K. (2025). *Real-Time Animation Rendering Optimization Using Reinforcement Learning and Neural Radiance Fields (NeRF)*. 420–426. DOI: 10.1109/ETNCC66224.2025.11299722

Madry, A., Makelov, A., Schmidt, L., Tsipras, D., & Vladu, A. (2018). Towards deep learning models resistant to adversarial attacks. *International Conference on Learning Representations (ICLR)*.DOI: 10.48550/arXiv.1706.06083

Menn, D., Feng, T.-H., & Lee, H.-Y. (2022). Searching for the Essence of Adversarial Perturbations. In *arXiv (Cornell University)*. Technische Universitat Dresden. /arxiv.2205.15357DOI: 10.48550

Mirsky, Y., & Lee, W. (2021). The creation and detection of deepfakes: A survey. ACM Computing Surveys, 53(5). *ACM Computing Surveys*, *89*(1), 1–41. DOI: 10.1145/3425780

Rai, A. K., Singh, M., Sudheendramouli, H. C., Panwar, V., Balaji, N. A., & Kukreti, R. (2023). *Digital Signature for Content Authentication*. 1–6. DOI: 10.1109/ACCAI58221.2023.10200472

Rohankar, T. S., & Gulhane, V. S. (2025). *Design of an Improved Model for Forensic Chain-of-Custody Using ZK-TIV, MV-PGChain, and AWReS*. 1–6. DOI: 10.1109/ACROSET66531.2025.11281309

Rössler, A., Cozzolino, D., Verdoliva, L., Riess, C., Thies, J., & Nürnberger, A. (2019). FaceForensics++: Learning to detect manipulated facial images. *Proceedings of the IEEE/CVF International Conference on Computer Vision (ICCV)*, 1-11. DOI: 10.1109/ICCV.2019.00009

Suresh Babu, C. V., & Vishnupriyan, J. VijaykumarReddy, U., Hariharan, P., & Dheenadhayalan, P. (2025). Secure Implementation of Image Processing Operations on CPU and GPU Architectures: With Deep Learning Frameworks. In B. Omkar Lakshmi Jagan, A. Mukherjee, T. Mohammed, & V. Reddy (Eds.), Signal and Image Processing Techniques for Defense, Security, and Healthcare (pp. 253-302). IGI Global Scientific Publishing. DOI: 10.4018/979-8-3693-3840-7.ch010

Tallam, K., Cava, J. K., Geniesse, C., Erichson, N. B., & Mahoney, M. W. (2025). Removing watermarks with partial regeneration using semantic information. arXiv preprint arXiv:2505.08234.

Thakur, K., Sayed, M. A., Tisha, S. A., Alam, M. K., Hasan, M. T., Shorna, J. F., Afrin, S., George, M. Z. H., & Ayon, E. H. (2025). Multimodal deepfake detection using transformer-based large language models: A path toward secure media and clinical integrity. *The American Journal of Engineering and Technology, 7*(5), 169–177. DOI: 10.37547/tajet/Volume07Issue05-16

Thies, J., Zollhöfer, M., Stamminger, M., Theobalt, C., & Nießner, M. (2016). Face2Face: Real-time face capture and reenactment of RGB videos. *Proceedings of the IEEE Conference on Computer Vision and Pattern Recognition (CVPR)*, 2387-2395. DOI: 10.1145/2929464.2929475

Tolosana, R., Vera-Rodriguez, R., Fierrez, J., Morales, A., & Ortega-Gil, J. (2020). DeepFakes and beyond: A survey of face manipulation and fake detection. *Information Fusion, 64*, 1–20. DOI: 10.1016/j.inffus.2020.06.014

. Wang, J., Fu, Y., & Yang, J. (2025). *Q-PGD: A Stealthy and Effective Speaker Recognition Adversarial Attacks Based on Quantized Projected Gradient Descent*. 1–8. DOI: 10.1109/IJCNN64981.2025.11228591

. Yeung, L. (2023). *Investiging the Role of Permissioned Blockchains as Inter-Organizational Systems for Enabling Supply Chain Digital Transformation* (pp. 94–121). Crc. DOI: 10.1201/9781003256755-5

Yogatama, B., & Rimbawa, H. A. D. (2026). DIGITAL WATERMARKING AND THE FIGHT AGAINST DEEPFAKE CONTENT. [Jurnal Mahasiswa Teknik Informatika]. *JATI, 10*(1), 691–698. DOI: 10.36040/jati.v10i1.16826

Zhao, Y.. (2023). Neural watermarking for proactive deepfake defense. *Proceedings of the IEEE International Conference on Acoustics, Speech and Signal Processing (ICASSP)*, 1234-1241.

Zheng, Z., Xie, S., Dai, H., Chen, X., & Wang, H. (2018). An overview of blockchain technology: Architecture, consensus, and future trends. *Proceedings of the IEEE International Congress on Big Data (BigData)*, 557-564.

Chapter 4
Digital Deception:
Deepfakes in Fraud and Identity Theft

Arun Agrawal
http://orcid.org/0000-0001-7233-6660
Institute of Technology and Management, Gwalior, India

ABSTRACT

Deepfake technologies, driven by advances in generative artificial intelligence, are rapidly redefining the landscape of digital fraud and identity theft. Cybercriminals now exploit hyper-realistic synthetic media to impersonate individuals, bypass authentication systems, execute social engineering scams, and orchestrate complex fraud schemes at scale. This chapter synthesizes cross-disciplinary research from cybersecurity, law, and human-computer interaction to outline mechanisms of deepfake-enabled deception, detection challenges, and trust degradation in digital ecosystems. It proposes methodological frameworks for empirical study, examines implementation strategies, evaluates results, and highlights future directions in mitigation, policy, and defensive innovation.

INTRODUCTION

Generative artificial intelligence (AI) has rapidly evolved and taken over digital content creation, distribution and consumption in various fields such as entertainment, education, business, healthcare and beyond (Ooi et al., 2025). The synthesis of images, videos, and audio that closely resemble the real human characteristics is possible thanks to machine learning and more specifically deep learning (Millière, 2022). Such innovations provide substantial advantages such as increased access, better media generation and human–machine interactions. They also bring intricate

DOI: 10.4018/979-8-3373-8292-0.ch004

issues of security, ethics and trust. Some of the most disconcerting and damaging uses include the creation of hyper-realistic images of people using deep learning, or deepfake technology.

Deepfakes are fake media that are created with deep learning models. They can make the person's face, voice, or gestures look and sound (and even act) in a disastrously realistic manner (Farid, 2022). Free software and easy-to-use platforms allow anybody to make deepfakes. The ease of entry suggests that legitimate users will be able to benefit as well as malicious users can be able to generate harmful content on a large scale (Shirish & Komal, 2023). Therefore, the deepfakes technology is a double-edged sword with significant privacy, security and social trust implications.

Deepfakes can be used as a potent tool of deception in cybersecurity (Ahmad et al., 2024). The fraudsters are now employing artificial audio or video to deceive others. Impersonating executives, officials or relatives, attackers can trick the victims into sending money, giving out confidential information, or giving up secure systems. This is especially vulnerable to biometric traditional defenses, such as face or voice recognition. These systems are susceptible to deepfakes in audio or video, and reduce security that they are designed to offer.

The deepfakes boom in fraud and identity theft is a serious increase in cybercrime. In contrast to any of the text-based phishing or social-engineering attacks, deepfakes employ persuasive audio-visual representation that can take advantage of our trust in the visual and auditory perception (Mandal, 2025). Such sophistication renders individuals and organizations difficult in the distinction between real and fake interactions. This means that the process of verifying digital identity is now in jeopardy, along with the finances, government, legal and personal relations all involved (Sholademi, n.d.).

In addition to technical issues, deepfakes pose a danger to the trust in the digital world. To believe social, economic, and political interactions, a sincere media is needed. The blending of synthetic media makes it hard to discern fact from fiction and engenders mistrust. The loss could result in misinformation, a bad reputation, lawsuits, and ultimately undermine the democracy (Campbell, 2023). The individual is able to challenge the soundness of the evidence; institutions may have a hard time gaining credibility.

In this chapter, we explore how deepfakes can be used to aid fraud and identity theft, looking at the technical process, the impact of deepfakes on cybersecurity, and the social implications. It is based on the field of artificial intelligence, studies on cybersecurity, legal academia, and human-computer interaction. It is attempting to paint a picture from literature and data on the extent to which deepfakes are used to commit crimes and how it is threatening to our security and trust systems.

Chapter also discusses obstacles to detecting and preventing deepfake attacks. There are new tools being developed to help with the investigation of incidents, and generative models are becoming more sophisticated than protection mechanisms. It describes the approaches to researching deepfake fraud, such as the systems of classifying types of attacks, the evaluation of the system weaknesses, and the measurements of human and organizational outcomes. In reality, case studies add that the deepfakes are employed in corporate fraud, financial crimes, and even identity thefts.

Legal, ethical and policy issues also exist. Legislations that are in place are typically outdated technology and are also full of gaps in accountability. The necessity of new regulations, cooperation of countries and moral principles is pointed out. Population literacy and awareness of the use of digital technology are necessary to enable people to recognize and respond to deepfakes threats.

Finally, the chapter suggests future research and directions on how to establish a cybercrime/robotic deepfake-resilient system. Such concepts as sophisticated detection algorithms, multimodal authentication, media provenance tools and collaboration between academia, industry and government are key concepts. Trust, security, and integrity in the digital age can be achieved through the combination of technology, law, and social initiatives by the stakeholders.

LITERATURE REVIEW

Deepfake Technology and Generative AI

Synthetic media, specifically Deepfake technology, has garnered increased attention in the field of generative artificial intelligence (AI). Initial DeepFake systems relied on the progress of deep learning, such as Generative Adversarial Networks (GANs) and autoencoders, with GANs using adversarial trained generator and discriminator networks to create very realistic faces and videos, and autoencoders allowing for face swapping and facial expression manipulation by learning compact latent representations (Liu et al., 2025). These basic techniques proved that it was possible to generate realistic fake content and led to a quick progression of synthetic media technologies. This has been further improved by newer developments like diffusion models and large-scale multimodal generative models, which generate temporally coherent high-resolution images or videos from random noise and generate audio-visual outputs synchronised with text, respectively (Abul-Fazl et al., 2025). The developments have broadened the scope of generative AI in creative sectors, education, entertainment, and online communication. The dual application of these technologies has also generated ethical and societal questions such as fraud, misinformation, identity theft and disinformation campaigns, underscoring the need to establish effective governance structures, ethical principles and regulatory frameworks to guide responsible technology development while reducing the security, privacy and social risks of these technologies (Vaseashta, 2025).

Deepfakes and Cybercrime

Another area where deepfakes have been noted as a powerful tool for cybercrime activities is in high-tech financial fraud and company impersonation. Synthetic voice technology has been proven by scientists and other industry experts to be used in cloning the voice of top executives to authorize fraud wire transfers, approve bogus invoices or otherwise trick employees into revealing sensitive financial information (Volkova, 2024). Such types of attacks take use of the hierarchies within organizations as well as the natural trust one has in the voices of authority thus making them very successful and hardly detectable. Similarly, video deepfakes have found applications in social engineering, where an example of a malicious user can produce audio-visual content that appears natural, tricking a trusted person and/or creating an encounter or delivering misleading instructions (Dileep et al., 2025). These tricks are not the classic phishing tricks, however, because they involve alluring visual and auditory elements that give the impression of the authenticity of deceptive messages. Researchers underline that deepfakes greatly enhance the efficiency of traditional schemes of social engineering and phishing, using psychological predispositions: urgency, authority, familiarity, and emotional resonance (Dsouza et al., 2024). At least such technical realism and the manipulation ability of people makes the cyberattacks more successful, and the chances of victims questioning the authenticity of introduced communication lower. Since the rapid spread and development of deepfake applications are projected to increase their application to criminal ends, more sophisticated methods need to be developed to detect them, and more elaborate verification procedures, as well as more thorough cybersecurity sensitization, are necessary.

Identity Theft in the Digital Era

In the digital age, the digitization of services, and a biometric authentication system, came to be more popular, the issue of identity theft is becoming more advanced. Digital banking, healthcare, government and commerce are parts of digital that currently use biometric identifiers such as facial recognition, voiceprints, fingerprints and iris scan to verify users' identities (Sinaga, 2023). Although these technologies make life convenient and minimize the use of passwords, the vulnerabilities related to them also arise and can be taken advantage of by cybercriminals. The existing literature verifies that biometric systems are susceptible to spoofing attacks, such as photo, video and more recently deep fake generated synthetic media presentation attack (Burrel, 2025). The attacks similar to Deepface can imitate facial expressions or voice patterns and make it highly realistic, which allows attackers to securely avoid authentication protocols that are meant to ensure that the authentic user and the attacker are two separate entities (Agarwal & Ratha, 2023).

The scholars believe this might be too weak to counter the processing of constantly evolving generative AI technologies. Biometric systems need to be augmented with liveness detection facilities to check if the biometric sample is a live person or from a synthetic or recorded source to increase the security level (Khan & Khan, 2025). These techniques involve recognizing eye blinks, micro expressions, pulse signals and facial depth and 3D images. Moreover, multimodal verification systems involving a combination of several biometric characteristics e.g. face, voice, and behavioral biometrics will considerably decrease the probability of successful identity spoofing. Protecting against identity theft is further ensured by continuous authentication methods where the behavior of the user is monitored with regard to time. Overall, it is crucial to strengthen the biometric authentication systems to mitigate the number of cases of identity thefts based on deepfakes, and loss of trust in the digital identity systems (Ayeswarya & Singh, 2024).

Trust in Digital Systems

Users, organisations, and government should have confidence in online platforms, automated systems, and online communications, and be able to make decisions that rely on these parts of a digital ecosystem, and engage with and through such platforms, systems and communications. Human-computer interaction and information systems research has discussed human trust creation across several factors that include reliability of the system, system transparency, usability, perceived security as well as the authenticity of the online content. Genuineness and trustworthiness have been essential in classic online space, and images, voice recognition, and registered online identities have been key. The ability to create synthetic images, videos and audio that have become increasingly realistic with the advent of deepfake technology, however, is one reason why these trust cues are being disrupted, allowing synthetic images and videos to be inserted into a convincing portrayal of real people and events. Consequently, users can become more suspicious of audio visual contents on how legitimate communications and evidence can be (Tiwari, 2025). Such loss of trust may result in a general mistrust of digital media, online platforms, and automated decision-making systems by the whole society. This mistrust is serious and has a negative impact on e-commerce, online governance, journalism, legal procedure and social relations, as it will be impossible to distinguish between truth and manipulation (Campbell, 2023). As a result, ensuring trust in the digital system is no longer about bases of technical security, including authentication, provenance tracking, and AI-based detection tools, but it is also believed in the transparency of the governance framework along with user education to strengthen confidence in digital technologies.

Legal and Ethical Implications

The legal and ethical implications of this deep fake technology have attracted a vast amount of attention from scholars, policy makers, and technology practitioners due to its staggering threats from synthetic media. The key regulatory issues that have been brought to the attention of legal scholars on relation to deepfakes are those pertaining to consent, defamation, misinformation, identity theft, and financial fraud. Deepfakes can facilitate non-consent synthetics, defamation, influence and impersonation-based crime, and the liability and jurisdiction and enforcement are complex issues that raise puzzling questions. The laws currently in force in most countries are focused on traditional media and cybercrime and their application may not be specific enough or provide problems with respect to hierarchies for AI-generated synthetic media (Tuysuz & Kılıç, 2023).

Another aspect of the ethical debate is the role of the developers, the platforms where they can be used, and the persons in charge of their policies in stopping the misuse of the deepfakes technology. (Kelley et al., 2025) recommend that generative AI developers should employ protective mechanisms as watermarking, or content-blocking and restrictions on its usage to curb malicious applications. Digital platforms are morally obliged to detect and remove harmful synthetic stuffs, users' privacy, and the discouragement of disinformation spreading. It is the role of policy makers to create fairer policies to protect individuals and the society while also promoting innovation and free expression. Legal and ethical regulatory frameworks play a crucial role together, ensuring that deepfake technologies are developed, deployed and controlled responsibly, minimizing the downsides of using the technology, and that society will not lose faith in digital ecosystems.

Detection and Forensic Techniques

The deepfakes detection research has tried many different approaches, some of which fall into the content-based or context-based categories. Content based approaches focus on intrinsic properties of the media such as visual objects, frequency domain issues, and biometric features such as blinking, head movements and subtle facial expressions, which are difficult to faithfully model with generative models. A number of research has been able to use deep learning models to automatically pick these anomalies and has shown promising results on benchmark data, however, performance usually tests when the model is presented high-quality or adversarial produced deepfakes. However, context-based approaches draw on analyses of extrinsic information, including file metadata, provenance, social media sharing patterns, and other data that might be considered as supportive elements and manipulated (Dubey et al., 2023). Studies have shown that the accuracy of detection can be improved in the case of content and context analyses, especially in practice, where deepfakes are popularized. With all these developments, the discipline is very antagonistic, as generative algorithms improve at a very high pace thus usually surpassing the available detection models. At present, literature also emphasizes hybrid and adaptive approaches, which integrate the multi-modal forensic information and strategies of on-going learning, and states that the key to the successful detection of a deepfake lies in the technical complexity and in having a thorough understanding of where and how the content has been created (Mubarak et al., 2023).

Biometric Security and Spoofing Attacks

Biometric security is one of the most delicate topic areas in research, where significant research work on this matter have given the indications of vulnerabilities to be looked into in the system using the techniques of facial recognition, voice recognition and fingerprint recognition. The initial investigations revolved around the susceptibility of authentication systems to the use of low-tech means such as printed photographic pictures, voice samples or spoof prints, which gave rise to liveness detection and anti-spoofing solutions. The introduction of deepfake technology has however, offered a more advanced category of spoofing attacks, which are now able to produce hyper-realistic facial, voice and even gait simulations which can defeat traditional biometric defenses (He et al., 2025). Literature has provided sufficient proof that such synthetic forgery is highly critical for any authentication system, particularly in a high security environment such as banking, mobile devices and access control. As a reaction, researchers have pointed out that their research has found that multimodal biometric systems are necessary, where multiple independent biometric characteristics are combined to ensure robustness, and continuous forms of authentication where variations in behavioral and physiological characteristics are observed over time as opposed to one verification attempt. Research also suggests that artificial intelligence detection models and context-aware analysis can be improved further, resulting in greater resistance to deep fakes in spoofing, and therefore, an integrated and dynamic approach to biometric security in the ever-evolving threat landscape is needed (Golea, 2025).

Social Engineering and Psychological Manipulation

A major problem with deepfakes is that they have introduced the risk of social engineering due to the cognitive bias and trust people have in the audio-visual media. Some other studies and research work in the field of psychology and cybersecurity have consistently resulted in higher number of people being more easily manipulated by the stimuli that present a realistic appearance and context and are presented by objects they are familiar with or objects that have authority over them (Dsouza et al., 2024). The Deepfake technology can be used to create extremely convincing videos or audio recordings of a known person, creating a scenario where the person will most likely be coerced into either fulfilling a scam or even revealing privileged information or harmful actions that result in their own damage. Studies have shown that even if it is the knowledgeable are easily deceived when what they see and hear agrees with their own perception of a situation that shows that the apparatus of conventional awareness defence has its limits (Blake, n.d.). What these types of manipulations exploit is the psychological shortcuts of power, exposure and connection to emotions and emotions, which means that social engineering using deep fakes is very powerful as compared to the standard phishing or impersonation attack. As a result, recent studies propose combined mitigation measures, such as real-time media checking tools, user behaviour analysis tools, and training of users that take into consideration the subtle details of how synthetic media may skew perception and decision-making (Siddiqi et al., 2022). Overall, the study has emphasized the need for a combination of technical and psychological solutions to combat the socially engineered behaviour of deepfakes with psychological weaknesses of humans.

Organizational and Economic Impacts

The deepfake technology can have a great impact on the organization and its economy, and researchers estimate that, depending on the capabilities of deep faking fraud, individuals, companies and monetary institutions could lose a significant amount of money. Studies note that complex impersonation attacks, business email compromise scams, and synthetic identity frauds are able to circumvent old security measures, causing a direct financial loss as well as reputation loss (Efthymiou & Egleton, 2025). The threat is not confined to short-term financial effects, it actually adds to the long-term economic impact by reducing investors' trust, brand reputation and trust of the stakeholders. To address some of these challenges, extensive organizational solutions are recommended, including employee training programs to raise awareness of the risks of deepfakes, establishing protocols for incidents depending on the type of synthetic media attack and actively managing risks through means of sensitive communication monitoring, authentication, etc. There are also signs of the need to have cross-functional teams (IT, legal, and compliance) to ensure that incidents involving deepfakes are identified and dealt with swiftly. Overall, the study reminds us that the reduction of the organizational and economic effects of deepfakes cannot be solely achieved through technological approaches but rather by a well-designed policy, preparedness among employees and adaptability to new threat environments, a reflection of the complexity of the proposed problem (Johri et al., 2025).

Societal and Democratic Risks

Deepfakes are a massive social and democratic problem, not just for an organization or money, but because they can be used to deceive a particular population, distort media and taint democracy. We have found that this omnipresence of synthetic media can lead to mistrust in news and political communication, and the rejection of the truth as fake information, the so called liar-dividend. In political science and media psychology research, the authors have highlighted that Deepfakes can be utilized in misinformation campaigns, propaganda and character assassination to influence public opinion, electoral processes, and even policy discussions (Misirlis & Munawar, 2023). It is also important to note that user perception of hyper-realistic fabricated material is further reinforced by cognitive biases like confirmation bias, and enhanced trust of audio-visual data makes the populations highly vulnerable to manipulation (Chaturvedi et al., 2025). The literature suggests that a multi-pronged mitigation is needed, including advanced detection systems, media literacy training sessions, regulations, and cooperation between governments, technology platforms and civil society organisations, as each will play a role in the mitigation effort. Overall, it is claimed by literature that deepfakes can be a social issue, as they may undermine accountability, divide and polarize society and threaten democratic processes, and that technological advances are needed along with a robust socio-political resilience at the system level (Pawelec, 2022).

METHODOLOGY

The chapter takes a multidisciplinary approach to research with both qualitative and quantitative methods, in order to provide a detailed study of the effect of deepfake technology on fraud and identity theft. Deepfake powered cybercrime is dynamic and complex and requires a combination of methods to tackle the technical, organizational, legal and human aspects of digital fraud. This methodology is useful to collect the prior knowledge, interpret empirical data and elaborate conceptual frameworks in future studies.

The research starts with a Systematic Literature Review (SLR) that is organized around topics like cybersecurity, artificial intelligence, legal and information systems studies, as well as human-computer interaction. The review comprises peer reviewed journal articles, sector papers, conference papers, and policy documents, to analyse trends, gaps in the research and key themes in deepfake technology, cyber fraud and identity theft. The literature review process validates content and allows for repeatability by applying keywords, inclusion/exclusion criteria, and coding and organizing themes. It assists in identifying technical issues, threats, detection methods and regulations concerning the misuse of synthetic media.

Then, qualitative case studies are done on actual cases of deepfake and identity theft fraud. The examination of reports on impersonation attacks, financial fraud, social engineering attacks, and biometric authentication attacks provides insight into the strategies used by attackers, vulnerabilities of organisations, and the effects of such attacks. The case studies offer context on the use of deepfakes in cybercrime and its response. They also provide input on identifying best practice and lessons learnt, which is essential for effective mitigation strategies.

To analyze deepfake-facilitated fraud, the chapter proposes a three-level conceptual model (Dehghani & Saberi, 2025):

- **Content generation level**: Emphasis on technical approach to generating content using synthetic media (GANs, diffusion models, voice cloning system). This level examines tools, datasets and algorithms employed to produce realistic material.
- **Attack deployment level:** Discusses the role of deepfake content in social engineering, biometric spoofing and financial crimes. This level integrates technical and behavioral perspectives, to gain insight into how attackers take advantage of human trust and organizational procedures.
- **Impact assessment level:** Assesses damage to finances, reputation, legal implications and psychological effects on victims. This model, which was structured, enables research to analyze the lifecycle of deepfake-enabled fraud and provides insights into possible prevention and detection points.

Along with the qualitative analysis, the chapter suggests quantitative as well as experimental studies. The vulnerability of user(s) and online resources to the use of deepfakes can be measured through controlled experiments, simulations and surveys. The methods can also be used to test the efficacy of biometric authentication systems with synthetic media, the trust they are placed in, and the decision making process they make when presented with synthetic AV content. These quantitative methods allow to measure the risk factors and create efficient security policies and technologies.

The methodology also focuses on interdisciplinary integration such as the legal analysis and the study of the existing regulations and gaps in the laws that cover deepfake misuse, identity theft and online fraud. Ethical aspects, including AI governance, privacy protection, and responsible innovation, are integrated. Human-computer interaction viewpoints are useful to understand the users' perception of authenticity, trust in digital media, and reactions to misleading content. To get the holistic picture of the deepfake-powered cybercrime, this approach brings together the technical, legal and social aspects.

Finally, the chapter proposes a research agenda for the future, such as longitudinal studies, cross-cultural studies, and studies in collaboration between academia, industry, and policy makers. The methodology offers a structured approach to the technical processes, human factors, and broader effects of deepfake technology, safeguarding researchers and practitioners to create trustworthy and secure digital environments.

EXPLOITATION OF DEEPFAKE TECHNOLOGY IN FINANCIAL AND IDENTITY CRIMES

Financial Fraud and Corporate Impersonation

The Deepfake voice iPAS has become a vital tool for the ability to fraud in finance and corporate impersonation, which makes it possible to create a top-level executive's voice with high fidelity and to make the delivery of fraudulent instructions by employees possible (Sholademi, n.d.). In these types of attacks, the cybercriminal pretends to be the voice of a CEO or CFO and gains permission to make emergency fund transfers, approve payments or request financial details or information that is confidential. All of which are based on the authority and trust that comes with the job. Being trained to follow the orders of the leaders without in-depth verification, employees can be most effective in such attacks. These incidences demonstrate severe weaknesses of conventional verification procedures which are based on voice recognitions, informal affirmation procedures or organizational trust frameworks. Synthetic voice generators are increasingly becoming more widely available, and more convincing to the point that it will be difficult to tell whether you are talking to a real person or fake person. Organizations should respond to such threats by enhancing internal controls by using multi-factor authentication, two-approval financial practices, call back verification rules, and offering extensive staff training on deepfake awareness and social engineering threats.

Biometric Authentication Bypass

A major challenge with deep fake videos and the creation of AI voices is their ability to evade biometric authentication mechanisms and circumvent facial recognition and voice authentication systems. Biometric identifiers can be abused by providing extremely realistic and convincing synthetic facial movement or synthesized speech to fool automated authentication systems that are based on the use of biometrics as proof of identity. The key vulnerability is a significant risk to critical platform operations such as those in the banking industry, government services, and any platform that relies on biometric authentication for remote access or for sensitive transactions. As deepfake technologies continue to advance, traditional biometric security measures are becoming increasingly ineffective. To protect against the spoofing attack with synthetic media (SMM), it is crucial to deploy liveness detection, multimodal authentication and continuous identity verification systems.

Social Engineering and Phishing

Deepfakes contribute to social engineering and phishing crimes a lot because they provide the audio-visual content of high levels of realism, which enhances the believability and persuasiveness of deceived messages. Unlike with text-based phishing, however, in the case of deepfakes, the victim's voice and face can be fabricated to make it easier for them to reply to a phishing request from a known and trusted individual, such as a manager or colleague, or even a family member (Schulte, 2025). Deepfakes can be generated on a person-by-person basis against specific individuals or organisations and employ tactics of the psyche (such as urgency, authority, emotional resonance etc) to enable access to sensitive information or incite actions without justification. The technical realism and the psychological manipulation make the phishing attack by means of a deepfake even more difficult to detect and hence the need for modern security awareness training, verification systems, and AI-based detection systems to combat the growing threat of social engineering using synthetic media (Gregory, 2022).

Disinformation and Reputation Attacks

Reputation based deepfake attacks and disinformation are slowly becoming one of the more prominent attack categories and, in most instances, can be a secondary problem to financial fraud, but in some instances it can result in identity theft and create severe social harm at a large scale. Attackers can discredit people by producing fake videos or audio recordings showing that people are involved in immoral, illegal or controversial behavior. This false information can lead to professional and personal damage, loss of employment position, court cases and social rejection (Günay & Alkan, 2026). In addition, if the reputation of a person is compromised, the attackers may benefit from the resulting confusion and mistrust, perpetrating identity theft, impersonation or fraud. Financial, emotional, psychological and social consequences cause extreme anxiety, depression and lower social status to the victims due to their experiences. These all highlight the need for good digital forensics, legal oversight, and social awareness of the dangers of fake news and the reputation adverse effects it can have on people and organizations to eradicate deepfakes as a source for disinformation.

CASE STUDY: DEEPFAKE-ENABLED CORPORATE FRAUD

An example of deepfakes being employed in the field of corporate fraud was a large-scale company in which cybercriminals used synthetic voice technology as the voice of the Chief Executive Officer (CEO) of the company. In this instance, the perpetrator made a very convincing faux copy of the chief executive's voice and one of the high-ranking staffers was hastily contacted, and ordered to wire a substantial sum into a designated account. In the elements of hierarchical authority and urgency that are intrinsic to the executive messages, the employee did what the message suggests; he/she followed the request as it seemed to be a command from the top management. It was later found out that the fraudulent transaction had took place, which cost the organization a lot of money. In this scenario, deepfake social engineering is demonstrated to effortlessly breach and penetrate the traditional mechanisms of trust-based verification, and to expose basic flaws in in-house financial procedures and communication methods.

It revealed some of the flaws in the organization, including the reliance on voice authentication and the lack of other secondary means of verification, and employees' lack of knowledge of the dangers of a synthetic media. It demonstrated that the traditional companies with its advanced cyber security solutions can be attacked by humans using the attack vectors which are based on human factor and backed by the technologies of artificial intelligence.

The other up-and-coming is identity theft on online banking and online services sites where a fake video and altered facial information is used to compromise remote identity verification checks. When it comes to registering a customer and gaining access to their financial accounts with the aid of video footage, hackers have been able to create a realistic video to trick facial recognition systems into granting them access and to obtain personal data. Such cases highlight the increasing vulnerabilities of biometric authentication systems which are not equipped with sufficient liveness detection and multimodal authentication methods.

The case studies show how essential it is to have more robust authentication systems, multi-factor authentication processes, and employee training programs. Companies should have call-back measures in place, a double-approval system to financial interactions, deepfake detection tools powered by AI, to reduce the risks of deepfake-facilitated fraud and identity theft.

SOCIAL IMPACTS AND TRUST DEGRADATION

The deepfake technology has far-reaching social consequences since it essentially questions the authenticity and trustworthiness of digital communication. In contemporary electronic cultures, an audio-visual production can provide authentic evidence, on which a reliance can be based for interpersonal communication, journalism, law and even governance. Nonetheless, the cornerstone of this trust is broken by deepfakes which have allowed one to create highly realistic synthetic media that can convincingly simulate real people and events. The more synthetic content gets, the closer it gets to the original recording, the harder it could be for people and organizations to distinguish between truth and fake the more the unbelievable number of people will become skeptical and doubtful about the online world.

One of the greatest impacts of deepfakes is the loss of trust in information ecosystems and media. News media and journalism are extremely reliant on audio-visual records to ensure that events are true and people and institutions are held responsible. Deepfakes could be used to spread fake news and disinformation in unprecedented ways and viewers will have trouble determining whether events described are true or not. It is the so called "liar dividend" where those who receive a tag for misconduct can claim to lack real evidence as a fake one, thus making the accountability systems weaker and weakening the discourse of the society as a whole.

Deepfakes have been problematic with regard to admissibility and credibility of online evidence in legal cases. Digital recordings, surveillance cameras and audio-visual evidence are increasingly being relied on as a foundation for criminal and civil cases in court. The evidence of realistic artificial media is difficult to prove, and can lead to misconvinctions, falses exoneration, or the legal finding of a case. The justice systems should thus respond by coming up with forensic tools, authentication standards as well as legal frameworks that guarantees integrity of digital evidence in the era of synthetic media.

Deepfake technology is also having an impact on communication and trust between people online. Personal and business communication is now done via digital messaging, video conferencing and social media. Deepfakes viewer can be spoofed, fake conversation can be used to manipulate a dialogue and fake information can be spread, thus creating mistrust in the users. Once people know they can be affected in a synthetic way, they'll be skeptical of legitimate communications, which will hinder them from working together, but also in their social and online interactions.

But there are deepfake implications for the way democracies work and for political stability as well. The impact of synthetic media can be used to alter perceptions of candidates, campaign messages, or media content including images and sounds. These disinformation campaigns can undermine citizens' confidence in political systems, dissension and polarization within societies and the legitimacy of democratic institutions. These effects are magnified by the massive proliferation of deepfake content on social networks that makes it hard to have a timely response from authorities and fact checkers.

Deepfake Attacks have the potential to inflict significant damage on companies, leading to repercussions of reputational harm, financial losses, and legal liability. Deepfakes can be used to make fraudulent payments, breach access to sensitive information, and gain control of corporate communications through impersonation. In case these incidences get publicity, organizations can find themselves damaged over the long run in their reputation, as well as the collapse in customer confidence and auditory examinations. Furthermore, if they fail to implement adequate security measures to prevent issues arising from deep fakes, organizations can be held legally liable for the misuses, or at least reduce their vulnerability, especially their financial systems, healthcare services and government operations.

A person's psychological, social and economic problems can be severe in the wake of deepfake victimization. Deepfake attacks that are based on reputation risks may result in social stigmatization, harassment, and work-related losses. It can trigger feelings of distress and anxiety for the people who are spreading it, and for victims who want to lie about their actions or personalities.It can cause distress and anxiety to the person spreading it and loss of self-esteem to the victim who wants to misrepresent their actions or personality. The financial losses may be incurred when engaging in identity theft, fraud or extortion using a deepfake. Psychological and financial evil is highlighted in this blend, highlighting the very personal and social impact of the misuse of synthetic media.

Together with the rapid growth of deepfake software, another issue is the lack of trust in the digital platform and social institutions. Use of too many synthetics in media will cause people to distrust all online media content; people will tend to distrust information they get from online media in general. This loss of trust has been able to have ripple effects on digital economies, governance and social cohesion. As a result of that, users may lose their eagerness to utilize online services, share information and become members of online groups, thereby delaying the technological progress and digital transformation.

To counter these problems, pressures are mounting on the implementations of regulatory interventions, technology protection and ethical governance sets. Policies to criminalize malicious deepfakes creation and sharing are under discussion by governments and international organizations, technology companies are making systems to detect them, and create media verification mechanisms. There is also the need to empower the people by providing them with public awareness and digital literacy programmes enabling them to recognize and take corrective action against the threats to the synthetic media.

In general, deepfakes are a disruptive, but transformative technology that has significant social implications. The loss of trust in the digital communication has become a threat to information ecosystems, law, democratic institutions and social relations. These challenges can be addressed through a multi-disciplinary approach that includes technology, legal, ethical regulation, and social education to ensure trust, security and integrity in the digital era.

FUTURE WORK AND RESEARCH DIRECTIONS

The ongoing development of deep fake technologies may be linked to an urgent need for ongoing research, innovation and policy development to mitigate future risks and loss of deep face benefits of generative AI. The future of the work should be interdisciplinary and future-oriented, covering technical, legal, ethical and social aspects of creating robust digital ecosystems, which are capable of countering synthetic media attacks.

A key point of research interest is the design of robust deepfake detectors that are multimodal (visual, auditory and behavioral). The classical methods of detection tend to target single-sample characteristics, e.g. pixel artifacts, spectral anomalies or temporal anomalies. However, as generative models get more sophisticated, they become more difficult to identify these artefacts. The new detection systems would have to be more robust and precise and, of course, multi-modal—with the addition of context-related behavioral and facial micro-expression and eye movement patterns, as well as prosodic speech. The detection results can be enhanced by ensemble learning models and multimodal fusion techniques, which can achieve the complementary signals and reduce the false negative (FN) and false positive (FP).

The deepfake detection systems should also incorporate explainable artificial intelligence (XAI) to improve the transparency, interpretability, and user trust. Most of the existing detection models are black-box systems, thus constraining their usage in areas that require it the most like law enforcement, the judiciary and in the finance field. Explainable AI techniques can also provide explanations on the decisions detected that are understandable and amenable to human interpretation, so that the stakeholders can have an idea of the accuracy of the system outputs. Future research might explore ways to represent model choice, and the important properties that could be used to characterize and quantify prediction uncertainty. This transparency is required in order to meet the requirements of regulations, forensics, and end user trust in automated detection systems.

Media provenance and content authentication systems that leverage blockchain can be another potential research direction. Content generation, modification and dissemination can be traced and documented with blockchain and distributed ledger technologies to ensure the immutability of content so that traceability and authenticity of digital media can be verified. Plataforms can provide proof of provenance and integrity in the following ways: digitally signing and adding content's provenance metadata to the content when it is created. In the future, scalable and privacy-conscious blockchain architectures, interoperability standards, and interactions between blockchain and existing media platforms should be explored. Also, the research must assess the usability and adoption issues of provenance systems in the real-life practice, such as journalism, social media and electronic forensics.

Additionally, policy and regulatory measures are key to preventing deep fake related fraud and identity theft. The existing legal frameworks are usually not clear on the definition, enforcement, as well as jurisdictional aspects of the misuse of synthetic media. Future law and policy research should include defining legal categories of malicious deepfakes creation and sharing, defining the frames of liability and creating measures to enforce them. Adverse deepfake practices like fraud, impersonation, and self-generation of such content without a person's consent should be criminalized with the implementation of due process protection and proportionate punishment. The observation of comparative legal studies in a cross- jurisdiction could shed light on the perfect activities and consolidated regulatory strategies.

Since cybercrime is transnational, cross-border collaboration is needed in overcoming threats through deepfakes. It should explore the cross border legal frameworks, mutual assistance treaties and cooperation of cybercrime task forces for helping in the investigation, prosecution and information sharing. Future research is recommended to assess the effectiveness of international governance model for cyber security, public-private relations and multinational regulatory bodies in fighting the synthetic media threats. Also, AI governance models should be created globally that will balance the factors of innovation, security, and human rights.

One more research and policy area are the activities for public awareness and digital literacy. As deepfakes become more common, individuals should be provided with information and expertise to help them discern their authenticity and respond. The educational interventions, awareness campaigns, and training programs that should be considered in the future are directed towards different populations like students, professionals and vulnerable populations. The science behind behaviour can be applied to understand people's perception and reaction towards deepfake material, understand the cognitive bias that a malicious party may use, and develop communication strategies that could be useful to increase people's awareness of risks. Engaging it into the curriculum, enterprises training and information sources for the population can make people less susceptible to deception.

Privacy-preserving authentication and identity verification measures should also be technologically innovated to fight against the spoofing attacks of a deepfake nature. The traditional biometric systems that rely on a set of facial and/or voice features are becoming vulnerable to artificial manipulation. The research work which should be done in the future should be related to the continuous authentication mechanism and should involve the analysis of dynamic behavioral biometrics such as typing, gait, interaction behavior and usage pattern of devices. As mentioned, federated learning and other methods of privacy-preserving strong authentication may be possible, such as secure multiparty computation and differential privacy. This is because as these measures are put in place, they will be able to enhance security without a breach of the data protection policies and ethical guidelines.

The other potential avenue in ensuring deepfake-enabled cybercrime is curbed is AI-driven systems to detect fraud. To detect fraud in real time, machine learning models are able to examine transaction patterns, communication patterns, as well as network aberrations. The deepfake detection results along with the rest of the fraud detection system can provide a comprehensive threat intelligence and automatic response. Adaptive learning models, adversarial robustness and real-time deployment systems of large-scale financial and governmental systems are future research areas to explore. Also, the solution of human-in-the-loop is possible to enhance decision-making through the automated detection that is accompanied by the expert control.

The development of the research and effective countermeasures will be a vital part of the work that will be accomplished through cooperation between academia, industry and government. The academic institutions' role will be the background research, the theoretical background and experimental validations, while the industrial partners' role will be the commercial data in real life situations, the implementation platforms and the technological background. The government agencies can help with the formulation of policies, enforcement of policies and funding of activities. Future research can explore collaborative research models, datasets, common benchmarks, standardization to move towards innovation and interoperable detection and authentication technologies.

Besides, it should be interdisciplinary research to respond to the socio-technological content of deep fake threats. Collaboration among computer scientists, cyber experts, lawyers, psychologists, sociologists and ethicists can provide a comprehensive knowledge of human behavior, legal implications, social ramifications and technical vulnerabilities. Future longitudinal and cross-cultural research can also focus on the dynamics of the overall perception of deepfakes over time and in various social situations and inform the global policy and technological responses.

Development in future research and development should be in a holistic and proactive manner to deal with the multifaceted challenges of deepfake technology. The stakeholders can come up with digital ecosystems that are resilient by creating multimodal detection techniques, AI systems with explanations, provenance systems, regulatory policies, public education programmes, and privacy-preserving authentication and AI systems to detect fraud. To ensure a future where trust, security, and integrity are maintained in the age of synthetic media, it is crucial that academics, industry, and government work together and interdependently.

CONCLUSION

This rapid development of the deep fake technology has created a multifaceted threat landscape which is both technical, organizational, sociocultural, and democratic. In both detection and forensics, research has progressed significantly, incorporating both content analysis of visual and physiological evidence and analysis of context of metadata dissemination; it continues to be challenged on an ongoing basis by the constantly changing generation models. Previously assumed to be a firm security, biometric security systems are now more susceptible to highly complex spoofing attacks made possible through deep fakes, thus leading to a move towards multimodal authentication and ongoing verification approaches. Furthermore, deepfakes add to the dangers of social engineering due to human biases and tendency to accept information in audio-visual form, and makes individuals vulnerable to impact and fraudulent control. Likewise, at the economic level deep fake fraud jeopardizes both organizations and people, and calls for systemized incident response frameworks, personnel awareness plans and thorough risk handling methods. Societal and democratic effects of synthetic media are tremendous: By effecting popular trust, synthetic media can put at risk journalistic integrity, polarise the community, and result in the so-called liar's dividend – information is called into question, responsibility is challenged and the social integrity is undermined. The overall findings suggest that deepfakes are a complex socio-technical phenomenon, which demands a multi-disciplinary approach to solve it. Effectiveness is the key to mitigation, and this includes implementation of technology linked to detection, policy and regulatory action, organizational readiness, and social education. New research that can be adapted, multi-modal and context-dependent should be conducted in the future, with a view of increasing the technical sophistication of deepfakes and the human and institutional vulnerabilities that they pose.

REFERENCES

Abul-Fazl, S. D., Dina, R., & Fairuza, H. (2025). *Diffusion Models at Scale: Techniques*. Applications, and Challenges.

Agarwal, A., & Ratha, N. (2023). Manipulating faces for identity theft via morphing and deepfake: Digital privacy. In *Handbook of statistics* (Vol. 48, pp. 223–241). Elsevier.

Ahmad, J., Salman, W., Amin, M., Ali, Z., & Shokat, S. (2024). A Survey on Enhanced Approaches for Cyber Security Challenges Based on Deep Fake Technology in Computing Networks. *Spectrum of engineering sciences, 2*(4), 133-149.

Ayeswarya, S., & Singh, K. J. (2024). A comprehensive review on secure biometric-based continuous authentication and user profiling. *IEEE Access : Practical Innovations, Open Solutions, 12*, 82996–83021. DOI: 10.1109/ACCESS.2024.3411783

Blake, H. (n.d.). AI-Powered Social Engineering: Understanding the Role of Deepfake Technology in Exploiting Human Trust.

Burrel, D. N. (2025). The Cyberpsychology and Criminal Psychology of Cyber Identity Theft and Criminal Reach in the Digital Era. *RAIS Journal for Social Sciences, 9*(2), 343–360.

Campbell, L. (2023). AI, Deepfakes, and Digital Trust Why Ethics Matter More Than Ever.

Chaturvedi, A., Raghani, K. N., Kumar, S., Choudhary, M., & Yakub, A. A. M. (2025). Deepfakes in Society: Risks and Realities.

Dehghani, A., & Saberi, H. (2025). Generating and detecting various types of fake image and audio content: A review of modern deep learning technologies and tools. *arXiv preprint arXiv:2501.06227*.

Dileep, M. R., Kansara, Y., & Suneel, J. S. (2025, August). Deepfake Technology and Online Cyber Crime: A Critical Analysis of AI Tools in Unethical Practices. In *2025 Control Instrumentation System Conference (CISCON)* (pp. 1-5). IEEE.

Dsouza, D. S., Hajjar, A. E., & Jahankhani, H. (2024). Deepfakes in social engineering attacks. In *Space Law Principles and Sustainable Measures* (pp. 153–183). Springer Nature Switzerland. DOI: 10.1007/978-3-031-64045-2_8

Dubey, H., Bhatt, S., & Negi, L. (2023). Digital Forensics Techniques and Trends: A Review. [IAJIT]. *The International Arab Journal of Information Technology, 20*(4).

Efthymiou, I. P., & Egleton, T. E. (2025). The Impact of Deep Fakes in Markets and Economies. In *Deepfakes and Their Impact on Business* (pp. 19–50). IGI Global Scientific Publishing.

Farid, H. (2022). Creating, using, misusing, and detecting deep fakes. *Journal of Online Trust & Safety, 1*(4). Advance online publication. DOI: 10.54501/jots.v1i4.56

Golea, D. G. (2025). CHALLENGES TO SECURITY POLICIES IN A DIGITAL ENVIRONMENT. GOLEA DANIELA GEORGIANA.

Gregory, S. (2022). Deepfakes, misinformation and disinformation and authenticity infrastructure responses: Impacts on frontline witnessing, distant witnessing, and civic journalism. *Journalism, 23*(3), 708–729. DOI: 10.1177/14648849211060644

GÜNAY, Z. H., & ALKAN, M. (2026). Exploring a deepfake attack: A multi-dimensional approach. *International Cybersecurity Law Review*, , 1–21.

He, S., Lei, Y., Zhang, Z., Sun, Y., Li, S., Zhang, C., & Ye, J. (2025). Identity Deepfake Threats to Biometric Authentication Systems: Public and Expert Perspectives. *arXiv preprint arXiv:2506.06825.*

Johri, A. Reepu, Taneja, S., & Shamsuddin, Z. (2025). A Study in Understanding the Measures Taken by Organizations Organization to Overcome the Effect of Deepfake on Corporate Image. In *Navigating the Deepfake Conundrum: A Manager's Roadmap* (pp. 127-134). Cham: Springer Nature Switzerland.

Kelley, P. G., Rousso-Schindler, S., Shelby, R., Thomas, K., & Woodruff, A. (2025). How Generative AI Empowers Attackers and Defenders Across the Trust & Safety Landscape. *arXiv preprint arXiv:2601.06033.*

Khan, F. A., & Khan, M. K. (2025). Generative AI and Deepfake Detection in Biometric Systems. *Cognitive Computation, 17*(3), 112. DOI: 10.1007/s12559-025-10469-3

Liu, B., Liu, B., Zhu, T., & Ding, M. (2025). A Review of Deepfake and Its Detection: From Generative Adversarial Networks to Diffusion Models. *International Journal of Intelligent Systems, 2025*(1), 9987535. DOI: 10.1155/int/9987535

Mandal, S. (2025). Deep Fake Technology and Identity Theft: An Emerging Challenge for Cyber Laws in India. Available at *SSRN* 5161545. DOI: 10.2139/ssrn.5161545

Millière, R. (2022). Deep learning and synthetic media. *Synthese, 200*(3), 231. DOI: 10.1007/s11229-022-03739-2

Misirlis, N., & Munawar, H. B. (2023). From deepfake to deep useful: risks and opportunities through a systematic literature review. *arXiv preprint arXiv:2311.15809.*

Mubarak, R., Alsboui, T., Alshaikh, O., Inuwa-Dutse, I., Khan, S., & Parkinson, S. (2023). A survey on the detection and impacts of deepfakes in visual, audio, and textual formats. *IEEE Access : Practical Innovations, Open Solutions, 11*, 144497–144529. DOI: 10.1109/ACCESS.2023.3344653

Ooi, K. B., Tan, G. W. H., Al-Emran, M., Al-Sharafi, M. A., Capatina, A., Chakraborty, A., Dwivedi, Y. K., Huang, T.-L., Kar, A. K., Lee, V.-H., Loh, X.-M., Micu, A., Mikalef, P., Mogaji, E., Pandey, N., Raman, R., Rana, N. P., Sarker, P., Sharma, A., & Wong, L. W. (2025). The potential of generative artificial intelligence across disciplines: Perspectives and future directions. *Journal of Computer Information Systems, 65*(1), 76–107. DOI: 10.1080/08874417.2023.2261010

Pawelec, M. (2022). Deepfakes and democracy (theory): How synthetic audio-visual media for disinformation and hate speech threaten core democratic functions. *Digital Society : Ethics, Socio-Legal and Governance of Digital Technology, 1*(2), 19. DOI: 10.1007/s44206-022-00010-6 PMID: 36097613

Schulte, E. (2025). The social consensus on truth in news-related deepfakes: Implications of public perception and media integrity (Master's thesis, Iowa State University).

Shirish, A., & Komal, S. (2023). A socio-legal inquiry on deepfakes. *Cal. W. Int'l LJ, 54*, 517.

Sholademi, D. B. (n.d.). Leveraging AI for Detecting Deep Fakes and Combating Financial Fraudulent Identity Schemes.

Sholademi, D. B. (n.d.). Leveraging AI for Detecting Deep Fakes and Combating Financial Fraudulent Identity Schemes.

Siddiqi, M. A., Pak, W., & Siddiqi, M. A. (2022). A study on the psychology of social engineering-based cyberattacks and existing countermeasures. *Applied Sciences (Basel, Switzerland), 12*(12), 6042. DOI: 10.3390/app12126042

Sinaga, H. (2023). Legal and Ethical Implications in Data Theft Cases in the Digital Era. *East Asian Journal of Multidisciplinary Research, 2*(11), 4585–4604. DOI: 10.55927/eajmr.v2i11.6791

Tiwari, S. (2025). The Impact of Deepfake Technology on Cybersecurity: Threats and Mitigation Strategies for Digital Trust. Available at *SSRN* 5259359. DOI: 10.2139/ssrn.5259359

Tuysuz, M. K., & Kılıç, A. (2023). Analyzing the legal and ethical considerations of deepfake technology. *Interdisciplinary Studies in Society, Law, and Politics, 2*(2), 4–10. DOI: 10.61838/kman.isslp.2.2.2

Vaseashta, A. (2025). Dual-Use Artificial Intelligence—Trends, Security Challenges, and Mitigation Strategies. In *Spectrum of Dual-Use Technologies: Unforeseen Risks Versus Returns* (pp. 3–37). Springer Nature Switzerland.

Volkova, S. (2024). Deepfakes: Fraud and Cybercrime. *Deepfakes and Their Impact on Business*, 221.

Chapter 5
Fingerprint Cryptography and the Culture of Digital Trust in Secure Communication

Sangeetha Ganesan
http://orcid.org/0000-0001-7347-2162
R.M.K. College of Engineering and Technology, India

G. Shanmugaraj
http://orcid.org/0000-0002-0601-4046
Velammal Institute of Technology, India

K. Mohanambal
Velammal Engineering College, India

ABSTRACT

The conventional methods for protecting digital data use either authentication or cryptography. The fundamental issue with these approaches is still securely storing or memorizing the user's credentials. The security of biometric data is ensured by neither storing it nor sharing it, and session keys are used to maintain perfect forward secrecy. The long-term security of messages exchanged between users is also guaranteed by this effort. This framework is privacy-preserving and might be used to actual access control systems, according to experimental evaluation over four datasets from FVC2002 and the NIST special database. A further examination of the method, which involves testing it out on several standard fingerprint photos, reveals startlingly that 99.83% of the time it is true positive and 0% for false negative. The

DOI: 10.4018/979-8-3373-8292-0.ch005

Metaverse strains sturdy safety to defend users from avatar spoofing, individuality theft, and illegal access. Integrating crypto-biometric key generation safeguards privacy-preserving verification and safe communication crossways virtual milieus.

1. INTRODUCTION

The different security concerns involved in safeguarding a user's document are extremely important to pay proper attention to in a time when Digital Document Management (DDM) acquires utmost importance. The safety of the digital document can be ensured by a number of ways. Among these are the venerable, classic Windows login process, security certificate-based article guard schemes, file level safety, Encrypting File Systems (EFS), disk encoding, and steganographic-based article protection schemes, among others. The username and password are used in Windows' login system to safeguard a user's document (also known as user authentication). To access their papers using this approach, users must enter their username and password. The user of this system must select a security credential (such as a password) to keep a document private. In other words, a security key is necessary to safeguard the document while it is being saved. It develops a system for document protection based on security certificates. The user must next install it on his computer. For any specific document, this certificate essentially offers a secrete key and document defense techniques. In EFS, a employer must fix an EFS certificate on his computer before using it to encrypt or decrypt documents with cryptographic keys that user has supplied. The steganography-based approach introduced by Choi et al. (2011) relies on a stego key to protect user information by hiding it within documents. Understanding the correct stegokey is a need in order to access the secret data. In addition to the studies discussed above, several biometric-based cryptosystems have been reported in the literature (Gottschlich & Huckemann, 2014; Li et al., 2012). All of these works have significant flaws that mostly relate to how cryptographic keys or biometric templates are stored. The aforementioned provides us with strong motivation to suggest a new digital document protection system that addresses the serious flaws that are now present. Information is secured using cryptographic methods both during transmission and storage. These strategies are based on cryptographic mechanisms. These kays need to be kept a secret. An exception that is shared publicly in an asymmetric key system is the public key. But keeping these keys secure is a problem. Biometric information about a user is employed in the field of study known as "bio-cryptosystem" to protect these cryptographic keys. Three different bio-cryptosystem approaches are possible: Key generation, key binding, and key release are three examples. This study explores a privacy-preserving biometric framework that enhances digital trust and identity protection in secure communications. By eliminating the need to store biometric templates and generating unique session-based cryptographic keys, the approach aligns with the growing societal demand for ethical and secure data practices.

2. RELATED WORKS

In the most recent literature, a amount of research projects have been documented. In the Crypto Biometric System (CBS), a user's biometric characteristics were recorded and saved as a pattern for a operator in the folder. Many different secure procedures are used to protect the biometric data that is saved. The production of cancelable biometric templates is common today (Haghighat et al., 2015) in order to safeguard the stored biometric template. Additionally, the database discreetly stores a user's private key. The user's data is secured (encrypted or decrypted) using this private key. Another strategy involved the system enrolling a user's biometric information. The recorded biometric information is used to generate the user's private key. The user validation and key release processes are carried out using the biometric data that has been stored (Li et al., 2012; Jain et al., 2005). In addition to the aforementioned, biometrics, a trustworthy authenticator, can be combined with conventional cryptography to strengthen the system (Stinson, 1997). By creating a tight connection between a key and a user's physiological attributes, biometrics are utilized in this type of CBS to manage cryptographic keys (Kanade et al., 2010), Beng et al., 2008). Either a user-defined method or any common hash function (one way) could be used to obtain a cryptographic key using biometric data (Al-Saggaf et al., 2012). A random cryptographic key created by a PRNG, for example (Upmanyu et al., 2010) can be protected using biometric technology. Another method uses biometric-based key publication to secure a cryptanalytic key that is created at random. In this system, a biometric data inaccuracy can lead to a cryptographic key error. Error correction coding (ECC) method(s) are used to tackle this error. It is common practice to syndicate biometric information with cryptography using a fuzzy commitment approach that corrects for errors in the cryptographic key (Kanade et al., 2010) sing (Stoianov, 2010) and Hadamard error correction coding (Jin et al., 2010). In addition to these, combinations of Reed-Solomon and Hadamard error alteration cipher (Kivinen, 2003; Alvarez & Li, 2006) and Reed-Solomon and BCH error alteration (Panchal & Samanta, 2018) are also frequently used to increase the accuracy in CBS. Additionally, programmers are employing various error-coding systems, such as Reed-Muller codes to deal with iris code errors. Currently, a key binding approach locks the encoded key with a binary string obtained from the operator's biometric information and encrypts a arbitrarily produced key with ECC.

Objectives

The purpose of this effort is to propose a fingerprint-based key generation system with the following goals:

- The first step in symmetric cryptography is to create a revocable but non-invertible key using the sender and receiver's fingerprint properties.
- Second, to guard the privacy and confidentiality of the fingerprint information for both communication parties. At the same time, securely share both users' fingerprint data using cryptographic techniques so that an attacker cannot access the users' biometric information.

3. PROPOSED SYSTEM

In the proposed work, the sender and recipient are first checked for pair-minutiae features. Quantization and binning result in the creation of a binary string. To create a commuted binary string, the feature bit string is then put through a random key-based permutation (Figure 1). The sender's and receiver's public keys are generated by feeding the binary string into the DH algorithm sideways with two predefined limits after it has been hashed with SHA256 to produce a 256-bit private key. In the proposed system, the sender and receiver first exchange their community keys. By means of the Diffie–Hellman procedure, each party generates the same symmetric key from its secluded key and the other gathering's community key. This common key is then hashed to create the final cryptographic key used for secure data encryption and decryption. To ensure secure communication, both users must authenticate themselves before exchanging information. A Central Authority (CA) is incorporated into the system to manage user registration and verify user identities during the authentication process. A operator creates an RSA key couple during registration and stocks it with the CA lengthways with some documentation. The CA records the operator with all of this data and issues the user a engaged certificate.

Authentication System

In crypto-biometric structures, a cryptographic key is either generated during transformation or is bound to the unique biometric, giving it revocability and non-invertibility. This key is easily obtained by adversaries, is used to authenticate users. The suggested framework, however, does not exchange or store biometric information. At both the transmitter and receiver ends, symmetric keys are created using the DH algorithm. Users can safely argument a cryptographical key ended open stations thanks to the DH procedure. For the users who use this private key, we create a public key using the DH algorithm. Additionally, a public-private key pair is used for CA authentication.

Figure 1. Proposed Crypto-Biometric system framework

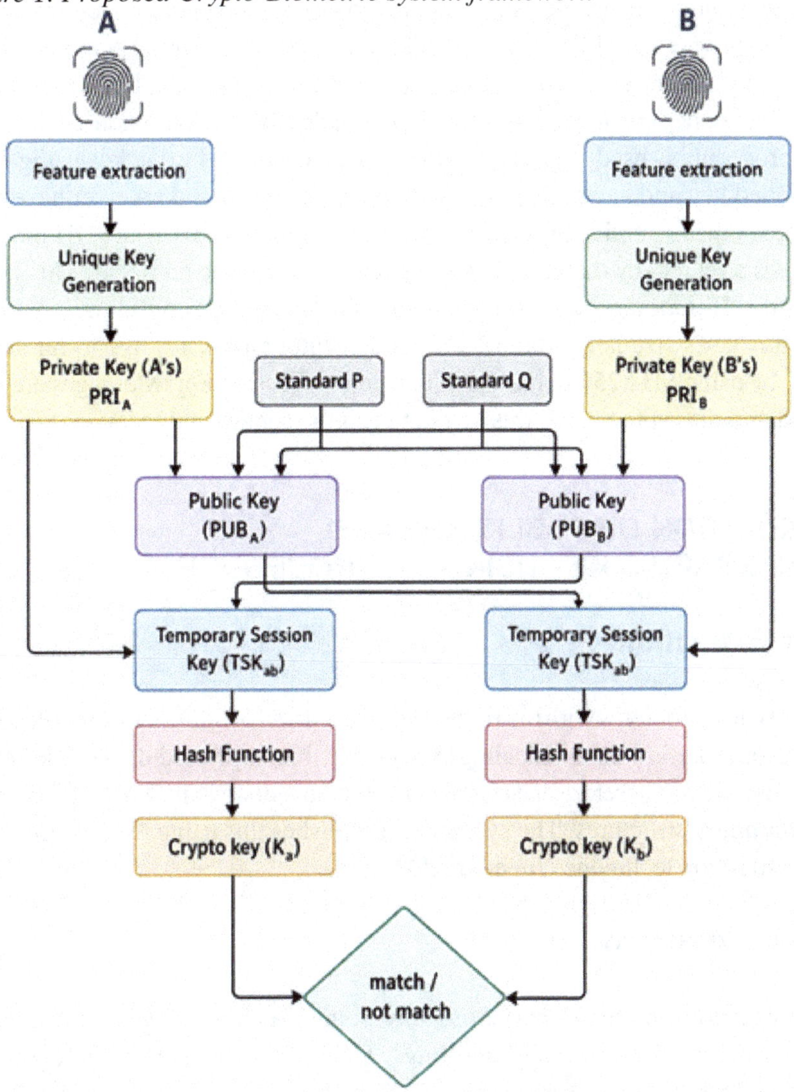

With the DH algorithm, calculating discrete logarithms is more difficult than calculating exponential modulo a prime. The latter task is thought to be impractical for big primes. Because the n in our method is 15, we can obtain a feature bit string with a length of 215. It is necessary to shorten this lengthy binary string so that it can be secondhanded as the key effort for the DH procedure. A SHA256 hash has been employed for this. This key is the user's private key. In this manner, the despatcher's (PRIVATE(A)) and headset's (PRIVATE(B)) private keys are created. The DH procedure also needs the huge prime integer q and its rude root. We can utilize a set value for these limits as opposed to having to generate them for every session. The private keys PRIVATE (A), PRIVATE (B), standard Q, and R are used to produce the sender's and receiver's respective public keys, PUBLIC (A) and PUBLIC (B). The sender and the recipient will then trade PUBLIC(A) and PUBLIC(B). The DH procedure is used at both trimmings to create a clandestine key using one's own secluded key and another's public key once the sender and receiver have both obtained the other's public keys, as elucidated in steps 9 and 10 of the DH method. This creates a secret key that is utilized by the sender and the recipient. This key is known as the "Temporary Session key" in the communication configuration. In our method, this key's size is 2048 bits. The final cryptographic key, a 256-bit key, is produced by using SHA256 to hash this Temporary Session key. Messages are then encrypted and decrypted using this key between the sender and receiver.

4. GENERATION OF PUBLIC KEY AND CRYPTOGRAPHIC KEY USING DH PROCEDURE

Feature Extraction

Performance problems with the fingerprint-based verification system could result from rotation, translation, and scaling distortions that happened during the image acquisition process. Therefore, it is crucial to assess conversion- and rotation-invariant fingerprint image structures. The system accomplishes this using the pair-minutiae feature abstraction technique (Jin et al., 2016).

Minutiae Extraction

In a fingerprint, there are numerous tiny points, such as islands, pores, lakes, core points, delta points, and ridge splittings. The Core point is the highest point on the inmost edge, while the Pore point is a minor hole in the ridge lines. The Delta point is a tri-radial point because it has three ridges emanating from it. In Figure 2, these points are displayed.

Reliable Selection of Minutiae Points

Afterward untrue minutiae points are removed, high calibre and genuine minutiae points remain. The suggested method must always use the same set of minutiae points for key group because its main objective is to produce a stable cryptographic key. As a result, in this technique, a collection of minute points is physically selected from the area that is present in all of the fingerprint photographs of the same individual.

Figure 2. Minutiae, delta and core points

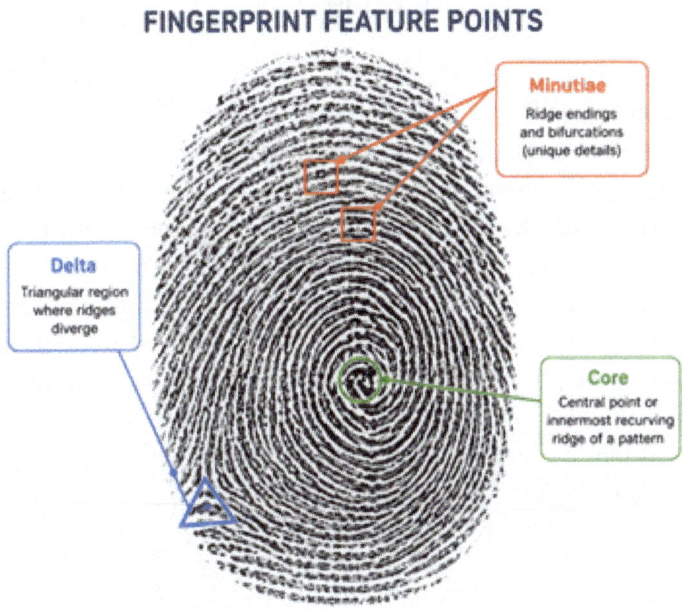

Euclidean Distance Calculation

The Euclidean detachment between each couple of points' coordinates is calculated after choosing the reliable set of details, core, and delta points. Let's say that two tiny points P_i and P_j are situated at (x_i, y_i) and (x_j, y_j), respectively. The calculation of the Euclidean distance is

$$d_{i,j} = \sqrt{\left(x_i - x_j\right)^2 \rightleftarrows +\left(y_i - y_j\right)^2}$$

M_D is equal to $M_1, M_2, ..., M_n$, where n is the quantity of minutiae points. Let C_D stand for a collection of core point distances. C_D is equal to $C_1, C_2, ..., C_n$, where n is the quantity of minutiae points. Let DD represent a collection of delta point distances. D_D is equal to D_1, D_2,... Dn, where n is the quantity of minutiae points.

Sorting of the Distances

When n minutiae, core, and delta points from a fingerprint are chosen, ${}^{n}c_{2}$ the detachment among each couple of minutiae points is taken into account to calculate ${}^{n}c_{2}$ these distances. The values of the distance are then arranged ascendingly.

Altering Distance Into Gary Code

Each detachment is transformed into an m-bit binary number, with a extreme detachment value of 2^m -1, using m bits. Due to the fact that the following cipher words only vary by one-bit, grey code is identified as a part detachment cipher. Due to the fact that a small alteration in the detachment value will have little effect on the bit string generated, the suggested method gains a significant advantage.

For instance, the distance values 11 and 12 are represented in 8-bit binary as '0001011' and '00001100', respectively. The corresponding binary string only differs by one position, contempt the fact that the distance from 11 to 12 increases by 1. These two grey code representations therefore reduce the error resulting from a small variation in the distance between two-minute points in two dissimilar examples of the fingerprint. Let the m-bit binary string be represented by 'b_0,$b_{1,}$$b_2$...$b_{m-1}$'. The corresponding grey code is "$g_{0,}g_{1,}g_{2,}...g_{m-1}$". Gray code is generated from a binary number using the conversion method described below.

$$g_0 = b_0$$
$$g_j = b_{j-1} \oplus b_j$$

Here, ⊕ represents the bitwise exclusive-OR (XOR) operator.

Key Generation Through Concatenation of Gray Codes

The bit string produced by concatenating the grey codes from the sorted distance serves as the cryptographical key. it should be renowned that N minutiae points have ${}^{n}c_{2}$ distance values,. The key therefore has the following length: m X ${}^{n}c_{2}$bits. A binary string is produced by concatenating all the bits obtained from the feature sets Md, Cd, and Dd. This binary string is provided to the S-box (substitution box) as input. In our method, the S-box's output binary string serves as the bio-crypto key. If the binary form of the bio-crypto key is denoted by Key, then

$$Key = EP[S - Box(M_d \| C_d \| D_d)]$$

In this instance, for a real number represented by T bits, where $S = S^m + S^c + S^d$, $|K| = S$ X T bits. Be aware that in this case the link among the feature groups and the bio-crypto key is being concealed by means of the S-box. This S-box, which necessity be selected during the deployment of the request, is typically the same for all users. Recommended using keys with a 1024-bit size. The key size must be increased if it is smaller than the desired size. Ensured the key scope by means of the expansion-permutation apparatus (EP) in the manner described below.

(ii) Guaranteeing key scope: If the key scope is less than 1024 bits, advised using the Expansion-Permutation (EP) method to add the last few bits. As part of our expansion-permutation apparatus, initial create two accidental arrays, Array1 and Array2, with indices from 1 to 1024. Add values to Array 2 in a similar way. Now seal each bit position of key K that is still empty by using K[i] = K[Array2[Array1[j]]], where i= (|K| + 1) 1024, K[Array2[Array1[j]] ≠ null, Array2[Array1[j]] ≤|K|, and j = 1 to 1024. During each stage of the key generation process, these arrays are used to expand the key bits as needed. It should be added that Array1 and Array2 are exclusive to the server. EP is a method that uses the output of an S-box as its input to produce a 1024-bit pattern. If a given fingerprint lacks a core and/or a delta point, Cd and/or Dd won't be calculated. Use an expansion-permutation mechanism to seal the hole and guarantee the key size. Give Cd xor Md as an effort to S-box if a core point is discovered but a delta point is not. Give Dd xor Md as an effort to S-box if a core point cannot be discovered but a delta point can. The Md feature set will always be generated by every fingerprint. Md is used as an input to S-box if neither the core nor the delta points are found. It should be noted that S-Box always guarantees the precise key size for a given input with a accidental bit design. Fig. 3 shows our method for producing bio-crypto keys. As a result, use an expansion-permutation instrument to fill the gap and guarantee the key size. Provide Cd xor Md as an input to S-box if a core point is found but a delta point is not. The S-box receives Dd ⊕ Md as input whenever a delta point is available and a core point is not noticed. We should be aware that every fingerprint will always generate the Md feature set. If neither the core nor the delta points are discovered, Md is provided to S-box as an input. It should be noted that S-Box continuously safeguards the precise key scope with a random bit pattern for a given input. Our strategy for creating bio-crypto keys is depicted in Figure 3.

5. SECURITY ANALYSIS

Users' biometric information is neither shared nor stored in our method. Without having to worry about storing or sharing their biometric information, two users can communicate with one another. This section focuses on the planned framework's security in contradiction of various potential attacks. Examination of numerous attacks demonstrates how effective our strategy is at preventing security breaches and invasions of privacy.

5.1. Security of DH Algorithm

While discrete logarithms are extremely difficult, DH key conversation makes it comparatively informal to compute exponentials modulo a prime. For larger primes, the latter task is regarded as being impractical. However, the assessment becomes impracticable for larger primes. This ensures that no information exists that a hacker could use to access the customers' original biometric information.

The tests were conducted using an Intel(R) Core (TM) i5-2400 processor running at 3.10 GHz. Under Windows 10 OS, developed our programme in MATLAB R2014a. In this section, the outline of the experiment and the findings of proposed approach is explained. The cryptographic key is created using the freely accessible public database Figure print Verification Competition (FVC) 2002 DB1 and DB2. The databases from which obtained the fingerprint images for experiments were: (i) DB2 database for optical sensors: 800 fingerprint images of 100 people with 8 instances of each in set A and 80 fingerprint images of 10 people with 8 instances of each in set B. Each image has a 388x374 (142 Kpixel) size and a 500 dpi resolution. (ii) DB2 database for optical sensors: In set A, there are 80 fingerprint images of 10 people and in Set B, 800 fingerprint images of 100 people, each with eight instances. Each image is stored in the NIST Special Database (DB5) and has a resolution of 569 dpi. Its size is 296x560 (162 Kpixels).

The ridge junction and ridge finish are taken as minutiae point in the proposed work. Using the NIST NBIS software implement FpMV (Fingerprint Minutiae Viewer), the minutiae points were removed from the fingerprint image (Murillo-Escobar et al., 2015). When using this tool, you can input fingerprint images and receive minutiae points with x and y coordinate values and various minutiae types as an output. The point-to-point correspondence between extracted minutiae points from different fingerprint images belonging to the same individual is taken. 10 minutiae points, 2 delta points, and 3 core points are chosen from individually fingerprint twin. Thus, 45 distances at10C2=1 distance at 2C2, and 3 distances at 3C2 are obtained. Experimental findings show that all distance measurements fall within the (0, 255) range.

The distances can therefore be represented using an 8-bit representation. This could be fixed by using error correction codes (such as the Reed-Seolomon or Hammaard codes). However, the effectiveness of the suggested scheme is assessed by computing the aforementioned difference between the kay strings For every 10 people, there are 8 fingerprint images stored in the DBI database. As a result, it is possible to determine the 10C2 = 45 Hamming distances between every pair of a person's fingerprints. There are therefore 300 such comparisons that can be made using the Hamming distance. However, 15 of those 80 fingerprint images have been found to be of low quality or to only contain a portion of a fingerprint. As a result, it was not possible to extract the desired minutiae points from those 12 images. In order to compare 205 pairs of keys (out of a possible 300 pairs), Hamming distance is used (Figure 3). The table 1 displays the measured hamming distances.

Figure 3. Key generation

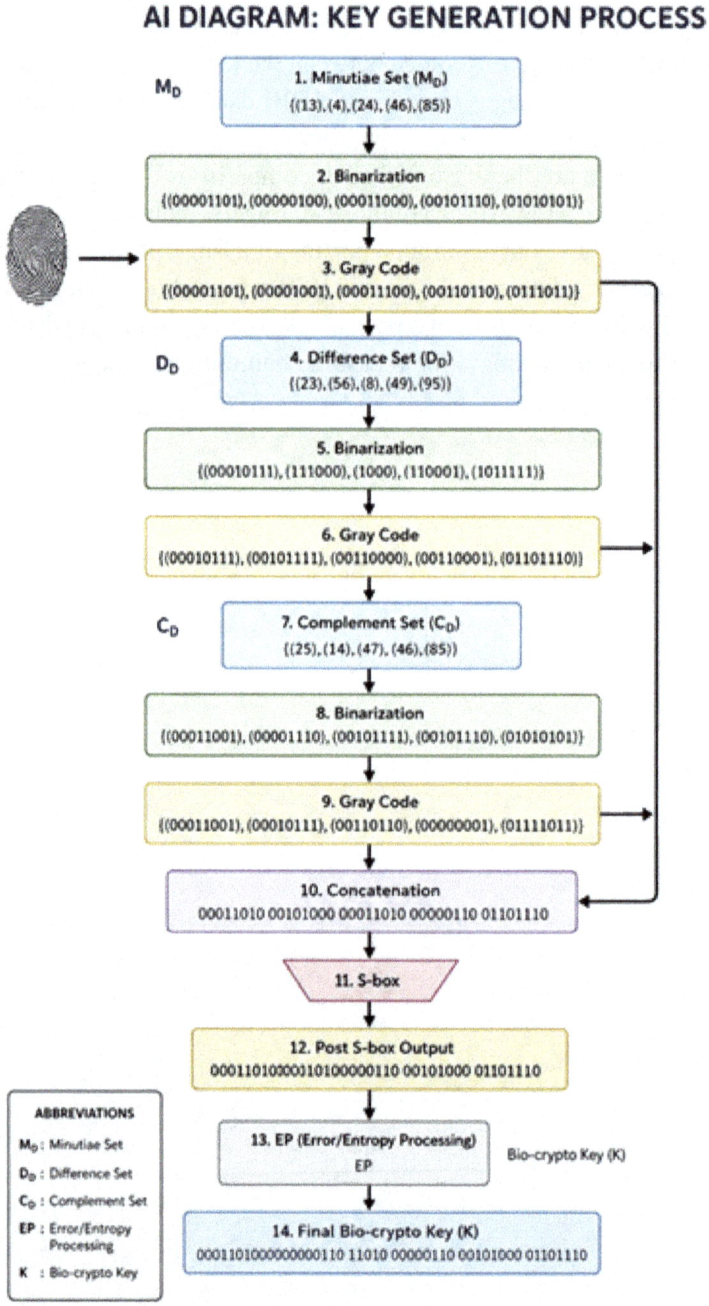

6. EXPERIMENTAL RESULTS

Table 1. Hamming distance – genuine fingerprint and impostor fingerprint

	FVC2002DB1 _Partial Data Base			FVC2002DB1_Full Data Base			FVC2002DB2_Partial Data Base			FVC2002DB2_Full Data Base		
	Min HD	Avg HD	Max HD	Min HD	Avg HD	Max HD	Min HD	Avg HD	Max HD	Min HD	Avg HD	Max HD
Genuine fingerprint	0.12	0.25	0.58	0.11	0.33	0.57	0.11	0.49	0.84	0.1	0.54	0.73
Impostor fingerprint	0.11	0.34	0.78	0.16	0.42	0.61	0.17	0.51	0.74	0.12	0.64	0.78

Table 2. NIST special data base _partial data base vs NIST special data base _full data base

	NIST Special Data Base _ Partial Data Base			NIST Special Data Base _Full Data Base		
	Min HD	Avg HD	Max HD	Min HD	Avg HD	Max HD
Genuine fingerprint	0.14	0.45	0.74	0.25	0.54	0.79
Impostor fingerprint	0.12	0.32	0.48	0.22	0.47	0.57

Additionally, it is determined whether the produced keys from the fingerprints of two dissimilar people will resemble one another (i.e., whether one is an authentic operator and the other is a forger). As a result, the Hamming distance between two keys made from two different people's fingerprints is compared. Since every fingerprint in the database is compared to every additional fingerprint in the record, a total of 6400 comparisons are possible.

As a result, there are a total of 6400 comparisons that can be made (80 comparisons per fingerprint X 80 fingerprints). However, since 15 out of the 80 fingerprints available did not yield the desired granular points, the actual 4200 judgements are performed for this imitator class.

Cryptanalytic Key Testing With NIST Geometric Test Suite

In the NIST- recommended arbitrariness extent data, from 800+274 fingerprint images, produced 1064 bio-crypto keys. NIST advises assuming the bit arrangement is chance if the P-value is less than 0.01. This approach was found to be successful in 13 out of the 16 tests. Therefore, the bio-crypto keys produced by this method meet the criteria for NIST's recommendations regarding the use of chance and pseudorandom designs in cryptanalytic applications (Figure 4).

Complexity of Computation

The difficulty of the encoding and decoding process is O(N2). The proposed encryption and decryption processes have been found to compute in 0.95 and 0.98 seconds, respectively. Giving to sophisticated encryption procedures, the encoding time and decryption time are 0.351 and 0.522 seconds as well as 0.217 and 0.511 seconds, respectively.

Figure 4. (a) Hamming Distances among unaffected pair of cryptograph keys (a) Minutiae points (b) Delta points (c) Core points

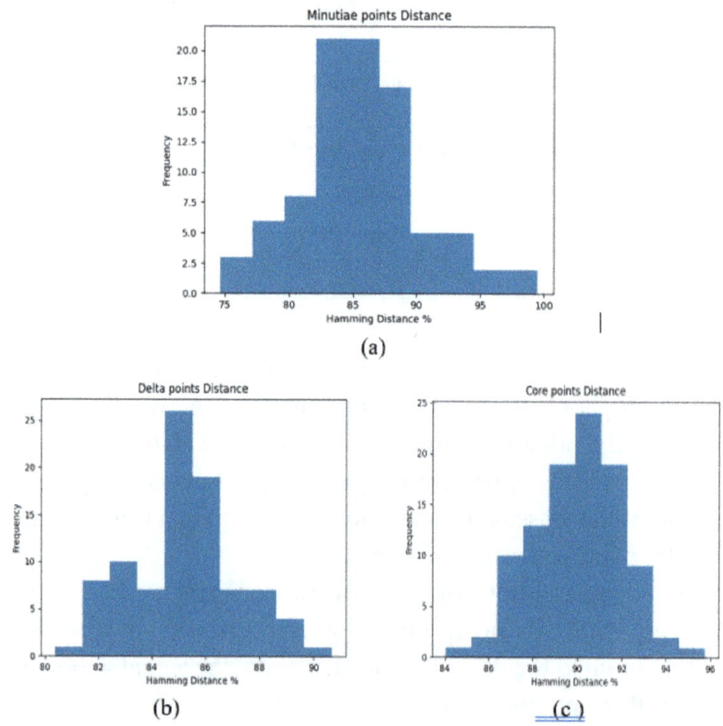

Randomness Analysis of Cryptographic Keys for Genuine Subject Pairs

In order to assess the randomness cryptographic key for such fingerprint pairings, the initial deuce fingerprints of individually theme from each of the four FVC2002 datasets DB1 and DB2 are taken into account as a legitimate pair. For the first two occurrences of each subject's fingerprint, a cryptographic key is generated. Consequently, 100 statistics facts are intended for each dataset as the proportion of identical bits out of all bits in the generated feature string. In Figure 4, histograms are used to display 7 data points out of 100 . The histogram shows that the average identical proportion for a real pair of fingerprints is 92.99%, corresponding to an average of 3986 identical bits out of 4096 total bits. With a standard deviation of 0.033, the proportion of identical bits is dispersed between the ranges of 81.37% and 99.83%. It follows that a genuine pair will have a enough number of bits that match for the couple's cryptanalytic key.

Randomness Analysis of Cryptographic Keys for Impostor Subject Pairs

To evaluate the randomness of cryptographic keys for imposter pairs of users, the datasets DB1 and DB2 are used. Each dataset is separated into 50 unique pairs. Each pair's remaining fingerprints are regarded as a forgery pair. There are a total of 50 x 48 = 2400 combinations for each genuine communication-engaged pair. As a result, a histogram in Fig. 4 shows a total of 2400* 8= 19200 hamming distances that have been calculated.

The average hamming distance between authentic and fake keys is 128 bits, as can be seen from the histogram, which shows that it is 46.19%. Hamming distances have a standard deviation of 0.041 and range from 38.89% to 62.72%. Additionally, it has been found that between 30% and 70% of the bits in real keys differ from those in 99.89% of fake keys, and that under 30% of fake keys (0.03%) have mismatched bits. Therefore, no 256-bit cryptographic key can be cracked using more than 128 matched bits.

Key Size Analysis

According to Alvarez and Li (2006), analysis of the literature, a verification scheme needs more than 2100 clandestine keys. Each key in his case must be vigorous sufficient and produce haphazard data to fend off an thorough attack. This technique uses a 256-bit cryptographic key, and its chance has been confirmed. As a result, 2^{256} unique keys can be retrieved.

Information Entropy Analysis

A cryptographic key's randomness serves as a proxy for information entropy; the more unpredictable the key, the higher the entropy. A key Public's entropy H(-PUBLIC) can be calculated using the formula below:

$$H(PUBLIC) = \sum_{j=0}^{2M-1} P(PUBLIC_j) \log_2(\frac{1}{PUBLIC_j})$$

where M is the key's bit count, 2M is the total number of bits that could be used, and $P(PUBLIC_j)$ denotes the likelihood that each bit in $PUBLIC_j$ is present. The ideal entropy for a key PUBLIC with 2^M possible bits would be H(PUBLIC)=M. The maximum entropy of the cryptographic key, which has 256 bits, is H = 8. This demonstrates that every bit has the same probability of appearing. When the parameter $P_M = 15$ is used, the generated cryptographic key has an entropy of 7.28 as opposed to the original template's H = 5.14. Thus, it can be determined that the proposed method generates keys in a highly pseudorandom manner.

Performance

All three databases—DB1, DB2, and the NIST Special database—were used to assess the suggested approach for FVC2002. Many different, excellent fingerprint images can be found in the datasets. This work uses the commercial VeriFinger SDK software to extract minute points (Figure 5). The hamming distances among the cryptanalytic keys created from a real couple of fingerprints and the cryptanalytic keys created from a fake couple of fingerprints are planned for each subject. For a couple of real fingerprints, the hammering distances must be as small as possible; in contrast, the distances must be greater for a pair of fake fingerprints. This instance serves as an example of a token theft scenario in which a fraudster has access to the alteration key. We have contrasted real and fake notches using the similar alteration key for each operator in the record. The ROC curves for the DB1, DB2, and NIST Special databases from FVC2002 are shown in Figure 5. The performance of proposed system and existing system is compared in tTable 2.

Figure 5. Comparison of TAR and FAR

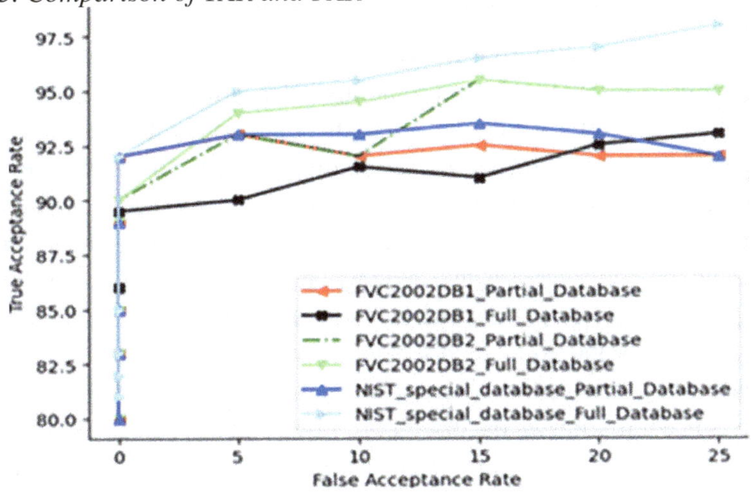

Table 3. Comparisons with respect to the accuracy measures

	Z. Jim et al., 2016	Y. Lim et al., 2017	Gaurang Panchal et al., 2018	Proposed Work
TAR	97.00%	95.7%	96.78%	99.83%
FAR	0.001%	0.01%	0.002%	0.00%

The datasets DB1 and DB2, which contain more high-quality images, allowed us to achieve TAR of 97.29% and 97.59%, respectively, as shown in Fig. 5. The decline in performance is caused by the dearth of reliable minutiae. In addition, we evaluate performance using 2900 x 4 = 11600 real key comparisons and 4050 x 4 = 16200 fake key comparisons, which are obtained by combining all two datasets from FVC2002. The proposed method is tested using NIST Special Record 4 in addition to the FVC2002 datasets (Ribouh et al., 2020). Figure 5 depicts the ROC arc for the NIST special record 4 (Ribouh et al., 2020). It is significant to note that the proposed method outperforms the previously reported 97.12% TAR in Mukhammadovich and Djuraevich (2023) by achieving a TAR of 95.73% for part NIST special database 4. However, because error-correction codes have not been practical over cryptanalytic keys, we find high FAR for the NIST special record. The approach addresses the growing need for ethical and secure data handling by avoiding biometric template storage and producing unique session-specific cryptographic keys.

6. CONCLUSION

The production of lengthy, robust cryptographic keys is difficult in cryptographic procedures. Additionally, there is a problem with how to store such a key. In this paper, we afford a idea for generating a lengthy, random cryptographic key from a user's fingerprint. Many concerns relating to the user's enrollment and key storage are automatically resolved because the same key does not need to be saved anywhere. The cryptographic key must be stored securely, which is a difficult undertaking. The suggested method addresses this issue by creating the cryptographic key from the fingerprint. As a effect, it makes it incredible for an attacker to steal the cryptographic key. The proposed method yields a single key string that may be utilized in a symmetric key arrangement. The proposed method's use of gray code is a vital component since it minimizes the discrepancy between keys produced from different occurrences of the same figure print. According to an analysis, the mismatch between a pair of keys caused by a forger is greater than the mismatch caused by the natural variance in the acquired figure print pictures. As a result, a fake person cannot produce the same key that a real person does. According to the suggested technique for generating a cryptographic key from a fingerprint biometric, a like feature course can be created through 99.83% accuracy. The approach addresses the growing need for ethical and secure data handling by avoiding biometric template storage and producing unique session-specific cryptographic keys. The findings contribute to discussions on digital privacy, trust, and the cultural shift toward secure biometric authentication in modern communication systems. The outcomes establish that integrating crypto-biometric key generation meaningfully reinforces Metaverse security by safeguarding dependable user verification and endangered virtual interactions.

REFERENCES

Al-Saggaf, A. A., Ghouti, L., & Acharya, H. S. (2012). Biometric cryptosystem with renewable templates. In *WIAR 2012: National Workshop on Information Assurance Research*. VDE.

Alvarez, G., & Li, S. (2006). Some basic cryptographic requirements for chaos-based cryptosystems. *International Journal of Bifurcation and Chaos in Applied Sciences and Engineering*, *16*(8), 2129–2151. DOI: 10.1142/S0218127406015970

Beng, A., Teoh, A. B. J., & Toh, K.-A. (2008). Secure biometric-key generation with biometric helper. In *2008 3rd IEEE Conference on Industrial Electronics and Applications* (pp. 2300–2305). IEEE. DOI: 10.1109/ICIEA.2008.4582898

Choi, H., Choi, K., & Kim, J. (2011). Fingerprint matching incorporating ridge features with minutiae. *IEEE Transactions on Information Forensics and Security*, *6*(2), 338–345. DOI: 10.1109/TIFS.2010.2103940

Gottschlich, C., & Huckemann, S. (2014). Separating the real from the synthetic: Minutiae histograms as fingerprints of fingerprints. *IET Biometrics*, *3*(4), 291–301. DOI: 10.1049/iet-bmt.2013.0065

Haghighat, M., Zonouz, S., & Abdel-Mottaleb, M. (2015). CloudID: Trustworthy cloud-based and cross-enterprise biometric identification. *Expert Systems with Applications*, *42*(21), 7905–7916. DOI: 10.1016/j.eswa.2015.06.025

Jain, A. K., Ross, A., & Uludag, U. (2005). Biometric template security: Challenges and solutions. In *Proceedings of the 13th European Signal Processing Conference (EUSIPCO)*. IEEE.

Jin, Z., Teoh, A. B. J., Goi, B. M., & Tay, Y. H. (2016). Biometric cryptosystems: A new biometric key binding and its implementation for fingerprint minutiae-based representation. *Pattern Recognition*, *50*, 50–62. DOI: 10.1016/j.patcog.2016.02.024

Jin, Z., Teoh, A. B. J., Ong, T. S., & Tee, C. (2010). A revocable fingerprint template for security and privacy preserving. *KSII Transactions on Internet and Information Systems*, *4*, 1327–1342. DOI: 10.3837/tiis.2010.12.020

Kanade, S., Petrovska-Delacrétaz, D., & Dorizzi, B. (2010). In *Proceedings of the 4th IEEE International Conference on Biometrics: Theory, Applications and Systems (BTAS)* (pp. 1–7). IEEE.

Kivinen, T. (2003). More modular exponential (MODP) Diffie-Hellman groups for Internet Key Exchange (IKE). Internet Engineering Task Force., RFC 3526. DOI: 10.17487/rfc3526

Li, P., Yang, X., Qiao, H., Cao, K., Liu, E., & Tian, J. (2012). An effective biometric cryptosystem combining fingerprints with error correction codes. *Expert Systems with Applications*, *39*(7), 6562–6574. DOI: 10.1016/j.eswa.2011.12.048

Mukhammadovich, N. M., & Djuraevich, A. R. (2023). Working with cryptographic key information. *International Journal of Electrical and Computer Engineering*, *13*(1), 911–919. DOI: 10.11591/ijece.v13i1.pp911-919

Murillo-Escobar, M. A., Cardoza-Avendaño, L., Méndez-Ramírez, R., & Cruz-Hernández, C. (2015). A robust embedded biometric authentication system based on fingerprint and chaotic encryption. *Expert Systems with Applications*, *42*(21), 8198–8211. DOI: 10.1016/j.eswa.2015.06.035

Panchal, G., & Samanta, D. (2018). A novel approach to fingerprint biometric-based cryptographic key generation and its applications to storage security. *Computers & Electrical Engineering*, *69*, 461–478. DOI: 10.1016/j.compeleceng.2018.01.028

Ribouh, S., Phan, K., Malawade, A. V., Elhillali, Y., Rivenq, A., & Al Faruque, M. A. (2020). Channel state information-based cryptographic key generation for intelligent transportation systems. *IEEE Transactions on Intelligent Transportation Systems*, *22*(12), 7496–7507. DOI: 10.1109/TITS.2020.3003577

Stinson, D. R. (1997). An introduction to visual cryptography. In *Public Key Solutions* (Vol. 97, pp. 28–30).

Stoianov, A. (2010). In *Proceedings of the 8th Annual International Conference on Privacy, Security and Trust (PST)* (pp. 231–235).

Upmanyu, M., Namboodiri, A. M., Srinathan, K., & Jawahar, C. V. (2010). Blind authentication: A secure crypto-biometric verification protocol. *IEEE Transactions on Information Forensics and Security*, *5*(2), 255–268. DOI: 10.1109/TIFS.2010.2043188

Chapter 6
Forensic Attribution of Deepfakes:
Tracing Synthetic Media to Model, Device, and Actor

Kiranbhai Dodiya
http://orcid.org/0009-0001-9409-7303
Gujarat University, India

Trilokkumar B. Akhani
Parul University, India

Shweta Javia
Sardar Patel University, India

Kowshika Prabhakar
Anglia Ruskin University, UK

Sudha Manjunath Shetty
Sigma University, India

Hitesh Vora
Regional Forensic Science Laboratory (RFSL), Rajkot, India

ABSTRACT

Deepfakes have become increasingly sophisticated, producing synthetic media that can mislead both humans and automated detectors. This chapter outlines a unified forensic attribution framework that identifies the creator, generative model, and production pipeline behind deepfakes by analysing model fingerprints, training artefacts, device metadata, and workflow traces. It integrates digital forensics, AI provenance analysis, cybercrime investigation, watermarking, and behavioural profiling, while addressing legal standards for evidence handling, authenticity, and admissibility. The chapter concludes with a roadmap advocating global model registries, standardised forensic metadata, and cross-sector collaboration to strengthen accountability in the deepfake era.

DOI: 10.4018/979-8-3373-8292-0.ch006

1. INTRODUCTION

1.1 The Proliferation of Deepfakes in Crime and Society

The advent of technology over the past several years has produced increasingly sophisticated deepfakes. Most people associate deepfakes with videos, images, and now audio, manufactured using machine learning processes, diffusion models, and Generative Adversarial Networks. Originally, the technologies that led to the fakes were those used to enhance films. However, these technologies are now being developed and deployed across a range of sectors, including but not limited to criminal activity, cyberspace, and the social fabric. The availability of datasets, open-source technologies, editing tools, and a means of posting content online allows people with no expertise to produce believable synthetic content. The spread and accessibility of deepfake technologies are clearly accelerating (Hancock & Bailenson, 2021). Deepfakes are uniquely positioned in modern-day cybercrime to facilitate identity and financial fraud and enable impersonation, blackmail, and social engineering attacks, contributing to the growth of cybercrime as a service industry. Synthetic media provides criminals with tools to more effectively impersonate almost any target, including political figures, executives, celebrities, or even private citizens. The negative effects of deepfakes extend beyond victimization. Deepfakes erode public trust in digital media and make information verification more difficult .<|join|>Deepfakes erode public trust in digital media and make information verification more difficult. They exacerbate the spread of false and misleading information, especially during turbulent times such as conflicts, crises, and public or political disruptions, including emergencies and elections. This makes deepfakes a multi-faceted challenge in technology and cybercrime that requires governance and regulatory oversight, framed within a cybercrime policy and forensic preparedness, to address their harmful effects (Singh & Dhumane, 2025).

1.2 Beyond Detection: The Demand for Attribution

Significant advancements have been made in tools for detecting deepfakes. However, detecting deepfakes is not enough to counter the challenges posed by synthetic media. Important questions, such as who the perpetrator is, which generative model or software was employed, what production process was followed, and which channels were used for dissemination, remain unaddressed and leave an unmeasured impact of deepfake-enabled crimes. The race to create a highly sophisticated detection tool for deepfakes is rapidly losing ground to the development and use of next-generation deepfake technology, counter-forensics, and avoidance techniques that will render traditional forensic tools obsolete. This continuously evolving situation is a strong indicator of the absolute necessity for trustworthy attribution mechanisms. Forensic attribution examines methods beyond identifying manipulated content. It focuses on linking synthetic media to certain models, devices, people, or operational infrastructures. This means reinterpreting detection results and converting them to useful intelligence. AI architecture, AI training methods, and metadata are examples of attributes that may provide useful information. Other attributes include the methods the AI uses to generate behavior and the digital signature it leaves. These may also be useful in determining the origins of synthetic content. Digital forensic investigators, cybersecurity professionals, and law enforcement personnel may find these attributes especially useful. Attribution may also improve the quality and integrity of evidence. Sometimes, determining the origins of digital evidence may be just as important as verifying the evidence's authenticity. Because of this, rigorous attribution may become necessary to establish responsibility in the digital world, to provide trust and safety in internet systems, and to discourage bad-faith actions involving synthetic media (Amerini et al., 2025).

1.3 The Scope, Importance, and Purpose of the Chapter

This chapter examines deepfake forensic attribution systems and emergent methods that integrate technological and investigative systems to probe the legal pathways for identifying the origin(s) of synthetic media. Rather than concentrating on conventional detection methods, this chapter investigates attribution methods. It examines advanced traces from generative models, device-specific traces, and operational pathways, as well as the threat actor's conduct. By bridging the domains of forensic attribution, digital investigations, advanced machine learning, and cybercrime, this chapter seeks to situate forensic attribution within the contemporary, evolving paradigms of digital investigations. This chapter examines attribution methods to address the challenges posed by deepfake technologies and sets the stage for future critical media studies that focus on the origins of media. It analyzes attribution at the model, device, and actor levels and addresses ongoing efforts to build attribution systems that can be legally and ethically employed at scale. This chapter also strengthens trust and resilience to synthetic media. This chapter also goes beyond most studies of deepfakes, which are primarily focused on detection. It integrates model-, device-, network-, and actor-level attribution within a forensic framework. Within this framework, the technical, behavioral, evidentiary, and legal dimensions of attribution are addressed to demonstrate how attribution can support accountability and trust in the digital realm while also strengthening the legal and ethical frameworks of generative AI. This chapter also addresses the many gaps in the literature concerning deepfakes and seeks to build a more solid and practical foundation for future forensic research and investigations.

Table 1. Major attribution types used in deepfake forensic investigations and the corresponding evidence sources

Attribution Type	Purpose	Typical Evidence
Model Attribution	Identify the AI model or architecture used to generate synthetic media	Neural fingerprints, watermarking artefacts, frequency-domain signatures, provenance indicators
Device Attribution	Identify the hardware or software environment involved in the generation	Metadata, system logs, GPU/TPU traces, cache remnants, rendering artefacts
Actor Attribution	Identify the individual, group, or organisation responsible	OSINT, SOCMINT, behavioural patterns, communication records, contextual intelligence
Network Attribution	Identify the infrastructure used for generation or dissemination.	

2. DEEPFAKE GENERATION PIPELINES

Figure 1. Overview of the deepfake generation pipeline showing GAN, diffusion, and multimodal generation paths

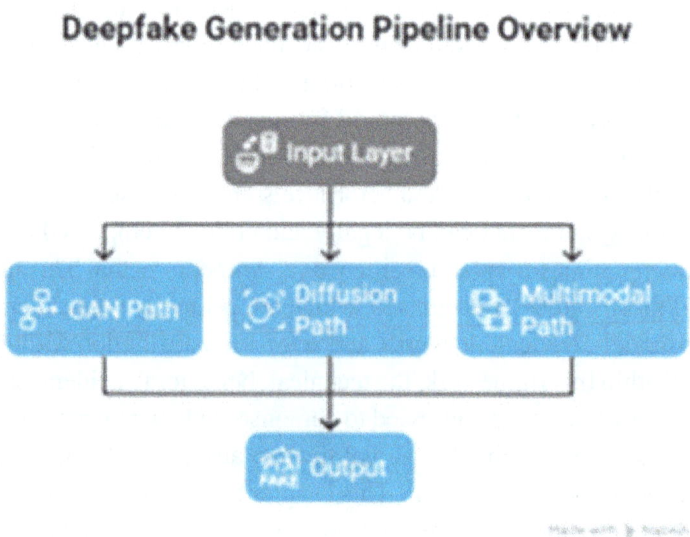

2.1 Multimodal Deepfake Generation and Diffusion Models

The rapid rise and growing popularity of deepfake technologies can be attributed to their use of multimodal content synthesis. Existing deepfake systems can use inputs of various data types, such as text, audio, video, images, and even motion, to produce coordinated, realistic synthetic content. For example, text-to-video systems can produce moving images in response to text input, and audio-based facial animation systems can produce synchronized speech along with speech-related gestures and facial movements. More advanced systems that perform identity swaps, voice cloning across languages, motion synthesis, and even the creation of virtual humans are now possible due to the fusion of Generative Adversarial Networks, diffusion systems, and autoregressive transformer systems. This combination of systems has led to a large increase in the tools available to practitioners. The increased use of deepfake technologies has created a significant gap in many existing legal, regulatory, and forensic frameworks and technologies for automatically differentiating and investigating media. There is an urgent need to develop automated attribution technologies and investigative methods to distinguish original media from sophisticated synthetic content. (Li et al. 2024) Recently, diffusion models have gained massive popularity. This stems from how different they are from other synthetic frameworks, such as Generative Adversarial Networks (GANs), which use adversarial learning to oppose a generator and a discriminator. Conversely, diffusion models add noise to the training images from the onset. The models then learn to remove the added noise in discrete steps. Diffusion models provide a framework for generating high-quality images that retain semantic meaning. Competitors to diffusion models include Stable Diffusion, DALL·E, and Imagen. Each of these models employs diffusion models and produces high-quality images and videos, exhibiting robust performance even with simple and incomplete prompts. Because diffusion models are modular and easy to implement, complex deepfakes depicting people and interactive environments can be generated easily by those without technical expertise. Unlike GANs, diffusion models are more reliable and do not suffer from problems such as mode collapse. (Cao et al. 2024).

2.2 Training Data, Hyperparameters, and Architectural Signatures

Deepfake generation encompasses various facets, including training data, hyperparameters, and model architecture. Training data encompasses a wide range of media, including facial image snapshots, voice recordings, videos, and synchronized multimedia, collected from public and private data libraries, social media, and other repositories. These datasets combine quality, quantity, and variety. Smaller or biased datasets often yield less convincing or duplicative outputs. Large and diverse datasets, in turn, are likely to yield highly realistic synthetic media outputs. Moreover, the nature of the training data often yields telltale signs or artifacts that can serve as valuable forensic tools in attribution investigations (Cassia et al., 2025). Hyperparameters are another important dimension to consider when evaluating the quality and characteristics of the model's outputs. The learning rate, batch size, training duration, choice of optimizers and regularizers, and the like influence characteristics of generative modeling. These can be the structural signatures that yield artifacts, noise, and patterns embedded in the outputs of the generation process. Such residue can provide important traces of the training and may help the forensic analyst to identify the specific model's signature configuration. Architecture additionally introduces idiosyncratic forensic features on a per-model basis. Choices regarding convolution and scaling, as well as activation functions, attention mechanisms, and representations within latent space, all impact the model's intrinsic behavior and workings. Structures yield patterns, both visually and statistically, that are likely unique to them. While many artifacts are imperceptible to the naked eye, a forensic analysis of the model may reveal them, for instance, a frequency domain analysis or temporal anomaly analysis conducted on video data (Yu et al., 2019). The development environment may impose its own idiosyncratic implementation signatures. Optimizing, executing, and parallelizing techniques that differ in how they harness hardware apply to development environments such as TensorFlow, PyTorch, and custom CUDA. Different versions of a model also affect the kind of math it uses, which in turn may alter the math in its outputs. These characteristics are model-specific and support attribution of the model at hand by determining its implementation frameworks and training pipeline. Therefore, the structure of a model may help identify specific development environments, model families, and potentially the developers, in the case of deepfakes (Yang et al., 2022; Liu et al., 2024).

2.3 Toolchains, Software Bundles, and Unregulated Markets

Deepfake technology has proliferated due to a growing network of specialized software toolchains, open-source repositories, and commercial or pirated bundles. Modular toolchains, such as DeepFaceLab, FaceSwap, and implementations of Avatarify and Stable Diffusion, provide adaptable platforms for face-swapping, voice cloning, lip-syncing, and avatar generation. Many of these technologies provide automated, streamlined procedures for collecting data, training models, and rendering media, thereby minimizing the technical expertise required to create synthetic media. To further compound the accessibility issues surrounding the creation of synthetic media, the availability of cloud computing services offers low-cost access to powerful, efficient computing systems. In addition to readily available software toolchains, deepfake technology has found its way into underground markets. Such markets encompass the dark web, various Telegram groups, and cybercrime-as-a-service platforms, to name just a few. Software toolchains for deepfake generation and counter-forensics that avoid detection are for sale in these markets. These services are used in numerous scams, including business email compromise, social engineering fraud, and financial fraud. Furthermore, these toolchains, software, and frameworks are often used to conduct cybercrime in conjunction with malware and phishing. This creates an ecosystem of cybercrime (Suleiman, 2025). A detailed study of deepfake generation systems and their pipelines shows how the creation of such systems, and the training, software, and techniques used to deploy them to the web, shape the systems and images in the designers' choosing. These elements leave traces and serve as the initial components of attribution forensics. Digital investigators can manipulate media and then determine the specific frameworks and hardware on which it was created, as well as the people responsible for its creation. Mechanisms of generation and design leave a forensic trace in the media they create and are therefore vital for attribution. A multitude of factors craft the deepfake content—dataset selection, Framework designs, hyperparameter configurations, development environments, among others. Provide a unique signature and, if possible, a persistent artifact in the synthetic media. These generation mechanisms are vital for forensic trace creation and provide comprehensive attribution at the model, device, and actor levels.

3. CONCEPT OF FORENSIC ATTRIBUTION

3.1 Definitions: Model, Device, and Actor Attribution

In the domain of deepfake media, forensic attribution entails the comprehensive and structured determination of the sources of synthetic media, linking them to the specific generative model, the relevant computing environment, and, in some cases, the creator or creators. Attribution endeavors to go beyond detection by providing technical and behavioral traces to establish media provenance and responsibility. Model attribution determines which generative architecture is responsible for producing a particular piece of synthetic content, whether that architecture is a framework or a generative pretrained model. In this context, the technicalities of latent models are studied. These include neural fingerprints, latent artifacts, spectral distortion, and statistical and GAN- or diffusion -related transformation irregularities. These traits may be used to classify synthetic media and to determine the model family or an identifiable AI framework, marking the initial step toward attribution. Distinguishing these traits helps constrain the available generation tools and determine the model origins of the synthetic content and its technology (Liu et al., 2024).

Figure 2. Layered attribution framework linking AI models, devices, and actors in synthetic media investigations

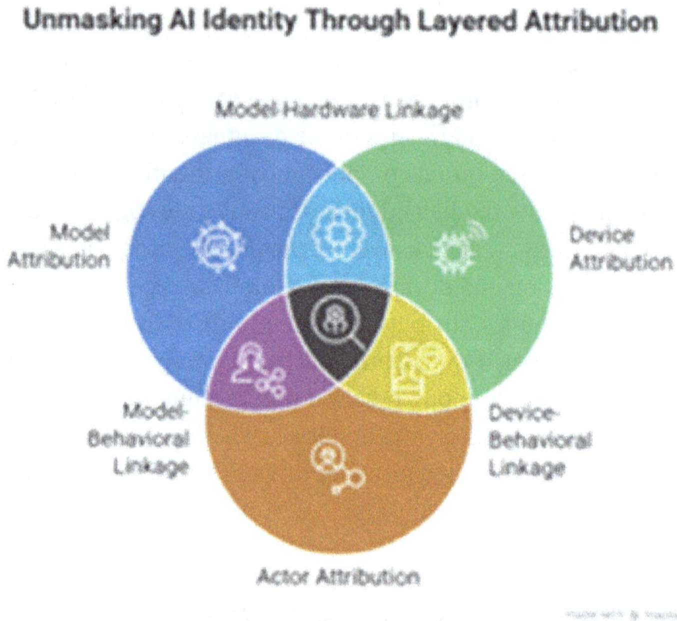

Attribution of devices refers to the specific computational systems or configurations identified as the sources of synthetic content. Such systems may be GPUs/TPUs, CPUs, cloud services, or local devices. Each of these systems leaves specific, identifiable traces in the configuration and operational footprints of the media or the virtual environment. These may include metadata imprints, rendering occlusions, and low-level executables with specific hardware and software bindings. For a particular deepfake instance, available metadata may assist forensic practitioners in determining the type of deepfake (i.e., a commercial, cloud, or custom-built workstation) based on the low-level operating signatures and trace evidence. Once the devices and algorithms are mapped, actor attribution focuses on identifying the individuals or groups (especially threat actors) responsible for creating and/or distributing deepfakes. This is the most defining and complicated element of the attribution process. This will be the result of a combination of digital forensics, cyber behavioral profiling, cybernetic intelligence, and contextual inquiries. Clues from linguistic, operational, and behavioral typologies may help identify actors and online personas on the deep web.

3.2 Attribution Challenges of Synthetic Media

Deepfake attribution encounters many technical, operational, and evidentiary hurdles. One of the more difficult challenges is that many open-source generative model architectures are publicly available. Many people use the same model and training set, thus resulting in the same outputs. Those outputs are less distinctive, which in turn makes attribution efforts more difficult. The problem compounds as newer generative models produce outputs in less detectable ways, highlighting the forensic challenges. Using generative models, novice forensic techniques have been introduced, including metadata removal, perturbations, and noise reduction, which together obscure the fingerprints of the generative architecture. That makes forensic and model analyses more difficult. The use of commercially available anonymization techniques, including VPNs, the Tor network, and disposable and compromised cloud services, provides multiple means to conceal the user's identity. Considering the decentralization and transience of cloud GPUs, attributing to the user makes it less feasible since the identifiers can be temporary or nonexistent. Coupled with the differentiating state legislation, it makes the deepfake user forensics even more challenging. With advances in deepfake technology, synthetic media becomes even more difficult to track. Because of this, new forensic methodologies are needed to ensure that deepfake technology is used responsibly. (Heidari et al., 2024).

3.3 The Intersection of Multiple Disciplines in Forensics

To successfully operationalize the crime of deepfake attribution, knowledge of digital forensics is necessary, as is an understanding of how forensic-valued digital evidence is captured, preserved, and subsequently analyzed, and how to search metadata for missing artifacts. This includes the formulation of digital forensics that pertains to the prospective witnessing or shadowing of a specific computing device or segment of digital infrastructure. Machine learning engineers may be called upon to analyze the models and algorithmic frameworks that enable the capture of so-called 'fingerprints' during the training of a specific neural net, as well as the novel 'generative' behaviors that may aid in differentiating one synthesis pathway from others. According to Amerini et al. (2025), net defenders receive attribution assistance by tracking digital assailants through a specific synthesis that correlates the distribution with the synapse of an attack and a campaign. In actor-level attribution, behavior analysts and criminologists consider the psychological, operational, and contextual factors of the Deepfake activity as they pertain to specific actors or groups. Meanwhile, legal scholars and forensic specialists are concerned with actor attribution, standards, and the admissibility and reliability of evidence. The intersection of these fields enhances attribution, advances the inquiry, and safeguards the defensibility of the results from technical and legal perspectives. These aspects of attribution, drawing on various fields, place interdisciplinary forensics at the core of expanding and resilient Deepfake attribution systems (Sandoval et al., 2024).

Table 2. Comparison of attribution methods used in deepfake forensic investigations

Attribution Method	Evidence Required	Strengths	Limitations
Watermarking & Provenance	Embedded signatures, metadata	Strong source verification	Can be removed or absent
Model Fingerprinting	Neural artefacts, frequency traces	Useful for model attribution	Reduced effectiveness after heavy processing
Metadata & Log Analysis	EXIF, system logs, cache data	Strong device-level evidence	Easily modified or deleted
OSINT and SOCMINT	Public information, social media data	Supports actor attribution	Time-intensive and indirect
Behavioural Profiling	Language, operational patterns	Useful for campaign attribution	May not uniquely identify actors

4. MODEL-LEVEL ATTRIBUTION METHODS

Table 3. Comparative fingerprint characteristics of GAN and diffusion-based deepfake models.

Fingerprint type	GAN models	Diffusion models
Pixel artifacts	Checkerboard artifacts	Smoother pixel patterns
Frequency domain signatures	Repeating noise patterns	Probabilistic denoising signatures
Training artefacts	Mode collapse patterns	Noise schedule identifiers

4.1 Neural Fingerprints and Model-Specific Artifacts

Neural fingerprints are presumed evidence of artificial neural networks and are significant for model-level forensic attribution. Rather than attempting to identify the creator of a product, as traditional forensic methods do, neural fingerprints look for the patterns that media synthesis and creation leave behind. These patterns are byproducts of the interaction among a model's architecture, its training data, its optimization, and the environment in which the model is implemented. Just as a manufacturing tool leaves traces on the product, generative AI will leave traces in the content it creates. AI will leave marks that may be seen as pixel-level irregularities, variations in texture, and odd statistical patterns. Forensic analysts may employ texture synthesis, frequency domain analysis, co-occurrence matrix analysis, and residual-noise learning to discover these traces. Both guided and autonomous methods may be employed. Guided methods work to discriminate between real media and AI-generated content, while autonomous methods work to find internal similarities. These methods may assist in attributing deepfakes to a specific model architecture and the environment in which they were created.

4.2 Watermarking, Invisible Tags, and Cryptographic Signatures

Watermarking and cryptographic methods take a proactive position on the forensic attribution of synthetic media and its governance. In contrast to post-generation forensic assessments, these techniques embed the means of identifying information within the content creation pipeline. Digital watermarks and invisible tags can be embedded in the media during generation or rendering, enabling investigators and verification frameworks to trace a content's origin and verify its authenticity. Attribution is further bolstered by cryptographic signatures, which provide mathematical certainty about the source and the integrity of the synthetic media. During the rendering stage, any instance of the model or a session of content generation may cryptographically sign the generated output. Such signatures ensure a tamper-proof record of content authorship and the provenance of its creation. In conjunction with verification frameworks, cryptographic signatures enable investigators to determine whether an authorized system generated the content and whether it has been altered after generation. The combination of digital watermarking and cryptographic signatures addresses an ever-growing governance challenge within the synthetic media ecosystem. These mechanisms enable trustworthy content verification and attribution and, therefore, justify the growing perception that watermarking and cryptographic methods for governance structures constitute a necessary framework for managing the risks associated with deepfake technologies.

4.3 Provenance Tracking in GAN and Diffusion Pipelines

Provenance tracking revolves around reconstructing the complete lifecycle of synthetic media, including its generation, modifications, and distribution. Watermarking techniques involve the insertion of overt markers into media content. In contrast, provenance tracking focuses on the operational, structural, and procedural markers left in the generation pipeline. Operational traces left in the generation pipeline may include execution logs, generation parameters, processing workflows, and artifacts of content synthesis. In GAN-based systems, provenance indicators often stem from features of the discriminator's behavior, the latent space, noise, and upsampling. The GAN training procedure often results in the insertion of artifacts characteristic of a particular model configuration and may reflect a specific training paradigm or domain of focus. Forensic systems may identify these artifacts and thereby distinguish between different GANs and/or determine the probable origin of the synthetic media (Amrouche et al., 2021). In contrast, Diffusion models produce a different set of provenance indicators since the task of content generation is performed by a series of iterative denoising operations. Each iterative generation cycle contains information on the sampling schedule, noise and guidance scale, denoising, and checkpoint parameters. The reverse diffusion paths may contain slight statistical differences that pertain to particular models and/or sampling methods. Further, the denoising correlation, feature-space transitions, and analyses of temporal coherence may yield pertinent information about the generation pathway. Provenance indicators signal to investigators the construction of aspects of the generation process and assist in refining attribution techniques of linking content to a particular generative pipeline.

4.4 Deepfake Quality Metrics as Attribution Evidence

Deepfake quality metrics enable qualitative assessments of the realism, coherence, and consistency of media. While these metrics facilitate content evaluation, they can also serve as secondary forensic attribution indicators by highlighting elements specific to particular generative models and development paths. Different families of models demonstrate distinct, and often inverse, profiles with respect to quality measurement. Thus, quality metrics can be employed to hypothesize the likely origin of the synthetic content. Common evaluation metrics include Fréchet Inception Distance (FID), Kernel Inception Distance (KID), and perceptual and temporal consistency metrics. Each of these metrics has been designed to quantitatively assess generated media with respect to realism, consistency, and coherence at the feature and frame levels. GAN-based approaches, for example, may introduce training artifacts or regions of inconsistency, coupled with a coherence failure. On the other hand, state-of-the-art diffusion models may introduce artifacts and denoising and smoothing effects, but generally achieve a higher degree of texture consistency and fidelity. Quality metrics may vary across specific architectures, and investigators can infer the generative model, its iterations, and its training methodologies. Quality metrics can be employed to indicate temporal characteristics of the media, such as frame and coherence failures, abrupt changes, and facial expression inconsistencies.

Quality metrics, combined with deepfake neural fingerprints, watermarking, and provenance analysis, formulate an attribution framework that identifies deepfake media and aids forensic analysis (Delibiss & Wen, 1997).

5. DEVICE-LEVEL AND ENVIRONMENT ATTRIBUTION

Figure 3. Device-level traceability framework for attribution of AI-generated content

5.1 Metadata Analysis and Device Attribution

At a general level, metadata analysis is a critical aspect of device-level attribution. It describes the environment, software, and hardware used to create deepfake content. Although malicious actors have been known to edit/remove metadata to avoid forensic analysis, digital files often contain traces that can be highly valuable to an investigation. These may be timestamps, software used, codecs, renders, device information, platform information, and geolocation. All of these help reconstruct the environment in which the synthetic media was created.

For image and video deepfakes, EXIF metadata includes information about the image's color profile and resolution, packing history, device, and software. Similarly, encoding methods leave behind signatures, quantization tables, and traces of the software used. Tools such as DeepFaceLab, FaceSwap, Stable Diffusion, and the like often produce outputs with patterns that can be valuable in attribution. In the same way, audio deepfakes exhibit compression artifacts and can be traced to voice-cloning software. These may also include background noise, compression, and synchronization methods. As a result, metadata analysis can be a useful way to link synthetic media to the environment and software used to create them.

5.2 GPU/TPU Usage Signatures and Local Hardware Artifacts

Forensic investigators examine file structures and low-level computational artifacts to spot indicators beyond metadata. These indicators, referred to as "implicit metadata," include byte-level abnormalities, binary header irregularities, execution traces, and formatting discrepancies, which may describe the operating system, rendering framework, or the hardware setup used to generate the content. Evidence may include model fingerprints and provenance indicators to constrain generation environments. Highly specialized hardware accelerators are integral to modern generative AI systems. Among these are NVIDIA and AMD GPUs, as well as Google TPUs. Each hardware implementation has its own nuances in executing tensor operations and floating-point computations. Precision formats used in computations may include FP16, FP32, FP64, and the recently proposed bfloat16. Artifacts may be introduced into generated outputs due to these nuances and the framework's parallel processing and kernel execution techniques. An example of such artifacts is half-precision computation, which can yield rounding effects and numerical discrepancies compared to full-precision environments. Incorporation of hardware-specific acceleration frameworks, such as cuDNN, TensorRT, and ROCm, as well as XLA, further increases the variability of computational behavior and, in turn, the variability of the framework's outputs. These frameworks may also introduce slight variability in timing, rendering, and computational noise, all of which become part of the synthetic media. Although these signatures may be hard to detect directly, advanced forensic investigation techniques may help identify patterns associated with consumer-grade GPUs, cloud-based accelerators, high-performance workstations (HPW), and distributed inference systems. When combined with metadata and provenance information, hardware artifacts will help forensic investigators understand the physical and/or virtual infrastructure used to generate deepfake content.

5.3 Log Files, Rendering Pipelines, Cache, Memory Forensics

At the system level, logs provide critical evidence for device attribution. Applications that produce deepfakes usually maintain logs of training sessions, training configurations, and even details such as training progress and the parameters of the hardware and software used. Users of these applications usually attempt to clean up logs; however, these deleted logs may still be documented in temporary files, caches, swap files, and even memory. Logs may reveal information about which deepfake creation tools the user employed, which software and training datasets were used, and the hardware the user used. Rendering pipelines create a series of artifacts that are further processed. In face-swapping applications, preprocessing may include generating aligned face images, segmentation masks, and transformation matrices. Likewise, diffusion model workflows may contain intermediate states for denoising and sampling in the latent space. These intermediate artifacts may be cached in memory. From Intermediate states, digital forensics tools may be employed to understand content generation and the processes behind it. Memory forensics strengthens device attribution because RAM snapshots and memory dumps provide significant insights into which files were accessed, which processes were executed, and which interactions were made with the operating system during the generation of deepfakes. This can link the creation of synthetic media to specific users, devices, software, and even a specific time. In a legal setting, generation logs provide strong evidence of attribution because they document the process of deepfake generation rather than pre-existing media (Xu et al., 2017).

5.4 Network-Level Traces and Cloud Attribution

Network-level attribution involves analyzing interaction patterns across cloud services and the infrastructure that generates and disseminates deepfakes. Most cloud-based services used today to generate deepfakes rely on a distributed set of graphics processing units. Some of the services include Amazon Web Services (AWS), Windows Azure, and Google Cloud, among others. These services generate a lot of logs including details of API calls, authentication logs, access token logs, bandwidth logs, timestamps, and logs of interactions with the cloud services. While a significant number of actors attempt to conceal their identities through various anonymization methods, cloud service providers retain backend logs and service usage records, which may become available following a legal inquiry and cooperation among the parties involved. The analysis of these logs may assist in identifying the location, time, account, and environment in which the deepfake was executed and made available to the public. Network forensics aims to uncover the infrastructure that supports the distribution of multiple deepfakes. This encompasses the range of deceptive hosting services, content delivery networks (CDN), instant messaging services, and social media services. By integrating network-level, model-level, and device-level forensics, investigators can determine the vast digital ecosystem used by multiple actors for deepfake operations (Bakla, 2019).

6. ACTOR ATTRIBUTION AND CYBERCRIME INVESTIGATION

6.1 Associating Deepfake Activities with Threat Actors

Actor attribution aims to identify the potential individuals and/or organizations responsible for the creation and/or distribution of deepfake content. In contrast to device- and model-level attribution, which focus on the technical elements of deepfake content, actor attribution integrates behavioral, contextual, and intelligence-based elements to provide a comprehensive profile of the threat. Consequently, malicious activities based on deepfake technology can be associated with campaigns that sustain operational homogeneity, characterized by the use of the same software, the same language, similar targeting and grouping tactics, and the same dissemination and operational techniques used by known threat groups. In such cases, attribution based on deepfake technology involves integrating model fingerprints, metadata, generation and dissemination patterns, and cybercriminal activities. Often, investigators combine technical evidence with auxiliary evidence, such as social media evidence, telecommunications evidence, dark web transactions, cryptocurrency transactions, and time-related evidence. The alignment of time zones, languages, themes, and campaign objectives can provide substantial evidence supporting the rationale and identity of the threat actors. When integrating the aforementioned elements, sufficient attribution of deepfake-enabled fraud, cybercrime, and influence operations can be achieved to facilitate law enforcement and counterintelligence operations (Kuźnicka-Błaszkowska & Kostyuk, 2025).

6.2 OSINT, SOCMINT, and Digital Footprinting

Open-Source Intelligence and Social Media Intelligence are pivotal to actor attribution investigations. They allow the study of dissemination, online persona construction, and influence networks of deepfake campaigns. OSINT is the collection of information from publicly available resources. This includes news articles, online discussions, posts, forum or field domain registrations, video sharing websites, and leaks. Deepfake campaigns leave numerous digital traces, such as upload metadata, usernames, embedded links, publication time stamps, and platform-specific identifiers.SOCMINT expands upon OSINT by examining social media and analyzing the structure of social media networks. In social network analysis, investigators examine the paths through which information is disseminated, identify influential nodes, and identify coordinated activities to enhance the impact of social media posts. This type of investigation can expose bot networks, coordinated inauthentic behavior, and influence operations intended to broaden the dissemination of deepfake content. Digital Footprinting examines the traces left by users' technology use in online activities and complements OSINT and SOCMINT. Relevant observations include IP address patterns, browser fingerprints, device fingerprints, the use of URL shortening services, and records of API Calls. It is possible that users of VPNs and anonymization services can be identified from the digital traces they leave, as well as their posting and interaction patterns. Combined with OSINT and SOCMINT, Digital Footprinting provides a powerful and comprehensive investigative framework for attribution of synthetic media campaigns (Rajak & Shaw, 2021).

6.3 Dark-Web Supply Chains and Tool-Sales Patterns

An expanding marketplace for deepfake technology is the dark web. It sells tools, training datasets, and pretrained models as well as technologies to avoid detection. These underground systems support advanced supply chains that facilitate the creation and distribution of deepfake content online. Subscription services offered by some vendors are akin to cybercrime-as-a-service models. Vendors provide cloud access to fully automated services for deepfake creation, identity manipulation, and the creation of custom synthetic media. These vendors engage in commerce that may even provide useful evidence for attribution. They may employ identifiable communication, branding, and customer support styles, as well as consistent pricing and cryptocurrency payment methods. These techniques may enable investigators to attribute users of the marketplace and identify links between different market participants. Typical customer activity may even result in payment for escrow services, the creation of a visible trace on the blockchain, participation in encrypted communication, and other evidence of commercial activity relevant to attribution investigations. Studying these commercial trends can help law enforcement understand and investigate the cybercrime infrastructure of deepfakes.

6.4 Deepfake Fraud, Extortion, and Disinformation: Case Studies

The number of cases of deepfake technology being used for cybercrime, finance, and geopolitical purposes is numerous. One well-known case is the voice deepfake of an executive that tricked the victim organization's staff into making an unauthorized payment exceeding $200,000. This case was later investigated, and the authors were identified as members of a financially motivated cybercrime group that used voice synthesis in their business email compromise scheme. The use of voice deepfake technology was an innovative and sophisticated method that significantly improved the fraud's believability. Another abusive practice involves generating synthetic sexual content of victims using images that are available in the public domain. In these situations, investigators have reported that their preliminary findings focused on analyzing metadata, OSINT conducted at the platform level, and tracing the infrastructure to establish connections to activities in a darknet marketplace. About political campaigning and more specifically elections, deepfakes have been employed to psychologically manipulate voters, propagate lies, and damage trust in the system. For these purposes, the account has relied on analysis of the communication, modeling of the dissemination network, assessment of the infrastructure, and, at times, coordination of "influence" operations and foreign state activities. These cases require the design of comprehensive and innovative deepfake actor attribution systems to address the many social challenges posed by deepfakes. (Temara, 2024).

7. FORENSICS WORKFLOWS FOR DEEPFAKE ATTRIBUTION

7.1 Multi-Layer Attribution Architecture

Deepfake attribution requires a multi-layered forensic model with interlocking elements for each attribution layer (Model, Device, Network, User). A single layer is often insufficient. Sophisticated adversaries are often capable of manipulating or concealing individual elements. A multi-layered model allows investigators to combine multiple indicators, increasing the reliability of the findings. The first layer addresses model attribution. Here, investigators are concerned with the presence of structural artifacts, neural fingerprints, and watermarks, among other generation-specific signatures. The second layer focuses on citing devices and environments. For this layer, investigators analyze metadata, hardware remnants, memory traces, rendering pipelines, and system logs to reconstruct the environment wherein the content was created virtually. From these, investigators can learn about the operating systems, hardware, and software used in the generation process and determine the cloud infrastructure used for it. The third layer is network targeting. This includes analysis of cloud service interactions, communication, and API usage patterns, traffic logs, and infrastructure distribution related to the creation and/or distribution of deepfake content. This layer is especially useful when remote inference services or a distributed cloud computing facility are used to generate synthetic media. Lastly, the fourth layer focuses on target identification, which combines technical evidence with information gathered through OSINT, SOCMINT, deep-web investigations, behavioral analysis, and contextual information. This layer aims to link the technical evidence to individuals, groups, or organizations that have executed the operation. By combining evidence from all four layers, forensic investigators can determine the environment in which deepfake campaigns were created, the distribution pathways, and the human actors involved, thereby creating a comprehensive evidentiary framework for assigning responsibility.

Figure 4. Hierarchical attribution framework for deepfake source identification

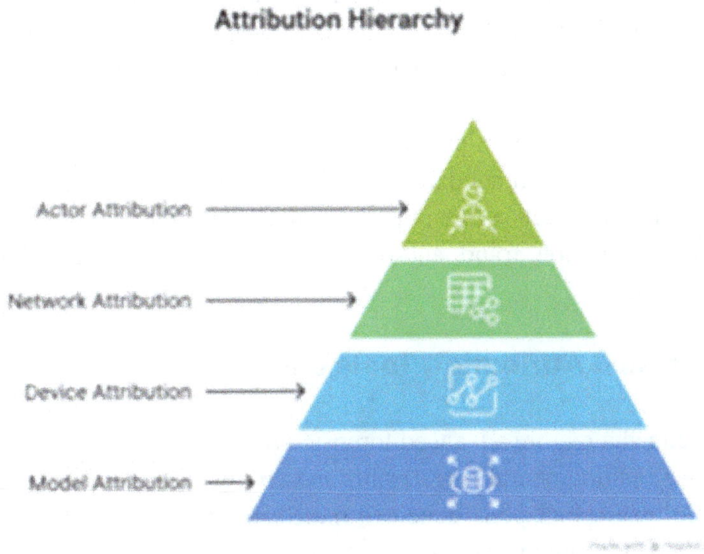

7.2 Evidence Acquisition and Preservation

Inquiries regarding the attribution of a deepfake necessitate the careful collection and preservation of evidence. Subsequent digital forensics findings will capture the integrity of the original evidence only if that evidence is authenticated and reproducible. The preservation of digital media files occurs during evidence collection by justifying the forensic preservation of the original media files and implementing post hoc measures to prevent intervention in the media files and their metadata. The use of write-blockers further supports the integrity of the evidence, the creation of hash values (e.g., SHA-256), and extensive chain-of-custody documentation. Once evidence is collected, investigators gather digital media along with related documentation, including but not limited to metadata, logs, thumbnails, temporary files, cache files, processing results, and intermediates. Video deepfakes often include frame extractions, motion vectors, and temporal codecs as digital artifacts. When conducting audio investigations, waveform and spectrogram analysis are often accompanied by acoustic markers. When deepfake content is captured from the Internet, investigators gather web archives, platform metadata, upload histories, and comment and Internet Protocol trace systems.

Preservation of volatile evidence is of great concern, as rapid collection is the only way to ensure it is not lost. This type of evidence typically includes RAM snapshots, GPU memory dumps, and the active state of processes and logs. When investigating a cloud-based system, the forensic investigator may need to capture snapshots of virtual machines and logs of the cloud system and infrastructure, as offered by the cloud service provider. All collections must be substantiated by a precise timestamp for the action, along with a documented, verifiable trail of the collection. Preservation activities should utilize established methods, such as ISO/IEC 27037, SWGDE recommendations, and NIST guidelines. Standards help maintain the integrity of evidence for court cases and reduce the likelihood of disputes caused by contamination, fraud, and/or failure to adhere to preservation methods (Siegel et al., 2021)

7.3. AI-Assisted Attribution Tools and Automation

Synthetic media require advanced forensic investigation methods using AI. For example, investigating neural fingerprints and family classifications of generative models while looking for inconsistencies is much easier for machines than for humans. Tools that use large training sets, such as CNNs, transformers, and frequency-domain classifiers, investigate artifacts left by model families specific to GANs, Diffusion models, and multimodal systems. Automated forensic platforms also aid specialists in the amalgamation of various sources of evidence, such as audio, video, text documents, their metadata, and network-related logs. Using automated interactive dashboards, analysts can visualize connections, spot trends, and streamline workflows to assign the appropriate actors. At the same time, the more automated the system is, the more necessary human oversight will be. The more expert the investigator, the better the system will assess algorithmic outputs, contextual factors, and the extent and significance of technical findings, while mitigating false positives. For this reason, and in this context, artificial intelligence is an augmentation that improves the system. (Thing, 2023).

7.4 Correlating Technical, Behavioral, and Contextual Evidence

The primary aim of deepfake attribution is to construct an attribution narrative that is both coherent and justifiable by linking technical, behavioral, and contextual evidence. Technical evidence may include synthetic media's neural fingerprints, metadata traces, and hardware provenance. Technical evidence may also include attribution calculation parameters and supporting computational evidence. Incorporating contextual evidence improves attribution by considering geopolitical contexts, target selection, sociocultural factors, information amplification techniques, and multiple layers of contextual framing. Investigators can develop a holistic attribution framework through an interdisciplinary examination of the fragmented information. Cross-domain correlation increases the evidential reliability of information and attribution by removing spurious relationships and reinforcing findings through multiple independent elements. Consequently, attribution results are more likely to withstand critical evaluation in judicial, intelligence, and policy contexts (Cassia et al., 2025).

7.5 Practical Deployment and Evaluation Considerations

The practical implementation of deepfake attribution systems demands a tradeoff between the systems' technical performance, legal integrity, and operational feasibility. Evaluating standard performance metrics, such as accuracy, precision, recall, F1-score, and false-positive rate, provides an objective assessment of attribution systems' performance. Particularly concerning is the taxonomic error; therefore, it is especially pertinent to minimize false-positive rates, as this error also carries severe financial and reputational consequences. To evaluate attribution systems across various contexts, operational systems need to process large collections of digital media while maintaining performance. Systems also need to be able to sustain their performance. Benchmark datasets that include a range of synthetic media generated by Generative Adversarial Networks (GANs), diffusion models, and other multimodal systems are vital for this. Attribution frameworks must resist adversarial and intentional system degradation, metadata manipulation, anti-forensic techniques, and other strategies to circumvent detection systems. In legal contexts, systems must provide explanations of attribution results and meet the needs of investigators, legal practitioners, judges, and jurors. Forensic systems that support transparent and interpretable findings will evidence admissibility. The successful implementation of deepfake attribution systems will rely on developing systems that are legally defensible, explainable, and robust.

8. LEGAL AND EVIDENTIAL CONSIDERATIONS

While notable improvements have been made in the forensic attribution of deepfake technologies, numerous technical, legal, and operational barriers remain. Given the advancements in generative models, which continue to produce more realistic synthetic media while embedding less detectable artifacts, attribution is becoming more probabilistic than certain. The use of similar systems, identical or closely related pre-trained models, and shared training resources may generate outputs that are virtually indistinguishable. Because of this, attribution will typically be derived from the presence of multiple independent indicators rather than from an unambiguous artifact. Forensics is often hindered further by the use of anti-forensic measures. These may include metadata adjustments, adversarial perturbations, lossy compression, various anonymization techniques, and intentional removal of artifacts. Anti-forensic measures are employed to diminish forensic evidence and lower confidence in attribution. Accordingly, any attribution becomes informative and meaningful only when placed within the context of the broader investigation and supported by as much evidence as possible. From a legal and ethical standpoint, incorrect attribution damages reputation, can lead to wrongful attribution, and can result in legal repercussions. For these reasons, the results of a forensic analysis need to be communicated openly, with as much certainty as possible, and with a clear identification of gaps and opposing views. The deepfake technologies under consideration are often multinational and operate across multiple jurisdictions; therefore, research into attribution methods for these technologies must remain focused on providing clear, unambiguous, and trustworthy attribution.

8.1 Authenticity and Reliability

Authenticity and reliability remain among the most substantial legal constraints regarding the admissibility of deepfake evidence. Courts must evaluate whether a piece of digital evidence is a genuine, unaltered product of a forensic process grounded in reliable science. According to most classical methods for evaluating evidence, one must demonstrate the integrity of the evidence, and the forensic methods must demonstrate validity and replicability. Synthetic media that closely replicate authentic recordings pose a particular challenge for legal attribution. An example of such media is deepfakes. To address this challenge, forensic scientists have begun employing techniques such as neural fingerprints, watermark retrieval, provenance and manipulation tracking, and attribution modeling. The courts have begun to expect attribution methods to satisfy the Daubert standards, which include elements such as a known error rate, testability, reproducibility, and the method's overall acceptance within the relevant scientific community. As a result, techniques for deepfake attribution must be documented extensively, leave a trail for others to follow, and be published in peer-reviewed literature, where expert testimony is necessary to explain the technique's findings in a way comprehensible to judges and juries. With the continued rapid evolution of synthetic media, the legal system will have to revise evidentiary standards to meet the new challenges posed by digital media and forensic attribution technologies (Delfino, 2025).

Attribution results must communicate confidence and uncertainty. Forensic examination reports should offer an assessment based on the evidence and be supported by technical, behavioral, and contextual clues.

8.2 Reliability Checklist

1. Verification methods and evidence sources are documented.
2. Whenever applicable, a known error rate is reported.
3. Repeatability and reproducibility are reported.
4. Confidence levels are reported.
5. Alternative methods were considered and explained.
6. Limitations and uncertainties are reported.

Findings are reported using validated forensic methods published in peer-reviewed literature.

The checklist offers a transparent accounting of attribution methods, which assists courts in evaluating the reliability and admissibility of attribution evidence. Verifiable chains of custody are necessary for the admissibility of deepfake evidence. A chain of custody spells out every step taken with evidence, from collection to analysis and every transfer and storage step in between. The lifecycle of any piece of digital evidence should be thoroughly documented. In the case of digital evidence, maintaining its integrity is indispensable. Whenever evidence is transferred, the handler must document the time, date, and their own name. Alongside evidence, an SHA-256 cryptographic hash must always be provided. These ensure that the evidence provided in court is the original evidence collected. In the case of online/deepfake evidence, the chain of custody must also include: volatile digital artifacts, web archives, and contextual metadata. The integrity of digital evidence is of utmost importance for its use in court. While society is beginning to recognize the peril posed by deepfake technology, many gaping holes in policy and governance facilitate its use. In many areas, the absence of legally codified definitions of synthetic media results in legally vacant, unaccountable, and unregulated domains. The current legal infrastructure provides frameworks for addressing injury caused by misinformation and defamation, privacy violations, fraud, etc. However, the current frameworks do very little to address model, governance, and developer concerns, as well as the broader issues of Generative AI systems.

The transnational aspect of deepfake technologies creates challenges for regulation. Synthetic material could be created in one region, sent across multiple different servers, and impact a variety of regions. Consequently, several different nations working together are complicated by inconsistencies in their laws. No governance model has been created to define a system for the responsible use of generative AI technologies and to establish standards for transparency, attribution, content verification, and validation. Legislatures, governments, tech producers, and intergovernmental organizations are necessary for the proper creation of governance systems. This involves establishing policy frameworks that support model transparency, attribution, development accountability, and the protection of innovation. The gaps in these policies must be addressed to reinforce trust in virtual systems and mitigate the threats posed by advanced synthetic media (Łabuz, 2023).

8.3 Resilience and Attribution in Real-Life Scenarios

In real-life scenarios, deepfakes usually undergo many changes before investigators see them. Common alterations include compression, re-encoding, resizing, cropping, screen recording, platform optimization, and content redistribution. All of these alterations affect the quality and amount of available forensic evidence for attribution. Certain forensic evidence, such as neural fingerprints, frequency-domain artifacts, behavioral traces, and dissemination patterns, can remain even after some alterations. However, metadata records, watermarks, and provenance information can be lost or diminished altogether during alteration. Because of this, attribution becomes more difficult as alterations become more extensive. In highly altered or partially damaged media, forensic evidence may be lacking or of poor quality. In these situations, investigators should not make too many assumptions and should express the level of uncertainty. The attribution of evidence that really does not exist should be considered a legitimate forensic outcome. Attribution of evidence should be done carefully and take the freedom of available evidence into account. This minimizes the risk of incorrect attribution and maintains the integrity of forensic evidence.

9. FUTURE DIRECTIONS AND RESEARCH ROADMAP

9.1 Global Model Registries and Authentication Protocols

Deepfake attribution systems are becoming increasingly sophisticated, and the best is yet to come. These systems are predicted to implement global model registries.

These registries will likely contain detailed descriptions of generative AI architectures, as well as histories, training data sets, developer names, and cryptographic hashes. Forensic analysts would have registries to reference their attribution results. At that point, analysts could improve model-level attributions. Authentication protocols would work in tandem with registries, implementing digital signatures and cryptographic certificates. Content would be generated with automated verifications. Forensic analysts could reference robust systems of secure provenance and verifiable content that provide frameworks for establishing trustworthy content and validating synthetic media. This body of work will benefit in particular from international co-operation. The synthetic media landscape would improve digital trust and systems for cross-border investigations. Additionally, it would provide an early governing structure for synthetic media ecosystems (Romero-Moreno, 2025).

9.2 Standardized Forensic Metadata

Another area of focus is the standardization of forensic metadata. Metadata should not be disjointed or inconsistent, as this can make attribution unreliable. In constructing a standardized metadata framework, model architectures, generation parameters, training datasets, software versions, computational environments, and content generation timestamps could be structured. Integrating synthetic media with such metadata would improve the tracing of origins, validation of accuracy, and forensic analysis. Standardization of metadata would also facilitate interoperability among forensic tools and promote automated processes to detect, classify, and identify synthetic media across diverse environments and multiple legal jurisdictions. Standardization of forensic metadata would likely be the core element of advanced attribution and the creation of trustworthy synthetic media ecosystems in the future (Gan et al., 2025).

9.3 Joint Governance in Attribution

The global reach of deepfake technologies means that a joint governance model is necessary. Governments, industry, academia, law enforcement, and international organizations must be part of the joint governance model. No single stakeholder has the expertise or resources to deal with the challenges of synthetic media in isolation. A joint governance model relies most on the participation of technology companies. They have the knowledge necessary to improve attribution through model governance and the responsible use of artificial intelligence. Effective joint governance also relies on the collaborative use of research, harmonized law, and response to cross-border activities. International joint governance on attribution, transparency, responsibility, and authentication of synthetic media would help establish effective governance to address the challenges posed by deepfakes and other synthetic media.

9.4 Emerging Challenges and the Future of Attribution Tools

The future of deepfake attribution looks difficult. Sophisticated artificial technologies present a new, difficult threat, including the real-time generation of deepfakes, autonomous deepfake agents, decentralized deepfake training, multimodal deepfake agents, and sophisticated models that will evade forensic detection. All of the aforementioned will create difficulty for current attribution and forensic capacity. Next-generation attribution systems may combine hybrid artificial intelligence, multi-layer forensic fusion, and continuous monitoring of huge portions of the public domain. Future systems may combine explainable AI, adaptive watermarking, blockchain and provenance systems, threat-intelligence automation, and beyond to improve the attribution systems. Research and development of self-verifying generative systems that create content while embedding evidence and traceable, trustworthy provenance may also be warranted. As synthetic media technologies develop, forensic science will need to develop with them. Integrative thinking will be needed to combine advanced technologies, new legal frameworks, and new operational forms to maintain the ability to establish the truth of matters, especially in complex digital situations.

10. CONCLUSION

The integration of deepfake technologies is one of the most serious threats to digital trust, cybersecurity, and legal accountability. Forensic attribution goes beyond detection to identify the generative models and actors behind the infrastructure and synthetic media. This technology shows an immense potential to alleviate the risks posed by artificial intelligence. This chapter outlines an attribution framework that includes investigations at the model, device, network, and actor levels. When combined with digital forensics, attribution aids the accountability and legal value of digital investigations. Methods such as neural fingerprinting, provenance tracking, watermarking, metadata hardware attribution, and AI forensics help identify the sources of synthetic media. There are many obstacles to attribution. The rapid pace of generative AI and anti-forensics, along with the limitations of current governance and jurisdictional issues, makes attribution difficult. To combat these issues, AI and platform developers must impose stricter restrictions and improve international collaboration. Forensic systems that support attribution, model registries that enable interoperability, and model systems that provide standardized forensic metadata will be priorities. The systems must also provide a basis for international and universal thresholds of evidence for investigations of synthetic media. Partnerships among researchers, industry, and law enforcement may provide the necessary systems to stabilize attribution methods and ensure security against threats. The ability to attribute deepfakes will help maintain the integrity of digital media, consumer trust, and the value of forensic investigations. Reliable attribution methods will protect the authenticity of the digital media and the integrity of digital societies.

REFERENCES

Amerini, I., Barni, M., Battiato, S., Bestagini, P., Boato, G., Bruni, V., Caldelli, R., De Natale, F., De Nicola, R., Guarnera, L., Mandelli, S., Majid, T., Marcialis, G. L., Micheletto, M., Montibeller, A., Orrù, G., Ortis, A., Perazzo, P., Puglisi, G., & Vitulano, D. (2025). Deepfake media forensics: Status and future challenges. *Journal of Imaging*, *11*(3), 73. DOI: 10.3390/jimaging11030073 PMID: 40137185

Amrouche, F., Erickson, P. A., Park, J. W., & Varnhagen, S. (2021). Performance comparison of a Wankel SI engine fuelled with gasoline and ethanol blended hydrogen. In *Proceedings* (pp. 315–321). DOI: 10.1007/978-981-15-6595-3_41

Bakla, A. (2019). A mixed-methods study of tailor-made animated cartoons in teaching punctuation in EFL writing. *ReCALL*, *31*(1), 75–91. DOI: 10.1017/S0958344018000046

Cao, H., Tan, C., Gao, Z., Xu, Y., Chen, G., Heng, P. A., & Li, S. Z. (2024). A survey on generative diffusion models. *IEEE Transactions on Knowledge and Data Engineering*, *36*(7), 2814–2830. DOI: 10.1109/TKDE.2024.3361474

Cassia, M., Guarnera, L., Casu, M., Zangara, I., & Battiato, S. (2025). *Deepfake forensic analysis: Source dataset attribution and legal implications of synthetic media manipulation* [Preprint]. arXiv. https://arxiv.org/pdf/2505.11110

Delfino, R. A. (2025). Loyola Law School [Legal studies research paper]. DOI: 10.13140/RG.2.2.12632.61447

Gan, Z., Liu, C., Tang, Y., Wang, B., Wang, W., & Zhang, X. (2025). *GenPTW: In-generation image watermarking for provenance tracing and tamper localisation* [Preprint]. arXiv. https://arxiv.org/pdf/2504.19567

Hancock, J. T., & Bailenson, J. N. (2021). The social impact of deepfakes. *Cyberpsychology, Behavior, and Social Networking*, *24*(3), 149–152. DOI: 10.1089/cyber.2021.29208.jth PMID: 33760669

Heidari, A., Jafari Navimipour, N., Dag, H., & Unal, M. (2024). Deepfake detection using deep learning methods: A systematic and comprehensive review. *Wiley Interdisciplinary Reviews: Data Mining and Knowledge Discovery, 14*(2), Article e1520. DOI: 10.1002/widm.1520

Kuźnicka-Błaszkowska, D., & Kostyuk, N. (2025). Emerging need to regulate deepfakes in international law: The Russo–Ukrainian war as an example. *Journal of Cybersecurity*, *11*(1), 8. Advance online publication. DOI: 10.1093/cybsec/tyaf008

Łabuz, M. (2023). Regulating deep fakes in the Artificial Intelligence Act. *Applied Cybersecurity and Internet Governance*, *2*(1), 252–291. DOI: 10.60097/ACIG/162856

Li, P., Zhao, H., Liu, Q., Tang, P., & Zhang, L. (2024). TellMeTalk: Multimodal-driven talking face video generation. *Computers & Electrical Engineering*, *114*, 109049. Advance online publication. DOI: 10.1016/j.compeleceng.2023.109049

Liu, C., Zhu, T., Zhao, Y., Zhang, J., & Zhou, W. (2024). Disentangling different levels of GAN fingerprints for task-specific forensics. *Computer Standards & Interfaces*, *89*, 103825. Advance online publication. DOI: 10.1016/j.csi.2023.103825

Rajak, M., & Shaw, K. (2021). An extension of technology acceptance model for mHealth user adoption. *Technology in Society*, *67*, 101800. Advance online publication. DOI: 10.1016/j.techsoc.2021.101800

Romero-Moreno, F. (2025). Deepfake detection in generative AI: A legal framework proposal to protect human rights. *Computer Law & Security Review*, *58*, 106162. Advance online publication. DOI: 10.1016/j.clsr.2025.106162

Sandoval, M. P., de Almeida Vau, M., Solaas, J., & Rodrigues, L. (2024). Threat of deepfakes to the criminal justice system: A systematic review. *Crime Science*, *13*(1), 41. Advance online publication. DOI: 10.1186/s40163-024-00239-1

Siegel, D., Kraetzer, C., Seidlitz, S., & Dittmann, J. (2021). Media forensics considerations on DeepFake detection with hand-crafted features. *Journal of Imaging*, *7*(7), 108. Advance online publication. DOI: 10.3390/jimaging7070108 PMID: 39080896

Singh, S., & Dhumane, A. (2025). Unmasking digital deceptions: An integrative review of deepfake detection, multimedia forensics, and cybersecurity challenges. *MethodsX*, *15*, 103632. Advance online publication. DOI: 10.1016/j.mex.2025.103632 PMID: 41080432

Suleiman, N. A. (2025). Deepfake-as-a-Service: The next challenge for enterprise cybersecurity. *Journal of Technology and Systems*, *7*(3), 47–59. DOI: 10.47941/jts.2752

Temara, S. (2024). The dark web and cybercrime: Identifying threats and anticipating emerging trends.

Thing, V. L. L. (2023). Deepfake detection with deep learning: Convolutional neural networks versus transformers. In *Proceedings of the 2023 IEEE International Conference on Cyber Security and Resilience (CSR)* (pp. 246–253). DOI: 10.1109/CSR57506.2023.10225004

Xu, H., Tang, X., Sun, H., Zhao, H., & Li, M. (2017). Conductivity of silver and copper film printed by particle-free reactive inks. In *18th International Conference on Electronic Packaging Technology (ICEPT)* (pp. 1470–1473). DOI: 10.1109/ICEPT.2017.8046713

Yang, T., Huang, Z., Cao, J., Li, L., & Li, X. (2022). Deepfake network architecture attribution. *Proceedings of the AAAI Conference on Artificial Intelligence*, *36*(4), 4662–4670. DOI: 10.1609/aaai.v36i4.20391

Yu, N., Davis, L., & Fritz, M. (2019). Attributing fake images to GANs: Learning and analysing GAN fingerprints. In *Proceedings of the IEEE International Conference on Computer Vision* (pp. 7555–7565). DOI: 10.1109/ICCV.2019.00765

Chapter 7
Future of Synthetic Media:
Toward a Trustworthy Digital Ecosystem

Deepak Gupta
http://orcid.org/0000-0003-3929-1362
Institute of Technology and Management, Gwalior, India

Mangubek Urazmetov
http://orcid.org/0009-0004-2155-7809
Urgench State University, Urgench, Uzbekistan

Azamat Abdurakhmanov
Termez University of Economics and Service, Termez, Uzbekistan

Yakitjon Turdiyeva
Termez University of Economics and Service, Termez, Uzbekistan

Valisher Sapayev
http://orcid.org/0000-0002-6751-5864
Mamun University, Khiva, Uzbekistan

Nilufar Rajabova
Pedagogical Institute, Uzbekistan

ABSTRACT

The proliferation of synthetic media technologies, particularly deepfakes, presents unprecedented challenges to digital trust, democratic institutions, and individual privacy. This chapter examines the trajectory of deepfake evolution through 2030, analyzing the convergence of advanced generative AI architectures, emerging regulatory frameworks, and societal adaptation mechanisms that will shape a trustworthy digital ecosystem. Drawing upon interdisciplinary research spanning computer vision, digital forensics, policy studies, and social psychology, we present a comprehensive framework for understanding how stakeholders—governments, technology platforms, civil society, and individuals—can collaboratively establish trust in an age of synthetic content. Our analysis reveals three critical dynamics: the accelerating sophistication of generative models outpacing detection capabil-

DOI: 10.4018/979-8-3373-8292-0.ch007

ities, the fragmented yet rapidly evolving regulatory landscape spanning the EU AI Act to emerging national frameworks, and the paradoxical effects of deepfake awareness on public trust.

1. INTRODUCTION

1.1 Historical Background and Technological Development

Sophisticated technologies for the synthesis of media types constitute a paradigm shift in the production and perception of truth in digital spaces as described by scholars Chesney & Citron (2019). Deepfakes – audio, video and images created using artificial intelligence and now accessible tools that make events that never happened look remarkably real – are from research curios to readily available tools that can produce content that could not distinguish itself from real footage. This technological democratisation has far-reaching impact for individual privacy, democratic processes, national security and the basic epistemic infrastructure that is fundamental to any society.

Synthetic media technologies have evolved at a very rapid pace since generative adversarial networks (GANs) were developed in 2014. Initial deepfake versions were very technical and demanded substantial expertise and computing power, keeping them out of the reach of lesser-known personae and research organizations. With the democratization of machine learning frameworks and improvements in consumer hardware skills, however, complex synthesis devices are now widely available.

1.2 The Context and Dimensions of the Impact Today

The extent of this challenge has recently been shown through empirical studies. The results of the survey showed that 1.8% of respondents reported the private use of a synthetic intimate image (NSII) for them and 2.2% for others, which is a high rate of victimization compared to other NSII victimizations in the literature (range: 1% to 27%). This data represents millions of people around the world who are being impacted by the misuse of synthetic media, which indicates the direct consequences on people's lives. At the same time, the findings from public perception studies show mixed sentiments with 47 percent positive attitudes linked with fascination with technological capabilities, and 37 percent negative attitudes focused on issues of misinformation and privacy issues Zhang et al. (2025).

There's been an explosion in synthetic media production scale. According to industry research, more than 143,000 deepfake videos were released online in 2023, a 900% rise from the total recorded during 2019. Of these, some 96% harboured non-consensual intimate imagery, highlighting a focus of harmful application opportunities, despite the that there are legitimate creative and education-focused models.

1.3 The Systemic Implications of Trust and Democracy

Synthetic media harms are more than just harms to particular individuals; they imperil the epistemic pillars of democratic society. No longer can it be assumed that the evidence is the same when the evidence is audiovisual in nature. There are fundamental issues for institutions relying on verifiable documentation. The rules of evidence existing under the law should be rethought, the way to verify legal information needs in journalism has to be rethought, and the democratic system has to be adapted to the possibility of manipulation in elections via synthetic content.

1.4 A Definition of the Trustworthy Digital Ecosystem

Digital trust is effected by a conceptual framework. In a sound digital environment for synthetic media, three core needs must be met: (1) The preservation of legitimate innovation and creative expression; (2) individuals and institutions protection from harmful manipulation; and (3) public trust in apparent evidence of the trustworthiness of digital media. Technical infrastructure for authentication of content; regulatory frameworks, covering specific harms, without impeding innovation; and social structures to face the uncertainty about media authenticity.

Sustainable use of digital media functions on a number of layered concepts. At the perceptual level, humans have learned to accept sensory input especially the conjoining of the senses of hearing and sight as proof of reality. These are deepfakes because they employ this cognitive architecture to generate signals that produce real or 'realistically real' perceptual experiences. On an institutional level, recordings have been the basis of evidence historically for media and law enforcement and for democratic processes.

1.5 The Key Role of the Stakeholder Ecosystem and Interdependencies

The synthetic media landscape is a complex of actors that have different interests and capacities. Content creators produce the tangible content that can be amplified with AI. Content developers construct the AI algorithms and devices behind content synthesis. Platform operators control over distribution channels, and the implementation of content moderation policies. Legal structures and controls are set up by the regulators. Civil societies push for the causes of the marginalized and democracy. Individually users have created and consumed synthetic content, and individually they have made decisions that collectively influence technology uptake and social norms.

There is complex interdependency amongst these stakeholders, which makes governance challenging. While developers rely on platform distribution, they face regulatory challenges as well. Platforms are aimed to hit a sweet balance between user engagement and legal compliance and the concerns of advertisers. Promoting innovations is a challenge for regulators who have to ensure they are not counterproductive for prevention of harm in fighting the regulatory battle within the boundaries of the constitution.

1.6 Trust Mechanisms and Authentication Paradigms

In the past, consumers based their trust of uncertainty on the fact that there are institutional filters that allowed or disallowed information, such as journalism, editing and broadcast professionals. This gatekeeping approach has been disrupted by the democratisation of content creation and distribution, and new content authenticity and credibility mechanisms are needed to restore this approach.

Three major types of authentication have resulted: reactive detection-based on content analy-sis in the search for manipulation artifacts; proactive authentication where verified provenance chains are formed; and distributed (collective intelligence) based authentication, where the intelligence is distributed across the community of users evaluating content. Both have their merits as well as drawbacks, meaning that healthy trust systems will likely need to be hybrid, incorporating several implementations of various trust models.

2. LITERATURE REVIEW AND THEORETICAL FOUNDATIONS

2.1 The Architecture of Digital Trust

2.1.1 Conceptual Foundations of Trust in Digital Systems

Díaz-Rodríguez et al. (2023) identify five Dimensions of trustworthy AI systems: Techni-cal robustness, Explainability, Human agency, Privacy protection and Fairness. When these dimensions apply to synthetic media, they imply specific requirements: abstracting from manip-ulation type for detection, ensuring verifiable provenance, maintaining meaningful control over consumption of content, ensuring verification while preventing disclosure of sensitive content information, and governance protections of vulnerable communities.

2.1.2 The Use of Trust Mechanisms in Mediated Environments

The research of computer-mediated communication notes that there are three main mechanisms of trust: institutional (trust based on formal commitment and monitoring); calculative (rational weighing of incentives and risks); and relational (trusting due to interaction and reputation). All three mechanisms are simultaneously targeted by synthetic media environments.

When traditional gateholders such as news outlets and media platforms, and the legal system, cannot reliably determine if the content is authentic or manipulated, they lose some of their trust. In cases where the expenses and likelihood of manipulation are nebulous to users, it becomes onerous to establish a calculative trust in the algorithms. Synthetic media makes impersonation and manipulation of identity possible, posing a challenge to relational trust.

2.1.3 Epistemic Dimensions of Media Trust

In addition to interpersonal and institutional trust, synthetic media also impacts epistemic trust (confidence in reliability of knowledge and evidence). If it is possible to fabricate convincing visual and auditory recordings, there is need for new models for the societies to establish common understanding about events and facts.

2.2 The Liar's Dividend and Epistemic Uncertainty

2.2.1 Comparative Conceptual Development and Empirical Validation

The "liar's dividend" is a concept introduced by Chesney and Citron (2019), which holds that bad actors can make it too easy to deny the reality of the evidence as possibly fabricated due to its ability to be detected. But it is not quite a straightforward picture from empirical studies in recent times. Experimental research suggests that deep news creates uncertainty, and viewers are not sure whether it is true or false information, but this does not mean that viewers are misled, as the deep news will not actually deceive them Hwang et al. (2021).

It is this uncertainty, though, and not any particular case of deception that will be more corrosive of democratic discourse. Significant studies have reported that the viewing of deepfakes leads to a greater general loss of trust in news on social media platforms, indicating that the greatest threat is that such exposures degrade overall trust in news and not individual incidences of lies or distorted information Kang & Valadez (2025). Overall, the results of the meta-analytic evidence confirm that the correlation remains consistent across deepfake types and sample groups – however, education in media literacy is found to moderate the correlation.

2.2.2 Psychological Mechanisms and Cognitive Biases

There are many cognitive biases and heuristics involved in the psychological processes that drive the 'liar's dividend' phenomenon. Availability bias leads to an overestimate of the prevalence of deepfakes and results in inappropriate skepticism of authentic content following exposure to examples of deepfakes. Confirmation bias leads to motivated reasoning: rejecting unwanted evidence, "might be manipulated."

Cognitive psychology research shows that uncertainty about authenticity of information causes different cognitive processing than certainty about falseness of information. When ambiguous information is presented, its processing is less expanded and has less impact on attitudes and behaviors.

2.3 Evolution of Technologies: From GANs to Diffusion Models

2.3.1 The Foundation Era: Generative Adversarial Networks

Since the first emergent ability of generative adversarial networks (GANs) to swap faces in 2017, much has changed in the deepfake landscape. Progress with early implementations of AE-Ds on small datasets yielded encouraging results, but were plagued by artifacts and the lack of subject and condition diversity.

GAN-related techniques took a very quick advance due to architectural advancements like progressive growing, spectral normalization, and attention mechanisms. The instability of the training, mode collapse and inconsistency of quality however severely restricted their use for meaningful tasks. These restrictions led to the use of alternative generative paradigms.

2.3.2 The Contemporary Paradigm: Diffusion Models

Though the GAN approach is still common, the diffusion approach has taken a prominent stage for high quality synthesis Li et al. (2023). The above-mentioned architectures are variations of the models that can be obtained from DALL-E, Stable Diffusion, and Midjourney, which have generated less arf and more coherent results than traditional GAN models. Research has shown that diffusion-based face generation methods offer superiority over GAN methods in terms of preserving identity and making style transfer.

Diffusion models consist of unfolded denoising processes that coarsely de-noise such that the content starts to take shape. Though it may be more costly at inference time, this is a better way to train than the adversarial training approach, allowing for better stability and quality consistency. Rapid adoption in commercial uses has been propelled by the quality to cost ratio.

2.4 Detection Issues and Technological Limitations

2.4.1 The Generalization Problem

Currently, researchers have successfully proposed a few detection networks that show high accuracy scores on various typical datasets, such as the space-frequency interactive convolution network (SF-CNN) proposed by Guo et al. (2024), which achieves an accuracy rate of 98.7% on FaceForensics++. However, it fails to achieve high accuracy when being tested on content of different types and creation methods.

This generalization challenge arises due to the basic asymmetric relationship between generation-detection. Perceptual models can be optimized for perceptual realism and might even use adversarial methods to avoid specific detection methods. In the case of detection model, however, they have to cater for an infinite number of manipulation variations to achieve high precision without false positives that would destroy the confidence in authentic content.

According to Gong and Li (2024), current deepfake detection methods can be classified into three broad categories: exploiting pixel-level differences (spatial domain analysis), compression artifacts (frequency domain analysis), and between frames (temporal domain analysis). Their considerations show, however, that detection models which were well optimized for a specific manipulation type tend to not perform well on new manipulation types.

2.4.2 Adversarial Robustness and Watermarking

Awareness of the limitations of detection has encouraged the study of pro-active instead of reactive methods. Watermarking methods make sure detectable watermarks are included in synthetic content during its generation, which could permit identification even if there are no visual watermarks. Additionally, as shown by Zhao et al. (2023), fundamental weaknesses generated by the presence of adversarial post-processing make it possible for state-of-the-art watermarks to be bypassed, albeit with some degradation in visual quality.

Adversarial robustness problem is a deep challenge of adversarial machine learning. The attacker with white box access to detection models can optimize imperceptible perturbations which lead to misclassification. High success rates can be had with deployed systems even for black-box attacks based on query analysis.

The aforementioned vulnerabilities indicate that technical solutions can't fully address the authentication issue. To be successful, strong authentication systems need to combine technical elements with procedural, legal and social mechanisms of verification.

3. METHODOLOGY

3.1 Research Design and Analytical Framework

3.1.1 Mixed-Methods Approach

This chapter is based on the mixed methods stages of systematic literature review, regulatory document analysis and scenario planning. The research design involves three levels of analysis, micro, meso and macro, encompassing the individual response to synthetic media, institutional adaptations and a societal trajectory respectively.

The mixed-methods design allows for triangulation from multiple data types, including: empirical data resulting from controlled experiments, observational data resulting from deploy-ment studies, regulatory data resulting from analysis of policy documents and predictive data using scenario planning. This approach strengthens results and conclusions in comparison with individual method studies.

3.1.2 Temporal Scope and Prediction Methodology

The timeframes presented here span the present state analysis, prediction and into 2030. This allows analysis of short-term developments and the understanding of difficulties and uncertainties in longer-term forecasts. The idea for the prediction methodology is based on already existing methods for scenario planning in other domains, in particular the Shell model for the analysis of energy markets that has been successful in the analysis of complex sociotechnical systems.

3.1.3 Comparative Case Study Integration

The research design consists of comparative case studies in various application contexts, techno-logical settings and jurisdictions. A comparison of approaches is carried out across jurisdictions on EU and US markets, as well as in the Asian markets. Technological comparison studies the various ways of generating and detecting technology. In Application comparison, it will look at various applications, from creative uses to malicious use.

3.2 Literature Review Protocol

3.2.1 Search Strategy and Database Selection

Literature review was conducted using PRISMA guidelines, using the databases IEEE Xplore, ACM Digital Library, Web of Science, Scopus and SSRN for the peer-reviewed publications, related to deep fake technology, detection, regulation, and societal impact covering the last five years (2021-2025). Some common keywords used were "deepfake," "synthetic media," "AI regulation," "digital trust," "content authenticity," and similar variations.

The search strategy used Boolean operators to identify relevant literature alongside remaining as specific as possible: (deepfake* OR "synthetic media" OR "artificial media") AND (detection OR regulation OR trust OR society OR ethics). Other subjects searched included technical methods (GAN, diffusion, detection) and regulatory policy (AI Act, transparency, governance).

3.2.2 Inclusion-Exclusion Criteria

The inclusion criteria included: (1) the study was published in an English-language peer-reviewed journal, (2) it was published between 2021 – 2025, (3) had primary relevance to syn-thetic media, deepfake or related technologies, and (4) empirical data or theoretical frameworks relevant to the study of trust, regulation, or the impact of synthetic media. Some conference proceedings from prestigious conferences (IEEE, ACM, AAAI) were also added.

Papers that were conference abstracts, non-peer-reviewed preprints, or involved only with the technical implementation and lacked broader implications were excluded.

3.3 Regulatory Analysis Framework

3.3.1 Document Selection and Coding Scheme

To analyze primary legal documents, regulatory document analysis focused on three legal systems: the European Union (AI Act), the United States (federal proposals and state laws) and selected Asian markets (China, South Korea and Singapore). Priority given to legal documents and instruments which select significant policy recommendations and guidance documents.

The coding scheme controlled three aspects: regulatory scope (coded technologies and appli-cations included); obligations for stakeholder(s) (coded requirements for developers, deployer(s), platform(s); relevant penalties; enforcement structures; and international coordination.

3.3.2 Cross-Jurisdictional Comparison Methodology

Cross-jurisdictional analysis utilized structured comparison which involves convergent and divergent strategies to synthetic media governance. The comparison framework evaluated the model of regulation (rights versus utility), the means of implementing it (prescriptive rules versus principles-based standards), and the way to enforce it (administrative measure versus criminal sanctions).

3.3.3 Industry Self-Regulation Assessment

The analysis covered study of industry practices, notably self-regulation efforts such as platform community standards, industry association standards and technical standards developing. This element evaluated the extent to which voluntary measures were implemented, their ability to achieve desired outcomes and the extent to which they integrated with formal regulatory measures.

3.4 Scenario Planning Methodology

3.4.1 Key Uncertainty Identification

The development of a scenario involved identifying key uncertainties concerning the develop-ment of synthetic media. Two main dimensions emerged from the expert interviews and literature review: technological development trajectories (detection capabilities versus generation quality) and regulatory coordination effectiveness (fragmented versus coordinated efforts at international level).

Other ambiguities ranged from public awareness evolution, converging platform policy, international cooperation and breakthrough technologies.

3.4.2 Building Scenarios and Checking for Logical Consistency

In the analysis of the two crucial dimensions, four scenarios resulted that differed in regard to technological and regulatory trajectories. For each scenario, the incentive of various stakeholders, technological restrictions and capabilities of institutions had to be internally consistent.

To create scenarios, a narrative description was constructed on how identified uncertainties may resolve in the future, while the stakeholders' behaviors and technological update were kept logically consistent.

4. THE EVOLUTION OF DEEPFAKE TECHNOLOGY AND CHALLENGES IN ITS DETECTION

4.1 Generation Technologies Today

4.1.1 Technical Skills and Performance Benchmarks

In the current state of deep-fake technology, realistic generation of multimodal content is currently possible to a high degree. Video synthesis with diffusion-based architectures can fool any untrained audiences, with accounts representing a decrease from 82% in 2019 to 53% in 2024 Stroebel et al. (2023). Moreover, voice cloning systems have reached unprecedented levels of naturalness (4.7/5.0 in comparison to human speech) in the case of audio deepfakes Jung et al. (2022).

Table 1. Deepfake generation capabilities by modality (2024)

Modality	Best Architecture	Training Time	Quality Score	Human Detection Rate	Commercial Availability
Video Face Swap	Diffusion + GAN	12 hours	4.6/5.0	53%	High
Full Body Video	Pose-Guided Diffusion	24 hours	4.2/5.0	67%	Medium
Voice Cloning	Neural Vocoder	2 hours	4.7/5.0	34%	High
Singing Voice	SingSynth	8 hours	4.4/5.0	41%	Medium
Lip Sync	Wav2Lip + Enhancement	4 hours	4.5/5.0	58%	High
Real-time Face	Live GAN	< 1 second	3.8/5.0	74%	Medium

Sources: Compiled from Gong & Li (2024), Jung et al. (2022), Li et al. (2023)

4.1.2 Accessibility and Democratization

The democratization of the generation tools is a qualitative change in terms of the threat landscape. This raises the bar for quality synthesis with low technical effort in consumer applications and gets rid of hardware effort in cloud-based applications. Research shows that generation qualities from consumer developed tools are greater than those from research tools developed in 2020.

It can be used in popular applications such as FakeApp, DeepFaceLab, or even commercial software such as Respeecher, and the obstacles involved are quite low.

The survey shows that 23% of the students at university have used face-swapping apps, as well as 8% of them creating a fake image to fool others. This is the universal accessibility, and thus the possibility of misuses and creative uses.

High quality synthesis, and cost of it, has reduced exponentially. In 2019, it cost a full $10,000 to perform the face-swapping from professional quality to be used for the film, but today, with the cloud service, that has been reduced to just under $50.

4.1.3 Quality Improvements and Artifact Reduction

Architectural advances in recent years have significantly reduced visual and auditory artifacts which facilitated detection. The diffusion models are able to generate more temporally consistent video synthesis sequences, and the attention models can preserve the identity across various poses and lighting.

Specific improvements include 3D-aware generation models for better eye gaze consistency, using semantic guidance to better preserve facial landmarks, using video-specific architec-tures for better temporal coherence, and perceptually-optimal training objectives for lower compression artefacts.

4.2 The Detection Challenge: Accuracy vs. Generalisation

4.2.1 Current Detection Approaches and Performance

There are several approaches to current detection: train classifiers with manipulation artifacts in deep learning-based methods, look at the biological signal and identify any physiological anomalies, in the frequency domain with spatial-frequency analysis, and in the time domain using temporal consistency analysis to identify inter-frame artifacts.

Research results on the benchmark datasets are outstanding, and the state-of-the-art meth-ods has achieved a detection rate above 95% on widely used benchmark test sets. However, evaluation on a different data set shows that dramatic degradation of accuracy occurs when the different types of manipulation are not covered by the training set.

4.2.2 Cross-Dataset Performance and Generalisation Issues

The generation challenge is due to basic disparities between the generation and detection relationship. The Generation models work best to optimize their perceptual realism and can utilize adversarial methods that defeat specific detection methods. Instead, models used for detection have to be stable with potentially infinite varieties of manipulation yet be precise to prevent false detection leading to the loss of trust.

Figure 1. Detection accuracy trends across datasets (2021-2024)

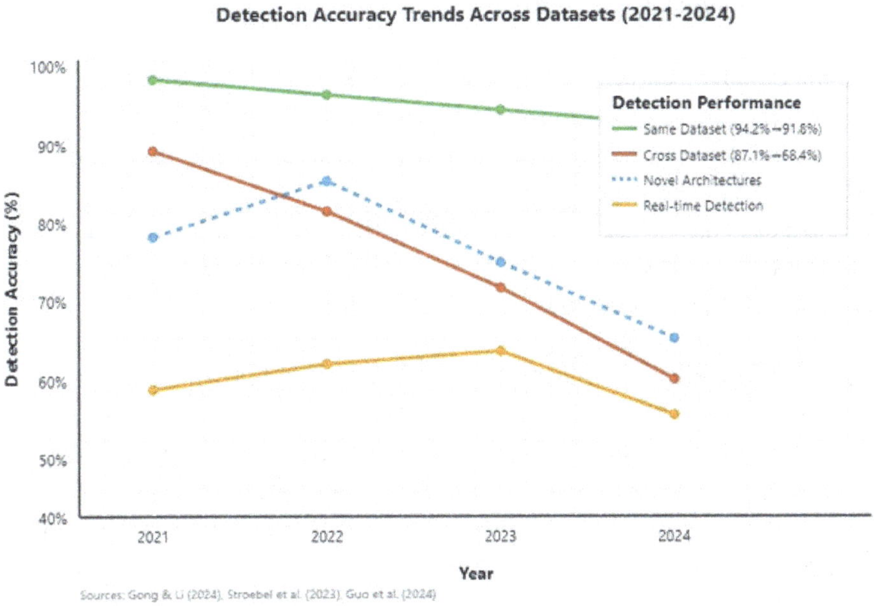

As demonstrated in Figure 1, patterns exist in each of these datasets across the systematic evaluation, and those are consistently found. The higher the accuracy of the detection (>90%), the more secure the manipulation type has been in the training data (the more common for some manipulation type), and the lower the accuracy (<70%), the more novel the manipulation type (the less common for some manipulation type). This is true irrespective of any detection architecture or training method.

5. REGULATORY FRAMEWORKS: GLOBAL APPROACHES AND CONVER-GENCE PATTERNS

5.1 European Union: The AI Act as Global Precedent

5.1.1 Regulatory Framework and Classification

The EU AI Act will create a comprehensive regulatory framework for synthetic media based on a risk-tailored approach. AI systems are categorised by Title IV as minimal risk, limited risk, high risk and unacceptable risk. The synthetic media systems are normally classified as "limited risk" systems, and are subject to the transparency requirements of Article 50.

To comply with Article 50(1) of their rules, deployers of AI systems that generate or manipulate image, audio or video content that appreciably resembles existing persons, objects, places or other entities or events and would falsely appear to a person to be genuine or true shall clearly and prominently inform that the content is artificial or has been manipulated.

The provision, however, offers important exceptions - the use is obviously creative, satirical, artistic or fictional or the content is created for educational or scientific purposes with suitable safeguards.

5.1.2 Implementation Challenges and Technical Requirements

There are implementation issues that need to be considered when applying the transparency approach from the AI Act as it may not be effective. The end-user is not considered a 'deployer', which leads to complexity of enforcement in peer-to-peer distribution scenarios. Also, the "clear and prominent" disclosure standard is not rooted in technical specifications.

According to Łabuz (2024), the constitutional dimension of the AI Act's framework on synthetic media has already attracted the attention. They ultimately suggest the requirements with respect to transparency are insufficient to guarantee respect for fundamental rights and are also seen as a potential restriction on legitimate expression.

5.1.3 Enforcement Mechanisms and Institutional Framework

There are significant differences in the enforcement challenges based on member state, with some jurisdictions being technically challenged to detect synthetic media on a large scale. The European AI Office, established under Article 65, will have a coordinating role for the enforcement.

The Act provides for administrative fines up to C35 million or 7% of total worldwide annual turnover for violations of transparency obligations. However, the deterrent effect depends on the enforcement of the law in all member states.

Member states need to build and strengthen technical capacity to ensure the compliance of AI systems, such as the detection of synthetic media and the evaluation of implementation of transparency.

5.2 United States: Fragmented Federal Structure and Sectoral Approaches

5.2.1 Federal Legislative Landscape

The regulatory environment in the United States reflects the challenges of regulation in a federalized space. Federal efforts, such as the DEEPFAKES Accountability Act and the AI Disclosure Act, are still in Congress and First Amendment protections for free speech have been stymied by constitutional concerns.

The requirements to disclose fake content would be akin to that existing in EU laws, however the DEEPFAKES Accountability Act would also offer safe havens for platforms to implement safety detection and labelling protocols. But tech industry groups are against forcing onerous requirements to implement.

5.2.2 State Level Initiatives and Variation

There has been a rapid growth of state-level systems, which introduced inconsistencies according to the context and location. California, Texas, and Virginia are just a few states that have passed laws that specifically address certain applications; other states have no synthetic media-specific laws.

Table 2. U.S. state-level deepfake legislation (2021-2024)

State	Legislation	Coverage	Criminal Penalties	Civil Remedies	Enforcement
California	AB 602, SB 155	Electoral, NCII	Misdemeanor	Injunction, Damages	AG, Private
Texas	SB 751	Electoral	Class A Misd.	None	Local DA
Virginia	HB 2678	NCII	Class 1 Misd.	Damages	Private
New York	Proposed A8155	Electoral + NCII	Felony	Damages	AG
Illinois	HB 3842	NCII	Class 4 Felony	Damages	Private
Florida	SB 1018	Electoral	3rd Deg. Felony	None	State AG

Sources: Van der Sloot & Wagensveld (2022), state legislative databases

5.2.3 Sectoral Regulation and Industry Standards

There is neither a single federal statute covering a single set of standards nor guidance for agencies and industry. Deepfake fraud falls within existing FTC industry regulations to safeguard consumers, and the Securities and Exchange Commission (SEC) has mentioned synthetic media in corporate communications.

The National Institute of Standards and Technology (NIST) has commenced technical work on standards for the evaluation of AI systems, including standards for detecting and authenticating synthetic media.

5.3 Asia-Pacific Approaches: Divergent Governance Philosophies

5.3.1 China's Comprehensive Control Framework

The spectre of threat and the philosophy of Asian governance is reflected in the way of regulation. Its approach is based on state control, with the control of content treated as part of the algorithmic system of content control. The Algorithmic Recommendation Management Provisions impose a number of technical safeguards on service providers.

The Draft Measures for Deepfake service providers set out a comprehensive list of require-ments for deepfake service providers such as real-name registration, labeling and required government certification for selected applications. The framework does not prioritize protecting individual privacy or promoting democratic transparency in information flows.

Pros and cons of centralized regulation are illustrated in the Chinese approach. The dis-tribution of deep falsely via platform by platform can be effectively controlled through fast implementation and uniform enforcement. But the approach is not necessarily compatible with democratic values.

5.3.2 South Korea's Rights-Based Framework

South Korea place a primary emphasis on individual dignity by emphasizing on wide-ranging privacy laws. Enforcement of the obligations contained in the amendments to the Personal Infor-mation Protection Act takes place at the level of synthetic media that impacts upon identifiable persons, while the provisions of the Information and Communications Network Act provide for a fast content removal process.

The Korean approach focuses on the priority of securing the protection of the victims through speeded up removal processes and criminal penalties for the dissemination of non-consensual intimate imagery. The civil penalties of up to 30,000,000 won ($23,000) offer effective deterrence.

But there's distribution issues and platform conformance that present problems to the Korean method. International platforms may not be able to do well with Korean removal procedures.

5.3.3 Singapore's Technology-Neutral Approach

Singapore has technology neutral strategies that leverage on technology to combat harmful content, irrespective of its source. The Protection from Online Falsehoods and Manipulation Act (POFMA) empowers government institutions to demand that false information be corrected or removed.

Rather than technology specific regulation, the Singaporean approach is one based on outcomes and is technology agnostic. But this is achieved at the expense of specificity in relation to media-specific requirements that may only be synthetic.

6. SOCIETAL ADAPTATION: PUBLIC PERCEPTION, MEDIA LITERACY AND INSTITUTIONAL RESPONSE

6.1 Public Perception and Awareness Evolution

6.1.1 Empirical Results With Regards to Public Attention and Attitudes

Empirical studies of public perception show some complexities with regard to simple binary descriptions of deepfakes awareness. In sum, even though large-scale studies have shown that human detections are better than chance, they are not 100% vulnerable.

Zhang et al. (2025) performed in-depth social media analysis of over 2.3 million posts of social media conversations on deepfakes. The study revealed a divided sentiment of public opinion where 47% of positive sentiment is from the fans of technological capabilities and 37% of negative sentiment is from the concern about misinformation and privacy issues.

Figure 2. Public sentiment toward deepfakes by application type

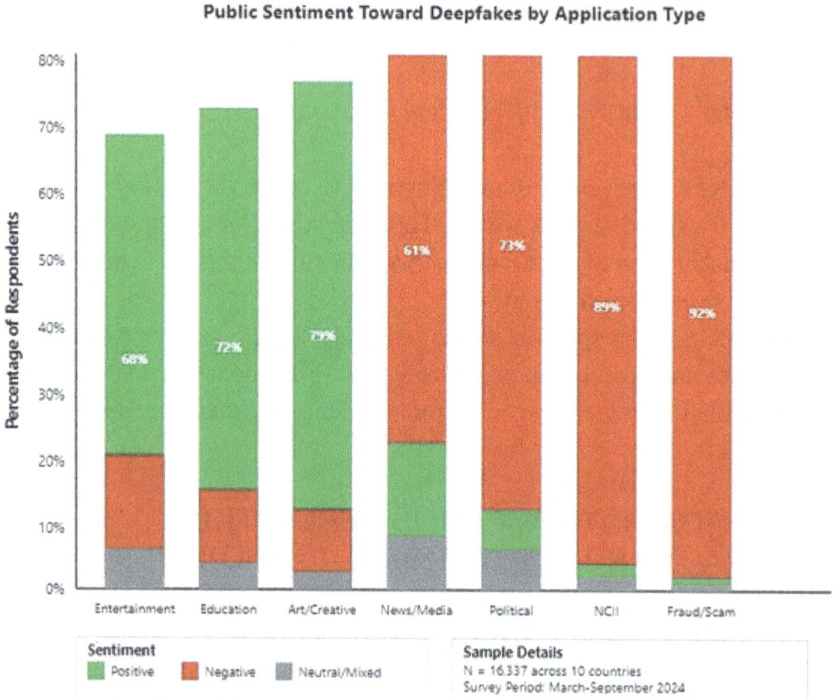

Geographic and demographical differences are significant as shown in Figure 2. The Europeans are somewhat more troubled by the infringement on privacy (62% negative sentiment compared with the Americans who are more troubled by the threat to democracy's electoral dimension (71% negative sentiment). Asians have more positive attitudes towards entertainment applications.

6.1.2 Detection Capabilities and Confidence Patterns

Human detection capabilities have been found to be quite complex when the content type is analyzed, exposure time is considered, and individual characteristics studied, with untrained humans still having an ability to discriminate between authentic and manipulated video content with an accuracy of 61% compared to chance performance of under 60% Groh et al. (2022).

In the study these machine-informed crowds achieve superior accuracy reaching 79%, promising a hybrid verification methods. The effectiveness relies, however, in designing the interface and the extent to which users trust algorithmic support.

6.2 The Liar's Dividend Effect

Experimental data supports the existence of liar's dividend effects but thus far reveals moderating factors. Overall, on average, exposure to deepfakes lowered levels of trust in authentic content by about 15% as a result of its exposure; however, the effect may vary according to the content type, the credibility of the source and media literacy.

Meta-analysis was performed by Kang and Valadez (2025) by analyzing 24 experimental studies on deepfake effects on trust and credibility judgments. The analysis shows that deepfake awareness yields differential effects: skepticism toward low credibility sources and cynicism toward high credibility.

6.3 Media Literacy as a Protective Intervention

6.3.1 Effectiveness of Educational Interventions

Experimental studies find that both media literacy and deepfake media literacy education significantly decreases the persuasiveness, credibility ratings, and intention to share deepfake disinformation Hwang et al. (2021).

The best interventions are using technical education on the creation of synthetic products complementing with critical education frameworks to evaluate the credibility of products. The combined intervention led to a 34% higher detection accuracy and a 28% lower false content sharing rate.

6.3.2 Challenges in Curriculum Design and Execution

The implementation challenges of media literacy interventions are significant such as the demands for the teacher training, the cost of curriculum development, and the need for both resources and the media itself to be up to date with respect to changes in technology. Good programs will be a balance of specific technological knowledge and transferable critical thinking skills.

Success in curriculum frameworks will focus on four technical skills: Technical understand-ing; Source evaluation; Verification; and Ethical reasoning.

6.3.3 Digital Literacy Integration and Lifelong Learning

Media literacy education needs to be internalized in the wider rubrics of digital literacy that cover various aspects of information evaluation and digital citizenship.

It remains to be seen whether standalone deepfake education is more effective integrated with other measures tackling misinformation.

There is evidence that professional development programs for teachers can be effective for scaling up media literacy interventions. Train the trainer has the potential to engage more populations, with quality and consistency of training.

6.4 Institutional Adaptation: Journalism, Law and Politics

6.4.1 Journalism and Verification Practices

Syndicated news outlets have started to seek to tackle synthetic media threats through verification processes and evidential standards. Reuters, Associated Press, BBC and CNN have created in-house source-confirmation and technical analysis verification teams.

Reuters verification refers to a blend of technical verification (via detection algorithms) and source verification (social media investigation and contact). The compromise ensures high accuracy rates but upholds the standards of journalism.

But, in scenarios such as breaking news where quick publication is a priority, verification practices encounter several troubles with scalability. There may be a balance between accuracy and timeliness.

6.4.2 Legal System Adaptations and Evidence Standards

As synthetic media challenges traditional notions of the documentary evidence, there are more fundamental issues for the legal system. As video evidence continues to be admitted in cases where deepfakes are technically feasible, U.S. courts have taken up questions regarding the standards for its admission.

Federal Rules of Evidence Rule 901 mandate proof by a process of "authentication" that the evidence is "what the proponent claims it to be." Courts are evolving views regarding the standard's meaning where "perfect" counterparts are likely available in practice.

The challenges are not limited to admissibility but also include jury instructions, expert testimony. Courts need to give some guidance to juries on the synthetic media, and not be too skeptical about the authenticity of evidence.

6.4.3 Political and Democratic Institutional Responses

Institutions of politics show a diverse range of adaptation patterns, in line with their democratic traditions and constitutional frameworks. A handful of legislatures have enacted laws banning the use of synthetic media in campaigns; others have taken a more circumspect approach that emphasizes disclosure.

The Federal Election Commission has taken the necessary steps to begin rulemaking about synthetic media in political advertising, but the need to respect the Constitution narrows the range of possibilities.

7. THE SYNTHETIC MEDIA TRUST FRAMEWORK (SMTF)

7.1 Conceptual Architecture and Design Principles

We introduce the Synthetic Media Trust Framework (SMTF) as an integrative framework to tackle multi-layered problems of building up trust in synthetic media environments. The frame-work acknowledges that trust is built through the relationship between technology, regulatory implementation, and social norms and practices.

The SMTF has three levels of interconnectedness, all of which need to work together to build sustainable trust:

- **Technical Layer**: Infrastructure and functionality for authentication and detection of content authenticity and manipulation.
- **Regulatory Layer**: Compliance and enforcement mechanisms and legal responsibilities.
- **Social Layer**: Society's capacity to exist within synthetic media environments, norms and literacy.

Theory of the framework is based on sociotechnical systems theory because the outcome is not simply a result of one facet of the system, but a function of interactions among the affordances, structure and behaviors of the system.

7.2 Systems Thinking and Interdependency Analysis

The SMTF follows the principles of systems thinking, which take account of complex inter-dependencies between the technological development, regulatory implementation and social adaptation. A change in one layer has effects on other layers, and thus involves co-ordinating changes.

For example, technical authentication processes provide both a basis for regulatory compli-ance, but social norms that confer a value on verification are required if such systems are to be widely adopted.

There are three key principles in designing the framework: creating modular components to support adaptation to different contexts; ensuring interoperability; and scaling to organizational and jurisdiction changes.

7.3 Stakeholder Integration and Governance Mechanisms

Recognizes five main stakeholder groups who have different roles and responsibilities: Tech-nology developers, platform operators, regulators, organisations of civil society, and individual users.

To have effective governance, there should be mechanisms for coordinating between the stakeholder that allow for respect of institutional capacities and democratic legitimacy. Multi-stakeholder governance models offer a means of cooperation.

Feedback mechanisms are included in the framework allowing for adaptive governance in the face of technological change and new evidence of effectiveness.

7.4 The Technical Layer: Authentication and Detection Infrastructure

7.4.1 Provenance Systems and Cryptographic Authentication

The technical layer provides infrastructure for content authentication and manipulation detection by means of four fundamental components. Provenance systems based on C2PA standards allows for cryptographic signing of content at creation to help create verifiable chains of custody. The C2PA manifests contain detailed information about the creation of the content, such as creation metadata from the devices used in the production process, editing history, and creators' attestation.

7.4.2 Robust Watermarking and Steganographic Approaches

Robust watermarking methods add detectable markers to synthetic content at generation time which are not affected by normal manipulation artifacts. The more advanced ones employ frequency domain embedding which is enhanced to remain resistant to compression, cropping, etc.

However, as demonstrated by Zhao et al. (2023), it is possible to insert basic weaknesses that can thwart state-of-the-art watermarks without compromising visual quality. This discovery points to the need for watermarking methods to be supplemented by other verification techniques.

Recently, other methods like semantic watermarking and perceptually-optimized embedding have been proposed to solve these challenges.

7.4.3 Detection Ensembles and Hybrid Approaches

Detection ensemble approaches are formed by integrating spatial, temporal, frequency and mul-timodal analysis to better generalise over types of manipulation. Machine learning architectures with uncertainty quantification yield confidence scores instead of simple classifications.

Hybrid human-AI verification systems take advantage of the synergy between human judg-ment and algorithmic analysis. Research shows that collaborative approaches can achieve higher accuracy.

7.4.4 Verification Services and API Integration

Some verification sites are open to journalists, researchers, civil society actors and any user in need of content verification. API-based services allow integration into social media platforms, news websites and other distribution channels.

Services have to be both user friendly and accurate. The educational elements enable users to understand the meaning of confidence scores.

Verification services need to be sustainable and adopted, influenced by business model considerations. General levies or subsidy might be essential for wide availability.

7.5 The Regulatory Layer: Risk-Proportionate Governance

7.5.1 Disclosure Requirements and Transparency Mechanisms

Four dimensions are used to implement the legal frameworks. Disclosure requirements call for clarity on the use of synthetic content distribution, while technical specifications guarantee that the synthesized content is disclosed in a readable way.

Risk-based exemptions allow for creative expression while assuring protection to high-stakes applications. A distinction might be warranted between educational and artistic practices, and applications that impact democracy.

Requirements for implementation are met only if technical standards are adopted outlining disclosure format, placement and persistence.

7.5.2 Specific Prohibitions and Targeted Enforcement

Specific criminalisation of specific deepfake applications that cause specific kinds of harm, such as intimate imagery without consent and electoral manipulation, can offer targeted deterrence without generalised restrictions.

Criminal sanctions should be commensurate with the gravity of the harm. In cases where prosecution will not provide sufficient protection, civil remedies are available.

Jurisdictional issues should be covered with enforcement mechanisms. Cross-border en-forcement is addressed under international cooperation agreements.

7.5.3 Platform Accountability and Intermediary Liability

Intermediary liability frameworks give instructions to entities to put in place proportionate measures to control harmful synthetic media. Notice and take down procedures ensure content is removed quickly.

Risks on platforms should be risk-proportioned and different for platforms with different functions and audience size.

Safe Harbor clauses encourage the implementation of good faith practices for limiting harmful content without imposing burdens to silence it.

7.5.4 International Coordination and Cross-Border Enforcement

Cross-border content distribution must rely on instruments of international co-operation that cover not only the uniformity of definitions but also cooperation in enforcement and the conflict of jurisdictions.

Capacity development support programmes enable developing countries to build up their capacity for synthetic media governance.

There are international mechanisms available for operational cooperation through organisa-tions such as Interpol, the UN Office on Drugs and Crime, and regional organisations.

7.6 The Social Layer: Collective Intelligence Mechanisms

7.6.1 Media Literacy Education and Critical Evaluation Skills

Media literacy education focuses on entire and transferable critical evaluation skills instead of recognizing deep fakes. Pedagogical strategies thick with contented evidence and not cynicism towards authentic media provide ways to build resilience.

Effective interventions involve integrating technical training on creating synthetic media with critical thinking skills.

Instructor training programs are needed and must be responsive to technology. Train-the-trainer methods may be used to expand educational programs.

7.6.2 Professional Standards and Verification Protocols

The institutional frameworks for content authentication are introduced by the development of verification protocols for journalism, law enforcement and other professions.

The journalistic verification process is a synthesis of technical analysis and the source checking process. Legal profession standards include attending to authentication issues of digital evidence.

Cross-professional collaboration allows best practice to be shared and common standards to be developed.

7.6.3 Collective Verification and Crowdsourced Authentication

Reputable crowdsourcing platforms are built with verification and trust systems. Seamless coordination of existing fact checking organisations gives institutional support.

The goal of collective verification systems is to deliver the benefits of collective, diverse perspectives and distribution of expertise. Reputation systems and algorithmic quality control can ensure accuracy.

But there are issues of scale and the risk of manipulation by organized groups. Mixed models of crowd verification and traditional methods could offer the best of both worlds.

7.6.4 Norm Development and Community Standards

Informal social sanctions reinforce legal requirements for social expectations about creation and consumption of synthetic content. Community consent and disclosure guidelines will change as technology advances.

Platform community standards and professional association standards are multiple paths to norm development. Active participation from communities is required.

Norm development trajectories are influenced by cultural differences. International gover-nance must allow space for respecting cultural differences.

8. FUTURE PREDICTIONS AND SCENARIO ANALYSIS

8.1 Methodological Approach to Prediction

8.1.1 Scenario Development and Probability Assessment

To forecast the evolution of synthetic media, we must accept basic uncertainty and recognize plausible scenarios. Our scenario methodology builds on existing ones used in strategic planning. Our two main dimensions are: technological development trajectories and regulatory coor-dination effectiveness. These dimensions were chosen because of their relevance to possible governance outcomes.

Other factors are public awareness evolution, convergence of platform policies, international collaboration and potential breakthroughs.

8.1.2 Expert Validation and Sensitivity Analysis

The expert review involved fifteen specialists from the fields of technology policy, computer security, digital media, and international law. Based on their input, we revised our assumptions regarding incentives and adjusted the technological constraints.

A sensitivity analysis was done on three advances at each of the primary dimensions and on the probabilities of transitions.

Important findings: technological breakthroughs may cause scenario paths to shift sharply, while coordinating regulatory action is more path-dependent.

8.1.3 Observable Indicators and Monitoring Framework

The scenarios have tangible signs to watch for. Technological indicators include the reliability of detection, the rate of adoption of content credentials, and the quality of AI-generated media. Signals from regulators include laws that come to pass, laws that are enforced, and international agreements that become effective.

8.2 Scenario 1: Technological Equilibrium (Optimistic Convergence)

8.2.1 The Story and What It Feels Like

That's the future we want, where we can catch manipulated media at the same speed at which they are being manipulated. It came out of a collaborative global process. It's a world where creative applications of synthetic media thrive without destroying shared reality.

What Life Looks Like by 2030:

- Detection tools are good at detecting most manipulation
- Majority of professional content is provided with content credentials
- Forty-plus countries have signed a decent agreement on synthetic media
- People have developed a useful and critical, but not cynical, relationship with digital media
- A flourishing creative economy has been built around synthetic media
- Non-consensual intimate imagery has declined precipitously

8.2.2 The Path Technology Takes

That future requires sustained financial commitment, estimated at $2 billion annually by 2027. Robust detection systems must withstand novel adversarial attacks.

Authenticators become expected parts of smart phones and cameras. One-click "check provenance" services verify content without trouble.

Processing becomes fast and inexpensive enough to scan synthetic content in real-time broadcasts.

8.3 Scenario 2: Adaptive Resilience (Innovative Transformation)

8.3.1 The Story and What It Feels Like

Progress in creating well-made deepfakes seems to stall. The "arms race" no longer exists. Truth is no longer an attribute of an individual file, but triangulation.

What Life Looks Like by 2030:

- An outgrown notion of an ideal false detector
- Reliance on mental shortcuts completely reframed
- Evidence standards in courts and newsrooms shifted toward skepticism-aware protocols
- Savvy individuals ask: who benefits if I believe this?
- New media platforms built on "provenance-first" principles

8.3.2 The Legal and Social Transformation

Definitions of "deepfake" are beginning to be replaced by laws aimed at redressing very real harms. The technological medium is irrelevant when it comes to fraud being legally actionable. Platforms are no longer considered the default truth-determining devices, but must instead have transparent and responsible governance mechanisms. In coordination with this, the international system is growing in its focus on protecting victims and encouraging joint measures for law enforcement.

8.3.3 The Story and What It Feels Like

If there is no breakthrough, this is the disappointing default road ahead. The truth becomes post-code dependent.

What Life Looks Like by 2030:

- Telling when a deepfake is being used is still not easy
- The universal "content credential" disappears
- The world map is a jumbled, unregulated set of laws
- Malicious creators jurisdiction-shop
- Public enthusiasm fades with each passing year

8.3.4 The Human Consequences and Risks

Protection depends on location. Risk concentrates in already marginalised communities. Plat-forms are cut down to compliance machines. The worst consequence is lawless enclaves.

8.4 Scenario 4: Trust Collapse (Pessimistic Outcome)

8.4.1 The Story and What It Feels Like

It is easy and near-perfect to create fake content, and just as easy for it to be missed. Society enters epistemic vertigo.

What Life Looks Like by 2030:

- The accuracy of detection falls below 60%
- Existing authentication methods apply only in professional settings
- Public trust drops below 40%
- The effectiveness of disinformation campaigns becomes unprecedented
- The legitimacy of democratic institutions is called into question

8.4.2 Systemic Consequences

The collapse of trust is a wound in the heart of democracy. Elections face convincing fake videos. Courts tremble. The financial impact spreads to personal and market levels.

9. CONCLUSION

9.1 The Story So Far

In this chapter, it has become clear that there is a clash between the speed of generative AI's progress and the slow pace of institutional adaptation. The attacker holds more of the cards. Legislation is coalescing around transparency but dividing on other aspects. The public is not a passive victim but an audience waiting to be made aware.

9.2 A Path That Demands We Walk Together

Interdependence can be seen in the Synthetic Media Trust Framework. Social resilience is our biggest weapon. The four futures are invitations rather than predictions.

9.3 The Moments Ahead, and the Choice

The five inflection points will address how we govern a technology moving at light speed. We must build the authentication structure before we need it. We must write laws before harms become endemic.

This is achievable. Technical standards are in place. Regulatory momentum is with the EU. Levels of public awareness are growing. Together we are creating the future of a trusted digital world.

REFERENCES

Chesney, B., & Citron, D. (2019). Deep fakes. *California Law Review*, *107*(6), 1753–1820.

Díaz-Rodríguez, N., Del Ser, J., Coeckelbergh, M., López de Prado, M., Herrera-Viedma, E., & Herrera, F. (2023). Connecting the dots in trustworthy artificial intelligence: From AI principles, ethics, and key requirements to responsible AI systems and regulation. *Information Fusion*, *99*, 101896. Advance online publication. DOI: 10.1016/j.inffus.2023.101896

Gong, L. Y., & Li, X. J. (2024). A contemporary survey on deepfake detection: Datasets, algorithms, and challenges. *Electronics (Basel)*, *13*(3), 585. Advance online publication. DOI: 10.3390/electronics13030585

Groh, M., Epstein, Z., Firestone, C., & Picard, R. (2022). Deepfake detection by human crowds, machines, and machine-informed crowds. *Proceedings of the National Academy of Sciences of the United States of America*, *119*(1), e2110013119. Advance online publication. DOI: 10.1073/pnas.2110013119 PMID: 34969837

Guo, Z., Jia, Z., Wang, L., Wang, D., Yang, G., & Kasabov, N. (2024). Constructing new backbone networks via space-frequency interactive convolution for deepfake detection. *IEEE Transactions on Information Forensics and Security*, *19*, 401–413. DOI: 10.1109/TIFS.2023.3324739

Hwang, Y., Ryu, J. Y., & Jeong, S.-H. (2021). Effects of disinformation using deepfake: The protective effect of media literacy education. *Cyberpsychology, Behavior, and Social Networking*, *24*(3), 188–193. DOI: 10.1089/cyber.2020.0174 PMID: 33646021

Jung, J.-W., Heo, H.-S., Tak, H., Shim, H.-J., Chung, J. S., & Lee, B.-J. (2022). AASIST: Audio anti-spoofing using integrated spectro-temporal graph attention networks. In *ICASSP 2022—2022 IEEE International Conference on Acoustics, Speech and Signal Processing* (pp. 6367–6371). IEEE. DOI: 10.1109/ICASSP43922.2022.9747766

Kang, S., & Valadez, K. (2025). Deepfakes' cognitive, emotional, and behavioral impact: A systematic review and meta-analysis of individual responses. *Journalism & Mass Communication Quarterly*, *102*(1), 45–72. DOI: 10.1177/10776990251357294

Łabuz, M. (2024). Deep fakes and the Artificial Intelligence Act—An important signal or a missed opportunity? *Policy and Internet*, *16*(4), 651–672. DOI: 10.1002/poi3.406

Li, Y., Ma, C., Yan, Y., Zhu, W., & Yang, X. (2023). DCFace: Synthetic face generation with dual condition diffusion model. In *Proceedings of the IEEE/CVF Conference on Computer Vision and Pattern Recognition* (pp. 12715–12725). IEEE. DOI: 10.1109/CVPR52729.2023.01222

Stroebel, L., Llewellyn, M., Hartley, T., Ip, T. S., & Ahmed, M. (2023). A systematic literature review on the effectiveness of deepfake detection techniques. *Journal of Cyber Security Technology*, *7*(2), 83–113. DOI: 10.1080/23742917.2023.2192888

van der Sloot, B., & Wagensveld, Y. (2022). Deepfakes: Regulatory challenges for the synthetic society. *Computer Law & Security Review*, *46*, 105716. Advance online publication. DOI: 10.1016/j.clsr.2022.105716

Zhang, Y., Chen, X., Wang, L., Liu, M., & Zhou, H. (2025). Public perception towards deepfake through topic modelling and sentiment analysis of social media data. *Social Network Analysis and Mining*, *15*(1), 45. Advance online publication. DOI: 10.1007/s13278-025-01445-8

Zhao, Z., Guan, J., Jiang, Z., & Gong, N. Z. (2023). Evading watermark based detection of AI-generated content. In *Proceedings of the 2023 ACM SIGSAC Conference on Computer and Communications Security* (pp. 3418–3432). ACM. DOI: 10.1145/3576915.3623189

Chapter 8
The Ethics of Deepfake Creation and Use:
Creativity Versus Harm, Boundaries of Free Expression, and Moral Dilemmas

Deepak Gupta
http://orcid.org/0000-0003-3929-1362
Institute of Technology and Management, Gwalior, India

Panjiyev Sukhrob
Termez University of Economics and Service, Termez, Uzbekistan

Valisher Sapayev
Mamun University, Khiva, Uzbekistan

Iroda Abdullaeva
Urgench State University, Urgench, Uzbekistan

Khudaybergen Kochkarov
Tashkent State University of Economy, Tashkent, Uzbekistan

Shoira Rakhimova
http://orcid.org/0009-0007-3154-7809
Pedagogical Institute, Uzbekistan

ABSTRACT

The proliferation of deepfake technology presents complex ethical challenges that span creativity, harm prevention, and free expression. This chapter examines the moral dimensions of synthetic media through philosophical frameworks, legal analysis, and empirical evidence. We explore the tension between legitimate creative applications and potential harms, analyze constitutional boundaries of regulation, and identify moral dilemmas faced by creators, platforms, and society. Drawing on recent scholarship (2021-2025), the chapter synthesizes deontological, consequentialist, and virtue ethics approaches to develop an integrated framework for understanding deepfake ethics. Key findings reveal that while deepfakes are not inherently wrong, their ethical status depends critically on consent, context, and

DOI: 10.4018/979-8-3373-8292-0.ch008

purpose. The analysis demonstrates how synthetic media threatens epistemic trust while simultaneously enabling beneficial applications in education, accessibility, and artistic expression.

1 INTRODUCTION

1.1 The Deepfake Revolution and the Ethics That Must Follow

DeepFake is a turning point if the image of synthetic media, authenticity, and morals are correlated with artificial intelligence.The DeepFake moment in the correlative image of synthetic media, authenticity and morals is a pivotal moment in the artificial intelligence correlation. Synthetic AV media, given its niche technological novelty has become a force that has now permeated the entire field of digital content—the production of advanced machine learning algorithms—has greatly affected our perception, creation and trust of digital content, and has become a world changing force. The analysis that is pursued by de Ruiter (2021) echoes the ethical challenges arising from deepfakes without setting the experience vile or low and realizing the piece's ethical status will rest on its producing, why, and how it would be used.

The deepfakes' production has got easier and quicker than before; it has become the latest men's trade of fascinating and influencing with deceptive impressions. It is now possible to perform work that was once harmed away of Hollywood resources in the comfort of the home office at a dip price using consumer equipment and consumer-level code. It has raised critical issues regarding limits of creative expression and potential for fabrication, boundaries of State and government oversight of digital speech, and moral obligations of creators, platforms, and users in a new era of proliferation of synthetic media.

1.2 Ethical Analysis is Used on a Variety of Issues and is Complex to Various Degrees

The implications of deep fakes are truly incredible, some of which are pro-social (for instance, providing features for the disabled and protecting historical stories), while others are easily concluded to be anti-social, namely intimate image creation without permission, particularly of the female and the marginalized communities. This report, written by Flynn et al. (2022), illuminates the prevalence, through scientific cross-national analysis, and the psychological and social harm that can be caused to individuals targeted by deepfakes. Between these extremes, applications in the fields of education, entertainment and art show more positive early social uses of the technology, with the permission of the user or user's parents.

This is an ethical complexity and considerations should be taken beyond the binary assess-ment, it is pertinent to take advanced philosophical considerations. A central problem is creating rules that can differentiate something that's morally acceptable from unacceptable use, and leave room for innovation and prolific creativity. As mentioned by Fallis (2021), the possibility of the 'information carrying capacity' being influenced by deepfakes, poses a threat to the acquisition of knowledge as well as to democracy. The same sets of technical skills, however, can be used to be helpful and useful for the conservation of a movie, the preservation of a language, and/or any changes for improved access.

1.3 Methodological Approach and Chapter Organization

The chapter adopts a multi-layered conceptual analysis comprising of philosophical ethical perspectives, technology and empirical social science analysis and assessments. It is worth briefly summarising recent scholarship from the past four years (2021-2025) to which we will refer, including a deontological view of the question, a consequentialist one and a virtue ethical one. This philosophical foundation is bolstered by research on constitutional constraints on the law of "deepfake" protection, social research examining effects and harms, and technical analysis on the technologies used to detect "deepfakes" and other security threats.

Table 1. Global survey data on deepfake victimization and perpetration (2024)

Country	Sample	Victimization	Perpetration	Female Victims
United States	1,600	2.8%	2.1%	89%
United Kingdom	1,600	2.4%	1.6%	92%
Canada	1,600	2.1%	1.4%	91%
Australia	1,600	2.6%	1.8%	88%
Germany	1,600	1.9%	1.2%	94%
France	1,600	2.2%	1.5%	90%
Japan	1,600	1.7%	1.3%	86%
Brazil	1,600	3.1%	2.4%	93%
India	1,600	2.9%	2.2%	87%
South Korea	1,600	2.0%	1.7%	91%
Overall	**16,000**	**2.2%**	**1.8%**	**90%**

Source: Umbach et al. (2024), Flynn et al. (2025)

The chapter is divided into eight substantive parts that examine the theoretical principles, conflict between creativity and harm, free expression versus legal limits, legal boundaries versus moral issues, social implications, literature regarding detection technology, and the role of policy. The sections are a mixture of philosophical analysis and empirical evidence to develop deeper understanding of the ethical connotations of deepfakes.

2 THEORETICAL FOUNDATIONS OF DEEPFAKE ETHICS

2.1 Deontological Perspectives: Dignity, Consent, and Moral Duties

2.1.1 Kantian Analysis of Synthetic Representation

The deontological ethics analysis of deontological deepfakes is the most in-depth philosophical study to this date conducted by de Ruiter (2021) and is perhaps the most Kantian line of thought. She argues with the universalizability principle of the categorical imperative which is the fundamental imperative of treating persons as ends in themselves as opposed to merely means. Lacking consent in the invention of synthetic representations situates the individual as an "object" in the process of technological manipulation – intended or not.

The Kantian structure highlighted the unique moral danger of deepfakes that de Ruiter calls the "phenomenal immediacy" problem. Deepfakes are a new type of misrepresentation, which unlike the more conventional ones, involve an interpretative mediation. The phenomenal directness bypasses usual cognitive filters related to the assessment of truthiness, capable of de-rationalizing viewers and violating their rational autonomy as an essential component of Kantian moral principles.

2.1.2 A Rights-Based Approach and Digital Self-Representation

Building on this deontological argument, Story and Jenkins (2023) advocate for a rights-based one underpinned by their rights-based notion of 'right to digital self-representation'. The second type of right is novel and is associated with the use of one's image, voice and identity in the digital environment. The non-consensual creation of a deep fake includes using and manipulating key aspects of someone's identity without permission, thus violating this right.

The right to digital self-representation goes beyond privacy and publicity rights to other issues related to the recognition of autonomy in digital domains. As the syntheses of increasingly complex synthetic media technologies have become available, controlling one's digital self has become an important aspect of one's personal integrity and social identity. This rights regime provides strong moral encouragement to help curb deepfakes, and provides enough deference to the lawful use of such technologies without harming individuals' right to consent and autonomy.

2.2 Consequentialist Approaches: Welfare, Harm, and Social Outcomes

2.2.1 Epistemic Consequentialism and Knowledge Threats

Fallis (2021) formulates a consequentialist perspective that addresses deepfakes' epistemic impacts, defined as the impacts on knowledge acquisition, belief formation, and information processing. Based on the study of information theory and epistemological analysis, he posits that the deepfake can pose a threat to social welfare in that digital media can no longer be trusted as a source of information or evidence. That "epistemic threat" has repercussions for democratic deliberation, judicial proceedings, and social coordination mechanisms that rely on common norms of evidence and truth.

The consequentialist approach shows a significant risk deepfakes pose of creating "infor-mational trust decay" Pawelec (2022), which includes a series of recurring fake instances that erode general trust in digital media. The presence of such deepfakes can introduce uncertainty over the veracity of what is actually authentic, which can have a negative impact on sources of information and evidence.

2.2.2 Welfare Maximization and Harm Prevention

In an utilitarian sense, the goal of a deepfake law should be to ensure that the total social welfare is maximized, while ensuring that some uses of deepfakes are not harmful. The groundbreaking interview study conducted by Flynn et al. (2025) gives valuable empirical support to this calculation, with interviews of both sexualized deepfake attackers and victims. Their work chronicles the significant psychological damage such as anxiety, depression, social isolation, experienced by the victims, as well as the victimizer's intentions to control, humiliate and gain money.

Deepfakes can have positive uses, making the welfare calculus complicated. As long as there are a variety of legitimate applications in education, accessibility, artistic and historical expression, etc., social advantages can be significant. The advantages of consequentialist analysis should be balanced with well documented disadvantages, paying particular attention to the impact that the regulatory measures might have on the distribution of both positive and negative consequences to different social groups.

2.3 Virtue Ethics and Character-Based Analysis

2.3.1 Virtue Frameworks for AI Ethics

Hagendorff (2022) elaborates a thorough virtue ethics framework for AI applications, such as synthetic media technologies. Just, honest, responsible, and caring are the four "basic AI virtues," in addition to two second-order virtues, prudence and fortitude, which instruct the ethical development and deployment of technology. The framework provides important guidance for deepfake creators and platforms, as well as those who create policy, on how to handle the complex ethical issues presented.

The virtue ethics approach has a focus on the development of character and moral virtue instead of rule following or the maximization of outcome. This lens has taught us to be accustomed to the use of deep fakes, so with this in mind, we now have to ask ourselves which characteristics are improved or jeopardized when creating and using synthetic media in different manners. The virtues of honesty and care involve being willing to act in a like manner, in line with consent, transparency, and benefit others; vices of honesty and care however involve engaging in deceptive, or otherwise doing applications that benefit others.

2.3.2 Practical Wisdom and Contextual Judgment

Reijers and Coeckelbergh (2024) further develop the concept of virtue ethics analysis with their "Virtuous Practice Design" (VPD) methodology, which is based on narrative ethics and the traditions of practical wisdom. It confirms that there are cases where ethical considerations of synthetic media applications are not algorithmically definable, or that result in mere simple utilitarian considerations.

The VPD approach focuses on how the different aspects of the narratives affect the ethical dimension of the uses of deepfakes. While the technology used might be the same, any photographic image of a deceased family member—intended to be used for memorialization purposes—has other issues than a photo being used in an unauthorized political parody. Virtue ethics provides principles that can help to resolve everyday practical issues in these context and allow the adherence to the same standards of moral judgment.

2.4 Integrative Approaches and Philosophical Synthesis

2.4.1 Multi-Framework Analysis

The current issue of deep fake ethics is so definite that it has many aspects and moral principles. Widder et al. (2022) illustrate this in their ethnographic study of the open source deep fake developers within a field that can be described as technology neutral, freedom of use (FOU) principles and draws attention to concerns about the harms that might arise.

The results of this study reveal that in the real world, ethical reflection regarding deepfakes is messy, and is complicated by trade-offs with competing deontological obligations, consequen-tialist considerations, and virtue considerations. Ethical guidelines must be capable to addressing the complexity, as also providing some actionable advice to creators, platform providers and policymakers.

2.4.2 Contextual and Relational Ethics

The new trend on deep fakes ethics calls to context and relation, taking into account the situationality of the ethical judgements. These are not strategies focused on generic principles that would apply to all situations of the making and receiving of synthetic media, but rather learning how to develop schemas or approaches that are attuned to the specific relationships, power relationships and communicative situations they involve.

This approach is in line with feminist ethics which place an emphasis on caring, relationships, and contextually situated knowledge in moral reasoning. In the context of deepfakes, contextual analysis prioritizes the contexts in which the image is created and the social status of the individuals in the image, as well as the context of the broader cultural issues surrounding gender, race, and marginalization in relation to the use of synthetic media.

3 THE CREATIVITY VERSUS HARM TENSION

3.1 Legitimate Creative Applications and Artistic Expression

3.1.1 Educational and Accessibility Benefits

While deepfake technology has some obvious uses in entertainment, it also offers a tremendous amount of potential in the educational realm and accessibility. Historical education programs are now more and more making use of synthetic media that are used to recreate the testimonies of deceased witnesses so that students can interact more compellingly and immersively with the primary source material. For endangered languages, a language preservation approach involves the use of deepfakes to preserve recordings of the languages, and thus to generate synthetic speakers, which can allow users to show pronunciation and linguistic patterns so that future generations can learn from and understand the languages.

Of particular allure are accessibility applications which exhibit the potential for deepfakes to benefit society. The synthetic media is used to produce sign language interpreters for content when live interpreters are not available, in organizations for deaf and hard-of-hearing. Likewise, when people have not been able to speak because of some type of medical issue, synthetic substitutes for their voices can be created based on a previous recording of their voice, thereby maintaining the important components of personal identity and self-expression.

3.1.2 Artistic Innovation and Creative Expression

With the emergence of deepfake technology in the art world, the creation of manipulated images has become a common method for contemporary artists to address issues related to identity, representation, and authenticity. Artworks in the Gallery are created with synthetic media and address cultural ideas about truth and documentation, and theatrical productions employ deepfake technology in innovative ways to highlight character development and narrative structure. These are applications where synthetic media is used for real art whose value adds to, not detracts from, the cultural discussion.

These are examples of "creative use of deepfake" in a movie. However, when dealing with populations at risk, and, in specific, with the identity of the subject to be anonymized and the testimony to be rendered in a faithful manner that would include the synthesis of the media employed by the subject, synthetic media could be used as a tool to achieve these goals. Such applications are meant to be transparent, safe: they are typically open about technical application processes and mention of protection motivations.

3.2 The Harmful Applications Spectrum

3.2.1 Non-Consensual Intimate Imagery and Gender-Based Violence

The most comprehensive cross national investigation of Deep fake abuse as an image form of sexual abuse to date conducted by Flynn et al. (2022) in the United Kingdom, New Zealand and Australia. The work brings to light that 96% of the deepfakes used in those sexed-up video clips was targeting women that were "fooled by their faces." It shows the gendered nature and systemic patterns of digital violence, which builds on traditional understanding of sexual harassment and abuse into the synthetic media spaces.

The psychological effects reported by the researchers Flynn et al. parallel the effects that have been reported in other GBV incidents, such as anxiety, depression, symptoms of post-traumatic stress and social withdrawal. Despite awareness of the synthetic nature of the content, victims still complain of feeling "violated" and "objectified", indicating that deepfake abuse can work by more complex means than just being deceptive or misrepresentative.

3.2.2 Political Manipulation and Democratic Threats

Pawelec (2022) offers a thorough theoretical examination of the ways deepfakes can harm key democratic functions: empowerment, inclusion, will formation, and legitimacy of decision making. Political deepfakes can compromise citizens' information literacy by infiltrating public message spaces with false content that can skew election results in a way that could be only marginally disprovable through discerning deepfake detection.

The actual data on political fake videos shows that their impact is not necessarily limited to persuasion effects. In the Russo-Ukrainian war, Twomey et al. (2023) look at tweets, and discover that the most damaging epistemic mistake is when someone calls real media fake, and not calling fake media real. This "liar's dividend" effect means that bad actors can benefit from these synthetic existences even if they don't produce them.

3.3 Distinguishing Creative Expression from Harmful Manipulation

3.3.1 Consent and Authorization Frameworks

The big difference in legitimate creative uses compared to harmful manipulation lies with the means of consent and authorization. Situations that are considered legitimate usually include informed consent by subjects of the media, a clear statement of why synthetic media was used, and a well-defined application that reflects a subject's interest and/or social good. Unlawful applications systematically transgress these principles by using the subjects' knowledge without their consent, by presenting it as a legitimate application, or by using it in an application that can harm the interest of the subjects.

The context of contemporary consent patterns should reflect the particular characteristics of the big data synthetic media which require overcoming the traditional rules of consent. Unlike images or traditional video captures, deep faces permits senseless manipulation and recombination of captured images, which can be hard to foresee when authorization hits the hook. It implies that consent should be dynamic; that is, that a consent model should be in place to enable the subjects to retain the right to control synthetic media with their likeness continuously.

3.3.2 Purpose, Context, and Social Function

In the vein of this, Murray (2025) contributes to the field of legal analysis of deepfakes by considering existing remedies in the field of IP and Privacy law and the value of purpose and context in determining ethics and laws. Even if the technical process of creating an image, product or textile is the same and uses an inauthentic or unauthorized image of a person as the source material, there are other considerations regarding possible commercial exploitation compared with educational or artistic purposes.

In the contextual approach, identical synthetic media content can be used for good or bad purposes depending on who creates, distributes and how the audience understands it. The role of a synthetic recreation designed for a memorial purpose is distinctly different from one designed for commercial exploitation and/or harassment purposes, with family consent as a key criterion.

3.4 Platform Governance and Content Moderation Challenges

3.4.1 Automated Detection and Human Review

In Fisher et al.'s (2024) work, they discuss synthetic content moderation on social media platforms, emphasizing the need to look through existing policies of content moderation instead of creating new policies to fight the threats posed by deepfakes. This view acknowledges that most deep fake applications—whether created synthetically or not—are likely in violation of the platforms' existing rules against harassment, intimate imagery taken without consent or misleading content.

However, platforms are also subject to governance issues, due to technical aspects of deepfakes. Unfortunately, there are no fully automated systems currently available to produce results for accurate classification and human media reviewers are often not technically proficient enough to do so. It can pose major challenges in terms of scalability for platforms trying to moderate deepfake content without compromising legitimate uses.

3.4.2 Model Governance and Creation Tool Oversight

This is a research paper by Gorwa and Veale (2024) regarding the new governance challenges for AI model hosting services like HuggingFace, GitHub and specialized platforms like Civitai that are used to generate deepfakes. These "model marketplaces" are confronted with having to decide which tool(s) to host, how to put in place restrictions on access to them, and whether to track any downstream use of models that have been hosted.

The model governance approach highlights the need for, and potential for, action not just with respect to content but also at the level of creation and propagation of models. A balance will need to be achieved as the platforms provide tools for accessing deceptive or preferential creation models, while ensuring researchers can have their creative freedoms and innovativeness respected.

4 FREE EXPRESSION AND LEGAL BOUNDARIES

4.1 First Amendment Analysis and Constitutional Constraints

4.1.1 Speech Classification and Protected Expression

Stewart and Littau (2025) has more than uncovered legal doctrine; they've discovered the human dilemma at the heart of American free speech. Their research shows that there is a painful irony in the First Amendment cases that argue for limiting deepfake regulation: The very principles that protect the freedom of an individual to broadcast an unpopular, fiery truth could be invoked also to protect a lie that could kill a person or an election. They studied proposed legislation and determined that the current civil laws actually provide protection for false political speech that would otherwise be hard to see how any law would successfully attempt to balance truth and falsehoods when it comes to restricting speech. The Supreme Court's famous ruling voiding the Stolen Valor Act reiterates this fact of law.

This puts the judges, legislators and public in a bind in the real world. How did we honor the legitimate and urgent concerns about preventing fraud, protecting personal dignity and ensure our elections and how can we reconcile our society's need for a robust, rough, sometimes unpleasant public debate with those goals? The issue is, when both are done with the same perfect deepfake, the distinction between them is a fine one, or it's lost altogether.

4.1.2 Content-Based Regulation and Strict Scrutiny

It is here that Weiner (2023) resides, with a very pragmatic idea: a "foreseeable harm" test. Instead of attempting to outlaw the deepfakes outright – as the Constitution bars – this approach considers a more human and context-based question: In this particular case, given all of the circumstances, did this deepfake present a significant threat to a vital public good or interest that the state had a legitimate right to address? It is a concept that recognises that we cannot regulate speech on the basis of an uncertain apprehension of its effect, but we can act when the harm is right in front of us.

The emergency brake on censorship as mandated by the Constitution of the United States. Law must be drawn with "surgical, narrow precision" for a good government interest not merely an important one, and be drawn "in the least restrictive way possible." For deepfakes' unsettling and serious impacts on humans, this is a sound moral and legal guideline. It puts an end to the wide government surveillance which chills satire, art, and dissent.

4.2 State Regulatory Approaches and Legal Landscape

4.2.1 Comprehensive Legislative Survey

Ugwuoke and Sanfilippo (2025) have undertaken the mapping exercise for us in the context of law and the internet. They have taken a systematic look at bills introduced in 2019–2024 in all 50 states and found that there's a picture of a country in an anxious state of scattered reaction, rather than a coherent strategy. In some states, dragging their feet on the issue simply to appease the pushers, it seems, is too much trouble. Laser-like focus is on non-consensual intimate imagery in some states, because it's a trauma they know their people are undergoing. Others, in a more sweeping gesture of alarm, make sweeping bans on "misleading synthetic media" in all its forms.

This survey shows how hugely expensive inhuman the federal inaction can be. This is often a patchwork end product that is constitutionally suspect and practically defies the constitution. Depending on where you live, the police might or might not pay attention to your case, or even have any law to which they can report it. It does not address the gravest of the harms: and it makes law unforgiving, leaving both good and bad uses of creativity in the same confusion.

4.2.2 Definitional Challenges and Technical Precision

This battle in these state capitals is no longer just political, it's existential. How to define a "deepfake" in a way that you're not capturing the parody, you're not capturing the homage, you're not capturing the historical documentary recreation, but you are capturing the thing that did the harm? Definitions provided are all broad brush, that is, they will capture legitimate expressions of creativity, or they represent a sieve, being too wide open to allow them to be consistently and fairly enforced. The artistry of technology is developing so rapidly that all formulaic terms of law are discredited. While it's certainly not the same as the state sponsored disinformation campaign of the past, the mere possibility of human harm is enough for law to govern the entire operation of the 'cheap fake' produced today by a jilted 'ex' lover using a mobile phone.

The law is under compulsion to draw a line, between a crime and a protected form of self-expression, on a technological spectrum. As any framework that comes out of this develops, it needs to be intelligent enough to take care of the harm on that whole spectrum, high tech to low tech, without tramping on the journalist trying to protect a source, on the artist trying to make a political point, or on the educator trying to bring history to life.

4.3 International and Comparative Legal Approaches

4.3.1 European Union Artificial Intelligence Act

Łabuz (2024) is an insight into a new constitutional spirit through a thorough examination of the European Union's Artificial Intelligence Act. The American instinct is to defend the speaker, the EU's first comprehensive legal definition of deepfakes bets on the listener's protection using transparency. The AI Act distinguishes between some deepfakes, which are not considered forbidden speech, but rather 'specific risk' systems, and imposes an obligation of disclosure: a responsibility for such systems to state that they are deepfakes.

The model of the EU is rooted in a different cultural and constitutional foundation. Doesn't assume the "marketplace of ideas" will naturally distinguish between fact and fiction; it feels citizens have a right to know when they are being spoken to by a machine. The law calls for the disclosure of users that they are viewing synthetic content and for creators to include protections. It's not prohibition it is a call to honesty.

4.3.2 International Law and Conflict Applications

The latest chapter of this technology is its use as a weapon in the Russo-Ukrainian war, as we are taken by Kuz´nicka-Błaszkowska and Kostyuk (2025) to its darkest frontier. The work they produce is both chilling and research into the way their synthetic media is being used not only to attack the dignity of individuals but against civilian populations, and the idea of international order. It is not only about misinformation in this case; it's about munitions. It is possible to produce a bogus surrender video of a surrendering leader, thereby deflating a civilian population. There can be fake evidence of atrocities that can be planted to quickly change international opinion and justify some real violence.

The solution they offer is the radical, and needful, idea of international rights over "cognitive liberty". It's a word that represents the numerous stakes that are new: the right to think, believe, remember, without being manipulated, influenced by technology and weaponized.

4.4 Platform Liability and Intermediary Governance

4.4.1 Section 230 and Content Moderation

Section 230 of the Communications Decency Act (CDA) is a law interpreted in an ever more "hands-off" and at times, heart-breaking way in America. In terms of legal protection, the robustness of protecting platforms from actual liability for providing a platform that facilitated the killing of someone from a deepfake is an important consideration as explained by Constantino (2024). This is one of the crucial policies that were designed in such a way that it shouldn't crush babyweb as it grows up, providing room for innovation. It is an experiment with liberty and risk of failure. Still present though, for deepfakes that will be both ethical and practical. As a result, the companies let other companies dictate the rules of cyberspace, rules that sometimes are even not visible, and capriciously enforce the rules, which are not fact-based but political instead of ethical.

4.4.2 Emerging Liability Frameworks

Murray (2025) offers a path away from this temptation of "one law to rule them all" and to a vision of a patchwork of existing legal strands for the future of real resilience. This is a profoundly human observation – harms of a significant complexity require a response to a significant complexity. What we need to do now is not look for a single "deepfake law" in the abstract, but see what can be done, using the tools we have, now. For instance, persons themselves have the right to their own voice and image being used in commercial pursuits (the right of publicity) and that right will be very powerful and quick to use to counteract the misuse of deepfakes.

This new perspective emphasizes the importance of a legal pluralist and ingenious approach. In some cases, the victim of dignitary harm where his or her image has been used without his or her permission can attempt to obtain relief through a privacy tort. The worst abuses can be dealt with by Criminal law. Intellectual Property right can be used to address commercial exploitation. None of these is a magic bullet, but it is a web of accountability.

5 MORAL DILEMMAS ACROSS STAKEHOLDER GROUPS

5.1 Creator Responsibilities and Ethical Obligations

5.1.1 Professional Ethics for Deepfake Developers

In an investigation of software development communities, Widder et al. (2022) have found that important lessons lie in understanding the ethical responsibilities of which open source deepfake creators consider themselves to be responsible for. The research exhibits elaborate and seamless interactions between "Freedom 0" principles and focus on free software use, Technology Neutrality beliefs and freedom from downstream application requirements, and greater recognition of potential harms associated with the use of synthetic media.

When dealing with professional developers, ethical questions are particularly difficult since a development is a work that may be done for good or for bad. The malicious uses of deep fake technology, like the creation of visual content depicting intimate actions without participants' consent, and the potential to use those same tools for good, such as creating visual aids that make things more accessible, for better or for worse reveal the dual nature of the technology.

5.1.2 Consent, Disclosure, and Transparency Obligations

There is a growing set of modern ethical standards that call on creators to secure meaningful consent from the people that are represented in the media, as well as for clarifying the use of synthetic media. Applying these principles in digital environments where content can be shared, edited, or otherwise recontextualised without the creator's control is difficult, however.

Figure 1. Stakeholder moral dilemmas in the deepfake ecosystem

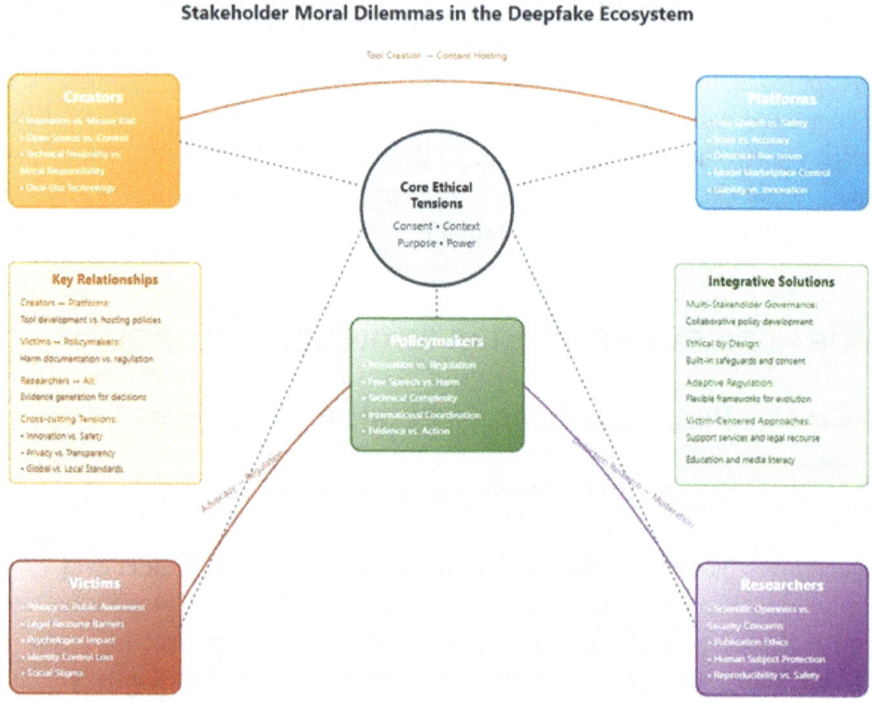

The consent process should incorporate the potential for continued modification and permu-tation of appropriated likenesses through the use of deepfake technology, which can be hard to predict in the context of the initial consent process. This points to the need for continued consent processes with users controlling synthetic media applications.

5.2 Platform Governance and Algorithmic Accountability

5.2.1 Content Moderation Challenges and Bias

In a recent paper, Fisher et al. (2024) look at the way platforms approach synthetic content moderation in the context of their existing policy frameworks and explore some of the challenges of creating scalable and accurate detection systems. The automated content-moderation systems sometimes fail to detect deepfake content, and human reviewers might lack the technical skills required to properly assess the content.

The results of the tests expose troubling bias in deepfake detection and modera-tion technolo-gies. Algorithmic decisions that are developed, tested and optimized mainly with content from specific demographic groups might not work out as well with synthetic content that represents content from underrepresented communities.

5.2.2 Transparency and Algorithmic Governance

In this article, Gorwa and Veale (2024) examine the governance issues around tools for creating deepfakes and the strategies adopted by prominent AI model hosting platforms such as Hugging Face, GitHub and dedicated communities like Civitai. Such platforms need to strike a balance between research freedom and values of innovation and with respect to possible misuse of the tools and models that they house.

The model marketplace analysis illustrates how intermediary platforms are exposed to new governance issues which go beyond content-moderation to tool design, access control and control of downstream platforms.

5.3 Victim Experiences and Support Needs

5.3.1 Psychological Impact and Recovery Challenges

In the study by Flynn et al. (2025), the researchers conduct a groundbreaking empirical study that uses interviews to gather insights into victims' experiences related to sexualised deepfake abuse. The research demonstrates the negative psychological health effects of the violence, such as anxiety, depression, post-traumatic stress disorder and social isolation, which are similar to the effects of other forms of gender-based violence. Even when victims are aware that it is synthetic content, they feel "violated" and "objectified."

The victim impact analysis showcases how far deceptive and misrepresentation cases go with respect to the role of deep fakes. It appears that the hurt is more psychological than content authenticity as it's the non-consensual stealing and sexualization of personal identity that hurts.

5.3.2 Legal Recourse and Institutional Response

Empirical research shows that there are serious obstacles in the way of victims seeking effective legal remedy and/or institutional assistance in cases of deepfake abuse. There is a lack of technical expertise within law enforcement to effectively investigate those who have been victimized, and a lack of understanding of the unique harms caused by synthetic media abuse in the legal system.

New practices of victim advocacy include specialized training for law enforcement, legal professionals and support services to gain competency in dealing with synthetic media abuse.

5.4 Researcher Ethics and Academic Responsibility

5.4.1 Research Ethics in Deepfake Studies

Ethical issues in deepfake technology research are intricate and involve striking a balance between scientific progress and the potential for its use in harmful ways. Researchers aiming to design new generation algorithms or detection systems will have to deal with dual-use issues as their work can lead to both positive applications and high-stakes usage.

The evaluation of deepfake research proposals, especially those involving human subjects and/or sensitive applications, is an issue that is increasingly under discussion among IRCs and RECs. Conventional research ethics may be inadequate to deal with the new problems emerging from synthetic media technologies.

5.4.2 Publication and Disclosure Practices

In the academic world, appropriate ways to publish deepfakes are still a topic of debate, specif-ically with respect to technical details that could help out in creating deepfakes with harmful intent. Some scientists have called for responsible disclosure strategies where sensitive tech-nical details are restricted, while others put a strong emphasis on open scientific inquiry and reproduction and requirements rules.

These conversations reflect a wider dichotomy in AI ideation between openness and security issues.

6 SOCIAL IMPACTS AND SECURITY IMPLICATIONS

6.1 Democratic Institutions and Information Trust

6.1.1 Electoral Integrity and Political Discourse

The profound, conceptual account of the ways deepfakes challenge fundamental democratic pro-cesses of "empowered inclusion," "collective will formation" and "decision-making legitimacy" is offered by Pawelec (2022). Political synthetic media threatens democratic deliberation by adding sophisticated means of deception to the public discourse, and can even affect electoral results with campaigns that can be hard to detect and counter.

The democratic impact analysis illustrates the exacerbation of the epistemic challenges faced by today's democracies with the help of deepfakes. When the facts or understandings of the information or accepted truths differ amongst political groups, the manipulation of these differences can further inform private issues related to a lack of shared fact bases crucial to democratic discourse.

6.1.2 The "Liar's Dividend" and Truth Decay

To provide important empirical evidence on epistemic effects of deepfakes, Twomey et al. (2023) analyzed 4,869 tweets during the Russo-Ukrainian war. What they discovered was that the primary epistemic problem posed by deepfakes was not when people think they perceive something that is in fact fake, but when they interpret something as real when it actually is fake. This "liar's dividend" effect enables bad elements to benefit from deepfake existence without having to produce synthetic content.

The empirical results point to what researchers describe as "truth decay": the fading relevance of that which is factual in society and the growing uncertainty regarding basic information standards.

6.2 Gender-Based Violence and Social Inequality

6.2.1 Systematic Targeting and Marginalization

Flynn et al. (2022) report, using detailed cross-country analysis, that deepfake abuse is a systemic form of gender-based digital violence that is focused on women and other marginalised groups. Of the 96% of identified deepfakes, all were of females without consent, showing that the technology to fake media content is being used to help promote gender prejudice and abuse. The gendered impact analysis underscores the fact that the use of deepfakes is intertwined with wider trends in online harassment targeting women and marginalized groups. The victims report social retreats, absence from online activities and self-censorship of their expression in order not to be targeted.

6.2.2 Intersectional Vulnerabilities and Compound Harms

The empirical research demonstrates how the victim of deep fake abuse can be compoundly exploited by gender, race, sexual orientation and other identity factors.

Synthetic media technolo-gies can be used to produce fake evidence of behaviours and statements that reinforce negative stereotypes, which can exacerbate discrimination and social disadvantage.

Finally, the intersectional analysis highlights the need to consider the impact of synthetic media beyond individual notions of privacy or dignity, as it can contribute to existing inequitable systems.

6.3 Detection Technologies and Security Architecture

6.3.1 Human versus Machine Detection Capabilities

In the PNAS study of deepfake detection capabilities with 15,016 participants, Groh et al. (2022) deliver landmark empirical evidence on the abilities of deepfake detection. The data shows that humans and the top machine learning classifiers perform the same accuracy at detecting a deepfake image, but that they commit different kinds of errors, indicating potential improvements from hybrid systems of human and machine.

The detection capability analysis revealed vulnerabilities in human and automated efforts in identifying synthetic media. While human reviewers will still be asking about technical artifacts and inconsistencies, which sophisticated deepfake systems are increasingly able to remove, machine learning systems also may be susceptible to adversarial attacks or may not be robust enough to perform well on tests utilizing differing deepfake generation techniques.

6.3.2 Technical Evolution and Arms Race Dynamics

Rana et al. (2022) carry out a thorough systematic literature review (SLR) of deep fake detection techniques and analyze 112 articles related to deep fakes, in order to gain insights on the current state-of-the-art and limitations. The analysis shows that there is still an "arms race" between the techniques of generating the attacks and the methods of detecting them, with each new generation technique continually pushing the detection methods of their time to new limits.

This technical discussion focuses on the key issues that must be overcome to create practical deepfake detection tools that are effective, regardless of the method used to generate a deepfake, the subject matter, or the conditions under which it is generated.

6.4 Trust Architecture and Verification Systems

6.4.1 Content Provenance and Blockchain Solutions

In response, cutting-edge technologies for addressing deepfakes have become more focused on content provenance and verification systems leveraging cryptography and distributed ledger technologies to verify media authenticity. These strategies aim to solve these limitations in detection by providing a list of changes to document and test content production and modification in a way that is clear to the user when it occurs without relying on detection algorithms.

However, the verification process using blockchain technology also presents a number of challenges in practice, such as user adoption level, computational load, and integration with current media delivery networks.

6.4.2 Social and Institutional Trust Implications

But new media technologies give rise to more fundamental problems for social mechanisms of trust beyond technical problems of entanglement. Institutions like journalism, education, and democratic governance rely on common, fundamental rules of evidence and truth, which can be undermined in the absence of general trust in the authenticity of media.

Rebuilding the social trust mechanisms in a deepfake context will most likely need institu-tional changes, media education, and verification mechanisms.

7 DETECTION TECHNOLOGIES AND TRUST FRAMEWORKS

7.1 Current Detection Methodologies and Limitations

7.1.1 Machine Learning Approaches and Performance Analysis

Malik et al. (2022) perform a thorough survey analysis of the face-based deep fake detection methods, thoroughly examine a variety of deep learning architectures and emphasize that there are still many challenges in the deep learning models to distinguish the fake and real face content. Many of the current methods of detection involve technical effects or inconsistencies in the generation processes and they are susceptible to eliminating these with the sophisticated generation algorithms.

The technical survey potentially shows that existing methods involving detecting generation artefacts are intrinsically poor detection methods. The ability to create deepfakes continues to grow, with traditional indicators such as temporal inconsistencies, compression artifacts, and physiological implausibilities growing less reliable.

7.1.2 Multimodal and Cross-Domain Challenges

Wang and colleagues (2024) review deepfake detection from the reliability perspective and con-clude that there are three key challenges: transferability between various generation techniques, decisions on detection and their interpretability, and the ability to resist adversarial manipulation. The analysis shows how "specific" detectors set to a certain dataset and/or generation procedure tend to not adapt to new synthetic data types.

This reliability analysis shows special difficulties in finding detection systems that work well on a variety of content modalities such as video, audio and text-based synthetic media.

7.2 Human Detection Capabilities and Hybrid Systems

7.2.1 Cognitive Psychology and Detection Accuracy

It's definitely a landmark study of deepfake detection ability of human subjects from Groh et al. (2022) published in PNAS (15,016 subjects). In general, accuracy of distinguishing between synthesized and real content in videos is at 0.65-0.7, and the accuracy for each content may differ significantly because of content characteristics, viewing conditions and personal characteristics. Human detection analysis shows that there are patterns in which people look for synthetic content, many preferring to use technical artifacts, inconsistencies in facial expressions or inconsistencies in the context rather than more complex analysis.

7.2.2 Human-Machine Collaboration Models

The findings indicate that hybrid systems (combining human and machine learning) might have a few benefits over automatic systems. There are some differences in the type of errors humans and algorithms can make and people might be more or less sensitive to some aspects of the synthetics, so systems could be built more accurately with a combination of humans and algorithms.

Hybrid system approach has many practical difficulties such as the scalability issue, training of human reviewers, and the complexity of integration for real-time applications.

7.3 Technical Evolution and Countermeasure Development

7.3.1 Generative-Adversarial Dynamics

Deep fakes are analysed and methods of detection by Masood et al. (2023), commenting on the "arms race" scenario which exists between generating deep fakes and detecting them. Such adversarial training methods are increasingly adopted in new generation techniques, posing a challenging hurdle when trying to build countermeasures.

This adversarial paradigm analysis reveals that a reactive detection strategy may not suffice when it comes to facing more advanced synthetic media attacks.

7.3.2 Proactive and Prevention-Based Approaches

Stroebel et al. (2023) discuss the literature on deepfake detection in 2021-2022 and state the traditional neural network techniques require ensemble or multi-attention techniques for being effective. The analysis reveals that there is a possibility of being proactive with respect to content authentication and provenance (synthetic materials are only part of the puzzle).

The prevention approach focuses on technical supporting infrastructure development for content verification and authentic media certification.

7.4 Trust Infrastructure and Verification Systems

7.4.1 Cryptographic Provenance and Content Authentication

Today's technical approaches are increasingly aimed at cryptographic content authentication systems which are capable of proving the provenance of the media to ensure who are the signatories on the media through digital signatures, timestamps and verification in a blockchain system. These approaches seek to provide a record of content creation or modification with the property of tamper proofness which can be used to make claims regarding content authenticity without depending on detection algorithms.

But the cryptographic approach has many practical limitations, including user acceptance, computation, and media distribution integration.

8 POLICY AND GOVERNANCE RESPONSES

8.1 Regulatory Framework Development and Implementation

8.1.1 European Union Artificial Intelligence Act Analysis

Łabuz (2023; 2024) provides the most detailed examination of the risk labelling, transparency and enforcement obligations related to deepfakes under the EU's Artificial Intelligence Act. The EU's approach is the first integrated jurisdiction-wide legal framework for synthetic media technologies which provides insight into potential solutions for other systems around the world. The AI Act, while not imposing prohibition, contains transparency and disclosure require-ments for certain deepfake applications considered as "specific risk" AI systems. Users should be alerted in the event that synthetic content is encountered, and proper technical measures should be taken by creators to ensure that content is properly labelled as synthetic.

8.1.2 United States State-Level Legislative Responses

Earlier, Ugwuoke and Sanfilippo (2025) expose the complex present state of US deepfake laws by analyzing 319 bills that have been introduced in all 50 states since 2019. There is a very wide range of regulatory approaches, many of them targeting only non-consensual intimate imagery and others trying to regulate deceptive synthetic media in a more general way.

The state legislative survey shows that to legalize and constitutionalize the deepfake regula-tions remains a challenge. Numerous bills are vague in their technical language, have too broad definitions, or contain policies that may be hard to enforce in an effective manner.

8.2 Platform Governance and Content Moderation Evolution

8.2.1 Existing Framework Adaptation

Fisher et al. (2024) discuss major social media platforms' response to addressing synthetic content in the current policy landscape, which does not focus on specific policies for deep-fakes. It acknowledges that the dangerous applications of deep fakes most often simply bear special characteristics towards harassment, personal photos or misleading content, and that will otherwise be restricted by existing platform rules, independently of its synthetic nature.

The platform governance analysis highlights several issues related to the actual imple-mentation of deepfake content moderation, such as the limitations of detection accuracy and the capacity drop in moderation processes that depend on human effort, in addition to the requirement of specific technical expertise in the team of content moderators.

8.2.2 Model Marketplace Governance

Gorwa and Veale (2024) study new governance concerns with platforms which make AI models accessible for deepfake creation, covering strategies implemented by widely used platforms such as Hugging Face, GitHub, and niche communities. The "model marketplaces" are required to make new choices regarding creation tools to serve on these marketplaces, access control and whether to audit the downstream uses.

This model governance approach is not limited to managing content—the upstream benefits of moderation at the creation and distribution points may also be seen.

8.3 International Cooperation and Cross-Border Challenges

8.3.1 Jurisdictional Coordination and Legal Harmonization

It shows how the world has been reshaped by digital media distribution, and the role it plays is problematic when it comes to effective governance of deep fakes that needs international cooperation and legal harmonisation. Platforms and content creators who operate across multiple jurisdictions will face compliance issues due to differences in approaches toward speech regulation, privacy protections, and technology governance.

Contemporary international cooperation efforts focus on developing shared technical stan-dards for content authentication, establishing mutual legal assistance frameworks for cross-border enforcement, and promoting best practices for platform governance.

8.3.2 Conflict and Information Warfare Applications

Kuz´nicka-Błaszkowska and Kostyuk (2025) examine deepfakes' implications for international law through analysis of synthetic media deployment during the Russo-Ukrainian war. Their research reveals novel challenges for international humanitarian law including civilian protection, cultural property preservation, and information warfare regulation during armed conflicts.

The international law analysis proposes regulation through establishing rights to "cognitive liberty" under existing legal frameworks.

8.4 Future Governance Directions and Policy Recommendations

8.4.1 Multi-Stakeholder Governance Models

Rather than using any single governance mechanism, a multi-stakeholder approach that coor-dinates responses at the government level, through self-regulatory frameworks of platforms, through industry standard-setting, and in the civil society sphere is likely more effective to ensure robust governance of deepfakes. Collaborative practice is a key part of contemporary policy development, and the capacity to meet the challenges of rapidly changing technologies without foreclosing the space where innovative and beneficial practice might emerge.

The multi-stakeholder model takes into account different typologies of governance actors and their complementary capabilities and limitations regarding deepfakes.

9 FUTURE DIRECTIONS AND RECOMMENDATIONS

9.1 Emerging Technological Developments and Ethical Implications

9.1.1 Next-Generation Synthesis Capabilities

The early uses for synthetic media give an indication that deepfake technology is still being developed and has made so much progress. But of course, synthetic multimodal productions that have the capacity to yield coordinated products in all three genres – video, sound and text – may play a key role in such misleading products, and may also have important educational, access and creative expression benefits.

Technological development in the future will likely concentrate on enhancing the quality of the synthesis, decrease the computational load and achieve real time generation.

9.1.2 Integration with Extended Reality and Immersive Media

However, the challenges and opportunities that deepfake technologies bring up, when merging with virtual and augmented reality platforms, are not only the ones that are broadly referenced in frameworks centered around digital media. Vivid deception and manipulation capabilities may be granted to synthetic media through immersion, but the potential exists there for helpful applications to education, therapy and social togetherness as well.

Extended reality use of synthetic media creates unique ethical questions of consent and identity and psychological effects which may need particular analysis.

9.2 Policy Innovation and Governance Evolution

9.2.1 Regulatory Experimentation and Adaptation

While some degree of governance on deepfakes is probably necessary, the process will likely require some trial and error with regulatory strategies and methods, and a degree of flexibility will be needed if technology changes and societal impacts turn out to be larger than originally predicted. Space for innovation and positive experimentation can be safeguarded while allowing for the development of evidence-based governance through regulatory sandboxes, pilot projects and controlled policy experiments.

New policy developments focus on adaptive regulation with feedback and periodic policy review.

9.2.2 International Cooperation and Standard Setting

Improved international coordination at global level on the governance of deepfakes is needed in terms of common technical standards, mutual legal assistance and cooperation for enforcement mechanisms. In the current governance architecture, fragmented across jurisdictions, compliance is a challenge, and potentially forum shopping of harmful applications is possible.

The next steps for international cooperation are to establish standards of baseline protection for vulnerable populations, develop interoperable content authentication systems, and implement response capabilities for fast initial mitigation.

9.3 Research Priorities and Knowledge Gaps

9.3.1 Empirical Studies of Social Impact

Lacking in-depth empirical research are the various impacts of Deepfakes on society, especially given the many different populations and application scenarios that could reveal impacts not yet observed or understood. Future studies should focus on longitudinal studies of victim experiences, cross-cultural studies of detection and impacts of trust and systematic studies on beneficial applications in education and accessibility settings.

Intersectional vulnerabilities and differential impacts across demographic groups, communi-ties, and cultural contexts should be targeted.

9.4 Educational and Social Adaptation Strategies

9.4.1 Media Literacy and Digital Citizenship Education

A true social adaptation to synthetic media technologies demands an extensive media literacy education to enable citizens to operate in an environment rich in deceptive possibilities. Practices that should be focused in education should include critical evaluation skills, awareness of technical skills and their limitations, and awareness of positive and negative uses.

Current media literacy frameworks need to move beyond the subjective framework of assessing media sources' reliability to include the understanding of how media are generated by algorithms, how they can be detected and how they can be verified.

9.4.2 Professional Training and Institutional Capacity Building

The specialized training of law enforcement, legal professions, educators, and other institutional actors is needed in order to build competency in coping with deepfake related issues. The documentation of current institutional responses is frequently beset by technical gaps and lack of knowledge that can affect response within the investigation, prosecution, education, and victim support settings.

Both technical knowledge of synthetic media technologies and suitable response strategies to various deepfake applications should be covered in professional development programs.

10 CONCLUSION

10.1 Synthesis of Key Findings and Normative Insights

In conclusion, the discussion on the Ethics of deepfake reveals a complex situation, where the ethical issues intersect with the technological possibilities and with some fundamental issues of morality, law, and society, in ways that are hard to classify and answer. The evidence confirms deepfakes are not an inherently good or bad use of technology and that consent, context, purpose and use style are all critically important to the ethical use of deepfakes.

The philosophical analysis reveals that the principles coming from various ethical theories (deontological ethics, utilitarianism and virtue ethics) are complementary but not equivalent, each of them should be considered in the synthesis of media application. In deontological approaches, principles of respect for individual autonomy and dignity are grounded in the principle of consent and transparency, and consequentialist analysis is focused on ensuring the maximization of social good, and how this requires a balancing of benefit and harm. Ethics of virtue emphasizes development of character and abilities to address contextual problems that are not algorithmically or rule-based.

In the charts for empirical evidence, the clear concrete harms include the systematic targeting of women and other marginalised groups such as the production of intimate images without consent. They are recognised harms and they are valid to discuss in an ethical context and to be acted on, but do not rule out legitimate uses in education, inclusion, art and other contexts. Structures for good governance should be able to differentiate the good and bad uses of the technology, and be flexible for innovation and creative expression.

10.2 Implications for Ethics Theory and Applied Philosophy

The deepfake case study illustrates theoretical understanding and insights for more general questions of ethics of technology, of digital rights and of moral responsibility in a more complex sociotechnical setting. The analysis illustrates the potential for new ethical guidelines to emerge in response to new technologies and the need to be flexible and normative thinking that can change with the technology.

With respect to the technology ethics of today, there is no single rule but multiple strategies. The deepfake case is interesting in that it demonstrates that "ethical thinking in the real world" is not a process of imposing universal rules, but is rather a negotiation process among conflicting moral considerations.

The analysis also reveals the relevance of structural inequalities, social position in the communities, and of power relations in building, using and managing technological capacities in different communities. Deepfakes are a case in point of how seemingly innocuous technology can contribute to and perpetuate existing patterns of marginalisation and oppression, with regards to gender-based violence.

10.3 Policy Recommendations and Governance Directions

The detailed examination found in this chapter suggests the following policy recommendations for effective deepfake governance which will take into account considerations of innovation, expression and protection:

- **Regulatory Approaches**: Jurisdictions should focus on narrow regulations that address harm and only prohibit specific harmful uses, instead of blanket technology prohibition. The most straightforward situation for regulatory action is with regard to non-consensual intimate imagery, whereas the case of political uses presents more nuanced concerns of freedom of expression, which could be addressed differently.
- **Platform Governance**: Platforms should create advanced content moderation strategies, combining automated identification with human moderation, maintaining appeals pro-cedures and transparency in content removal decisions. Access controls and monitoring should be strengthened on model marketplaces that provide access to creation tools.
- **International Cooperation:** Given the global nature of the distribution of digital media, it is important to enhance international cooperation in terms of technical standards, legal frameworks and enforcement coordination. Content authentication systems, mutual legal assistance and victim support services are among the priority areas.

Education and Capacity Building: There needs to be extensive education and capacity building activities to equip institutions and persons with the knowledge and skills they need to operate in synthetic media environments.

10.4 Future Research Directions and Ongoing Challenges

There is also a substantial lack of understanding regarding how deepfakes affect society, what are the best governance solutions, and what are the best technical solutions. Research priorities identified are in relation to longitudinal victim impact studies, cross-cultural analysis of detection capabilities and the effects of trust, assessment of the beneficial uses of the system and evaluation of various regulatory options.

The deepfake challenge finally is a miniature of the challenges set before democratic societies to adapt their institutions, norms and practices to fast technological change without sacrificing their fundamental values of dignity, autonomy, truth and social cooperation. Cooperation must be strong, cross-disciplinary, inter-stakeholder and intergovernamental, in order to arrive at technically feasible, normatively acceptable solutions. It highlights the potential ethical, legal and societal dangers and boundaries of using deepfakes, but also demonstrates how these dangers can be overcome with attention to consent, transparency, harm prevention and adaptive governance. The challenge is to develop this sense of estimation, making distinctions between good and evil, and to maintain fundamental moral principles such as dignity of the human person, respect for the person, informed consent and social justice. If an ethical examination, empirical investigation and a participatory building process of governance are used, the positive potential of the synthetic media technologies could be tapped and a strategy developed to counter the most pressing threat and harm.

REFERENCES

Constantino, I. (2024). REAL PEOPLE IN FAKE PORN: HOW A FEDERAL RIGHT OF PUBLICITY COULD ASSIST IN THE REGULATION OF DEEPFAKE PORNOGRAPHY. *Jurimetrics: The Journal of Law, Science & Technology, 64*(3).

De Ruiter, A. (2021). The distinct wrong of deepfakes. *Philosophy & Technology, 34*(4), 1311–1332. DOI: 10.1007/s13347-021-00459-2

Fallis, D. (2021). The epistemic threat of deepfakes. *Philosophy & Technology, 34*(4), 623–643. DOI: 10.1007/s13347-020-00419-2 PMID: 32837868

Fisher, S. A., Howard, J. W., & Kira, B. (2024). Moderating synthetic content: The challenge of generative AI. *Philosophy & Technology, 37*(4), 133. DOI: 10.1007/s13347-024-00818-9 PMID: 39555113

Flynn, A., Powell, A., Eaton, A., & Scott, A. J. (2025). Sexualized deep-fake abuse: Perpetrator and victim perspectives on the motivations and forms of non-consensually created and shared sexualized deepfake imagery. *Violence Against Women*. Advance online publication.

Flynn, A., Powell, A., Scott, A. J., & Cama, E. (2022). Deepfakes and digitally altered imagery abuse: A cross-country exploration of an emerging form of image-based sexual abuse. *British Journal of Criminology, 62*(6), 1341–1358. DOI: 10.1093/bjc/azab111

Gorwa, R., & Veale, M. (2024). Moderating model marketplaces: Platform governance puzzles for AI intermediaries. *Law, Innovation and Technology, 16*(2), 341–391. DOI: 10.1080/17579961.2024.2388914

Groh, M., Epstein, Z., Firestone, C., & Picard, R. (2022). Deepfake detection by human crowds, machines, and machine-informed crowds. *Proceedings of the National Academy of Sciences of the United States of America, 119*(1), e2110013119. DOI: 10.1073/pnas.2110013119 PMID: 34969837

Hagendorff, T. (2022). A virtue-based framework to support putting AI ethics into practice. *Philosophy & Technology, 35*(3), 55. DOI: 10.1007/s13347-022-00553-z

Kuźnicka-Błaszkowska, D., & Kostyuk, N. (2025). Emerging need to regulate deepfakes in international law: The Russo–Ukrainian war as an example. *Journal of Cybersecurity, 11*(1), tyaf008. DOI: 10.1093/cybsec/tyaf008

Kuźnicka-Błaszkowska, D., & Kostyuk, N. (2025). Emerging need to regulate deepfakes in international law: The Russo–Ukrainian war as an example. *Journal of Cybersecurity*, *11*(1), tyaf008. DOI: 10.1093/cybsec/tyaf008

Łabuz, M. (2023). Regulating deep fakes in the Artificial Intelligence Act. *Applied Cybersecurity & Internet Governance*, *2*(1), 1–42. DOI: 10.60097/ACIG/162856

Łabuz, M. (2024). Deep fakes and the Artificial Intelligence Act—An important signal or a missed opportunity? *Policy and Internet*. Advance online publication.

Malik, A., Kuribayashi, M., Abdullahi, S. M., & Khan, A. N. (2022). DeepFake detection for human face images and videos: A survey. *IEEE Access : Practical Innovations, Open Solutions*, *10*, 18757–18775. DOI: 10.1109/ACCESS.2022.3151186

Masood, M., Nawaz, M., Malik, K. M., Javed, A., Irtaza, A., & Malik, H. (2023). Deepfakes generation and detection: State-of-the-art, open challenges, countermeasures, and way forward. *Applied Intelligence*, *53*(4), 3974–4026. DOI: 10.1007/s10489-022-03766-z

Murray, M. D. (2025). Deceptive exploitation: Deepfakes, the rights of publicity and privacy, and trademark law. IDEA: The Law Review of the Franklin Pierce Center for Intellectual Property, 65.

Pawelec, M. (2022). Deepfakes and democracy (theory): How synthetic audio-visual media for disinformation and hate speech threaten core democratic functions. *Digital Society : Ethics, Socio-Legal and Governance of Digital Technology*, *1*(2), 19. DOI: 10.1007/s44206-022-00010-6 PMID: 36097613

Rana, M. S., Nobi, M. N., Murali, B., & Sung, A. H. (2022). Deepfake detection: A systematic literature review. *IEEE Access : Practical Innovations, Open Solutions*, *10*, 25494–25513. DOI: 10.1109/ACCESS.2022.3154404

Reijers, W., & Coeckelbergh, M. (2024). Virtuous practice design in AI ethics. *AI and Ethics*, *4*, 487–502.

Stewart, D., & Littau, J. (2025). The right to lie with AI? First Amendment challenges for state efforts to curb false political speech using deepfakes and synthetic media. Colorado Technology Law Journal, 24.

Story, D., & Jenkins, R. (2023). Deepfake pornography and the ethics of non-veridical representations. *Philosophy & Technology*, *36*(3), 1–22. DOI: 10.1007/s13347-023-00657-0

Stroebel, L., Llewellyn, M., Hartley, T., Ip, T. S., & Ahmed, M. (2023). A systematic literature review on the effectiveness of deepfake detection techniques. *Journal of Cyber Security Technology*, *7*(2), 83–113. DOI: 10.1080/23742917.2023.2192888

Twomey, J., Ching, D., Aylett, M. P., Quayle, M., Linehan, C., & Murphy, G. (2023). Do deepfake videos undermine our epistemic trust? A thematic analysis of tweets that discuss deepfakes in the Russian invasion of Ukraine. *PLoS One*, *18*(10), e0291668. DOI: 10.1371/journal.pone.0291668 PMID: 37878559

Ugwuoke, V., & Sanfilippo, M. R. (2025). The current landscape of deepfake legislation in the United States: Analysis of state-level responses. Journal of Information Policy, 15.

Umbach, R., Henry, N., Beard, G. F., & Berryessa, C. M. (2024). Non-consensual synthetic intimate imagery: Prevalence, attitudes, and knowledge in 10 countries. In Proceedings of the CHI Conference on Human Factors in Computing Systems (CHI '24) (Article 779, pp. 1–20). Association for Computing Machinery.

Wang, T., Liao, X., Chow, K. P., Lin, X., & Wang, Y. (2024). Deepfake detection: A comprehensive survey from the reliability perspective. *ACM Computing Surveys*, *57*(3), 1–35.

Weiner, M. D. (2023). Destined to deceive: The need to regulate deepfakes with a foreseeable harm standard. Mich. L. Rev., 122, 771.

Widder, D. G., Nafus, D., Dabbish, L., & Herbsleb, J. (2022). Limits and possibilities for "ethical AI" in open source: A study of deepfakes. In *Proceedings of the 2022 ACM Conference on Fairness, Accountability, and Transparency (FAccT '22)* (pp. 2035–2046). Association for Computing Machinery. DOI: 10.1145/3531146.3533779

Chapter 9
Utilizing Fuzzy AI to Find Relative Desirability of Online Threats on Social Media

Seema Khanum
http://orcid.org/0000-0002-2933-2717
Indian Computer Emergency Response Team (ICERT), MeitY, Electronics Niketan, Lodhi, India

A. Firos
http://orcid.org/0000-0003-4207-713X
Rajiv Gandhi University, India

ABSTRACT

We developed a research on Privacy and Ethical Norms where we quantifies these values using Bipolar Fuzzy Sets to ensures that modern systems behaves according to human values. For any specific context, we defines a bipolar state where a positive membership represents the presence of an ethical value like trust or anonymization and a negative membership represents a counter-value such as sadness or breach risk. We calculates the positive function as the average rating divided by ten and we represents the negative function as the negative average rating divided by ten. For example, if we have an AI that manages data with a high anonymization score of 8 but a risk of 2, we obtains a bipolar state showing strong positive presence and low negative risk. We utilizes t-cuts to filter out con-texts that does not meet our rigorous ethical standards, ensuring that only states with robust privacy measures is allowed to proceed in the decision-making pipeline.

DOI: 10.4018/979-8-3373-8292-0.ch009

1 INTRODUCTION

1.1 Fuzzy-Based Approach for Understandings Online Threats on Social Media Platforms

We developed a research on Generative Models for Understanding Online Threats on Social Media Using Fuzzy Logics because we knows that traditional security systems fails to captures the nuanced and evolving nature of digital dangers in social environments. Falana et al. (2024) proposed a hybrid fuzzy-AHP and game theory model to assess privacy risks on social media platforms, demonstrating improved risk prioritization . We utilizes generative models like Generative Adversarial Networks and Variational Autoencoders to discern complex patterns in data that resembles various online threats such as misinformation, cyberbullying, or phishing. Since social media be vast and full of anonymous interactions, we identifies unique challenges in recognizing threats that is buried in text sentiment or hidden interaction patterns. Duan et al. (2022) developed a q-rung double hierarchy linguistic fuzzy AHP model for evaluating security threat features in social media systems. Fuzzy Logic is used as a mathematical model by We in order to deal with the uncertainty and imprecision of the definition of a threat, and thus to represent the degrees of membership of a threat rather than just being true or false. This integration presents a finer method wherein the fuzzy concept is applied to the model to further the capability of the model to deal with the ambiguous security cues that give a better understanding of the subtle differences in the expression of threats across the platforms.

We also train our generative model in our methodology to apply the Fuzzy Logic principles to it; we train it with various datasets of threat expressions that are the result of real social media situations. The described work in Saeed and Shareef (2021) used the methods of artificial intelligence to anticipate security threats in the social media space. We carries out a training procedure which encompasses learning of the fuzzy association amid the input features such as user text, metadata and the resultant threat conditions. We discovered that this enables the model to represent the fuzzy delimitation of the various forms of harm that might not be mathematically relevant in a digital environment where sarcasm or context reforms all things. In Korkmaz et al. (2024), fuzzy N-soft sets were proposed to detect and authorize cyber harassment in social media networks. We test the efficacy of our suggested strategy with the help of stringent testing on actual social media data collections based on the metrics of accuracy, precision, and recall. We also ensures through validation procedures that our model generalizes well to unseen data, which proves its robustness in capturing the complexity of online malicious behaviors. By leveraging these advanced computational techniques, we seeks to provides a more nuanced understanding of digital risks to foster improved security outcomes and safer user experiences for everyone. Luo and Luo (2024) utilized fuzzy neural networks to analyze social media user behavior and support accurate online marketing strategies.

Arpaci (2023) employed a SEM-ANN approach to examine the social sustainability of AI chatbots under cybersecurity considerations. Here we believes that this cutting-edge research initiative significantly enhances the adaptability and responsiveness of cybersecurity technology in the modern era. Bouramdane (2023) addressed cyberattack challenges in smart grids using an AHP-based multi-criteria decision-making framework. Here they uses the fuzzy logic to process the vagueness associated with online threats, enabling a context-aware analysis that traditional binary models cannot achieves because they is too rigid. See that the authors in Mehlawat et al. (2021) proposed a multiobjective fuzzy vehicle routing model using Twitter data for efficient delivery of essential goods. In our analysis, we observes that identifying threats plays a crucial role in maintaining user trust and mental well-being, and our system helps to bridge the gap created by the high volume of automated spam and fake news. Alguliyev et al. (2018) developed an MCDM model for evaluating security threats in social networks. Here we found that the resulting model be capable of generating responses that align with identified threat nuances, making the social media environment feels more secure and trustworthy for the public. We conducts these operations in order to make sure that each user gets a secure and morally sound experience as they interact on line. This model changes the way we perceive the grey spaces of online safety, which makes the social media scene more accommodating and safe to everyone involved.

1.2 Using Deep Neural Network to Find Mean Peoples and Keep Social Media Safe

We discovered that an intelligent computer system known as Deep Neural Network is highly effective at discovering average things and tricks on social media. Kumar et al. (2020) suggested a hybrid approach of utilizing hesitant fuzzy sets, AHP, and TOPSIS to evaluate the web application security. These intelligent computer brains are able to discern trends in large stacks of data that peoples may overlook. As an example, a brain can scan the way a person posts and whether he or she is a bully or an attempt to steal passwords. This becomes important in ensuring the internet is safe to all. We uses a special way to give posts two scores called a Bipolar Fuzzy Set. One score is for how much we can trust the post and the other score is for how much danger it has. Sangaiah et al. (2020) introduced a big data-driven cognitive computing system for optimizing social media analytics. We have made a plan with five big steps. The research in Ashraf et al. (2023) proposed circular spherical fuzzy aggregation operators for uncertainty handling in social media programming environments. First, we chose which apps to watch. Second, we took the data from those apps. Third, we looked at how people from different places talk. Fourth, we built the big brain. Fifth, we checked our work to make sure it was correct.

The computer brain has many layers that works together like a big team. Each layer looks at the data to find different kinds of mean talk or lies. Ali et al. (2022) analyzed the growing threat of deepfake technologies to individual and national security using AI perspectives. Here we uses a way to see where safety rules for different apps meet up. The authors in Ognibene et al. (2023) proposed recommendation algorithms to mitigate social media threats while promoting collective well-being. This help the brain learn from one app to help another one stay clean. Shahzad et al. (2024) examined the impact of artificial intelligence and social media on students' academic performance and mental well-being. We also looks at the leftover parts to see how new kinds of tricks fit into our safety rules. Our math shows that the core parts of the brain, which we call prime states, stay steady even when there is too much data. The research in Hameed et al. (2025) proposed an explainable AI-driven framework for depression detection from social media using NLP techniques. We uses special cuts to block any post that has a high danger score. Our rules proves that these safety states will always work right.

Such an arrangement of big computer brains makes the internet a better place to spend the time with (Wang et al., 2023). It makes individuals feel positive and secure when they are speaking with friends. The brain can learn and change for each person to make the warnings better over time. O'Meara and Murphy (2023) explored co-creation of surrealist body horror imagery using AI-based text-to-image generation models. It helps the people who run the apps make good choices to stop bad guys fast. We have seen that this smart way finds more tricks than old ways did before. It keeps the web safe from mean words and lies so nobody gets hurted while they is online. We keeps making the brain smarter so it can find new tricks that bad guys might try tomorrow. Hameed et al. (2025) proposed an explainable AI framework for detecting mental illness from social media using machine learning techniques.

1.3 Fuzzy AI for making safe Social Media transactions

We made a smart Fuzzy AI system to understand and find threats on social media. Sharma et al. (2024) analyzed the influence of digital assistant attributes on intentions using PLS-SEM and ANN. This system is very good because it deals with things that is not simple or clear. Online places can be messy with many mean words and tricks. Our system uses a way called a bipolar fuzzy set to look at two sides of every post. Hsu and Lin (2006) utilized fuzzy set theoretic techniques to empirically analyze travel risk perception. We gives each post a score for being helpful and a score for being a threat. We calculates the threat score by seeing how many people get hurt and how often the bad thing happens. This help us see the grey areas where a post might be a little bit bad but not a total lie. We have seen that this way is much better than just saying something is all good or all bad. Gwassi et al. (2025) proposed an end-to-end cyber threat detection and risk assessment framework using XAI and blockchain technologies.

Our fuzzy brain can do many things to keep people safe. It can find mean bullies by looking at how they talk and if they is trying to make others sad. It also catches the fake stories and individuals who attempt to steal passwords. The flexibility of the system allows it to alter on a case-by-case basis. On one of the applications, it could look at mean pictures. On another, it may be on the lookout of fake news. We provides a special syntax known as an intersection to determine the safety rules that are applicable to all apps simultaneously. This is the reason why when we combine data around different locations the safety remains quite high. We also have what is referred to as a t-cut to mark out a line. Any post that exceeds the danger line is immediately halted before it can cause harm to anybody. To make this system work we have a plan with five big steps. First, we chose which apps to watch. Second, we took the data from those apps. Third, we looked at how people from different places talk. Fourth, we built the big computer brain using our math rules. Fifth, we checked if the brain was right. We checked our work with real apps to see if it works. See the study (Haddadpajouh et al., 2020) introduced a multi-view fuzzy consensus clustering model for malware threat attribution . We found that our fuzzy way is swifter and more reliable than the old ways that people used to use. Our math rules shows that the system stays steady even when there is millions of posts every second. We have proven through Theorem 3.1 that these safety states is stable and stays strong.

We also found that our system reduces "digital friction," which is a simple way of saying it stops people from getting into fights online. It also assists the individuals running the apps make good decisions by providing them with clear scores of all the risks that they observe. The fuzzy system also considers the feelings of people so as to know more about the threats. It examines the text typed by people to determine whether they are pleased or angry. In case the system notices that a post is hurting a lot of people the post may be a threat. We discovered such an attitude towards feelings is overly significant to a secure internet. With such intelligent regulations, we transform the digital world into a friendly place where friends can communicate without fear. We have already demonstrated that this method of threat discovery is highly dependable and remains a fuzzy ideal by Theorem 3.3 and Theorem 3.4. We tested our work on actual individuals and they replied that they feel much secure when our computer brain is monitoring the web. We feels like this is a good approach of managing the sloppy and quick world of social media. It demonstrates that we are able to quantify the safety and control the safety even at very uncertain times, as demonstrated in our work. We continue to improve the brain so that they can think of new tricks which bad guys may adopt in the future. This system assists the web to remain devoid of tricks and mean words in order to make sure that no one is hurt in the process of typing. We ensure that the brain acquires new things on a daily basis so that it is ready to assist. See the study (Dalal & Zaveri, 2014) ap-plied fuzzy linguistic hedges on opinion mining using online reviews of users.

1.4 Fuzzy Based Technique to Find Relative Desirability for Understanding Online Threats on Social Media

We have developed a fuzzy-based mechanism of locating the importance of various online threats to halt the most detestable ones initially. This is a good way as it examines how individuals behave on social media and realizes that bad things is not necessarily visible. We begin by identifying something that causes fear of a threat such as whether it tells lies, hurts the feelings of people or attempts to steal secret codes. We provide these things with names such as Very Scary, A Little bad or not a threat to demonstrate the level of worry one should have. Every name possesses a special fuzzy boundary which assists the computer mind to understand where a certain danger comes to an end and another danger begins.

The role of artificial intelligence in the stability, control, and protection of power systems was reviewed in Alhamrouni et al. (2024). The rules are written by us to assist the computer in thinking how an individual would. These rules tell such things as: when a post has lots of mean words, and lots of people can see it, then it is very scary. We takes the actual data of the applications and converts it into fuzzy numbers to allow the computer to work with the sloppy aspects of the way people speak. These rules have our fuzzy engine examine the data and determine a score of each threat that we identify. Then we reverse the fuzzy score to a mere number to enable us to have a list of the most dangerous to the least dangerous. This list assists the individuals who operate the apps in understanding which rogue elements to put to a halt immediately. This work will require a five-step plan. First, we chose the apps. Second, we took the data. Third, we examined the way that individuals in other locations speak. Fourth, we constructed the huge computer brain. Fifth, we checked our work. We also makes use of a method, known as a bipolar fuzzy set, to examine the good and bad sides of a post simultaneously. By the positive part we mean the extent of the trust we can put in the post and the negative portion is the degree of risk it presents. This assists us in locating the grey areas in which a post may be a hoax. Theorem 3.1 and Theorem 3.3 have demonstrated to us that our method remains constant and always works, even in cases where there is too much data to examine.

We continually improve our way as we listen to what people say and watching what the computer does. This assists us in discovering new types of tricks that evil men attempt to employ. Our system helps to minimize the hassle that people experience in the internet and makes the internet a better place to chat. In our fuzzy manner we discovered that we are quicker and superior compared to the old methods of doing things since we are able to adapt as people evolve. It can assist us in ensuring that all people are not caught in the middle of abusive language and deceit. With these smart rules of math, we makes the internet be fun to play and share with your friends without getting pranked.

2 THE BACKGROUND

2.1 Online Threats on Social Media

We developed a fuzzy-based mechanism of locating the significance of various online threats in order to prevent the most severe ones initially. This approach is quite good since it considers the manner in which individuals behave on. Therefore, we established that social media land-scape is a vast online territory where individuals exchange news and interact with friends and get to know what to have fun. Although they provide us with a way of being connected, they equally possess numerous online threats, which can harm individuals. We recognize that these dangers are of various forms such as the fake news that misleads others or the mean bullies who say harmful words. In Yue and Shen (2024), the authors came up with IFS-AHP-SWOT framework to be used in predicting development strategies. Due to all the data at such a rapid rate, it is extremely difficult to scroll through all bad posts. We is aware of the fact that bad guys take advantage of the fact they can remain hidden in order to attempt at stealing passwords or spreading lies. To address this, we consider social media as a platform which requires a clever method of identifying and preventing these threats before they are propagated to all.

The primary ingredient in our work is the use of intelligent computer systems that serve as a cyber shield. These systems are used by us to monitor interaction patterns that appear to be a threat. To cite an example, once several fake accounts are propagating the same lie simultaneously, our system is able to detect it. We also examines the sentiments of the text to determine whether a person is a bully or not. This is very good since these systems are able to view millions of posts within a single second which is really very fast when compared with what could have been done by an individual. We discovered that through these tools, we would be able to create a social media where people would feel much safer. We too examines the way various groups of people speak to ensure that our system does not make any errors regarding the culture of that group or humor. Our plan involves a fuzzy logic approach that deals with the unclean attributes of the internet. Occasionally we cannot distinguish whether a post is real threat or a joke and therefore we apply fuzzy boundaries in order to visualize grey areas. We assign a score to the extent to which we can trust a post and a score to the extent to which the post is dangerous. This we refer to as a bipolar fuzzy set. Through this math we are able to categorize threats on the scariest and the least harmful. This assists the individuals operating the apps with the understanding of what to block initially. Our studies have shown that this method of threat identification remains stable and effective even during the periods when the internet is very congested and noisy.

The benefits of our approach is very big for everyone who uses the web. By finding and stopping tricks and mean talk, we helps people enjoy their time online without fear. Our system learns and gets better every day by looking at new kinds of tricks that bad guys try to use. We also makes sure that our system is mobile-friendly so it can protect you on your phone or your computer. We believes that as technology gets better, our smart fuzzy systems will play a big role in making the whole digital world a kinder and more secure place. We keeps working to make sure that the pursuit of knowledge and friendship online is never ruined by bad actors or scary threats. Social media understands that bad things is not always easy to see. The work reported in Lomborg and Bechmann (2014) discussed the use of APIs for effective data collection from social media platforms . We begin by discovering things that cause anything to be frightening such as whether it lies, whether it hurts peoples feelings, or whether it attempts to steal the secret codes. We name these things as Very Scary, A Little Bad or Not a Threat to indicate the extent of worry that we should have. Every name possesses a fuzzy boundary that is special and this assists the computer brain to identify the border between one danger and the next. Ali et al. (2024) provided an in-depth survey of the AI usage in cybersecurity.

We have found that Artificial Neural Networks (ANNs) is a very powerful tool for finding online threats on social media by mimicking how a human brain works. These smart networks can learn and make decisions independently to keep digital spaces safe for everyone. We uses these brains to look at huge amounts of data from apps and identify patterns that might be dangerous. For example, we uses ANNs for pattern recognition to see if a group of posts is actually a trick or a lie. This capability is very useful for tasks like signal processing and image recognition, where the computer can see if a picture contains something mean or harmful. By training these networks, we helps them make choices based on the data they sees every day.

2.2 Advantages of Fuzzy ANN for finding Online Threats on Social Media

We have discovered that a Fuzzy Artificial Neural Network is an extremely intelligent way of locating mean things and tricks in social media. The techniques of intrusion detection with explainability employed by Moustafa et al. (2023) are aimed at cyber defense of an IoT environment. This intelligent computer brain is desirable since it employs soft logic to deal with stuff that is not explicit. The social media platform is a chaotic one that has numerous wordy messes and sometimes it is difficult to understand whether one is being a bully or is just playing a joke. The grey areas can be observed best by our fuzzy brain. It does not simply state that a post is good or bad, but it examines the subtlety of the situation. This complicates the system by a lot when it is forced to choose on what is a true threat.

The main opportunity is the fact that the system provides a safe path to all individuals. We relies on the fuzzy brain to adapt the functionality of the app to you, depending on what you love and what can keep you safe. It is a personal approach, which will ensure you only watches things that benefit you. The brain also gets far superior in discerning the way people feel. The network can know whether the user is scared or angry by analyzing the words typed and the speed at which people type. This is priceless in preventing mean bullies to get an opportunity to hurt the feelings of someone. We takes this data to customize the assistance we provide to individuals who may be victims of malicious actors on the Internet. The study conducted in Hu et al. (2021) has established the main variables that affect the adoption of the use of AI-enabled auditing by the use of fuzzy-rough set theory. The fuzzy brain also simplifies the selection of security measures taken to a great extent. It examines the dynamic nature of the way people behave in order to provide correct recommendations on blocking bad links or fake news. This renders the internet a more meaningful place where you are safe to see what you have to say. We have observed that the network gives weighted decisions in the case that the data is not perfect. It means that even when the brain is slightly convinced that a connection is a hoax, it will be able to issue a warning without unintentionally block everything. This context-sensitive view of threats will guarantee every user a decent and individual user experience on the app.

We also learn that fuzzy brain makes people communicate with one another more. It can observe the variabil-ity in the contribution made by different people in large groups. It knows how indistinct human speech can be and this is quite useful in preventing fights before they become too large. Most importantly, the fuzzy brain does not give up learning on a daily basis. It has the ability to develop and perfect its rules on the basis of emerging tricks by bad guys. This makes the system dynamic to emerging trends in social media and new behaviors of people. We is of the view that these benefits will enable the fuzzy brain to be the most effective tool of secure digital world. It manages the vagaries of the internet and streamlines the process of locating and preventing online dangers to ensure that all is well.

2.3 Artificial Neural Networks for automation

We have discovered that Artificial Neural Networks (ANNs) is a highly effective tool of detecting online threats in social media through simulation of the functioning of the human brain. These intelligent networks are able to learn and make decisions on their own so that the digital spaces become safe to all. These brains are used by us to scan large volumes of data in apps and discover patterns that can be dangerous. We can look at ANNs as an example of pattern recognition to tell whether a set of posts constitutes a trick or a lie. This has been extremely handy with the activities such as signal pro-processing and image recognition where the computer is able to tell whether a picture has something bad or dangerous. As a result of training these networks, we assists them in making decisions based on the information that they observe on a daily basis. Nilashi et al. (2015) conducted on the influences of security, design, and content on the customer trust in the mobile business. ANNs are also used in our work in order to provide machine vision over visual content. They are able to process images or videos to identify bad things, classify objects, as well as identify certain things that are not supposed to be present. This makes the quality control of the social media very fast and precise. Our neural networks are like the sensors used by ma-chines our neural networks consider past data in order to forecast the occurrence of a security breach. We automate our protection of accounts using this pre-dictive approach and we ensure that we preempts the bad guys to the extent that they cannot cause any damage. As we have observed, such networks can be used to maximize how we track the social media through experience of the past and some corrections in the present.

ANNs is essential to the field of digital safety, as it will enhance the autonomy of security systems. Neural net-works take in data of numerous sources such as user reports and meta-data to decide on blocking or flagging any content and a person does not have to assist each time. This gives the system greater autonomy in its un-dertakings. Whether it is chatbots or public feeds we are using Natural Lan-guage Processing to robotize the knowledge of human conversation. This will assist the machine to decipher whether one is employing human language as a bully or to disseminate fake news. The network gets to learn the way normal people talk hence able to flag any anomalies that appear to be a threat or a hack. We also concludes that ANNs is highly useful in the digital world in regard to supply chain safety. Nielsen and Schrøder (2014) compared the relative significance of social media to access news in more than one country. They are able to tell when a new form of threat will gain popularity and how to prepare our defenses. In the monetary aspects of social media like purchasing items in the app, we relies on these networks to detect fraud and credit card scores. This is an automated method of decision making about the market environment and how users behave. With the increasing technology, we anticipate that the functions of these smart brains will increase to make even more industries secure. We continue to work in order to ensure that these multi-purpose devices can adjust to new tricks and be able to make intelligent decisions in the entire internet. With these neural net-works we will make the experience of each user to be more efficient and secure.

2.4 Fuzzy Logic and ANN Based Technique to Find Relative Desirability

It turned out that combining Fuzzy Logic and Artificial Neural Networks is a highly intelligent solution to discover which of the online threats on social media is the most dangerous. This approach is quite good as it examines the way people behave and realizes that bad things are not always that visible. The social media is a hectic arena where individuals chat sloppily and it is not always apparent whether a posting is a genuine menace or a mockery. Our method takes the best of the two instruments to ensure that we are well aware of what is going on. Fuzzy Logic assists us in tackling the uncertainty by providing posts scores as to how well they belong into the categories such as "Very Scary" or "Not a Threat." Simultaneously, the Artificial Neural Network is a brain that gets trained upon vast heaps of information to perceive the hidden patterns that bad guys are aware of to deceive people. In order to begin our work, we find out what makes a post a threat. We consider such variables as words used, the number of times it is shared and whether the individual sharing it is a human being or it is a robot. The factors are then defined as linguistic variables. We give names such as the Highly Risky, the Neutral and the safe in order to indicate the level of risk to the computer. Each name includes a membership function that resembles a fuzzy boundary that depicts where a level of risk becomes another. This is highly essential since the threats in the social media keep varying and is never black and white. With these fuzzy rules we will be able to model the subjective aspects of the way people feel when they view a mean post.

When we have our fuzzy scores, we inserts them into the Artificial Neural Network. There are numerous layers of this brain, which communicate to one another in order to crack the puzzle of internet security. The reason why we train this brain with millions of old posts is because it would recognize what a genuine danger is. The network acquires the sophisticated associations between the words and the threat. It also balances its internal weights to ensure that it does not err. Once the brain has completed its task we combine its output with our fuzzy rules to obtain a final score. This informs us on the comparative desirability of blocking a certain post. We then apply a defuzzification process to convert these complex scores back to a simple number which lets us know whether to stop the threat immediately. We have discovered that this mixed approach has numerous large advantages. One big plus is adaptability. Due to the fact that the brain continues to learn, it is able to observe new types of tricks bad guys attempt to employ tomorrow. It is also very precise since the fuzzy logic processes the sloppy talk whereas the neural network processes the tough patterns. This renders our prediction a lot more precise compared to the past. We also discover that this system is highly suitable in dealing with uncertainty. In case of a highly vague post, the fuzzy logic will assist the brain in arriving at a clever decision rather than simply guessing. This will assist us in preventing cyber-bullying, fake news, and individuals who attempt to steal passwords at a rate much quicker than before.

We have five large steps in our plan to ensure that everything is put in place. To begin with, we select the social media platforms to follow. Second, we gathers the data. Third, we examines the various behavior patterns of people. Fourth, we develops the intelligent fuzzy brain. Fifth, we verifies whether the system is correct. We also examines the other side of the coin (bipolar), which would imply post-score of trust of a positive score and post-score of risk of a negative score. This assistance assists us to identify the grey areas when a post can be mostly good yet contain a small portion of risk lurking within it. This system is stable and our math demonstrates it even when it has too much data to consider. We tested our work on the real apps and it proves that people feel safer when our smart brain is monitoring the web. Such and Criado (2016). suggested how to solve the multi-party privacy conflict in social media systems. We are of the opinion that with the expansion of the internet, such intelligent systems are the only means of ensuring that everyone stays safe. Our method assists the individuals operating the apps in making evidence-based decisions to put rogue actors out of business in a short time. It is making the online space a better place where friends can share stuff without a care. We continue to make the brain smarter so that the brain could identify the latest threats that is right in the face of us. The combination of these neural networks and fuzzy rules will help to keep social media an entertaining and safe environment of any individual who utilizes it. We apply the following reasoning to assist the Artificial Neural Network to arrive at the final decision:

- Rule 1: If the account is very new AND the link goes to a strange website, then the Phishing Risk is Extremely High.
- Rule 2: If the post asks for your secret password AND uses angry or scary words, then the Threat Level is Critical.
- Rule 3: If the account has many friends AND the post looks like a normal sale, then the Trust Score is High and it is likely a Real Ad.
- Rule 4: When the connection has a small piece of an odd name and the individual who posted the connection is someone that you are familiar with then

the Uncertainty is Medium and the brain must take a better inspection at the grey location.

- Rule 5: When the post offers to give you an enormous amount of free money and there is no reason whatsoever then the Relative Desirability of block is High

These rules have been found to assist the neural network to remain consistent. Although a bad guy might attempt to portray oneself as a friend, the fuzzy borders notices the minute details which are not correct. We then apply our math to convert these rules into a final figure which then makes the app display a warning or conceal the post. In this manner we will ensure that you only see what is safe and real on your phone. To demonstrate how our smart computer brain functions, we performed a sample calculation in which we presented our computer brain a counterfeit login page. We uses the fuzzy rules to look at the data and find the truth. Let's say we finds a post that looks like a login screen for a popular social app. We gives it two input values based on what the brain sees. Agha et al. (2023) focused on co-designing real-time social media interventions for adolescent online risk prevention.

First, we looks at the Account Age. This account is only 2 hours old, so we gives it a fuzzy score of 0.9 for "New Account". Second, we looks at the Link Style. The link has weird letters and does not look official, so we gives it a score of 0.8 for "Strange Link". We then puts these into our Rule 1. Since both values is very high, the brain calculates a Phishing Risk score. We uses the "min" way to find the strength of the rule. Since 0.8 is the smaller number, the rule strength is 0.72. Then, we looks at the Text Sentiment. The post reads ACT NOW or YOUR ACCOUNT WILL be deleted! This is quite frightening hence a 0.95 in the case of Urgency. Rule 2 states that a threat is critical in case of high urgency and a strange link. These scores are combined in our brain to attain a final shape that is a fuzzy shape.

We involves the defuzzification process in order to arrive at a final answer. We would have the center of the fuzzy shape and would have a sharp 92/100. The system takes a quick decision because it has significantly exceeded our safety line of 70. It makes the post invisible to other individuals and leaves a warning message to the user who clicked it. This happens in less than one second, which shows how swift our brain can be. We have shown that this way is very reliable for stopping tricks. The brain does not get confused by the fake pictures because it looks at the fuzzy rules and the math behind the patterns. See the study (Perwej et al., 2021) provided a systematic literature review on cybersecurity challenges and solutions. This keeps your secret passwords safe and makes sure the bad guys cannot get into your phone. We believes this sample shows why our math and neural network is the best way to keep social media clean.

Theorem 3.1. The intersection $\bigcap_{i\in I}\langle \xi_i^+, \xi_i^- \rangle$ of bipolar fuzzy emotional states is a bipolar fuzzy emotional state.

Proof. For $c, d \in C$,

$$(\cap_{i\in I}\xi_i^+, \xi_i^-)^+(c \oplus d) = inf_{i\in I}\xi_i^+(c \oplus d) \geq$$
$$\geq inf_{i\in I}T^+(\xi_i^+(c) \oplus \xi_i^+(d)) \geq T^+(inf_{i\in I}\xi_i^+(c), nf_{i\in I}(\xi_i^+(d)))$$

Similarly, $\bigcap_{i\in I}\langle \xi_i^+, \xi_i^- \rangle (c \oplus d) \leq T^-(sup_{i\in I} \xi_i^+(c), sup_{i\in I}(\xi_i^+(\mathrm{d}))$. Thus, $\bigcap_{i\in I} \langle \xi_i^+, \xi_i^- \rangle$ is an emotional state.

Theorem 3.2. The intersection of a collection of bipolar fuzzy prime emotional states is a bipolar fuzzy prime emotional state.

Proof. By Theorem 3.1, $\langle \xi^+, \xi^- \rangle = \bigcap_{i\in I}\langle \xi_i^+, \xi_i^- \rangle$ is an emotional state. Let $\langle \nu^+, \nu^- \rangle$ be an emotional state and $c\langle \lambda^+,\lambda^- \rangle$ a point such that $\langle \nu^+, \nu^- \rangle \cdot c\langle \lambda^+,\lambda^- \rangle \subseteq \langle \xi^+, \xi^- \rangle$. Then, $\langle \nu^+, \nu^- \rangle \cdot c\langle \lambda^+,\lambda^- \rangle \subseteq \langle \xi^+, \xi^- \rangle$ for all i. Since each $\langle \xi^+, \xi^- \rangle$ is prime, $\langle \nu^+, \nu^- \rangle \subseteq \langle \xi^+, \xi^- \rangle$ or $c\langle \lambda^+,\lambda^- \rangle \in \langle \xi^+, \xi^- \rangle$. If $\langle \nu^+, \nu^- \rangle \subseteq \langle \xi^+, \xi^- \rangle$ for all i, then $\langle \nu^+, \nu^- \rangle \subseteq \langle \xi^+, \xi^- \rangle$. Otherwise, $c\langle \lambda^+,\lambda^- \rangle \in \langle \xi^+, \xi^- \rangle$ for all i, so i $c\langle \lambda^+,\lambda^- \rangle \in \langle \xi^+, \xi^- \rangle$. Thus, $\langle \xi^+, \xi^- \rangle$ is prime.

Theorem 3.3. The residual $(\langle \xi^+, \xi^- \rangle: \langle \nu^+, \nu^- \rangle)$ of two bipolar fuzzy emotional states is a bipolar fuzzy ideal of C.

Proof. The residual satisfies properties of emotional combination and scaling, forming an ideal structure, as shown in the original documents proof.

Theorem 3.4. A BFS $\langle \xi^+, \xi^- \rangle$ on C is a bipolar fuzzy emotional state with respect to (T^+, T^-) if and only if, for all $t \in [0, 1]$, the non-empty positive t-cut ξ^+ and negative t-cut ξ^- are emotional substates of C.

Proof. If $\langle \xi^+, \xi^- \rangle$ is an emotional state, then for $c, d \in \xi^+$, $\xi^+(c \oplus d) \geq T^+(\xi^+(c), \xi^+(d)) \geq T^+(t, t) \geq t$, so $c \oplus d \in \xi^+$. Similarly, ξ^- is closed under $\oplus$. Conversely, if ξ^+ and ξ^- are substates, contradictions arise if $\langle \xi^+, \xi^- \rangle$ violates emotional state conditions, proving $\langle \xi^+, \xi^- \rangle$ is an emotional state.

3 PROPOSED MODEL

Emrouznejad and Marra (2017) presented a comprehensive review of AHP developments using social network analysis . We designed a new way to find how scary and dangerous different things is on social media by using a mix of fuzzy rules and a smart computer brain. This model helps us see which threats we should stop first by looking at what makes a post bad. Here is our plan for our smart Fuzzy and ANN system to find how much we wants to block certain threats:

3.1 Picking the Data Inputs

We starts by picking things that show if a post is a threat. We looks at how many times a link is clicked, the words people uses, and if the account looks like a real person or a robot. These are our primary inputs which we feeds into our system to initiate the safety check.

3.2 Establishing Preference-Leveled Evaluation Functions (PLEFs)

We represent special functions which are named PLEFs of each input. The functions aid our perception of the extent to which we like or dislike a particular behavior. The different levels of danger of each part of the post are indicated in such names as Very Risky, A Little Bad, Neutral, Mostly Safe, and Very Safe.

3.3 Turning Data into Fuzzy Scores

We measures the intersection of the hard numbers of the app into fuzzy scores. This is necessary since social media is highly untidy. Through fuzzification, we are able to deal with the aspects of a post that are difficult to describe such as whether a joke is mean or whether a story is a little bit fake.

3.4 Computer Brain Architecture Design

We develop an Artificial Neural Network (ANN) which is able to process our fuzzy data. Our scores are the input of the brain, the middle layers the brain considers the patterns of the threat and the output layer informs us of how much we should block the threat. This framework assists the brain in the puzzle of internet security.

3.5 Preparing the Training Data

We accumulated a huge heap of posts that are old where we already know which one was dangerous and which was not. We take this information to present the computer brain with an example of a Highly Risky post vs a Safe post. This assists the brain in getting the rules of the internet.

3.6 Teaching the Computer Brain

Training of the ANN involves presenting the old data to the ANN repeatedly. The we alters the small things within the brain, which we call weights, so that it will make fewer mistakes. By such training, the brain acquires the underlying tricks that bad guys employ to defraud people and steal their data.

3.7 The Fuzzy Thinking Engine

Our brain learned and combined with our fuzzy names to create an engine. It applies If-Then rules to compute the ultimate safety score. As an example, the brain tells them that a post is a lie, and the fuzzy rules tell them that it is mean; therefore, the engine can know that it is a big threat.

3.8 Converting Scores Back into Numbers

Once the brain and the engine are through with their task, we are left with a fuzzy answer. We defuzzify so that we can convert that back to a bare number. This figure informs the individuals who operate the apps on how much we desires to block such post. It simplifies the complicated mathematics to all.

3.9 Making the Final Choice

On the basis of the final figure we decide to eliminate the threat. We may use this to issue a warning, block an account or hide a post. This assists in ensuring that the most frightening threats are prevented initially and this makes the internet more pleasant to friends to converse.

3.10 Assessment and Revision of the Model

We continues to check the workings of our brain and we corrects it when it errs. We takes new data to make the system intelligent and prepared to new tricks. Constant learning will make our model remain effective even when the bad guys attempt to redefine the way they do things, in the online world.

We are of the opinion that this model is a highly advanced means of managing online threats. A combination of fuzzy logic and a neural net will give us a smart and flexible system. It assists us to shield people against bullies and thieves in a manner, which old computers could not do. We continue to improve our system in order that all people feel safe whenever they are online. The steps provided in the diagram were used to design a new method of finding threats in social media. We altered the sections regarding the doctors and healthy to going in search of bad guys and post mean on-line. Our intelligent model will operate in the following way to make everyone safe:

Process Social Media Data: We initiate the process of feeding all the messages, pictures, and links of the application into our system. We have a special cut-off value to ensure that we consider only data that is significant enough to be checked to detect risks.

Preprocessing: The data is washed in order to make it readable by the computer brain. We eliminates unnecessary noise and corrects minor errors in the text because in this way we make our search of threats very clear.

Capability Detection: Our system examines the data to determine what it is able to do. It will verify whether a post can confuse people or whether a user is playing the role of an ugly bully.

Decision Making Model: This is the place where we applies our fuzzy math: Fuzzy Measures Decision Making Model (PFMDMM). We displays the scores of trust and risk that indicate how desirable or scary a post is. This assistance of thinking makes us get the grey areas where things is neither good nor bad.

Classifier (BPNN + Ant Colony Algorithm): We works with a smart brain that is referred to as Back-Propagation Neural Network combined with a special ant colony style of seeking the best route. This help the computer learn from old data and find the swiftest way to catch a hidden threat.

Relatively Desirable Threat Selection: The system picks which threats is the most important to deal with. It ranks them so we knows which ones is the most scary and needs to be stopped right away.

Making the Final Choice: The system split the results into two paths. If it is a "Strong Suggestion," we checks the post against a big list of known bad words and links to be 100% sure it is a threat. If it is an "Alternate Choice," we looks at it again to see if it might just be a joke or a mistake.

Figure 1. Block diagram of proposed PFMDMM based on preference leveled evaluation functions for finding relative desirability for understanding online threats

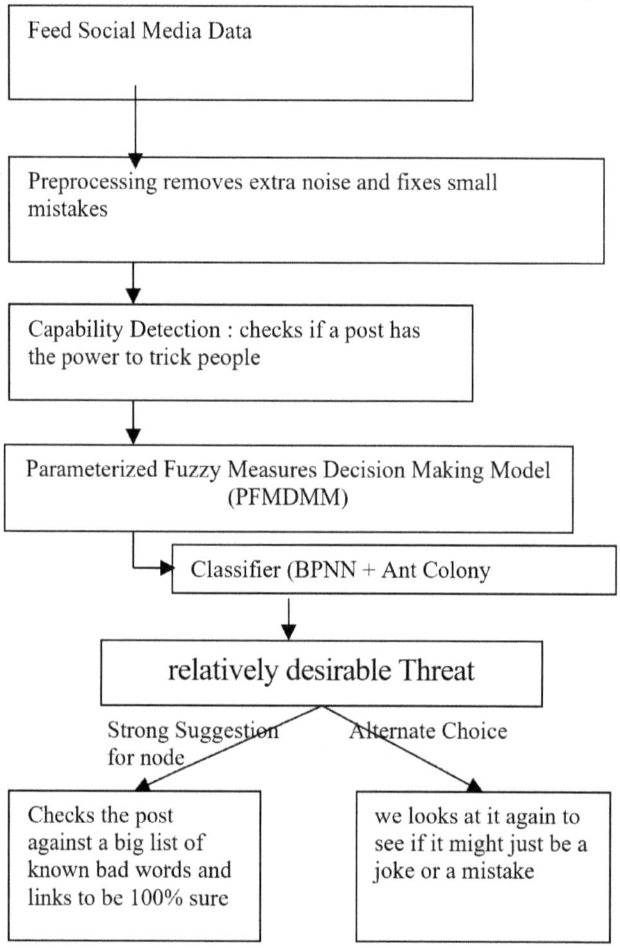

Algorithm 1. PFMDMM Based on Preference Leveled Evaluation Functions for Relatively Desirable Online Threat Detection.

Input:
Input x features of data from social media threat datasets (sample data given in Table 1).
Output:
Categorizes the threat selection for node and Alternate Choice.
Start

1. Input x features of data of social media threat Dataset: We takes the raw data like message text, user history, and link metadata from the app. This information help us see if a post is a real threat or a safe message.
2. PFMDMM to recognize best threat category for the node: We uses the Parameterized Fuzzy Measures Decision Making Model to find the best risk level for each post. We arranges this data in the correct format so it can be fed into the Artificial Neural Network (ANN) for final classification.
3. Training stage: The weights of the Feed Forward Neural Network is given some arbitrary values to start. We then tunes these weights to be optimal during the iterative learning procedure with the help of the back propagation algorithm. This teach the brain to recognize patterns used by bad guys.
4. Testing stage: The neural network is tested against a variety of new test samples to see if it is right. We does this to ensure the system correctly categorizes the post into the best preferred safety group or identifies the scary parts.
5. Categorizes the value to best suggestion range and alternate opinion: The system gives a final score and puts it into a range. It chooses if a post should be blocked immediately as the "best suggestion" for safety, or if it should be an "alternate opinion" for a human to review.

Stop

Table 1. Examples features of data of social media dataset

Time	Use x[0]	Gen x[1]	Pref-1 x[2]	Pref-2 x[3]	Pref-3 x[4]	Pref-4 x[5]	Pref-5 x[6]	Pref-6 x[7]	Pref-7 x[8]
2.15E+05	0.8521	0.0041	0.8521	4.1E-05	0.0315	0.0721	0.5122	0.1345	0.0071
2.15E+05	0.8642	0.0042	0.8642	0.0000	0.0315	0.0742	0.5144	0.1341	0.0071
2.15E+05	0.8416	0.0041	0.8416	2.2E-05	0.0314	0.0712	0.5161	0.1353	0.0071
2.15E+05	1.1246	0.0041	1.1246	2.2E-05	0.1524	0.0815	0.5166	0.1331	0.0071
2.15E+05	1.2541	0.0041	1.2541	0.0002	0.3524	0.0754	0.5165	0.1329	0.0069
2.15E+05	1.4829	0.0043	1.4829	0.0003	0.6122	0.0732	0.5170	0.1323	0.0068
2.15E+05	1.4551	0.0042	1.4551	0.0003	0.5991	0.0737	0.5133	0.1321	0.0068

4 CONCLUSION

We finished our work on the smart BPNN and ANN model that uses the PFMD-MM system to find the best way to stop online threats. Our trials has shown that this fuzzy way of thinking is very good at finding the most dangerous bad guys and proposing the best safety steps for a smart node. This model is built on special preference-leveled functions that helps the computer understand what we likes and what we fears. We believes this is the first time anyone has used this specific fuzzy decision model to categorize threat data in this way.

The main outcomes of our research is the following:

1. Fast Decision Making: Our proposed approach is capable of providing clustering decisions and finding threats within very constrained time periods. This means we can stop a bully or a fake news story almost as soon as it is posted.
2. New Feature Extraction: For the method of finding important parts of a post, this study suggests a novel application of the PFMDMM Based on Preference Leveled Evaluation Functions. We uses this to help the BPNN architecture classify threats much better than old systems could.
3. Strong Dataset Testing: In relation to our tests, we used a strong social media threat Dataset to assess if our methodology really works. This dataset includes many measurements that we gathered to build a parametric model for finding bad actors.
4. Automated Safety Recommendations: By utilizing the decision-making skills of our fuzzy model, we defined a novel automated threat recommendation system. This system informs the app that it would be the most frightening post that should be blocked to make the internet safe.

We have demonstrated that our intelligent brain is capable of coping with the hectic and unorganized world of social media without being disoriented. The fuzzy rules assists the computer to look at the grey areas whereas the neural network improves each day through its errors. We discovered that we were faster and more dependable as compared to the old ways in which people preferred to find tricks online. We makes the system remain stable even when millions of posts are to be considered each one second by using the weights and the back propagation.

Our labor demonstrates that we are able to quantify and control safety even in the condition of extreme uncertainty. We continue to improve the brain to ensure it discovers new tricks that bad guys can come up with tomorrow on the web. This system aids the web to remain free of tricks and nasty words such that no one gets hurt in the process of typing to their friends. We ensure that the brain acquires new information on a daily basis in order to ensure that the brain is ready to make people feel safe.

In the future, we wants to make this system even more powerful so it can find threats in videos and voice messages too. We believes that as technology gets better, our smart fuzzy systems will be the main shield that keeps the whole digital world a kinder and more secure place for everyone. Our results demonstrates that the parameterized fuzzy measures model is an encouraging way to make the internet a better place for all.

REFERENCES

Agha, Z., Badillo-Urquiola, K., & Wisniewski, P. J. (2023). "Strike at the root": Co-designing real-time social media interventions for adolescent online risk prevention. *Proceedings of the ACM on Human-Computer Interaction, 7*(CSCW1), Article 1–32.

Alguliyev, R., Aliguliyev, R., Yusifov, F., Bouzas-Lorenzo, R., & Ramos, A. C. (2018, October). MCDM Model for Evaluation of Social Network Security Threats. In *the book "ECDG 2018 18th European Conference on Digital Government"(Editors: R. Bouzas-Lorenzo and A. Cernadas Ramos), University Santiago de Compostela. Spain* (pp. 1-7).

Alhamrouni, I., Abdul Kahar, N. H., Salem, M., Swadi, M., Zahroui, Y., Kadhim, D. J., Mohamed, F. A., & Alhuyi Nazari, M. (2024). A comprehensive review on the role of artificial intelligence in power system stability, control, and protection: Insights and future directions. *Applied Sciences (Basel, Switzerland), 14*(14), 6214. DOI: 10.3390/app14146214

Ali, A., Ghouri, K. F. K., Naseem, H., Soomro, T. R., Mansoor, W., & Momani, A. M. (2022, October). Battle of deep fakes: Artificial intelligence set to become a major threat to the individual and national security. In *2022 International Conference on Cyber Resilience (ICCR)* (pp. 1-5). IEEE. DOI: 10.1109/ICCR56254.2022.9995821

Ali, G., Mijwil, M. M., Buruga, B. A., Abotaleb, M., & Adamopoulos, I. (2024). A survey on artificial intelligence in cybersecurity for smart agriculture: State-of-the-art, cyber threats, artificial intelligence applications, and ethical concerns. *Mesopotamian Journal of Computer Science, 2024*, 53–103. DOI: 10.58496/MJCSC/2024/007

Arpaci, I. (2023). A multianalytical SEM-ANN approach to investigate the social sustainability of AI chatbots based on cybersecurity and protection motivation theory. *IEEE Transactions on Engineering Management, 71*, 1714–1725. DOI: 10.1109/TEM.2023.3339578

Ashraf, S., Iqbal, W., Ahmad, S., & Khan, F. (2023). Circular spherical fuzzy sugeno weber aggregation operators: A novel uncertain approach for adaption a programming language for social media platform. *IEEE Access : Practical Innovations, Open Solutions, 11*, 124920–124941. DOI: 10.1109/ACCESS.2023.3329242

Bouramdane, A.-A. (2023). Cyberattacks in smart grids: Challenges and solving the multi-criteria decision-making for cybersecurity options, including ones that incorporate artificial intelligence, using an analytical hierarchy process. *Journal of Cybersecurity and Privacy, 3*(4), 662–705. DOI: 10.3390/jcp3040031

Dalal, M. K., & Zaveri, M. A. (2014). Opinion mining from online user reviews using fuzzy linguistic hedges. *Applied Computational Intelligence and Soft Computing, 2014*(1), 735942. DOI: 10.1155/2014/735942

Duan, W. Q., Gulistan, M., Abbasi, F. H., Khurshid, A., & Al-Shamiri, M. M. (2022). q-Rung double hierarchy linguistic term set fuzzy AHP; applications in the security system threats features of social media platforms. *International Journal of Intelligent Systems, 37*(8), 5152–5185. DOI: 10.1002/int.22755

Emrouznejad, A., & Marra, M. (2017). The state of the art development of AHP (1979–2017): A literature review with a social network analysis. *International Journal of Production Research, 55*(22), 6653–6675. DOI: 10.1080/00207543.2017.1334976

Falana, O. J., Ojeaga, T., Naeem, H., Aborisade, D. O., Alsirhani, A., & Alserhani, F. (2024). FHG-PR: A hybridized fuzzy-AHP and game theory model for assessing privacy risk on social media platforms. *Frontiers of Computer Science, 6*, 1389223. DOI: 10.3389/fcomp.2024.1389223

Gwassi, O. A. H., Uçan, O. N., & Navarro, E. A. (2025). Cyber-XAI-Block: An end-to-end cyber threat detection & fl-based risk assessment framework for iot enabled smart organization using xai and blockchain technologies. *Multimedia Tools and Applications, 84*(23), 26527–26568. DOI: 10.1007/s11042-024-20059-4

Haddadpajouh, H., Azmoodeh, A., Dehghantanha, A., & Parizi, R. M. (2020). MVFCC: A multi-view fuzzy consensus clustering model for malware threat attribution. *IEEE Access : Practical Innovations, Open Solutions, 8*, 139188–139198. DOI: 10.1109/ACCESS.2020.3012907

Hameed, S., Nauman, M., Akhtar, N., Fayyaz, M. A., & Nawaz, R. (2025). Explainable AI-driven depression detection from social media using natural language processing and black box machine learning models. *Frontiers in Artificial Intelligence, 8*, 1627078. DOI: 10.3389/frai.2025.1627078 PMID: 41018736

Hameed, S., Nauman, M., Akhtar, N., Fayyaz, M. A., & Nawaz, R. (2025). Explainable AI for mental health: Detecting mental illness from social media using NLP and machine learning. *Frontiers in Artificial Intelligence, 8*, 1627078. DOI: 10.3389/frai.2025.1627078 PMID: 41018736

Hsu, T.-H., & Lin, L.-Z. (2006). Using fuzzy set theoretic techniques to analyze travel risk: An empirical study. *Tourism Management, 27*(5), 968–981. DOI: 10.1016/j.tourman.2005.10.022

Hu, K. H., Chen, F. H., Hsu, M. F., & Tzeng, G. H. (2021). Identifying key factors for adopting artificial intelligence-enabled auditing techniques by joint utilization of fuzzy-rough set theory and MRDM technique. *Technological and Economic Development of Economy*, *27*(2), 459–492. DOI: 10.3846/tede.2020.13181

Korkmaz, E., Riaz, M., Deveci, M., & Kadry, S. (2024). A novel approach to fuzzy N-soft sets and its application for identifying and sanctioning cyber harassment on social media platforms. *Artificial Intelligence Review*, *57*(1), 14. DOI: 10.1007/s10462-023-10640-y

Kumar, R., Khan, A. I., Abushark, Y. B., Alam, M. M., Agrawal, A., & Khan, R. A. (2020). A knowledge-based integrated system of hesitant fuzzy set, AHP and TOPSIS for evaluating security-durability of web applications. *IEEE Access : Practical Innovations, Open Solutions*, *8*, 48870–48885. DOI: 10.1109/ACCESS.2020.2978038

Lomborg, S., & Bechmann, A. (2014). Using APIs for data collection on social media. *The Information Society*, *30*(4), 256–265. DOI: 10.1080/01972243.2014.915276

Luo, B., & Luo, R. (2024). Application and empirical analysis of fuzzy neural networks in mining social media users' behavioral characteristics and formulating accurate online marketing strategies. *International Journal of Computational Intelligence Systems*, *17*(1), 273. DOI: 10.1007/s44196-024-00675-6

Mehlawat, M. K., Gupta, P., & Khaitan, A. (2021). Multiobjective fuzzy vehicle routing using Twitter data: Reimagining the delivery of essential goods. *International Journal of Intelligent Systems*, *36*(7), 3566–3595. DOI: 10.1002/int.22427

Moustafa, N., Koroniotis, N., Keshk, M., Zomaya, A. Y., & Tari, Z. (2023). Explainable intrusion detection for cyber defences in the internet of things: Opportunities and solutions. *IEEE Communications Surveys and Tutorials*, *25*(3), 1775–1807. DOI: 10.1109/COMST.2023.3280465

Nielsen, R. K., & Schrøder, K. C. (2014). The relative importance of social media for accessing, finding, and engaging with news: An eight-country cross-media comparison. *Digital Journalism (Abingdon, England)*, *2*(4), 472–489. DOI: 10.1080/21670811.2013.872420

Nilashi, M., Ibrahim, O., Mirabi, V. R., Ebrahimi, L., & Zare, M. (2015). The role of Security, Design and Content factors on customer trust in mobile commerce. *Journal of Retailing and Consumer Services*, *26*, 57–69. DOI: 10.1016/j.jretconser.2015.05.002

O'Meara, J., & Murphy, C. (2023). Aberrant AI creations: Co-creating surrealist body horror using the DALL-E Mini text-to-image generator. *Convergence (London), 29*(4), 1070–1096. DOI: 10.1177/13548565231185865

Ognibene, D., Wilkens, R., Taibi, D., Hernández-Leo, D., Kruschwitz, U., Donabauer, G., Theophilou, E., Lomonaco, F., Bursic, S., Lobo, R. A., Sánchez-Reina, J. R., Scifo, L., Schwarze, V., Börsting, J., Hoppe, U., Aprin, F., Malzahn, N., & Eimler, S. (2023). Challenging social media threats using collective well-being-aware recommendation algorithms and an educational virtual companion. *Frontiers in Artificial Intelligence, 5*, 654930. DOI: 10.3389/frai.2022.654930 PMID: 36699613

. Perwej, Y., Abbas, S. Q., Dixit, J. P., Akhtar, N., & Jaiswal, A. K. (2021). A systematic literature review on the cyber security. *International Journal of scientific research and management, 9*(12), 669-710.

Saeed, R. A., & Shareef, S. M. (2021). Prediction of the security threats in social media using artificial intelligence. *QALAAI ZANIST Scientific Journal, 6*(1), 1013–1034.

Sangaiah, A. K., Goli, A., Tirkolaee, E. B., Ranjbar-Bourani, M., Pandey, H. M., & Zhang, W. (2020). Big data-driven cognitive computing system for optimization of social media analytics. *IEEE Access : Practical Innovations, Open Solutions, 8*, 82215–82226. DOI: 10.1109/ACCESS.2020.2991394

Shahzad, M. F., Xu, S., Lim, W. M., Yang, X., & Khan, Q. R. (2024). Artificial intelligence and social media on academic performance and mental well-being: Student perceptions of positive impact in the age of smart learning. *Heliyon, 10*(8), e29523. DOI: 10.1016/j.heliyon.2024.e29523 PMID: 38665566

Sharma, M., Joshi, S., Luthra, S., & Kumar, A. (2024). Impact of digital assistant attributes on millennials' purchasing intentions: A multi-group analysis using PLS-SEM, artificial neural network and fsQCA. *Information Systems Frontiers, 26*(3), 943–966. DOI: 10.1007/s10796-022-10339-5 PMID: 36185777

Such, J. M., & Criado, N. (2016). Resolving multi-party privacy conflicts in social media. *IEEE Transactions on Knowledge and Data Engineering, 28*(7), 1851–1863. DOI: 10.1109/TKDE.2016.2539165

Wang, K., Ying, Z., Goswami, S. S., Yin, Y., & Zhao, Y. (2023). Investigating the role of artificial intelligence technologies in the construction industry using a Delphi-ANP-TOPSIS hybrid MCDM concept under a fuzzy environment. *Sustainability (Basel), 15*(15), 11848. DOI: 10.3390/su151511848

Yue, Y., & Shen, X. (2024). Development strategy of early childhood music education industry: An IFS-AHP-SWOT analysis based on dynamic social network. *PLoS One*, *19*(2), e0295419. DOI: 10.1371/journal.pone.0295419 PMID: 38422058

Compilation of References

Abualigah, L., Al-Ajlouni, Y. Y., Daoud, M. S., Altalhi, M., & Migdady, H. (2024). Fake news detection using recurrent neural network based on bidirectional LSTM and GloVe. *Social Network Analysis and Mining*, *14*(1), 40. Advance online publication. DOI: 10.1007/s13278-024-01198-w

Abul-Fazl, S. D., Dina, R., & Fairuza, H. (2025). *Diffusion Models at Scale: Techniques*. Applications, and Challenges.

Agarwal, A., & Ratha, N. (2023). Manipulating faces for identity theft via morphing and deepfake: Digital privacy. In *Handbook of statistics* (Vol. 48, pp. 223–241). Elsevier.

Agha, Z., Badillo-Urquiola, K., & Wisniewski, P. J. (2023). "Strike at the root": Co-designing real-time social media interventions for adolescent online risk prevention. *Proceedings of the ACM on Human-Computer Interaction, 7*(CSCW1), Article 1–32.

Ahamad, R., & Mishra, K. N. (2024). Hybrid approach for suspicious object surveillance using video clips and UAV images in cloud-IoT-based computing environment. *Cluster Computing*, *27*(1), 761–785. Advance online publication. DOI: 10.1007/s10586-023-03977-0

Ahmad, J., Salman, W., Amin, M., Ali, Z., & Shokat, S. (2024). A Survey on Enhanced Approaches for Cyber Security Challenges Based on Deep Fake Technology in Computing Networks. *Spectrum of engineering sciences, 2*(4), 133-149.

Ahmed, S. R. A., & Sonuç, E. (2023). *Deepfake detection using rationale-augmented convolutional neural network*. Applied Nanoscience., DOI: 10.1007/s13204-021-02072-3

Aldausari, N., Sowmya, A., Marcus, N., & Mohammadi, G. (2023). Video Generative Adversarial Networks: A Review. In *ACM Computing Surveys*. DOI: 10.1145/3487891

Alguliyev, R., Aliguliyev, R., Yusifov, F., Bouzas-Lorenzo, R., & Ramos, A. C. (2018, October). MCDM Model for Evaluation of Social Network Security Threats. In *the book "ECDG 2018 18th European Conference on Digital Government"(Editors: R. Bouzas-Lorenzo and A. Cernadas Ramos), University Santiago de Compostela. Spain* (pp. 1-7).

Alhamrouni, I., Abdul Kahar, N. H., Salem, M., Swadi, M., Zahroui, Y., Kadhim, D. J., Mohamed, F. A., & Alhuyi Nazari, M. (2024). A comprehensive review on the role of artificial intelligence in power system stability, control, and protection: Insights and future directions. *Applied Sciences (Basel, Switzerland)*, *14*(14), 6214. DOI: 10.3390/app14146214

Ali, A., Ghouri, K. F. K., Naseem, H., Soomro, T. R., Mansoor, W., & Momani, A. M. (2022, October). Battle of deep fakes: Artificial intelligence set to become a major threat to the individual and national security. In *2022 International Conference on Cyber Resilience (ICCR)* (pp. 1-5). IEEE. DOI: 10.1109/ICCR56254.2022.9995821

Ali, G., Mijwil, M. M., Buruga, B. A., Abotaleb, M., & Adamopoulos, I. (2024). A survey on artificial intelligence in cybersecurity for smart agriculture: State-of-the-art, cyber threats, artificial intelligence applications, and ethical concerns. *Mesopotamian Journal of Computer Science*, *2024*, 53–103. DOI: 10.58496/MJCSC/2024/007

Ali, R., & Cha, Y. J. (2022). Attention-based generative adversarial network with internal damage segmentation using thermography. *Automation in Construction*, *141*, 104412. Advance online publication. DOI: 10.1016/j.autcon.2022.104412

Allaparthi, S. (2024). AI in Supply Chains: Transforming Fraud Detection and Authenticity Verification. *International Journal of Supply Chain Management*, *9*(6), 1–7. DOI: 10.47604/ijscm.3131

Al-Saggaf, A. A., Ghouti, L., & Acharya, H. S. (2012). Biometric cryptosystem with renewable templates. In *WIAR 2012: National Workshop on Information Assurance Research*. VDE.

Alvarez, G., & Li, S. (2006). Some basic cryptographic requirements for chaos-based cryptosystems. *International Journal of Bifurcation and Chaos in Applied Sciences and Engineering*, *16*(8), 2129–2151. DOI: 10.1142/S0218127406015970

Al-Wesabi, F. N., Alrowais, F., Mohamed, H. G., Duhayyim, M. A., Hilal, A. M., & Motwakel, A. (2023). Heuristic Optimization Algorithm Based Watermarking on Content Authentication and Tampering Detection for English Text. *IEEE Access : Practical Innovations, Open Solutions*, *11*, 86104–86111. DOI: 10.1109/ACCESS.2023.3297263

Amerini, I., Barni, M., Battiato, S., Bestagini, P., Boato, G., Bruni, V., Caldelli, R., De Natale, F., De Nicola, R., Guarnera, L., Mandelli, S., Majid, T., Marcialis, G. L., Micheletto, M., Montibeller, A., Orrù, G., Ortis, A., Perazzo, P., Puglisi, G., & Vitulano, D. (2025). Deepfake media forensics: Status and future challenges. *Journal of Imaging*, *11*(3), 73. DOI: 10.3390/jimaging11030073 PMID: 40137185

Amrouche, F., Erickson, P. A., Park, J. W., & Varnhagen, S. (2021). Performance comparison of a Wankel SI engine fuelled with gasoline and ethanol blended hydrogen. In *Proceedings* (pp. 315–321). DOI: 10.1007/978-981-15-6595-3_41

Arpaci, I. (2023). A multianalytical SEM-ANN approach to investigate the social sustainability of AI chatbots based on cybersecurity and protection motivation theory. *IEEE Transactions on Engineering Management*, *71*, 1714–1725. DOI: 10.1109/TEM.2023.3339578

Arshed, M. A., Mumtaz, S., Ibrahim, M., Dewi, C., Tanveer, M., & Ahmed, S. (2024). Multiclass AI-Generated Deepfake Face Detection Using Patch-Wise Deep Learning Model. *Computers*, *13*(1), 31. Advance online publication. DOI: 10.3390/computers13010031

Arslan, R. Ş., & Yurttakal, A. H. (2020). K-nearest neighbour classifier usage for permission based malware detection in android. *Icontech International Journal*, *4*(2), 15–27. DOI: 10.46291/ICONTECHvol4iss2pp15-27

Ashraf, S., Iqbal, W., Ahmad, S., & Khan, F. (2023). Circular spherical fuzzy sugeno weber aggregation operators: A novel uncertain approach for adaption a programming language for social media platform. *IEEE Access : Practical Innovations, Open Solutions*, *11*, 124920–124941. DOI: 10.1109/ACCESS.2023.3329242

Ayeswarya, S., & Singh, K. J. (2024). A comprehensive review on secure biometric-based continuous authentication and user profiling. *IEEE Access : Practical Innovations, Open Solutions*, *12*, 82996–83021. DOI: 10.1109/ACCESS.2024.3411783

Bakla, A. (2019). A mixed-methods study of tailor-made animated cartoons in teaching punctuation in EFL writing. *ReCALL*, *31*(1), 75–91. DOI: 10.1017/S0958344018000046

Beng, A., Teoh, A. B. J., & Toh, K.-A. (2008). Secure biometric-key generation with biometric helper. In *2008 3rd IEEE Conference on Industrial Electronics and Applications* (pp. 2300–2305). IEEE. DOI: 10.1109/ICIEA.2008.4582898

Bhandari, M., Neupane, A., Mallik, S., Gaur, L., & Qin, H. (2023). Auguring Fake Face Images Using Dual Input Convolution Neural Network. *Journal of Imaging*. Advance online publication. DOI: 10.3390/jimaging9010003 PMID: 36662101

Blake, H. (n.d.). AI-Powered Social Engineering: Understanding the Role of Deepfake Technology in Exploiting Human Trust.

Bouramdane, A.-A. (2023). Cyberattacks in smart grids: Challenges and solving the multi-criteria decision-making for cybersecurity options, including ones that incorporate artificial intelligence, using an analytical hierarchy process. *Journal of Cybersecurity and Privacy*, *3*(4), 662–705. DOI: 10.3390/jcp3040031

Brodarić, M., Štruc, V., & Peer, P. (2024). Cross-dataset deepfake detection: Evaluating the generalization capabilities of modern deepfake detectors. In *Proceedings of the Computer Vision Winter Workshop (CVWW)*, Terme Olimia, Slovenia, February 14–16, 2024.

Burrel, D. N. (2025). The Cyberpsychology and Criminal Psychology of Cyber Identity Theft and Criminal Reach in the Digital Era. *RAIS Journal for Social Sciences*, *9*(2), 343–360.

Campbell, L. (2023). AI, Deepfakes, and Digital Trust Why Ethics Matter More Than Ever.

Cao, H., Tan, C., Gao, Z., Xu, Y., Chen, G., Heng, P. A., & Li, S. Z. (2024). A survey on generative diffusion models. *IEEE Transactions on Knowledge and Data Engineering*, *36*(7), 2814–2830. DOI: 10.1109/TKDE.2024.3361474

Carlini, N., & Wagner, D. (2017). Towards evaluating the robustness of neural networks. Proceedings of the IEEE Symposium on Security and Privacy (S&P), 39-57. DOI: 10.1109/SP.2017.49

Cassia, M., Guarnera, L., Casu, M., Zangara, I., & Battiato, S. (2025). *Deepfake forensic analysis: Source dataset attribution and legal implications of synthetic media manipulation* [Preprint]. arXiv. https://arxiv.org/pdf/2505.11110

Cen, L., Gates, C. S., Si, L., & Li, N. (2014). A probabilistic discriminative model for android malware detection with decompiled source code. *IEEE Transactions on Dependable and Secure Computing*, *12*(4), 400–412. DOI: 10.1109/TDSC.2014.2355839

Chao, C., & Zheng, W. (2014). Android malware detection based on APIs. In *2014 International Conference on Machine Learning and Cybernetics (ICMLC)* (Vol. 1, pp. 82–87). IEEE. DOI: 10.1109/ICMLC.2014.7009683

Chaturvedi, A., Raghani, K. N., Kumar, S., Choudhary, M., & Yakub, A. A. M. (2025). Deepfakes in Society: Risks and Realities.

Chen, J., Dong, J., Hou, Q., Li, S., Gao, X., & Niu, S. (2022). *Semi-supervised Generative Adversarial Network for Face Anti-spoofing*. Lecture Notes in Electrical Engineering., DOI: 10.1007/978-981-16-6963-7_11

Chesney, B., & Citron, D. (2019). Deep fakes. *California Law Review, 107*(6), 1753–1820.

Chintha, A., Thai, B., Sohrawardi, S. J., Bhatt, K., Hickerson, A., Wright, M., & Ptucha, R. (2020). Recurrent Convolutional Structures for Audio Spoof and Video Deepfake Detection. *IEEE Journal of Selected Topics in Signal Processing, 14*(5), 1024–1037. Advance online publication. DOI: 10.1109/JSTSP.2020.2999185

Choi, H., Choi, K., & Kim, J. (2011). Fingerprint matching incorporating ridge features with minutiae. *IEEE Transactions on Information Forensics and Security, 6*(2), 338–345. DOI: 10.1109/TIFS.2010.2103940

Coccomini, D. A., Messina, N., Gennaro, C., & Falchi, F. (2022). *Combining EfficientNet and Vision Transformers for Video Deepfake Detection*. Lecture Notes in Computer Science. Including Subseries Lecture Notes in Artificial Intelligence and Lecture Notes in Bioinformatics., DOI: 10.1007/978-3-031-06433-3_19

Constantino, I. (2024). REAL PEOPLE IN FAKE PORN: HOW A FEDERAL RIGHT OF PUBLICITY COULD ASSIST IN THE REGULATION OF DEEPFAKE PORNOGRAPHY. *Jurimetrics: The Journal of Law, Science & Technology, 64*(3).

Dalal, M. K., & Zaveri, M. A. (2014). Opinion mining from online user reviews using fuzzy linguistic hedges. *Applied Computational Intelligence and Soft Computing, 2014*(1), 735942. DOI: 10.1155/2014/735942

De Ruiter, A. (2021). The distinct wrong of deepfakes. *Philosophy & Technology, 34*(4), 1311–1332. DOI: 10.1007/s13347-021-00459-2

Dehghani, A., & Saberi, H. (2025). Generating and detecting various types of fake image and audio content: A review of modern deep learning technologies and tools. *arXiv preprint arXiv:2501.06227*.

Delfino, R. A. (2025). Loyola Law School [Legal studies research paper]. DOI: 10.13140/RG.2.2.12632.61447

Deressa, D. W., Lambert, P., Van Wallendael, G., Atnafu, S., & Mareen, H. (2024). Improved Deepfake Video Detection Using Convolutional Vision Transformer. *2024 IEEE Gaming, Entertainment, and Media Conference. GEM: International Journal on Geomathematics, 2024*, 1–6. Advance online publication. DOI: 10.1109/GEM61861.2024.10585593

Díaz-Rodríguez, N., Del Ser, J., Coeckelbergh, M., López de Prado, M., Herrera-Viedma, E., & Herrera, F. (2023). Connecting the dots in trustworthy artificial intelligence: From AI principles, ethics, and key requirements to responsible AI systems and regulation. *Information Fusion*, *99*, 101896. Advance online publication. DOI: 10.1016/j.inffus.2023.101896

Dileep, M. R., Kansara, Y., & Suneel, J. S. (2025, August). Deepfake Technology and Online Cyber Crime: A Critical Analysis of AI Tools in Unethical Practices. In *2025 Control Instrumentation System Conference (CISCON)* (pp. 1-5). IEEE.

Dsouza, D. S., Hajjar, A. E., & Jahankhani, H. (2024). Deepfakes in social engineering attacks. In *Space Law Principles and Sustainable Measures* (pp. 153–183). Springer Nature Switzerland. DOI: 10.1007/978-3-031-64045-2_8

Duan, W. Q., Gulistan, M., Abbasi, F. H., Khurshid, A., & Al-Shamiri, M. M. (2022). q-Rung double hierarchy linguistic term set fuzzy AHP; applications in the security system threats features of social media platforms. *International Journal of Intelligent Systems*, *37*(8), 5152–5185. DOI: 10.1002/int.22755

Dubey, H., Bhatt, S., & Negi, L. (2023). Digital Forensics Techniques and Trends: A Review. [IAJIT]. *The International Arab Journal of Information Technology*, *20*(4).

Efthymiou, I. P., & Egleton, T. E. (2025). The Impact of Deep Fakes in Markets and Economies. In *Deepfakes and Their Impact on Business* (pp. 19–50). IGI Global Scientific Publishing.

El-Gayar, M. M., Abouhawwash, M., Askar, S. S., & Sweidan, S. (2024). A novel approach for detecting deep fake videos using graph neural network. *Journal of Big Data*, *11*(1), 22. Advance online publication. DOI: 10.1186/s40537-024-00884-y

Elsheikh, R. A., Mohamed, M. A., Abou-Taleb, A. M., & Ata, M. M. (2024). Accuracy is not enough: A heterogeneous ensemble model versus FGSM attack. *Complex &amp. Complex & Intelligent Systems*, *10*(6), 8355–8382. DOI: 10.1007/s40747-024-01603-z

Emrouznejad, A., & Marra, M. (2017). The state of the art development of AHP (1979–2017): A literature review with a social network analysis. *International Journal of Production Research*, *55*(22), 6653–6675. DOI: 10.1080/00207543.2017.1334976

Falana, O. J., Ojeaga, T., Naeem, H., Aborisade, D. O., Alsirhani, A., & Alserhani, F. (2024). FHG-PR: A hybridized fuzzy-AHP and game theory model for assessing privacy risk on social media platforms. *Frontiers of Computer Science*, *6*, 1389223. DOI: 10.3389/fcomp.2024.1389223

Fallis, D. (2021). The epistemic threat of deepfakes. *Philosophy & Technology, 34*(4), 623–643. DOI: 10.1007/s13347-020-00419-2 PMID: 32837868

Farid, H. (2022). Creating, using, misusing, and detecting deep fakes. *Journal of Online Trust & Safety, 1*(4). Advance online publication. DOI: 10.54501/jots.v1i4.56

Fisher, S. A., Howard, J. W., & Kira, B. (2024). Moderating synthetic content: The challenge of generative AI. *Philosophy & Technology, 37*(4), 133. DOI: 10.1007/s13347-024-00818-9 PMID: 39555113

Flynn, A., Powell, A., Eaton, A., & Scott, A. J. (2025). Sexualized deep-fake abuse: Perpetrator and victim perspectives on the motivations and forms of non-consensually created and shared sexualized deepfake imagery. *Violence Against Women*. Advance online publication.

Flynn, A., Powell, A., Scott, A. J., & Cama, E. (2022). Deepfakes and digitally altered imagery abuse: A cross-country exploration of an emerging form of image-based sexual abuse. *British Journal of Criminology, 62*(6), 1341–1358. DOI: 10.1093/bjc/azab111

Gan, Z., Liu, C., Tang, Y., Wang, B., Wang, W., & Zhang, X. (2025). *GenPTW: In-generation image watermarking for provenance tracing and tamper localisation* [Preprint]. arXiv. https://arxiv.org/pdf/2504.19567

Golea, D. G. (2025). CHALLENGES TO SECURITY POLICIES IN A DIGITAL ENVIRONMENT. GOLEA DANIELA GEORGIANA.

Gong, L. Y., & Li, X. J. (2024). A contemporary survey on deepfake detection: Datasets, algorithms, and challenges. *Electronics (Basel), 13*(3), 585. Advance online publication. DOI: 10.3390/electronics13030585

Goodfellow, I., Pouget-Abadie, J., Mirza, M., Xu, B., Warde-Farley, D., Ozair, S., Courville, A., & Bengio, Y. (2020). Generative adversarial networks. *Communications of the ACM, 63*(11), 139–144. Advance online publication. DOI: 10.1145/3422622

Goodfellow, I., Shlens, J., & Szegedy, C. (2015). Explaining and harnessing adversarial examples. *International Conference on Learning Representations (ICLR).*

Gorwa, R., & Veale, M. (2024). Moderating model marketplaces: Platform governance puzzles for AI intermediaries. *Law, Innovation and Technology, 16*(2), 341–391. DOI: 10.1080/17579961.2024.2388914

Gottschlich, C., & Huckemann, S. (2014). Separating the real from the synthetic: Minutiae histograms as fingerprints of fingerprints. *IET Biometrics, 3*(4), 291–301. DOI: 10.1049/iet-bmt.2013.0065

Gregory, S. (2022). Deepfakes, misinformation and disinformation and authenticity infrastructure responses: Impacts on frontline witnessing, distant witnessing, and civic journalism. *Journalism*, *23*(3), 708–729. DOI: 10.1177/14648849211060644

Groh, M., Epstein, Z., Firestone, C., & Picard, R. (2022). Deepfake detection by human crowds, machines, and machine-informed crowds. *Proceedings of the National Academy of Sciences of the United States of America*, *119*(1), e2110013119. Advance online publication. DOI: 10.1073/pnas.2110013119 PMID: 34969837

Guarnera, L., Giudice, O., & Battiato, S. (2020). *Fighting deepfake by exposing the convolutional traces on images*. IEEE., DOI: 10.1109/ACCESS.2020.3023037

GÜNAY, Z. H., & ALKAN, M. (2026). Exploring a deepfake attack: A multidimensional approach. *International Cybersecurity Law Review*, , 1–21.

Guo, Z., Jia, Z., Wang, L., Wang, D., Yang, G., & Kasabov, N. (2024). Constructing new backbone networks via space-frequency interactive convolution for deepfake detection. *IEEE Transactions on Information Forensics and Security*, *19*, 401–413. DOI: 10.1109/TIFS.2023.3324739

Gwassi, O. A. H., Uçan, O. N., & Navarro, E. A. (2025). Cyber-XAI-Block: An end-to-end cyber threat detection & fl-based risk assessment framework for iot enabled smart organization using xai and blockchain technologies. *Multimedia Tools and Applications*, *84*(23), 26527–26568. DOI: 10.1007/s11042-024-20059-4

Haddadpajouh, H., Azmoodeh, A., Dehghantanha, A., & Parizi, R. M. (2020). MVFCC: A multi-view fuzzy consensus clustering model for malware threat attribution. *IEEE Access : Practical Innovations, Open Solutions*, *8*, 139188–139198. DOI: 10.1109/ACCESS.2020.3012907

Hagendorff, T. (2022). A virtue-based framework to support putting AI ethics into practice. *Philosophy & Technology*, *35*(3), 55. DOI: 10.1007/s13347-022-00553-z

Haghighat, M., Zonouz, S., & Abdel-Mottaleb, M. (2015). CloudID: Trustworthy cloud-based and cross-enterprise biometric identification. *Expert Systems with Applications*, *42*(21), 7905–7916. DOI: 10.1016/j.eswa.2015.06.025

Hak, J. W. (2024). *Legal Considerations for Bloodstain Pattern Analysis Evidence and Expert Testimony* (pp. 561–581). Crc. DOI: 10.4324/9781003163695-38

Hameed, S., Nauman, M., Akhtar, N., Fayyaz, M. A., & Nawaz, R. (2025). Explainable AI-driven depression detection from social media using natural language processing and black box machine learning models. *Frontiers in Artificial Intelligence*, *8*, 1627078. DOI: 10.3389/frai.2025.1627078 PMID: 41018736

Hancock, J. T., & Bailenson, J. N. (2021). The social impact of deepfakes. *Cyberpsychology, Behavior, and Social Networking*, *24*(3), 149–152. DOI: 10.1089/cyber.2021.29208.jth PMID: 33760669

Hariharan, B., Karthic, S., Indra Priyadharshini, S., Nalina, E., Wilfred Blessing, N. R., & Senthil Prakash, P. N. (2022). Hybrid Deep Convolutional Generative Adversarial Networks (DCGANS) and Style Generative Adversarial Network (STYLEGANS) Algorithms to Improve Image Quality. *3rd International Conference on Electronics and Sustainable Communication Systems, ICESC 2022 - Proceedings*. DOI: 10.1109/ICESC54411.2022.9885611

He, S., Lei, Y., Zhang, Z., Sun, Y., Li, S., Zhang, C., & Ye, J. (2025). Identity Deepfake Threats to Biometric Authentication Systems: Public and Expert Perspectives. *arXiv preprint arXiv:2506.06825*.

Heidari, A., Jafari Navimipour, N., Dag, H., & Unal, M. (2024). Deepfake detection using deep learning methods: A systematic and comprehensive review. *Wiley Interdisciplinary Reviews: Data Mining and Knowledge Discovery, 14*(2), Article e1520. DOI: 10.1002/widm.1520

Heidari, A., Navimipour, N. J., Dag, H., Talebi, S., & Unal, M. (2024). A Novel Blockchain-Based Deepfake Detection Method Using Federated and Deep Learning Models. *Cognitive Computation, 16*(3), 1073–1091. Advance online publication. DOI: 10.1007/s12559-024-10255-7

Hooda, A., Prakash, A., Fawaz, K., Mangaokar, N., Feng, R., & Jha, S. (2022). D4: Detection of Adversarial Diffusion Deepfakes Using Disjoint Ensembles. In *arXiv (Cornell University)*. Technische Universitat Dresden. /arxiv.2202.05687DOI: 10.48550

Hsu, T.-H., & Lin, L.-Z. (2006). Using fuzzy set theoretic techniques to analyze travel risk: An empirical study. *Tourism Management*, *27*(5), 968–981. DOI: 10.1016/j.tourman.2005.10.022

Huang, Y., Juefei-Xu, F., Guo, Q., Liu, Y., & Pu, G. (2022). FakeLocator: Robust Localization of GAN-Based Face Manipulations. *IEEE Transactions on Information Forensics and Security*, *17*, 2657–2672. Advance online publication. DOI: 10.1109/TIFS.2022.3141262

Hu, K. H., Chen, F. H., Hsu, M. F., & Tzeng, G. H. (2021). Identifying key factors for adopting artificial intelligence-enabled auditing techniques by joint utilization of fuzzy-rough set theory and MRDM technique. *Technological and Economic Development of Economy*, *27*(2), 459–492. DOI: 10.3846/tede.2020.13181

Hwang, Y., Ryu, J. Y., & Jeong, S.-H. (2021). Effects of disinformation using deepfake: The protective effect of media literacy education. *Cyberpsychology, Behavior, and Social Networking*, *24*(3), 188–193. DOI: 10.1089/cyber.2020.0174 PMID: 33646021

Jain, A. K., Ross, A., & Uludag, U. (2005). Biometric template security: Challenges and solutions. In *Proceedings of the 13th European Signal Processing Conference (EUSIPCO)*. IEEE.

Jeong, Y., Kim, D., Ro, Y., & Choi, J. (2022). FrePGAN: Robust Deepfake Detection Using Frequency-Level Perturbations. *Proceedings of the 36th AAAI Conference on Artificial Intelligence, AAAI 2022*. DOI: 10.1609/aaai.v36i1.19990

Jin, Z., Teoh, A. B. J., Goi, B. M., & Tay, Y. H. (2016). Biometric cryptosystems: A new biometric key binding and its implementation for fingerprint minutiae-based representation. *Pattern Recognition*, *50*, 50–62. DOI: 10.1016/j.patcog.2016.02.024

Jin, Z., Teoh, A. B. J., Ong, T. S., & Tee, C. (2010). A revocable fingerprint template for security and privacy preserving. *KSII Transactions on Internet and Information Systems*, *4*, 1327–1342. DOI: 10.3837/tiis.2010.12.020

Johri, A. Reepu, Taneja, S., & Shamsuddin, Z. (2025). A Study in Understanding the Measures Taken by Organizations Organization to Overcome the Effect of Deepfake on Corporate Image. In *Navigating the Deepfake Conundrum: A Manager's Roadmap* (pp. 127-134). Cham: Springer Nature Switzerland.

Jung, J.-W., Heo, H.-S., Tak, H., Shim, H.-J., Chung, J. S., & Lee, B.-J. (2022). AASIST: Audio anti-spoofing using integrated spectro-temporal graph attention networks. In *ICASSP 2022—2022 IEEE International Conference on Acoustics, Speech and Signal Processing* (pp. 6367–6371). IEEE. DOI: 10.1109/ICASSP43922.2022.9747766

Kaddar, B., Fezza, S. A., Akhtar, Z., Hamidouche, W., Hadid, A., & Serra-Sagristà, J. (2024). Deepfake Detection Using Spatiotemporal Transformer. *ACM Transactions on Multimedia Computing Communications and Applications*, *20*(11), 1–21. Advance online publication. DOI: 10.1145/3643030

Kanade, S., Petrovska-Delacrétaz, D., & Dorizzi, B. (2010). In *Proceedings of the 4th IEEE International Conference on Biometrics: Theory, Applications and Systems (BTAS)* (pp. 1–7). IEEE.

Kang, S., & Valadez, K. (2025). Deepfakes' cognitive, emotional, and behavioral impact: A systematic review and meta-analysis of individual responses. *Journalism & Mass Communication Quarterly*, *102*(1), 45–72. DOI: 10.1177/10776990251357294

Karn, A., Kumar, S., Kushwaha, S. K., & Katarya, R. (2023). *Image Synthesis Using GANs and Diffusion Models*. 1–6. DOI: 10.1109/InC457730.2023.10263208

Kas, M., El-merabet, Y., Ruichek, Y., & Messoussi, R. (2022). Generative adversarial networks for 2D-based CNN pose-invariant face recognition. *International Journal of Multimedia Information Retrieval, 11*(4), 639–651. Advance online publication. DOI: 10.1007/s13735-022-00249-2

Kelley, P. G., Rousso-Schindler, S., Shelby, R., Thomas, K., & Woodruff, A. (2025). How Generative AI Empowers Attackers and Defenders Across the Trust & Safety Landscape. *arXiv preprint arXiv:2601.06033.*

Khan, F. A., & Khan, M. K. (2025). Generative AI and Deepfake Detection in Biometric Systems. *Cognitive Computation, 17*(3), 112. DOI: 10.1007/s12559-025-10469-3

Khormali, A., & Yuan, J. S. (2021). Add: Attention-based deepfake detection approach. *Big Data and Cognitive Computing*, *5*(4), 49. Advance online publication. DOI: 10.3390/bdcc5040049

Kim, E., & Cho, S. (2021). *Exposing Fake Faces through Deep Neural Networks Combining Content and Trace Feature Extractors*. IEEE., DOI: 10.1109/ACCESS.2021.3110859

Kivinen, T. (2003). More modular exponential (MODP) Diffie-Hellman groups for Internet Key Exchange (IKE). Internet Engineering Task Force., RFC 3526. DOI: 10.17487/rfc3526

Kohli, A., & Gupta, A. (2022). Light-weight 3DCNN for DeepFakes, FaceSwap and Face2Face facial forgery detection. *Multimedia Tools and Applications, 81*(22), 31391–31403. Advance online publication. DOI: 10.1007/s11042-022-12778-3

Komashinskiy, D., & Kotenko, I. (2010, February). Malware detection by data mining techniques based on positionally dependent features. In *2010 18th Euromicro Conference on Parallel, Distributed and Network-based Processing* (pp. 617-623). IEEE. DOI: 10.1109/PDP.2010.30

Korkmaz, E., Riaz, M., Deveci, M., & Kadry, S. (2024). A novel approach to fuzzy N-soft sets and its application for identifying and sanctioning cyber harassment on social media platforms. *Artificial Intelligence Review, 57*(1), 14. DOI: 10.1007/s10462-023-10640-y

Kumar Sharma, S., Ahmad Khan, W., Kumar, M., & Bali, R. (2024). Estimation and Concealment Deep Fake Detection in Images using Hybrid LSTM. [IJISAE]. *Journal of Intelligent Systems and Applications in Engineering*, *2024*(2), 505–522. www.ijisae.org

Kumar, R., Khan, A. I., Abushark, Y. B., Alam, M. M., Agrawal, A., & Khan, R. A. (2020). A knowledge-based integrated system of hesitant fuzzy set, AHP and TOPSIS for evaluating security-durability of web applications. *IEEE Access : Practical Innovations, Open Solutions*, *8*, 48870–48885. DOI: 10.1109/ACCESS.2020.2978038

Kuźnicka-Błaszkowska, D., & Kostyuk, N. (2025). Emerging need to regulate deepfakes in international law: The Russo–Ukrainian war as an example. *Journal of Cybersecurity*, *11*(1), 8. Advance online publication. DOI: 10.1093/cybsec/tyaf008

Łabuz, M. (2023). Regulating deep fakes in the Artificial Intelligence Act. *Applied Cybersecurity and Internet Governance*, *2*(1), 252–291. DOI: 10.60097/ACIG/162856

Łabuz, M. (2024). Deep fakes and the Artificial Intelligence Act—An important signal or a missed opportunity? *Policy and Internet*, *16*(4), 651–672. DOI: 10.1002/poi3.406

Li, Y., Chang, M. C., & Lyu, S. (2018). In Ictu Oculi: Exposing AI created fake videos by detecting eye blinking. *10th IEEE International Workshop on Information Forensics and Security, WIFS 2018*. DOI: 10.1109/WIFS.2018.8630787

Li, J., Sun, L., Yan, Q., Li, Z., Srisa-An, W., & Ye, H. (2018). Significant permission identification for machine-learning-based android malware detection. *IEEE Transactions on Industrial Informatics*, *14*(7), 3216–3225. DOI: 10.1109/TII.2017.2789219

Li, P., Yang, X., Qiao, H., Cao, K., Liu, E., & Tian, J. (2012). An effective biometric cryptosystem combining fingerprints with error correction codes. *Expert Systems with Applications*, *39*(7), 6562–6574. DOI: 10.1016/j.eswa.2011.12.048

Li, P., Zhao, H., Liu, Q., Tang, P., & Zhang, L. (2024). TellMeTalk: Multimodal-driven talking face video generation. *Computers & Electrical Engineering*, *114*, 109049. Advance online publication. DOI: 10.1016/j.compeleceng.2023.109049

Liu, B., Liu, B., Zhu, T., & Ding, M. (2025). A Review of Deepfake and Its Detection: From Generative Adversarial Networks to Diffusion Models. *International Journal of Intelligent Systems*, *2025*(1), 9987535. DOI: 10.1155/int/9987535

Liu, C., Zhu, T., Zhao, Y., Zhang, J., & Zhou, W. (2024). Disentangling different levels of GAN fingerprints for task-specific forensics. *Computer Standards & Interfaces*, *89*, 103825. Advance online publication. DOI: 10.1016/j.csi.2023.103825

Li, Y., Ma, C., Yan, Y., Zhu, W., & Yang, X. (2023). DCFace: Synthetic face generation with dual condition diffusion model. In *Proceedings of the IEEE/CVF Conference on Computer Vision and Pattern Recognition* (pp. 12715–12725). IEEE. DOI: 10.1109/CVPR52729.2023.01222

Lomborg, S., & Bechmann, A. (2014). Using APIs for data collection on social media. *The Information Society*, *30*(4), 256–265. DOI: 10.1080/01972243.2014.915276

Luo, B., & Luo, R. (2024). Application and empirical analysis of fuzzy neural networks in mining social media users' behavioral characteristics and formulating accurate online marketing strategies. *International Journal of Computational Intelligence Systems*, *17*(1), 273. DOI: 10.1007/s44196-024-00675-6

Lu, Y., & Ebrahimi, T. (2024). Assessment framework for deepfake detection in real-world situations. *EURASIP Journal on Image and Video Processing*, *2024*(1), 6. Advance online publication. DOI: 10.1186/s13640-024-00621-8

Madry, A., Makelov, A., Schmidt, L., Tsipras, D., & Vladu, A. (2018). Towards deep learning models resistant to adversarial attacks. *International Conference on Learning Representations (ICLR)*.DOI: 10.48550/arXiv.1706.06083

Maheshwari, R. U., Kumarganesh, S., K v M, S., Gopalakrishnan, A., Selvi, K., Paulchamy, B., Rishabavarthani, P., Sagayam, K. M., Pandey, B. K., & Pandey, D. (2024, July 05). K V M, S., Gopalakrishnan, A., Selvi, K., Paulchamy, B., Rishabavarthani, P., Sagayam, K. M., Pandey, B. K., & Pandey, D. (2025). Advanced Plasmonic Resonance-enhanced Biosensor for Comprehensive Real-time Detection and Analysis of Deepfake Content. *Plasmonics*. Advance online publication. DOI: 10.1007/s11468-024-02407-0

Malik, A., Kuribayashi, M., Abdullahi, S. M., & Khan, A. N. (2022). DeepFake detection for human face images and videos: A survey. *IEEE Access : Practical Innovations, Open Solutions*, *10*, 18757–18775. DOI: 10.1109/ACCESS.2022.3151186

Mandal, S. (2025). Deep Fake Technology and Identity Theft: An Emerging Challenge for Cyber Laws in India. Available at *SSRN* 5161545. DOI: 10.2139/ssrn.5161545

Masood, M., Nawaz, M., Malik, K. M., Javed, A., Irtaza, A., & Malik, H. (2023). Deepfakes generation and detection: State-of-the-art, open challenges, countermeasures, and way forward. *Applied Intelligence*, *53*(4), 3974–4026. DOI: 10.1007/s10489-022-03766-z

Mehlawat, M. K., Gupta, P., & Khaitan, A. (2021). Multiobjective fuzzy vehicle routing using Twitter data: Reimagining the delivery of essential goods. *International Journal of Intelligent Systems*, *36*(7), 3566–3595. DOI: 10.1002/int.22427

Millière, R. (2022). Deep learning and synthetic media. *Synthese*, *200*(3), 231. DOI: 10.1007/s11229-022-03739-2

Mirsky, Y., & Lee, W. (2021). The creation and detection of deepfakes: A survey. ACM Computing Surveys, 53(5). *ACM Computing Surveys*, *89*(1), 1–41. DOI: 10.1145/3425780

Misirlis, N., & Munawar, H. B. (2023). From deepfake to deep useful: risks and opportunities through a systematic literature review. *arXiv preprint arXiv:2311.15809.*

Mittal, T., Bhattacharya, U., Chandra, R., Bera, A., & Manocha, D. (2020). Emotions Don't Lie: An Audio-Visual Deepfake Detection Method using Affective Cues. *MM 2020 - Proceedings of the 28th ACM International Conference on Multimedia.* DOI: 10.1145/3394171.3413570

Moustafa, N., Koroniotis, N., Keshk, M., Zomaya, A. Y., & Tari, Z. (2023). Explainable intrusion detection for cyber defences in the internet of things: Opportunities and solutions. *IEEE Communications Surveys and Tutorials*, *25*(3), 1775–1807. DOI: 10.1109/COMST.2023.3280465

Mubarak, R., Alsboui, T., Alshaikh, O., Inuwa-Dutse, I., Khan, S., & Parkinson, S. (2023). A survey on the detection and impacts of deepfakes in visual, audio, and textual formats. *IEEE Access : Practical Innovations, Open Solutions*, *11*, 144497–144529. DOI: 10.1109/ACCESS.2023.3344653

Mukhammadovich, N. M., & Djuraevich, A. R. (2023). Working with cryptographic key information. *International Journal of Electrical and Computer Engineering*, *13*(1), 911–919. DOI: 10.11591/ijece.v13i1.pp911-919

Mukta, M. S. H., Ahmad, J., Raiaan, M. A. K., Islam, S., Azam, S., Ali, M. E., & Jonkman, M. (2023). An Investigation of the Effectiveness of Deepfake Models and Tools. *Journal of Sensor and Actuator Networks.* DOI: 10.3390/jsan12040061

Murillo-Escobar, M. A., Cardoza-Avendaño, L., Méndez-Ramírez, R., & Cruz-Hernández, C. (2015). A robust embedded biometric authentication system based on fingerprint and chaotic encryption. *Expert Systems with Applications*, *42*(21), 8198–8211. DOI: 10.1016/j.eswa.2015.06.035

Murray, M. D. (2025). Deceptive exploitation: Deepfakes, the rights of publicity and privacy, and trademark law. IDEA: The Law Review of the Franklin Pierce Center for Intellectual Property, 65.

Nguyen, H. H., Yamagishi, J., & Echizen, I. (2019). Capsule-forensics: Using Capsule Networks to Detect Forged Images and Videos. *ICASSP, IEEE International Conference on Acoustics, Speech and Signal Processing - Proceedings*. DOI: 10.1109/ICASSP.2019.8682602

Nielsen, R. K., & Schrøder, K. C. (2014). The relative importance of social media for accessing, finding, and engaging with news: An eight-country cross-media comparison. *Digital Journalism (Abingdon, England)*, *2*(4), 472–489. DOI: 10.1080/21670811.2013.872420

Nilashi, M., Ibrahim, O., Mirabi, V. R., Ebrahimi, L., & Zare, M. (2015). The role of Security, Design and Content factors on customer trust in mobile commerce. *Journal of Retailing and Consumer Services*, *26*, 57–69. DOI: 10.1016/j.jretconser.2015.05.002

Nirkin, Y., Wolf, L., Keller, Y., & Hassner, T. (2022). DeepFake Detection Based on Discrepancies Between Faces and Their Context. *IEEE Transactions on Pattern Analysis and Machine Intelligence*, *44*(10), 6111–6121. Advance online publication. DOI: 10.1109/TPAMI.2021.3093446 PMID: 34185639

O'Meara, J., & Murphy, C. (2023). Aberrant AI creations: Co-creating surrealist body horror using the DALL-E Mini text-to-image generator. *Convergence (London)*, *29*(4), 1070–1096. DOI: 10.1177/13548565231185865

Ognibene, D., Wilkens, R., Taibi, D., Hernández-Leo, D., Kruschwitz, U., Donabauer, G., Theophilou, E., Lomonaco, F., Bursic, S., Lobo, R. A., Sánchez-Reina, J. R., Scifo, L., Schwarze, V., Börsting, J., Hoppe, U., Aprin, F., Malzahn, N., & Eimler, S. (2023). Challenging social media threats using collective well-being-aware recommendation algorithms and an educational virtual companion. *Frontiers in Artificial Intelligence*, *5*, 654930. DOI: 10.3389/frai.2022.654930 PMID: 36699613

Ooi, K. B., Tan, G. W. H., Al-Emran, M., Al-Sharafi, M. A., Capatina, A., Chakraborty, A., Dwivedi, Y. K., Huang, T.-L., Kar, A. K., Lee, V.-H., Loh, X.-M., Micu, A., Mikalef, P., Mogaji, E., Pandey, N., Raman, R., Rana, N. P., Sarker, P., Sharma, A., & Wong, L. W. (2025). The potential of generative artificial intelligence across disciplines: Perspectives and future directions. *Journal of Computer Information Systems*, *65*(1), 76–107. DOI: 10.1080/08874417.2023.2261010

Pan, D., Sun, L., Wang, R., Zhang, X., & Sinnott, R. O. (2020). Deepfake Detection through Deep Learning. *Proceedings - 2020 IEEE/ACM International Conference on Big Data Computing, Applications and Technologies, BDCAT 2020*. DOI: 10.1109/BDCAT50828.2020.00001

Panchal, G., & Samanta, D. (2018). A novel approach to fingerprint biometric-based cryptographic key generation and its applications to storage security. *Computers & Electrical Engineering*, *69*, 461–478. DOI: 10.1016/j.compeleceng.2018.01.028

Passos, L. A., Jodas, D., Costa, K. A. P., Souza Júnior, L. A., Rodrigues, D., Del Ser, J., Camacho, D., & Papa, J. P. (2024). A review of deep learning-based approaches for deepfake content detection. *Expert Systems: International Journal of Knowledge Engineering and Neural Networks*, *41*(8), e13570. Advance online publication. DOI: 10.1111/exsy.13570

Pawelec, M. (2022). Deepfakes and democracy (theory): How synthetic audio-visual media for disinformation and hate speech threaten core democratic functions. *Digital Society : Ethics, Socio-Legal and Governance of Digital Technology*, *1*(2), 19. DOI: 10.1007/s44206-022-00010-6 PMID: 36097613

Qi, H., Guo, Q., Juefei-Xu, F., Xie, X., Ma, L., Feng, W., Liu, Y., & Zhao, J. (2020). DeepRhythm: Exposing DeepFakes with Attentional Visual Heartbeat Rhythms. *MM 2020 - Proceedings of the 28th ACM International Conference on Multimedia*. DOI: 10.1145/3394171.3413707

Rai, A. K., Singh, M., Sudheendramouli, H. C., Panwar, V., Balaji, N. A., & Kukreti, R. (2023). *Digital Signature for Content Authentication*. 1–6. DOI: 10.1109/ACCAI58221.2023.10200472

Rajak, M., & Shaw, K. (2021). An extension of technology acceptance model for mHealth user adoption. *Technology in Society*, *67*, 101800. Advance online publication. DOI: 10.1016/j.techsoc.2021.101800

Rana, M. S., Nobi, M. N., Murali, B., & Sung, A. H. (2022). Deepfake detection: A systematic literature review. *IEEE Access : Practical Innovations, Open Solutions*, *10*, 25494–25513. DOI: 10.1109/ACCESS.2022.3154404

Rehaan, M., Kaur, N., & Kingra, S. (2024). Face manipulated deepfake generation and recognition approaches: a survey. In *Smart Science*. DOI: 10.1080/23080477.2023.2268380

Reijers, W., & Coeckelbergh, M. (2024). Virtuous practice design in AI ethics. *AI and Ethics*, *4*, 487–502.

Ribouh, S., Phan, K., Malawade, A. V., Elhillali, Y., Rivenq, A., & Al Faruque, M. A. (2020). Channel state information-based cryptographic key generation for intelligent transportation systems. *IEEE Transactions on Intelligent Transportation Systems*, *22*(12), 7496–7507. DOI: 10.1109/TITS.2020.3003577

Rohankar, T. S., & Gulhane, V. S. (2025). *Design of an Improved Model for Forensic Chain-of-Custody Using ZK-TIV, MV-PGChain, and AWReS*. 1–6. DOI: 10.1109/ACROSET66531.2025.11281309

Romero-Moreno, F. (2025). Deepfake detection in generative AI: A legal framework proposal to protect human rights. *Computer Law & Security Review*, *58*, 106162. Advance online publication. DOI: 10.1016/j.clsr.2025.106162

Rossler, A., Cozzolino, D., Verdoliva, L., Riess, C., Thies, J., & Niessner, M. (2019). FaceForensics++: Learning to detect manipulated facial images. *Proceedings of the IEEE International Conference on Computer Vision*. DOI: 10.1109/ICCV.2019.00009

Saeed, R. A., & Shareef, S. M. (2021). Prediction of the security threats in social media using artificial intelligence. *QALAAI ZANIST Scientific Journal*, *6*(1), 1013–1034.

Sandoval, M. P., de Almeida Vau, M., Solaas, J., & Rodrigues, L. (2024). Threat of deepfakes to the criminal justice system: A systematic review. *Crime Science*, *13*(1), 41. Advance online publication. DOI: 10.1186/s40163-024-00239-1

Sangaiah, A. K., Goli, A., Tirkolaee, E. B., Ranjbar-Bourani, M., Pandey, H. M., & Zhang, W. (2020). Big data-driven cognitive computing system for optimization of social media analytics. *IEEE Access : Practical Innovations, Open Solutions*, *8*, 82215–82226. DOI: 10.1109/ACCESS.2020.2991394

Schulte, E. (2025). The social consensus on truth in news-related deepfakes: Implications of public perception and media integrity (Master's thesis, Iowa State University).

Shahzad, M. F., Xu, S., Lim, W. M., Yang, X., & Khan, Q. R. (2024). Artificial intelligence and social media on academic performance and mental well-being: Student perceptions of positive impact in the age of smart learning. *Heliyon*, *10*(8), e29523. DOI: 10.1016/j.heliyon.2024.e29523 PMID: 38665566

Sharma, M., Joshi, S., Luthra, S., & Kumar, A. (2024). Impact of digital assistant attributes on millennials' purchasing intentions: A multi-group analysis using PLS-SEM, artificial neural network and fsQCA. *Information Systems Frontiers*, *26*(3), 943–966. DOI: 10.1007/s10796-022-10339-5 PMID: 36185777

Shende, S. W., Tembhurne, J. V., & Ansari, N. A. (2024). Deep learning based authentication schemes for smart devices in different modalities: Progress, challenges, performance, datasets and future directions. *Multimedia Tools and Applications*, *83*(28), 71451–71493. Advance online publication. DOI: 10.1007/s11042-024-18350-5

Shen, F., Del Vecchio, J., Mohaisen, A., Ko, S. Y., & Ziarek, L. (2018). Android malware detection using complex-flows. *IEEE Transactions on Mobile Computing*, *18*(6), 1231–1245. DOI: 10.1109/TMC.2018.2861405

Shirish, A., & Komal, S. (2023). A socio-legal inquiry on deepfakes. *Cal. W. Int'l LJ*, *54*, 517.

Sholademi, D. B. (n.d.). Leveraging AI for Detecting Deep Fakes and Combating Financial Fraudulent Identity Schemes.

Siddiqi, M. A., Pak, W., & Siddiqi, M. A. (2022). A study on the psychology of social engineering-based cyberattacks and existing countermeasures. *Applied Sciences (Basel, Switzerland)*, *12*(12), 6042. DOI: 10.3390/app12126042

Siegel, D., Kraetzer, C., Seidlitz, S., & Dittmann, J. (2021). Media forensics considerations on DeepFake detection with hand-crafted features. *Journal of Imaging*, *7*(7), 108. Advance online publication. DOI: 10.3390/jimaging7070108 PMID: 39080896

Sinaga, H. (2023). Legal and Ethical Implications in Data Theft Cases in the Digital Era. *East Asian Journal of Multidisciplinary Research*, *2*(11), 4585–4604. DOI: 10.55927/eajmr.v2i11.6791

Singh, S., & Dhumane, A. (2025). Unmasking digital deceptions: An integrative review of deepfake detection, multimedia forensics, and cybersecurity challenges. *MethodsX*, *15*, 103632. Advance online publication. DOI: 10.1016/j.mex.2025.103632 PMID: 41080432

Sornavalli, G., & Vijaybaskar, P. (2024). DeepFake Detection by Prediction of Mismatch Between Audio and Video Lip Movement. *2024 International Conference on Advances in Data Engineering and Intelligent Computing Systems, ADICS 2024*. DOI: 10.1109/ADICS58448.2024.10533515

Srivastava, A., Pandey, M., & Sahu, S. K. (2022). *A Review on Deepfakes Detection Using Machine Learning Techniques*. Lecture Notes in Electrical Engineering., DOI: 10.1007/978-981-19-5037-7_46

Stewart, D., & Littau, J. (2025). The right to lie with AI? First Amendment challenges for state efforts to curb false political speech using deepfakes and synthetic media. Colorado Technology Law Journal, 24.

Stinson, D. R. (1997). An introduction to visual cryptography. In *Public Key Solutions* (Vol. 97, pp. 28–30).

Stoianov, A. (2010). In *Proceedings of the 8th Annual International Conference on Privacy, Security and Trust (PST)* (pp. 231–235).

Story, D., & Jenkins, R. (2023). Deepfake pornography and the ethics of non-veridical representations. *Philosophy & Technology, 36*(3), 1–22. DOI: 10.1007/s13347-023-00657-0

Stroebel, L., Llewellyn, M., Hartley, T., Ip, T. S., & Ahmed, M. (2023). A systematic literature review on the effectiveness of deepfake detection techniques. *Journal of Cyber Security Technology, 7*(2), 83–113. DOI: 10.1080/23742917.2023.2192888

Such, J. M., & Criado, N. (2016). Resolving multi-party privacy conflicts in social media. *IEEE Transactions on Knowledge and Data Engineering, 28*(7), 1851–1863. DOI: 10.1109/TKDE.2016.2539165

Suleiman, N. A. (2025). Deepfake-as-a-Service: The next challenge for enterprise cybersecurity. *Journal of Technology and Systems, 7*(3), 47–59. DOI: 10.47941/jts.2752

Sunil, R., Mer, P., Diwan, A., Mahadeva, R., & Sharma, A. (2025). Exploring autonomous methods for deepfake detection: A detailed survey on techniques and evaluation. *Heliyon, 11*(3), e42273. DOI: 10.1016/j.heliyon.2025.e42273 PMID: 39968137

Suresh Babu, C. V., & Vishnupriyan, J. VijaykumarReddy, U., Hariharan, P., & Dheenadhayalan, P. (2025). Secure Implementation of Image Processing Operations on CPU and GPU Architectures: With Deep Learning Frameworks. In B. Omkar Lakshmi Jagan, A. Mukherjee, T. Mohammed, & V. Reddy (Eds.), Signal and Image Processing Techniques for Defense, Security, and Healthcare (pp. 253-302). IGI Global Scientific Publishing. DOI: 10.4018/979-8-3693-3840-7.ch010

Tallam, K., Cava, J. K., Geniesse, C., Erichson, N. B., & Mahoney, M. W. (2025). Removing watermarks with partial regeneration using semantic information. arXiv preprint arXiv:2505.08234.

Tan, M., & Le, Q. V. (2019). EfficientNet: Rethinking model scaling for convolutional neural networks. *36th International Conference on Machine Learning, ICML 2019*.

Temara, S. (2024). The dark web and cybercrime: Identifying threats and anticipating emerging trends.

Thakur, K., Sayed, M. A., Tisha, S. A., Alam, M. K., Hasan, M. T., Shorna, J. F., Afrin, S., George, M. Z. H., & Ayon, E. H. (2025). Multimodal deepfake detection using transformer-based large language models: A path toward secure media and clinical integrity. *The American Journal of Engineering and Technology, 7*(5), 169–177. DOI: 10.37547/tajet/Volume07Issue05-16

Thies, J., Zollhöfer, M., Stamminger, M., Theobalt, C., & Nießner, M. (2016). Face2Face: Real-time face capture and reenactment of RGB videos. *Proceedings of the IEEE Conference on Computer Vision and Pattern Recognition (CVPR)*, 2387-2395. DOI: 10.1145/2929464.2929475

Thing, V. L. L. (2023). Deepfake detection with deep learning: Convolutional neural networks versus transformers. In *Proceedings of the 2023 IEEE International Conference on Cyber Security and Resilience (CSR)* (pp. 246–253). DOI: 10.1109/CSR57506.2023.10225004

Tiwari, S. (2025). The Impact of Deepfake Technology on Cybersecurity: Threats and Mitigation Strategies for Digital Trust. Available at *SSRN* 5259359. DOI: 10.2139/ssrn.5259359

Tolosana, R., Vera-Rodriguez, R., Fierrez, J., Morales, A., & Ortega-Gil, J. (2020). DeepFakes and beyond: A survey of face manipulation and fake detection. *Information Fusion*, *64*, 1–20. DOI: 10.1016/j.inffus.2020.06.014

Tuysuz, M. K., & Kılıç, A. (2023). Analyzing the legal and ethical considerations of deepfake technology. *Interdisciplinary Studies in Society, Law, and Politics*, *2*(2), 4–10. DOI: 10.61838/kman.isslp.2.2.2

Twomey, J., Ching, D., Aylett, M. P., Quayle, M., Linehan, C., & Murphy, G. (2023). Do deepfake videos undermine our epistemic trust? A thematic analysis of tweets that discuss deepfakes in the Russian invasion of Ukraine. *PLoS One*, *18*(10), e0291668. DOI: 10.1371/journal.pone.0291668 PMID: 37878559

Ugwuoke, V., & Sanfilippo, M. R. (2025). The current landscape of deepfake legislation in the United States: Analysis of state-level responses. Journal of Information Policy, 15.

Umbach, R., Henry, N., Beard, G. F., & Berryessa, C. M. (2024). Non-consensual synthetic intimate imagery: Prevalence, attitudes, and knowledge in 10 countries. In Proceedings of the CHI Conference on Human Factors in Computing Systems (CHI '24) (Article 779, pp. 1–20). Association for Computing Machinery.

Upmanyu, M., Namboodiri, A. M., Srinathan, K., & Jawahar, C. V. (2010). Blind authentication: A secure crypto-biometric verification protocol. *IEEE Transactions on Information Forensics and Security*, *5*(2), 255–268. DOI: 10.1109/TIFS.2010.2043188

van der Sloot, B., & Wagensveld, Y. (2022). Deepfakes: Regulatory challenges for the synthetic society. *Computer Law & Security Review*, *46*, 105716. Advance online publication. DOI: 10.1016/j.clsr.2022.105716

Vaseashta, A. (2025). Dual-Use Artificial Intelligence—Trends, Security Challenges, and Mitigation Strategies. In *Spectrum of Dual-Use Technologies: Unforeseen Risks Versus Returns* (pp. 3–37). Springer Nature Switzerland.

Vimala, M., Nandhini, M., Jasmine, S., Kumar, P. R., & Ramasamy, S. (2026). Implementation of a lightweight deep learning model for detecting driver fatigue. *Franklin Open, 15*(October 2025), 100547. DOI: 10.1016/j.fraope.2026.100547

Vinayakumar, R., Alazab, M., Soman, K. P., Poornachandran, P., & Venkatraman, S. (2019). Robust intelligent malware detection using deep learning. *IEEE Access : Practical Innovations, Open Solutions*, *7*, 46717–46738. DOI: 10.1109/ACCESS.2019.2906934

Volkova, S. (2024). Deepfakes: Fraud and Cybercrime. *Deepfakes and Their Impact on Business*, 221.

Wang, R., Juefei-Xu, F., Huang, Y., Guo, Q., Xie, X., Ma, L., & Liu, Y. (2020). DeepSonar: Towards Effective and Robust Detection of AI-Synthesized Fake Voices. *MM 2020 - Proceedings of the 28th ACM International Conference on Multimedia*. DOI: 10.1145/3394171.3413716

Wang, K., Ying, Z., Goswami, S. S., Yin, Y., & Zhao, Y. (2023). Investigating the role of artificial intelligence technologies in the construction industry using a Delphi-ANP-TOPSIS hybrid MCDM concept under a fuzzy environment. *Sustainability (Basel), 15*(15), 11848. DOI: 10.3390/su151511848

Wang, T., Cheng, H., Chow, K. P., & Nie, L. (2023). Deep Convolutional Pooling Transformer for Deepfake Detection. *ACM Transactions on Multimedia Computing Communications and Applications*, *19*(6), 1–20. Advance online publication. DOI: 10.1145/3588574

Wang, T., Liao, X., Chow, K. P., Lin, X., & Wang, Y. (2024). Deepfake detection: A comprehensive survey from the reliability perspective. *ACM Computing Surveys*, *57*(3), 1–35.

Weiner, M. D. (2023). Destined to deceive: The need to regulate deepfakes with a foreseeable harm standard. Mich. L. Rev., 122, 771.

Widder, D. G., Nafus, D., Dabbish, L., & Herbsleb, J. (2022). Limits and possibilities for "ethical AI" in open source: A study of deepfakes. In *Proceedings of the 2022 ACM Conference on Fairness, Accountability, and Transparency (FAccT '22)* (pp. 2035–2046). Association for Computing Machinery. DOI: 10.1145/3531146.3533779

Xu, H., Tang, X., Sun, H., Zhao, H., & Li, M. (2017). Conductivity of silver and copper film printed by particle-free reactive inks. In *18th International Conference on Electronic Packaging Technology (ICEPT)* (pp. 1470–1473). DOI: 10.1109/ICEPT.2017.8046713

Xu, P., Mei, X., Wei, Y., & Qian, T. (2021). Robust Facial Manipulation Detection via Domain Generalization. *ACM International Conference Proceeding Series.* DOI: 10.1145/3467707.3467736

Yang, J., Xiao, S., Li, A., Lan, G., & Wang, H. (2021). Detecting fake images by identifying potential texture difference. *Future Generation Computer Systems*, *125*, 127–135. Advance online publication. DOI: 10.1016/j.future.2021.06.043

Yang, J., Xiao, S., Li, A., Lu, W., Gao, X., & Li, Y. (2022). MSTA-Net: Forgery Detection by Generating Manipulation Trace Based on Multi-Scale Self-Texture Attention. *IEEE Transactions on Circuits and Systems for Video Technology*, *32*(7), 4854–4866. Advance online publication. DOI: 10.1109/TCSVT.2021.3133859

Yang, T., Huang, Z., Cao, J., Li, L., & Li, X. (2022). Deepfake network architecture attribution. *Proceedings of the AAAI Conference on Artificial Intelligence*, *36*(4), 4662–4670. DOI: 10.1609/aaai.v36i4.20391

Yang, Z., Liang, J., Xu, Y., Zhang, X. Y., & He, R. (2023). Masked Relation Learning for DeepFake Detection. *IEEE Transactions on Information Forensics and Security*, *18*, 1696–1708. Advance online publication. DOI: 10.1109/TIFS.2023.3249566

Yogatama, B., & Rimbawa, H. A. D. (2026). DIGITAL WATERMARKING AND THE FIGHT AGAINST DEEPFAKE CONTENT. [Jurnal Mahasiswa Teknik Informatika]. *JATI*, *10*(1), 691–698. DOI: 10.36040/jati.v10i1.16826

Yue, Y., & Shen, X. (2024). Development strategy of early childhood music education industry: An IFS-AHP-SWOT analysis based on dynamic social network. *PLoS One*, *19*(2), e0295419. DOI: 10.1371/journal.pone.0295419 PMID: 38422058

Yu, N., Davis, L., & Fritz, M. (2019). Attributing fake images to GANs: Learning and analysing GAN fingerprints. In *Proceedings of the IEEE International Conference on Computer Vision* (pp. 7555–7565). DOI: 10.1109/ICCV.2019.00765

Yu, Y., Zhao, X., Ni, R., Yang, S., Zhao, Y., & Kot, A. C. (2023). Augmented Multi-Scale Spatiotemporal Inconsistency Magnifier for Generalized DeepFake Detection. *IEEE Transactions on Multimedia*, *25*, 8487–8498. Advance online publication. DOI: 10.1109/TMM.2023.3237322

Zhang, H., Luo, S., Zhang, Y., & Pan, L. (2019). An efficient Android malware detection system based on method-level behavioral semantic analysis. *IEEE Access : Practical Innovations, Open Solutions, 7*, 69246–69256. DOI: 10.1109/ACCESS.2019.2919796

Zhang, Y., Chen, X., Wang, L., Liu, M., & Zhou, H. (2025). Public perception towards deepfake through topic modelling and sentiment analysis of social media data. *Social Network Analysis and Mining, 15*(1), 45. Advance online publication. DOI: 10.1007/s13278-025-01445-8

Zhao, H., Zhou, W., Chen, D., Wei, T., Zhang, W., & Yu, N. (2021). Multi-attentional Deepfake Detection. *Proceedings of the IEEE Computer Society Conference on Computer Vision and Pattern Recognition*. DOI: 10.1109/CVPR46437.2021.00222

Zhao, Y.. (2023). Neural watermarking for proactive deepfake defense. *Proceedings of the IEEE International Conference on Acoustics, Speech and Signal Processing (ICASSP)*, 1234-1241.

Zhao, Z., Guan, J., Jiang, Z., & Gong, N. Z. (2023). Evading watermark based detection of AI-generated content. In *Proceedings of the 2023 ACM SIGSAC Conference on Computer and Communications Security* (pp. 3418–3432). ACM. DOI: 10.1145/3576915.3623189

Zheng, Z., Xie, S., Dai, H., Chen, X., & Wang, H. (2018). An overview of blockchain technology: Architecture, consensus, and future trends. *Proceedings of the IEEE International Congress on Big Data (BigData)*, 557-564.

Zhou, P., Han, X., Morariu, V. I., & Davis, L. S. (2017). Two-Stream Neural Networks for Tampered Face Detection. *IEEE Computer Society Conference on Computer Vision and Pattern Recognition Workshops*. DOI: 10.1109/CVPRW.2017.229

About the Contributors

Manoj Kumar completed his Ph.D. from Northcap University and M.Sc. (Information Security and Digital Forensics) from Technological University Dublin, Ireland in 2013. Dr. Kumar has more than 15 years of research, teaching, and corporate experience. Currently, Dr. Kumar holds the position of Associate Professor at the University of Wollongong in Dubai. In addition, he serves as the Research Cluster Head for Network and Cyber Security @UOWD. Dr. Kumar is listed among the top 2% of computer scientists worldwide. He published over 265 research articles in international refereed journals and conferences. He published over 12 patents, delivered five research-funded projects, and released three authored and forteen edited books. In addition, he acts as an associate editor, guest editor, and editorial board member for various scientific journals. Dr. Kumar is a member of numerous renowned professional bodies, including IEEE, ACM, IAENG, ISTS, and UACEE. Dr. Kumar received the Best Researcher Award in 2020, an Outstanding Scientist Award, and a Young Researcher Award in 2021 from recognized international professional bodies. His specializations are Digital Forensics, Machine Learning, Information Security, Image Processing, IOT and Networks.

May El Barachi is Director of Computer Science & IT Programs at University of Wollongong in Dubai. An Egyptian Canadian Computer Scientist, and Smart Technology Expert with degrees in Telecom. Engineering, Computer Engineering, and Computer Science, Dr. El Barachi possesses width and breadth of knowledge in the areas of Computer Science, IT, and Engineering. Dr. El Barachi is also a public speaker who participates in large-scale public events and speaks about technology-related topics, such as: Digital transformation, smart cities, emerging technologies & their related opportunities, demystifying complex technologies, and professional training in alignment with the industry needs. Using her knowledge and experience, she conducts large scale multi-disciplinary projects in the areas of BioTech, Smart Transportation, Smart cities, Inclusion & Innovation. With collaborators spanning the globe, and a large group of researchers under her supervision, she tackles challenging real-life problems using a combination of legacy and emerging technologies. She is involved in industry collaborations with the telecom and health industries and was able to raise more than 3 million Dirhams in the last 5 years to support her research work. In addition to being a professor and active researcher, Dr. El Barachi holds leadership roles in teaching/learning and research. In her current role, she defines the research strategy for the faculty and ensures that the right eco-system is established for conducting high-impact research. She is also a champion and certified trainer in emerging technologies and have spearheaded a successful executive learning program in collaboration with IBM, currently offering 10 professional training modules ranging from AI, data science, and big data, to cloud, IOT, security and Blockchain, and design thinking. The idea of the program is to equip students and working professionals with important skills that are needed in the industry and complement conventional academic programs with professional hands on training.

Preeti Sharma is an accomplished Assistant Professor in the School of Computing at DIT Dehradun, with a distinguished academic and research background in neural networks, deep learning, and generative adversarial networks (GANs). She earned her Ph.D. in Deepfake Detection from UPES Dehradun, where her doctoral work focused on designing robust ensemble-based architectures to enhance the precision and generalizability of deepfake image recognition models. She holds an M.Tech in Computer Science and Engineering from UTU, where she was awarded the Gold Medal for academic excellence. With over seven years of rich academic and research experience, Dr. Sharma has made significant contributions to the fields of artificial intelligence, machine learning, and digital forensics. Her research is particularly noted for introducing VOTSTACK, a novel hybrid ensemble model designed to detect GAN-generated fake images with high accuracy and low computational cost. Dr. Sharma has authored and co-authored numerous research papers in peer-reviewed journals and international IEEE conferences, including presentations at prestigious forums such as the IEEE International Conference on Signal Processing and Advanced Research in Computing. Her impactful work has been recognized with several accolades, most notably the Best Oral Presentation Award at the Research Conclave 2024 organized by UPES. In addition to her research, Dr. Sharma is actively engaged in curriculum development, lab manual design, and academic mentorship. She is a Technical Committee Member for international conferences such as ICDTA 2025 (Morocco) and is frequently involved in interdisciplinary research projects, including AI-based systems for crop health monitoring and fruit ripeness detection. Known for her academic rigor, innovative thinking, and commitment to teaching, Dr. Preeti Sharma continues to inspire students and researchers alike, contributing to the advancement of trustworthy AI systems in critical areas such as media authenticity, healthcare diagnostics, and intelligent automation.

Keshav Kaushik is an Associate Professor at the Center for Cyber Security and Cryptology, Sharda School of Computing Science & Engineering, Sharda University, India. He holds a Ph.D. in Computer Science and Engineering and has around 12 years of full-time academic, research, and teaching experience. His research interests include cybersecurity, digital forensics, IoT and firmware security, AI/ML for cybersecurity, blockchain-enabled trust, cyber-physical systems, UAV/6G security, and quantum/post-quantum security. He has published 280+ research papers, authored/edited 50 books, and holds multiple granted patents and copyrights. He has been listed among the World's Top 2% Scientists by Stanford University/ Elsevier for 2024 and 2025.

***

Trilokkumar Akhani is the Dean of the Faculty of Applied Sciences at Parul University, Vadodara, Gujarat, India. He has extensive academic, research, and administrative experience in the fields of applied sciences and interdisciplinary research. His areas of interest include forensic science, biotechnology, environmental sciences, analytical sciences, and emerging technologies in scientific research. He has actively contributed to higher education through teaching, curriculum development, research supervision, and academic leadership. Dr. Akhani has authored and co-authored numerous research papers, book chapters, and scholarly publications in reputed national and international journals. He has participated in and organized several conferences, workshops, and faculty development programs, promoting innovation and scientific excellence. His research focuses on advancing applied scientific methodologies and fostering interdisciplinary collaborations to address contemporary challenges in science and technology. As an academic leader, Dr. Akhani is committed to strengthening research culture, enhancing industry–academia partnerships, and mentoring students and young researchers. He continues to contribute to scientific advancement through research, innovation, and educational excellence.

Kiranbhai Dodiya is an experienced Cyber Forensic Expert and Assistant Professor specializing in cyber security and digital forensics. He has taught at prestigious institutions and is currently pursuing a PhD in Biochemistry and Forensic Science. With a strong background in ethical hacking and malware analysis, Kiranbhai is passionate about educating students and contributing to the field of cyber forensics. His expertise includes malware forensic, computer forensics, and data recovery software. Kiranbhai's commitment to professional growth is evident through his participation in workshops, seminars, and research publications. He is dedicated to shaping the next generation of professionals in the field and combatting cybercrimes.

Deepak Gupta is a distinguished academician with over 20 years of teaching experience and expertise in Computer Science and Engineering. He holds a Ph.D. in Computer Engineering and has an extensive research portfolio, including many international journal papers, multiple conference proceedings, and several books. His research interests span machine learning, artificial intelligence, and data mining. Currently, Dr. Gupta serves as an Associate Professor and Head of Department of CSE (Emerging Branches) at ITM Gwalior, MP, India. He has also contributed significantly to the field through patents and copyrights and actively engages as a reviewer, conference chair and editor.

Shweta Javia is associated with the B.R. Doshi School of Biosciences, Sardar Patel University, Vallabh Vidyanagar, Anand, Gujarat, India. She is actively engaged in academic and research activities in the field of biosciences, with interests spanning biotechnology, molecular biology, microbiology, environmental sciences, and interdisciplinary life science research. Her work focuses on advancing scientific knowledge through research, innovation, and practical applications in biological sciences. She has participated in various academic and scientific programs, including seminars, workshops, conferences, and research initiatives, contributing to the dissemination of scientific knowledge and collaborative research efforts. Ms. Javia is committed to promoting excellence in education and research while fostering interdisciplinary approaches to address contemporary challenges in health, environment, and biotechnology. Her academic pursuits emphasize scientific inquiry, laboratory-based research, and the application of emerging technologies in biosciences. Through her contributions to research and scholarly activities, she continues to support the advancement of life sciences and the development of innovative solutions for societal and environmental well-being.

Mohanambal K was born in Tamil Nadu in 1983. He has received the M. E. degree in Computer Science from Anna University, India in May 2007, and B. E. degree in Information Technology from Bharathiyar University in April 2004. He has published papers in various International Conferences and International Journals in the domain of Machine Learning and IoT.

Nilufar Rajabova is working at the Department of Primary Education Methodology, Urgench State Pedagogical Institute, Uzbekistan.

Shoira Rakhimova is working at the Department of Primary Education Methodology, Urgench State Pedagogical Institute, Khiva, Uzbekistan.

Sudha Shetty is an Assistant Professor at Sigma University, Vadodara, where she actively contributes to academic excellence and the professional growth of students in the field of science and technology. With a dedicated passion for teaching and a strong commitment to fostering innovation, she guides students in research, project development, and innovative problem-solving approaches. Her mentorship has helped many budding researchers explore emerging domains and translate their ideas into impactful academic contributions. Ms. Shetty continues to play an influential role in shaping future professionals by encouraging curiosity, scientific thinking, and a research-oriented mindset.

C.V. Suresh Babu is a pioneer in content development. A true entrepreneur, he founded Anniyappa Publications, a company that is highly active in publishing books related to Computer Science and Management. Dr. C.V. Suresh Babu has also ventured into SB Institute, a center for knowledge transfer. He holds a Ph.D. in Engineering Education from the National Institute of Technical Teachers Training & Research in Chennai, along with seven master's degrees in various disciplines such as Engineering, Computer Applications, Management, Commerce, Economics, Psychology, Law, and Education. Additionally, he has UGC-NET/SET qualifications in the fields of Computer Science, Management, Commerce, and Education. Currently, Dr. C.V. Suresh Babu is a Professor in the Department of Information Technology at the School of Computing Science, Hindustan Institute of Technology and Science (Hindustan University) in Padur, Chennai, Tamil Nadu, India. For more information, you can visit his personal blog at https://sites.google .com/view/cvsureshbabu/.

Kowshika Thota is affiliated with Anglia Ruskin University, Cambridge, United Kingdom. She is actively involved in academic and research activities with interests in emerging technologies, data science, artificial intelligence, cybersecurity, digital innovation, and interdisciplinary research. Her work focuses on exploring the application of advanced technologies to address contemporary challenges in education, industry, and society. She has participated in various research, academic, and professional development initiatives, contributing to knowledge creation and collaborative scientific endeavors. Her research interests include technology-driven solutions, digital transformation, machine learning applications, and the ethical implications of emerging technologies. Through her academic pursuits, she seeks to bridge theoretical knowledge with practical applications that support innovation and sustainable development. Ms. Prabhakar is committed to continuous learning, research excellence, and interdisciplinary collaboration. She actively engages in scholarly activities, conferences, and research projects that foster innovation and contribute to the advancement of science and technology. Her work reflects a dedication to developing impactful solutions that address global technological and societal challenges.

Hitesh Vora is associated with the Regional Forensic Science Laboratory (RFSL), Rajkot, Gujarat, India. He is an experienced forensic scientist with expertise in forensic investigations, scientific evidence examination, and the application of advanced analytical techniques in criminal justice. His professional interests include forensic science, forensic chemistry, crime scene investigation, evidence analysis, and emerging technologies in forensic investigations. Throughout his career, Dr. Vora has contributed to forensic casework, scientific research, and the advancement of forensic methodologies. He has been actively involved in supporting law enforcement agencies through the examination and interpretation of forensic evidence, thereby assisting in the administration of justice. His work emphasizes scientific accuracy, quality assurance, and the integration of innovative technologies into forensic practice. Dr. Vora has participated in various academic, professional, and research activities, including conferences, workshops, and training programs related to forensic science. He remains committed to promoting excellence in forensic investigations, scientific research, and capacity building within the forensic science community.

Index

A

B

C

D

F

www.ingramcontent.com/pod-product-compliance
Lightning Source LLC
LaVergne TN
LVHW080858300926
849162LV00003B/463